Divine Aporia

Divine Aporia

Postmodern Conversations about the Other

Edited by
John C. Hawley

Lewisburg
Bucknell University Press
London: Associated University Presses

Associated University Presses
440 Forsgate Drive
Cranbury, NJ 08512

Associated University Presses
16 Barter Street
London WC1A 2AH, England

Associated University Presses
P.O. Box 338, Port Credit
Mississauga, Ontario
Canada L5G 4L8

The paper used in this publication meets the requirements of the American National Standard for Permanence of Paper for Printed Library Materials Z39.48–1984.

Library of Congress Cataloging–in–Publication Data

Divine aporia: postmodern conversations about the other / edited by John C. Hawley.
    p. cm.
Includes bibliographical references and index.
ISBN 0–8387–5449–X (alk. paper)
    1. Theology, Doctrinal. 2. Critical theory—Religious aspects—Christianity. 3. Postmodernism—Religious aspects—Christianity. I. Hawley, John C. (John Charles), 1947–
BT85 .D57 2000
230—dc21
                                                                00–023624
PRINTED IN THE UNITED STATES OF AMERICA

For Edward T. Oakes, S.J.

Lucky: "Given the existence as uttered forth in the public works of Puncher and Wattmann of a personal God quaquaquaqua with white beard quaquaquaqua outside time without extension who from the heights of divine apathia divine athambia divine aphasia loves us dearly with some exceptions for reasons unknown but time will tell. . . ."

—Samuel Becket, *Waiting for Godot*

The only strict and honest way. Have *no* finite exigency. Do not admit a limit in any sense or direction. Not even in the direction of the infinite. Demand of the individual what he is or what he will be. *Know nothing*, unless it be fascination. Never stop at the apparent limits.

—Georges Bataille, *On Nietzsche*

CONTENTS

ETHICAL MAPS ON SHIFTING GROUNDS

Acknowledgments

Carol J. Adams's chapter appeared in her book *Neither Man Nor Beast: Feminism and the Defense of Animals*, New York: Continuum (1994): 179–98. Copyright is held by The Continuum Publishing Company, which granted permission for the reprinting of this essay.

Kenneth Reinhard's essay, "Kant with Sade, Lacan with Levinas," appeared in *Modern Language Notes* 110 (1995): 785–808, copyright by The Johns Hopkins University Press.

Susan Handelman's chapter appeared in *Religion and Literature* 22.2–3 (1990): 61–84. Reprint permission was granted by the University of Notre Dame.

Divine Aporia

1
Waiting For

John C. Hawley

This collection of essays offers itself as a forum on some of the most interesting developing areas of interchange between critical theory and theology, joining such other recent studies as Philippa Berry and Andrew Wernick's *Shadow of Spirit: Postmodernism and Religion* (1992), Terrence Tilley's *Postmodern Theologies: The Challenge of Religious Diversity* (1995), Phillip Blond's *Post-Secular Philosophy: Between Philosophy and Theology* (1998), John C. Caputo and Michael J. Scanlon's *God, the Gift, and Postmodernism* (1999), and Merold Westphal's *Postmodern Philosophy and Christian Thought* (1999). Certainly one of the first things that such collections demonstrate to scholars in the humanities is that theology ought not to be conceived as a monolithic, static, or fossilized discipline, but rather as a dynamic and expansive one in which certain trends in philosophy, literary criticism, and feminist and critical theory have been established. Thus, the anthology as a whole might best be viewed as a collection of essays celebrating these inevitable marks of differences and pluralities within the postmodern landscape. The essays in the three sections portray the theoretical, textual, and ethico-social implications of acknowledging otherness or radical differences among us, and reflect upon the fact that certain authoritative forms of thought and practice have historically transformed differences into dichotomous oppositions, or reduced multiplicities and pluralities into a single oppositional norm. Several of the essays in *Divine Aporia* increase our awareness of the limitations of such binarism and the ambiguities of traditional theological claims, but most actually show the contradictions, pluralities, and paradoxes inherent in *all* our various systems of signification. They also focus upon the difficulties in understanding and (correctly?) appropriating the concept of the Other within a wide range of disciplinary fields. The book, sometimes by inference and sometimes by sustained analysis, brings together postmodern theory, philosophy, psychoanalysis, anthropology, literature, cultural studies, and women's studies, to show how a persistent and classical theme in Western theological studies (that is, the alterity of the divine reality) has become creatively transcribed and theorized anew within the postmodern landscape.

In an age in which fascination with margins and with the transgressing of borders enlivens fields of enquiry as divergent as physics and anthropology, many works of literature and religion variously focus on the pilgrim approaching holy ground, glimpsing the grail or facing the dragon looming on the horizon. Surprising to many who look with suspicion upon critical theory, sociologist Zygmunt Bauman describes the thinker in this age as rappeling down the side of the mountain of Enlightenment fact and into a realm of "re-enchantment," in which the emotional and experiential are revalorized, the ambiguous is embraced, and morality is once again rendered personal. Lying behind this re-enchantment, writes Graham Ward, is "the re-evaluation of ambivalence, mystery, excess and aporia as they adhere to, are constituted by, and disrupt the rational" (Ward 1996, 132).

As a hopeful David Griffin remarks, "the emerging postmodern worldview allows for the recovery of belief in God while eliminating the fatal problem inherent in the traditional idea of God. . . . In short, the postmodern worldview has a God-shaped hole in it" (1989, 51, 66). Whether this image is more akin to a black hole or a doughnut remains in dispute, but Griffin's suggestion offers a rationale for the title of this collection. In the words of Mario Valdes, an *aporia* is "an insoluble philosophical problem which nevertheless continues to draw thinkers. . . . To bring the question face to face with an aporia is the goal of the Socratic method: only then does the questioner realize that he does not know; the realization of not-knowing is the beginning of concerted searching" (Makaryk 1993, 507).[1]

Philippa Berry describes what she considers to be the central aporia that marks our age. "Could an apparently nihilistic tradition of thought," she asks, "a thought ostensibly *shaped* by that darkness of *angst*, of meaninglessness and abjection, which shrouds the 'end' of the modern era, paradoxically have acquired a new religious or spiritual dimension?" (Berry and Wernick 1992, 4). Her question arises from the observation that deconstructive thinking has blurred or even dissolved the Kantian distinction between secular and religious thinking—placing us, again, in some other, some in-between, space, like that described by Michel de Certeau, Mark Taylor, Graham Ward, and a good many others. In the process, increasing attention is being paid to Heidegger's foundational work, to the connections between Derridean thought and earlier work on the *via negativa* (see Coward and Foshay 1992), and to Emmanuel Levinas and Luce Irigaray. One result of these developments, therefore, has been an encouragement of less dualistic thinking and another, in Berry's view, has been "the attainment of a new capacity for ethical action" (1992, 5) and a reemergence of creative thinking on *agape*. As Krzysztof Ziarek has asserted, "the novelty of both Levinas's and [Jean-Luc] Marion's thinking lies in its focus on the primacy of the ethical, on the relation to the other, and on how this exposition of alterity traces itself in language" (Ziarek 1990, 93). Ziarek's summary statement provides a schema for this collection of essays, which seeks to suggest the contemporary discussion of issues of alterity especially as they manifest themselves in theology, literature, and ethics.

But any single volume must be modest in its approach to this complex of questions, acknowledging from the start that many nuances may be trampled in the march from one interesting connection to another. We do well to alert the reader to somewhat more formal outlines of the current theological terrain, as, for example, Phillip Blond's analysis of the influence of Enlightenment philosophy on contemporary theology (Blond 1998, 1–66) or Terrence Tilley's interesting schema for the only-sometime compatible agendas of contemporary theologians—those with "constructive theologies" (Helmut Peukert, David Ray Griffin, David Tracy), those with "postmodernisms of dissolution" (Thomas J. Altizer, Mark C. Taylor, Edith Wyschogrod), those with "postliberal theologies" (George Lindbeck), and those with a "communal praxis" (Gustavo Gutierrez, James W. McClendon, Sharon Welch) (Tilley 1995). We will here make reference to many of these writers, and to others, but cannot do any one of them full justice except in their capacity as one member of the choir.

To set the stage for the conversation that follows, therefore, imagine any tabernacle of your choosing as the bed of Procrustes, as the symbol for our attempt to set limits to that which remains inscrutable, and ourselves as highwaymen waiting to waylay the stray passerby who *will* not acknowledge our right to tribute. Would we have an accurate image for the human tendency to confirm its tenuous hold on mystery by the premature justification of "revelation"? At the outside edge of this domestication, marveling that some mundane place (a burning bush, a tattered shroud) has been touched by the timeless and the sacred, we nonetheless warily sustain the conviction of Samson-like potential within the tabernacle, "unconceivably" ready to burst its chains asunder. The history of theology suggests that any God worth his or her salt escapes such prisons—and will again be tracked down, domesticated anew. Ours seems to be an age in which the escape has, again, been discovered with fascination and dismay. In the ensuing silence, as much as in the babble—*there* is this book's implied object of study. What is *not* said (what *can*not be said?) may ultimately be the book's central concern. But charting that space and delimiting its expanse will lead us into such rocky shoals as Mark C. Taylor's atheology and Charles Winquist's death of God theology; into Luce Irigaray's ethics and René Girard's mimesis; into gendered theologies and into subaltern studies; into the performative and the intertextual.

Modern or Postmodern?

One debate that these essays will not end, but that nonetheless informs and shapes their various arguments, is the extent to which any of the thinkers whose work remains influential may be considered modern rather than "post" modern. Catherine Bell puts the question very well:

> On one level, a significant number of scholars of religion are still heavily invested in aspects of the great modernist debate, namely, demonstrating the superiority of the application of scientific methods and frameworks to the study of religion in place of more theological or confessional frameworks. In response to what they see as troubling trends, these scholars champion the validity of what is understood as the Enlightenment paradigm for the study of religion, explicitly criticizing the ways its application has been curtailed or undermined. They call for, indeed, they *plead* for, a real liberation from the lingering theological premises, perspectives, and even liberal tolerances that have kept the professional study of religion muddled and uninfluential. While they diagnose the problems and define the prescriptions differently, these advocates appear to share a consensus on the importance of "explanation."
>
> On another level, however, a rather different group of scholars is debating so-called postmodernist issues. They assume that the modernist debate has been long settled—in favor of the Enlightenment paradigm in theory, with various modifications toward interpretation in practice. Hence, they focus on the model's problems— the political, cultural, and epistemological dynamics involved in the generation of universal categories like "religion" and their application in explanations and interpretations of other cultural practices. Their provocative deconstructions of categories have raised both ethical and pragmatic questions for the field. (1996, 179) [2]

Such an analysis wars with the self-definition of several prominent theologians, but finds confirmation in the analyses of various others. Although David Griffin, Mark C. Taylor, Charles Winquist, Don Cupitt, Carl Raschke, and Thomas Altizer describe themselves as postmodern, for example, Graham Ward classes them as late modernists, and their relationship to postmodernism as epiphenomenal: "Their work," he writes, "does not issue from postmodern philosophy, its insights and methodologies; [instead,] postmodern philosophy substantiates their theses concerning contemporary culture." But this focus on culture, he writes, is a liberal move—theology is demythologized and takes on the garb of present cultural concerns. Such philosophical support might be offered by the radical Nietzscheans—Gilles Deleuze, the early paganism of Jean-Francois Lyotard, the work on hyper-reality and seduction by Jean Baudrillard. It would not receive support from some of the postmodern thinkers they wish to enlist—Derrida, for example. Secondly, they each affirm a radical immanentalism, a nihilistic monism or ontology which is at odds with what is evidently a search for a transcendental empiricism (to use a phrase coined by Vincent Descombes) in postmodern thinking. (Ward 1997, xl)

The theologians singled out by Ward would respond in various ways. David Griffin, for example, calls himself a certain *kind* of postmodern: He rejects "that type of postmodernism [which] should really be called ultramodernism, or mostmodernism, because it results from taking some of the presuppositions of modernity to their logical conclusions. In contrast with this relativistic, nihilistic, deconstructive postmodernism, [he speaks] of a constructive, reconstructive, or revisionary postmodernism, in which many of the presuppositions of modernity are challenged and revised " (Griffin 1990, 6–7). Craig Westman further refines this distinction, noting that Griffin "defines his 'postmodernism' over against three other forms: deconstruction [Mark Taylor], liberationist [Harvey Cox, Cornel West], and restorationist" (Tilley 1995, 18). His is a communalistic approach (hippie-like?) grounded in a process theology based upon Whitehead and Hartshorne. "Griffin's vision and style," writes Westman, "are finally much more characteristic of a modern neo-romantic communal vision than of postmodern forms of thought" (Tilley 1995, 26). In fact, Griffin's type of postmodernism is often classified as a neo-Whiteheadian or Process-oriented type of religious discourse, and hence still very much wedded to modern sensibilities and trappings.

For his part, Carl Raschke builds on Heidegger and Umberto Eco and notes that "postmodernity is the transcendence, or 'overcoming,' of all archaic or 'legendary' orders of significance that have underwritten cultural discourse. Understood superficially, the 'postmodern' represents a transition from the highly formalized, or 'modern,' understanding of things to the 'carnival' of popular culture. . . [but] it is the *power of performance* that appears to have emerged as the common denominator among the variegated 'postmodernisms' of art, philosophy, theology, textual criticism, and the like" (Raschke 1992, 94–95). He is rather dismissive of Griffin's work ("little more than process thought—a modernist metaphysic—leavened with the politics and eco-mysticism of the ageing 1960s counterculture" [97]),[3] but "true" postmodern thought, he writes, is of another "meta-phorical" sort: "Just as the movement over a generation ago from abstrac-tion to 'pop' can be construed as a revolt against the discreet nihilism of purely formal painting, so postmodern religious thinking no longer takes as its 'texts' the recondite writings of the so-called 'deconstructionalists'" (Raschke 1992, 98). Building on Umberto Eco, he writes that "one prob-lem of [Mark] Taylor's work, and with the now expiring fashion of 'deconstructionism' in religious writing for that matter, is that it has reached a seemingly insurmountable impasse, so far as the critical task is con-cerned, largely as a result of its inability to embrace the 'metaphoric postmodern,' which ultimately harks back to the desire of Nietzsche's Zarathustra to *dance*. The metaphoric postmodern rests on a profound post-metaphysical insight. . . . [It] is Eco's 'travels in hyper-reality.' It is the transcendence of nihilism—a nihilism that is the hidden agenda behind what Derrida calls the 'truth in painting,' the emptiness of all frames and representations, including the dys-representative entropy of the deconstructive campaign" (1992, 102). Following David Levin, Raschke distinguishes between the analytic postmodern and the metaphoric postmodern, and suggests that the former, evincing itself as deconstruction, has mistakenly taken the ascendant. And following Eco and Kristeva, Raschke notes that *metaphoric* postmodernism emphasizes somatology: "The language of the body, together with the ontological category of 'em-bodiment,' tracing the origin of that peculiar polylogical style of communi-cation that embraces psychology, philosophy, theology and aesthetics, thus emerges as its own distinctive *lingua franca* for 'postmodernist' conver-sation" (1992, 103).

Graham Ward makes a similar point, with a nuance:

> [I]t is the puncturing of the circle of immanence which the work of
> the postmodern philosophers of difference is attempting to sketch.
> This work draws attention to an aporetics—ambivalences, gener-
> ated by difference—which cannot be named. This presents its own
> problems: difference can never be overcome. Difference offers us
> the trace of that which is the condition for all things, a heteroge-
> neous origin. In the work of Bataille, Levinas, Girard, Certeau,
> Derrida, Irigaray, Cixous, and Jean-Luc Nancy discussions of this
> originating space, this destabilizing, differentiating source employs
> theological metaphors—metaphors that cannot function according
> to some opposition between the metaphorical and the literal, since
> metaphoricity is the nature of language itself. We cannot say, then,
> that they are simply using metaphors but they are not referring to
> God or the divine. The theological cannot be left out of their ac-

counts. Their accounts call forth the theological without attempting to view the problematics of late modernity which they are alert to from an explicitly theological (that is, faith) perspective and praxis. Yet neither can these thinkers complete the postmodern project they call for—the end of metaphysics as the ordering of what is according to human reason. They have no position from which to surmount such an overcoming. (1997, xli) [4]

Paul Lakeland suggests something that may, at this point in our discussion, be clear: that individual writers might actually situate themselves, willy-nilly, on a sliding scale of philosophical modernity, or sit Janus-faced looking both ways. Lakeland views their varying positionalities through a hermeneutical filter. "To put the difference between the late moderns and the radicals in the context of metanarratives," he writes, "it is fairly clear that the former wish to retain *some* metanarrative, albeit a highly sophisticated, 'weak,' or 'thin' account, while the radicals want to settle for swapping stories. The late moderns are promodern in their continued attention to metanarrative, postmodern in their willingness to accept its historicity and fragility" (Lakeland 1997, 33).

But can one *logically* remain in such a tenuous position? On the one hand, Graham Ward suggests that "the surrender of the subject—a certain kenosis which will bring about the final collapse of secular space itself—is both necessary and impossible for the realization of the postmodern project," but, on the other hand, he notes that "only theology can embark on such a project, for theology cannot conceive of a secular space at all, nor an autonomous subject" (1997, xlii). In seeking to deal with the aporia implied in such an apparent split between the sacred and the profane, Ward imagines a "cyberspatial city" that is "political, embodied, and sexed" (1997, xliii). If this may be, finally, not too distant from what St. Augustine had in mind, it at least seems a *highly* metaphoric metanarrative, if not an awfully uninviting metaphysic. But perhaps we do well to remain there, in its rather bleakly honest appraisal of the position of waiting in which we find ourselves today. "We have not yet attained to the postmodern," Ward writes, "until we recover for our time the world before and beyond the secular. Until then theology has constantly to engage with and critique that which calls itself postmodern" (1997, xlii).

Negative Theology?

[N]o matter how much spiritual understanding a man may have in the knowledge of all created spiritual things, he can never, by the work of his understanding, arrive at the knowledge of an uncreated spiritual thing, which is nothing except God. But by the failing of it, he can. For where his understanding fails is in nothing except God alone; and it was for this reason that Saint Denis [the Areopagite] said, "The truly divine knowledge of God is that which is known by unknowing." (*The Cloud of Unknowing* 1981, 256)

The significance of every organism of utilitarian technology has the same object and intention. It seeks an opportunity to penetrate into the area which we see on a Suprematist canvas. What, in fact, is such a canvas and what is pictured on it? If we analyse a canvas we primarily see in it a window through which we discern life. A Suprematist canvas is a representation of white—but not blue— space. The reason for this is clear: blue does not provide an actual representation of the infinite. It is as though the shafts of vision strike a dome and cannot penetrate into the infinite. Infinite Suprematist white enables the shaft of vision to advance without meeting a boundary. We perceive moving bodies, but what their motion is, and their nature, is a matter for discovery. (Malevich 1982, 285)

There are those who think that theology can only be defended in a negative fashion and indeed that this form of negation or doubt concerning grounds is the only discourse that will allow a theology at all. However, these theological sceptics (if I can call them that) lack a cataphasis. They lack an understanding that the *via negativa* itself requires a positum, a positum reserved for theology alone. However, this positum is not simply there as a fully replete phe- nomenon, it is rather more correctly conceived of as an inexhaust- ible plenitude and negation which expresses our inadequacy of re- ception (our inability, that is, to be equal to what we are given) and hence our need for further negation in order to ascend to an ever greater and ever more mediated account of what we have indeed been given. Negative theology requires a positive discourse about God, if, that is, this form of negation is to be recognizably about God at all. Only then can negative theology take its place in the peculiar grammar and comportment of religious affirmation. (Blond 1998, 5)

In an age delighting in verbal play and relishing prolonged deferrals of mean- ing, we may find a bracing transparency or comforting opacity in the writ- ings of those who ponder a mysticism they describe as inevitable. Inevi- table, they say, because the pure object of faith is *beyond*, by definition unattainable yet irresistibly attractive. If we may grant the unresolved na- ture of the position of "God talk" in postmodernism, this may be an approach that opens a pathway among many of the otherwise inaccessible positions.[5] Negative theology continues to be a topic of fruitful reflection (see, for example, Zornado 1998, Salomon 1998), but Thomas Carlson notes that it "does not amount to a pure emptiness or silence but rather marks the ever ambiguous edge where language wavers between its own production and failure, the unstable border where language is generated precisely—and impossibly—with the aim of undoing itself" (Carlson 1998, 168). "Exceeding articulate speech, understanding, comprehension," Fred Botting writes, "certain experiences disclose an 'unknowing' at the heart of experience that denotes the limit of language, discourse, culture" (Botting and Wilson 1998, 3). Influenced by Maurice Blanchot, such writers as Maria Lichtman ponder "the postmodern deconstructionist theme of a presence that is an absence in continual dialectical relation" (Lichtman 1998, 214). Many of our contemporaries ask, as others have before them, "is God that which eludes conceptualization and categorization?" (M. Taylor 1994, 594), and in the shuffle at the close of a millennium we find ourselves rubbing elbows with Meister Eckhart, John Tauler, Julian of Norwich, John of the Cross, and Teresa of Avila.

Do they dance on the only lasting plane of theological imagining—that of dumbstruck awe? As Louis Dupré observes, "what was once the arduous route traveled only by a religious elite is now, in many instances, the only one still open to us" (1998, 139). Apparently liberated from niceties of dogma, there should be no wonder that our own age might turn with renewed interest to a consideration of the alterity of God and to the "question" of the other (see Todorov 1984). In his introduction to contemporary philosopher/theologian Jean-Luc Marion, David Tracy points out that "since Schleiermacher and Hegel, Christian theology has been in intense internal conflict over its proper response to modernity (and more recently . . . to postmodernity)" (Marion 1991, ix); Tracy further notes that this crisis has elicited two strategies of response. One approach attempts to reconcile the claims of *reason* with the disclosures of revelation. The other approach believes that "reason functions best in theology by developing rigorous concepts and categories to clarify theology's sole foundation in *revelation*" (x, emphasis added). Fundamental to this second approach is the decision that revelation alone is theology's foundation, and that, therefore, "any attempt at correlation [of rationality and revelation] is at best a category mistake—at worst, an attempt to domesticate the reality of God by means of reason and being" (x).

In Tracy's words, the approach relying more heavily on revelation than upon reason proposes that "theology needs to cease being modern theo-*logy* in order to become again *theo*-logy" (Marion 1991, xii); it needs to become "noncorrelational" and "postmetaphysical." Such a theology, arguably the sort practiced by theologians as disparate as Marion, Hans Urs von Balthasar, and Karl Barth,[6] focuses on "the reality of God's revelation as pure gift," as "excess" and as Love (xii). And from such thinkers a disturbing question threatens to upset the metaphysician's applecart; again in Tracy's rewording of Marion, the question might take this shape:

> Is Platonic "goodness," or Christian "agape," or postmodern "excess" appropriately understood through any notion of Being—whether Scholastic "common being," Thomist *esse*, or even Heideggerian *Sein*? . . . Heideggerian manifestation (*Offenbarheit*) of *Sein* is not equivalent to Christian revelation (*Offenbarung*), that is, of God's disclosure of God's reality as radically, excessively, Agape beyond Being. (Marion 1991, xiv-xv)

In Marion's own mystical expression of the philosophical mystery: "If, to begin with, 'God is love,' then God loves before being. He only is as He embodies himself—in order to love more closely that which and those who, themselves, have first to be" (xx). This refers to us, of course, who must first *be* before we love—but God *is* love.

   John Milbank would be among those who assert that "traditional theology never entertained a 'metaphysics' or 'ontology' in autonomy from a discourse illuminated by God" (1997, 2), and yet he would advance an agenda that tries to take into account the critical objections coming from outside. "Theology," he writes,

> should recognize the primacy of linguistic mediation, but at the same time must develop its own construal of the meaning of this mediation—and so of the "meaning of meaning"—which in rational terms is as valid as a more sceptical, nihilistic construal. This attempt is seen as in keeping with traditional attempts to elaborate a specifically *theological* ontology, but departs from them in so far as it is only since the Renaissance that we have fully recognized the inescapability of culture: the way we make signs, yet signs make us and we can never step outside the network of sign-making. (1997, 2)

   When such encounters with our own ground of being raise more questions than they answer about how we are to "understand" the source or process of that ground, they are reflecting and refracting, like a circus mirror (or like a Byzantine icon),[7] back upon the observer. Many who begin by seeking to describe divine characteristics end by discovering that their god looks a lot like them. In his imaginative account of the gradual transformation of God's identity in the Jewish Bible, for example, Jack Miles shows a transmigration of images that would please Jean-Luc Marion and those with anthropomorphic metaphors for the divine. God is successively described in the Old Testament as Creator, Destroyer, Creator/Destroyer, Friend of the Family, Liberator, Lawgiver, Liege, Conqueror, Father, Arbiter, Executioner, Holy One, Wife, Counselor, Fiend, Sleeper, Bystander, Recluse, Puzzle, Absence, Ancient of Days, Scroll, Perpetual Round. If there is a progression here, it is perhaps in the direction of increasing abstraction and distance. Perhaps this makes the incarnational imagination of the Christian New Testament all the more striking, though the "degree" or *purpose* of incarnation, as reflected in the early Christian's reinterpretation of the notion of Messiah, also suggests less compulsive activity by Yahweh in the world. In Miles's words,

> [I]n the days of Abraham, Moses, Joshua, and David, the Lord took mighty action on behalf of Israel. In the days of Ezra and Nehemiah, Israel takes energetic action on behalf of the Lord. They become covenant partners again, but on a distinctly different basis. . . . As the Tanakh [the Hebrew Bible] ends, the mind of God has been objectified in law, the action of God incarnated in leadership, and now, finally, the voice of God transferred to prayer. David's last prayer [RSV; I Chron. 29:10-19] is the Lord God's farewell speech. The voice is the voice of the old king, but the desire is the desire of the eternal God. (Miles 1995, 372, 396)

Miles notes that the real crisis in this collective reimagination of (by?) God takes place in the book of Job: "After Job, God knows his own ambiguity as he has never known it before" (1995, 327). Less fictively, Miles's conclusions regarding the effect on *humanity* of such a series of divine "self-definitions" is telling: "Other things being equal, protracted exposure to a God in whom several personalities coexist and alongside whom no other god is ever portrayed even for the folkloric fun of it must foster a way of thinking of the self as similarly composite and similarly alone" (1995, 407). Yet there is something of a chicken-or-the-egg conundrum set up here, since the various authors of the books Miles describes are writing from the social context that produces the Yahweh by which they are themselves subsequently defined and "judged."

God as mirror, then?—as inkblot? Anthropomorphism that begins to describe a lonely God soon describes one that is neurotic and increasingly reclusive, one that has cast off responsibility for his/her works and has passed the baton to the next generation—like the Titans heading off for retirement as Zeus and company take up residence on Olympus. But appropriating the divine to this extent offers cold comfort indeed, and cries out for some *Other*, some *defamiliarizing* invasion by a God who may, in fact, appear more psychotic than neurotic. A God who has become one of us, filled with existential Angst, seems not far from the dead God portrayed in Peter Shaffer's *The Royal Hunt of the Sun* (1964), a God rendered powerless by his own decision not to act. At play's end, having successfully killed off the leader/god of the Incas, Pizarro considers the attractions of the graven image, the creation of a God of his own design:

> You have no peace for me, Atahuallpa: the birds still scream in your forest. . . . God's just a name on your nail; and naming begins cries and cruelties. But to live without hope of after, and make whatever God there is, oh, that's some immortal business surely. . . . I'm tired.
> (2. 12)

The quotidian creation Pizarro has in mind, one that will surely cause him little confusion or challenge and no ecstasy at all, recalls the bloodless God Kierkegaard so completely ridiculed and rejected: "Assuming that no God exists," Kierkegaard writes,

> no eternity, no accounting, then the official Christianity is a perfectly charming and elegant invention for very sensibly making this life as enjoyable as possible, more enjoyable than the pagan could have it. . . .The Christianity of Christendom . . . takes away from Christianity the offense, the paradox, etc., and instead of that introduces probability, the plainly comprehensible. (1944, 158, 162–63)

Pizarro's cynical proposal, made in the afterglow of his pyrrhic victory over God, is precisely opposite to the mystical experience; exhaustion in the face of his suggestion reflects despair in the face of a successful usurpation of the other.

Confusion, cynicism, exhaustion—one might hope that Pizarro's entropic decline is not typical of the human story, and that the life-project may move, for some, in quite an "other" direction. Tzvetan Todorov envisions this alternative future as a procession in self-knowledge through other-discovery:

[F]or the newborn child, *his* world is *the* world, and growth is an apprenticeship in exteriority and sociality; we might say, somewhat cavalierly, that human life is confined between these two extremes, one where the *I* invades the world, and one where the world ultimately absorbs the *I* in the form of a corpse or of ashes. And just as the discovery of the other knows several degrees, from the other-as-object, identified with the surrounding world, to the other-as-subject, equal to the *I* but different from it, with an infinity of intermediary nuances, we can indeed live our lives without ever achieving a full discovery of the other (supposing that such a discovery can be made). Each of us must begin it over again in turn; the previous experiments do not relieve us of our responsibility, but they can teach us the effects of misreading the facts. (1984, 247)

Todorov might grant Pizarro's observations, while describing them as partial and suggesting the explorer become a closer reader of the text. As Emmanuel Levinas puts it,

Desire is desire for the absolutely other. Besides the hunger one satisfies, the thirst one quenches, and the senses one allays, metaphysics desires the other beyond satisfactions, where no gesture by the body to diminish the aspiration is possible, where it is not possible to sketch out any known caress nor invent any new caress. . . . For Desire this alterity, non-adequate to the idea, has a meaning. It is understood as the alterity of the Other and of the Most-High. (1979, 34)

Little wonder, then, that contemporary audiences find themselves almost literally onstage with the disoriented (or, perhaps, disturbingly oriented) characters in Brian Friel's *Dancing at Lughnasa* (1990), who exist in some strangely transmogrifying realm of memory, forgetting, degradation, and reinvention. At this close of the century western audiences must quietly ask if they too dance on the edge of sanity with a sense that that is exactly where we inevitably must be, where we, in fact, might wish to be—at the edge, like a whirling dervish, joyously piercing the veil into a shapeless, musical energy beyond. In retrospect, at play's end, Michael, the central narrator of Friel's deeply resonant drama, muses over the implosion of rational systems:

But there is one memory of that Lughnasa time that visits me most often; and what fascinates me about that memory is that it owes nothing to fact. In that memory atmosphere is more real than inci-

dent and everything is simultaneously actual and illusory. In that
memory, too, the air is nostalgic with the music of the thirties. . . .
And what is so strange about that memory is that everybody seems
to be floating on those sweet sounds, moving rhythmically, languor-
ously, in complete isolation; responding more to the mood of the
music than to its beat. When I remember it, I think of it as dancing.
Dancing with eyes half closed because to open them would break
the spell. Dancing as if language had surrendered to movement—as
if this ritual, this wordless ceremony, was now the way to speak, to
whisper private and sacred things, to be in touch with some otherness. . . . Dancing as if language no longer existed because words
were no longer necessary. . . [*Slowly bring up the music. Slowly
bring down the lights.*]   (2)

A world of swelling music and dimming lights, words no longer available
and no longer necessary; and we unable, of course, to tell the dancer from
the dance, but unable, more pertinently, to tell the dance from the dancer.

God as process, then, a temporal event and mesh of experience; but
God as spatial horizon, as well, toward which all creation tends, the "tend-
ing" itself an immanent horizon like that of Charles Sanders Peirce proph-
esying that "ignorance and error are all that distinguish our private selves
from the absolute *ego* of pure apperception" (1960, CP5.235). But how
absolute might this ego be? And does "pure apperception" imply identification? Jean-Paul Vernant is among those who meditate on this conundrum,
knowing that our age is certainly not the first to look at extreme human
conditions as symptoms of some sort of horizon—as liminal gateways to a
purer apperception. Peter Mason summarizes Vernant as follows:

As the incarnation of the Other, Dionysos [for example] reveals the
possibility of a joyous alterity as another dimension of the human
condition. . . . His function is precisely to confuse the boundary line
between human and divine, between human and animal, between
here and beyond. Dionysos thus also reveals the multiple forms of
the Other, the ultimate failure of any attempt to pin the Other down
to some simple form of self/other binary opposition. (1990, 1)

The suggestion, as in Michel Foucault, seems to be that one does not find
oneself in exteriority, but finds the other in oneself (Mason 1990, 182).[8]

Alterity, by definition, is not easily imagined. As Foucault considers in
his history of the institutionalization of "madness": "We want to provide
some sort of account of that which is beyond the boundaries of self and
sameness, of that which is *radically and gloriously other*" (Mason 1990,

3). "The God of the Bible, whose ways are unknown," writes Levinas, "whose presence may be but absence and whose absence may impose itself as presence, to whom the faithful is both faithful and unfaithful, reveals himself in the interruption of coherent speech. And yet the Westerner, irreversibly a philosopher, does not consent to that separation between faith (or what is left of it) and philosophy. He desires a discourse capable of incorporating that interruption" (1996a, 90). Again, we are urged to return to the condition of "not-knowing," of entering into a foreign land where we become strangers to others and to ourselves—a land in which, in the words of Charles Winquist, we learn to "stammer in our own language" (Winquist 1995, 129). Michel de Certeau describes an exclusionary principle of mysticism that, he suggests, may offer a helpful barrier to the absorption of the other: "The *neither . . . nor* constitutes an interspace, a *zwischenraum*, the converse equivalent of a position that overcomes difference" (1986, 114)—an entering into the ambivalent in-between space. Mark Taylor is also helpful in mapping a strategy for maintaining integrity in imagining *where* the Other is to be not-found in his tortuous neologizing and demand for insulating doubly-negating no-man's-lands. "In the odd play of denegation," he writes, "nothing remains even; opposites are not reconciled but are held together in their belonging apart. . . . The sacred is. . . that which allows God to be God by enabling God to be other than everything that is not God" (1994, 595).

Such "stammering" to give shape to that which defies definition challenges traditional epistemologies, and obviously, in day-to-day lives, has pressing ethical demands. This combination is most clearly seen in Levinas's work:

> From the depths of the muddy, miasmatic swamps . . . can the name of God resound? . . . It is not necessary and it is not possible for this name to resound in being through demonstrations or actuality, nor for its "kingdom" to be manifestation and miracle. The youthfulness of its transcendent meaning does not signify in beliefs or hopes, but in the excessive expenditure of the human, in *the-one-for-the-other*, destroying the balance of accounts; in the "meaningfulness freely bestowed," without expectation of thanks, in the hyperbole exceeding long life and eternity. A project that moves not in the direction of being or non-being, but toward an excluded middle; even if language states it as *a being* or as *being*, in calling it God. Language, ambiguous *per se* (ancillary and indiscreet), that betrays the ineffable, but thus revealing it and offering it to the "reduction" of metaphysics. (1996a, 88)

The ethical component of this thinking is discussed at greater length later in this essay, but the "imagining" of the other is what we wish to address here. If "the sacred" forms this cushion against a merging with the other, then mundane experiences (*pace* experiences of a Thou) hammer away at any temptation we might have towards a solipsism that devours all it encounters. Sounding a bit as though he were arguing with Bishop Berkeley, Winquist notes that

> understanding can at least experiment with the possibility that the heterogeneity of the phenomenality of experience may be implicated in that which is other than subjectivity. It is the impurities in discursive practices that are most interesting for this thinking and might be thought of as secular traces within the discourse. . . . In a contemporary context . . . the figurations of otherness that trope the discourse and disrupt the hegemony of the subject are not going to be traditional theological formulations, even though they may function like Descartes's God.[9] . . . [For example,] experiences that resist shaping and persist in pressuring the differential play of consciousness mark the incorrigibility of the other of the body and the economy of forces in which it is situated. . . . We have trouble convincing ourselves that images and ideas at play in these experiences are either innate within or invented by our subjectivity. (1995, 35, 37)

Thus, for Winquist, "the markings of the incorrigibility of the other are an elementary transcendence of the subject" (1995, 37), but the phenomenality of these markings is complex. In the first place, it is not an isolating experience, but one that "implicate[s] the other of the body with the bodies of others"; secondly, the markings are always spatial, including one's "place" in history, so that travel beyond one's identifying space is self-confrontational, self-confirming; and thirdly, our libidinal forces, because of their intensity, "can be elaborated narratively into a story," and then "these stories are not descriptions of the other of thinking so much as constructions that can be inhabited by these forces of alterity" (38). Not too surprisingly, taking into account these "markings," Winquist follows Freud and Lacan to carve out an imaginative erotic space for theology, taking seriously the notion of God as love. "Theology," he writes,

> is a minor literature in the dominant community, but it also transforms the meaning of community. Within the dominant community there is a desiring community that makes concrete a vision of finitude that is beyond despair. The minor intensive theological use of

> language pressures the ordinary weave of discourse and opens it to desire. Meaning is intensified. Theology is a work against the disappointment of thinking. (1995, xi)

The "disappointment of thinking" is a very suggestive phrase, again almost echoing Levinas's simple acceptance of such "failure" as an acceptable parameter of human existence, almost beautiful in its melancholy disavowal of strict rationality. But Levinas's notion of "the excessive expenditure of the human" may suggest a way out of our heads and into a less rationalistic encounter with the other. We have noted above Kevin Hart's discussion of the dubious nature of Derrida's relationship with negative theology.[10] Perhaps it should be given another look. James Olthuis makes another pass at the question: "I do believe that Derrida goes a long way in showing that language and metaphysics cannot provide privileged access to self-present meaning. But does that mean access to the mysterious, sacred desert place is impossible?" (Derrida, as a displaced North African Jew, speaks of "a certain void, the place of an internal desert" where this sort of question will "resonate.") "Perhaps there are other ways and means to enter that space beyond or before. Can we agree with Derrida that another philosophy/theology will not help? Reason is im/potent [*sic*]. But what about an approach that sees access as a non-philosophical/non-theological gift to be received rather than a way to be engineered?" (1997, 241–42). Something to wait for.

But the waiting that writers like Olthuis and Levinas have in mind is quite active, and the route to the encounter may be disturbing. Georges Bataille, at least, paid a rather high price for the guidelines he offered.[11] Regretting the fact that "humanity recognizes the right to acquire, to conserve, and to consume rationally, but it excludes in principle *nonproductive expenditure*," he emphasized that cultures nonetheless undertake such expenditures: "luxury, mourning, war, cults, the construction of sumptuary monuments, games, spectacles, arts, perverse sexual activity (i.e., deflected from genital finality)—all these represent activities which, at least in primitive circumstances, have no end beyond themselves" (1985, 117–18). He attempted to explain the tension by offering a philosophy of the human person:

> [H]uman life cannot in any way be limited to the closed systems assigned to it by reasonable conceptions. The immense travail of recklessness, discharge, and upheaval that constitutes life could be expressed by stating that life starts only with the deficit of these systems; at least what it allows in the way of order and reserve has

> meaning only from the moment when the ordered and reserved forces
> liberate and lose themselves for ends that cannot be subordinated to
> anything one can account for. It is only by such insubordination—
> even if it is impoverished—that the human race ceases to be isolated
> in the unconditional splendor of material things. (1985, 128)

Hardly a likely candidate for Sunday school teacher, Bataille urged on this "insubordination," this apparently pointless activity, as a self-defining pushing against definition. Michel Beaujour, calling Bataille "a very quiet lunatic" who "skips and hops imperceptibly over the boundaries of reason in his criticism" praises him for "insisting that man can experience sovereignty in the face of an Absence." But the method employed, it seems, comes close to a blueprint for the flower-power of the 1960s:[12] "There are limits which must remain limits," Beaujour writes, "although, like all limits, these must repeatedly be overstepped, in fear and trembling. In other words, Bataille clings to guilt, he accepts his guilt, man's guilt. In a sense, guilt becomes a positive value" (1971, 150, 168). Perhaps this might be said of anyone who writes both "pornography" and "theology," but in Bataille this conflation, which does seem to appear quite insistently throughout history, achieves consciousness. As Jürgen Habermas notes, "Eroticism led [Bataille] to the insight that knowledge of what is essential is reserved for mystical experience, for an illuminated silence." This typifies some erotic writers, who "can still use language in a poetic way, such that the reader, assaulted by obscenity, gripped by the shock of the unexpected and unimaginable, is jolted into the ambivalence of loathing and pleasure" (1998, 187–88). And it is this ambivalence that a writer like Bataille seeks to evoke,[13] a destabilization, a breaking of codes. An unknowing.

Questions and Approaches

As we move now to a consideration of the first essays in *Divine Aporia*, two aspects of Bataille's thinking beyond his notion of excess deserve emphasis. The first is its preoccupation with the moment, and the second is its war against institutionalization. As with many writers who deal with ecstasy, Bataille recognizes that it is a sometime thing. As one writer noted, "the 'religion' into which Bataille advanced can best be described as a godless mysticism, whose highest value is the breakout from self." For this reason, "he greeted Christian mystics as kindred spirits because they had undermined orthodox religion's reinforcement of the individual ego and often described their moments of self-surrender in revealingly carnal terms" (Anon. 1972, 234). "He works to restore the prerogatives of unreason" the writer continues, "for the serious purpose of revitalizing reason itself." It is supremely important to Bataille that those who seek "God" never imagine that their success in the quest is anything other than momentary:

> If one now wants to represent, with an initial clarity, the "grail" obstinately pursued through successive, deceptive, and cloudy depths, it is necessary to insist upon the fact that it could never have been a *substantial* reality; on the contrary, it was an element characterized by the impossibility of its enduring. The term *privileged instant* is the only one that, with a certain amount of accuracy, accounts for what can be encountered *at random* in the search; the opposite of a *substance* that withstands the test of time, it is something that flees as soon as it is seen and cannot be grasped. The will to fix such instants, which belong, it is true, to painting or writing is only the way to make them *reappear*, because the painting or the poetic text *evokes* but does not *make substantial* what once appeared. This gives rise to a mixture of unhappiness and exultation, of disgust and insolence; nothing seems more miserable and more dead than the stabilized thing, nothing is more desirable than what will soon disappear. (Bataille 1985, 241)

His final words here lead to the second point of emphasis. As he notes, "[I]t is decisively important in this movement that the search, intellectually undertaken at the promptings of unsatisfied desire, has always preceded theory's delineation of the object sought." This is an intriguing idea: a search without an object or, perhaps, an object only theorized in retrospect. But, of course, that is not what usually happens—and, perhaps, that is why various grails are so fitfully encountered and then so half-heartedly remembered. The search for the uncanny is too canny. And perhaps that is one reason we don't all agree on the object of the quest. ("At the moment when the priest, armed with a knife (and with the priest, a dirty death) heads toward the cow, which is just a random animal, undifferentiated from any other cow that ruminates in a field, it becomes a divinity because of the circle traced around its legs" [Bataille 1985, 73].) It is not, perhaps, the priest's choice of a *cow* that Bataille finds objectionable, but rather the *priest's* choice of a cow. It is the institution's de-othering of the object that overturns the milkpail:

> The supreme being of theologians and philosophers represents the most profound introjection of the structure characteristic of *homogeneity* into *heterogeneous* existence: in his theological aspect, God

preeminently fulfills the sovereign form. However, the counterpart
to this possibility is implied by the fictitious character of divine
existence, whose *heterogeneous* nature, lacking the limitative value
of reality, can be overlooked in a philosophical conception (reduced
to a formal affirmation that is in no way lived). In the order of free
intellectual speculation, the idea can be substituted for God as supreme existence and power; this implies the admittedly partial revelation of a relative *heterogeneity* of the Idea. (Bataille 1985, 153)

One wonders, though, if Bataille must, by this logic, disgard all theologians. At any rate, he would certainly hold up what Winquist has called
"the disappointment of thinking" as a move in the right direction, and the
complaints of contemporary theologians like the following as misplaced
(because so true):

The problem of the perceived *loss of a framework* is widely
recognised as severe, because postmodern criticism of the principle
of subjectivity and its successor concepts seem to undercut any
possibility for clearing a foundation on which a framework could be
constructed. (Klemm 1993, 180)

We begin the first section of this book with Paul Lakeland's introduction to the recent writing of Jean-Luc Marion and John Milbank on the
question of whether or not a Christian God stands outside any metaphysical or ontological framework. Lakeland offers a critical questioning of the
connection between theological truth and foundationalism, and the depen-
dency of theology upon rationalist philosophies. This is very much in tune
with Kevin Hart's ongoing project, which contends that deconstruction
has been mistakenly framed in two ways: as a refinement of the Nietzschean
doctrine that God is dead, and as a displaced negative theology. Hart argues that deconstruction, while targeting metaphysics rather than theology, allows for reemphasis upon a nonmetaphysical theology that may be
reminiscent of negative theology (Hart 1989, x–xi).[14] And, Hart argues,
this is something of a two-way street. "From Descartes to Russell," he
writes, "mysticism has often been represented as philosophy's 'other,' as
that which must at all costs be excluded from philosophical discourse.
Deconstruction enables us to trace the effects within a discourse of precisely this kind of exclusion" (xi). Ed Block's introduction to one aspect of
Hans Urs von Balthasar's system demonstrates this theologian's quite different approach, a fascination with drama as a means of awakening a sense
of otherness and of eliciting an attempt at engagement through beauty and

love. The reader is redirected away from the traditional theological task of determining truth verification and objectivity in theological systems and toward drama and theater. According to Block, Balthasar's precursory postmodern aesthetic theory points to an immanentist theology that locates the encounter between the finite and the infinite, or the human and the transcendent Other, in the social form of drama known as theater. The mystery and sacredness of life is most brilliantly enacted in the words and deeds of human actors, not the Divine Author. Andrew McKenna's essay on René Girard's mimetic theory proposes "interindividuality," an other-centered one-anotherness, in preference to an intersubjectivity that would imply a greater integrity to the individuated subject than Girard finds evidence for. With echoes of Bakhtin and Levinas, the concept underscores the process of engagement as determinative of identity and illuminative of alterity. T. R. Wright suggests a debate between Julia Kristeva and Emmanuel Levinas on the respective merits of intertextuality and intersubjectivity. In Wright's illuminating essay on the correlation between Midrash and modern literary theory, the reader is encouraged to think about the illusions of theological discourse conceived as full and final revelatory truth, or as a totalizing system. This essay also points to the excess (or the exteriority) that always accompanies the idea of a closed, intact system of meaning. Wright's essay shows that the processes of reinterpretation and reevaluation celebrated in modern literary theory are endemic to understanding textual interpretation in certain biblical traditions.

Voices from the Margin

> The postmodern God . . . cannot emerge as anything other than an idol until theological discourse articulates its own spatiality and temporality, its own personhood and body, its own ethos. Theology must announce doctrines of creation and incarnation beyond the onto-theologies and humanisms of modernity. (Ward 1997, xli)

> In a secular culture theology cannot easily delimit a *place* of it *own*. There is no sanctuary for theological reflection. The locus of a theology is the space of the other. (Winquist 1995, x)

In the times of Ignatius of Loyola and Teresa of Avila, in the midst of degeneracy in the cities, Michel de Certeau records that there arose a

> movement that led "spiritual" scholars and theologians to seek wit-
> ness among people far below them in social status—maidservants,
> cowherds, villagers, etc. Real or fictional, these . . . stories tell of
> pilgrimages toward a different kind of "illumination." . . . [T]hose
> "spiritual" intellectuals who converted to the "barbarians," . . . were
> expressing the insufficiency of their knowledge in the face of a
> disaster in the system of reference. . . . These Magi go among the
> "little people" to hear that which still speaks. A field of knowledge
> takes leave of its textual "authorities" to turn to the exegesis of
> "wild" voices. (1986, 86)

The result was the production of innumerable biographies of these "others" who encountered a transcendent reality, happily naive to the cynical
demands of educated rationality. "In these writings," de Certeau concludes,
"a tradition, humiliated after having functioned as the court of reason, awaits
and receives from its other the certitudes that escape it" (1986, 87). This
"certitude" involves the experience of having spoken and having been heard,
or having listened, and having been spoken to. "Mysticism," de Certeau
writes, "is the anti-Babel. It is the search for a common language, after
language has been shattered. It is the invention of a 'language of the angels' because that of man has been disseminated" (88).[15] Again, as with so
many of the authors who address this topic, a kind of exhaustion of rational avenues—without giving leave of one's senses—seems to be the acceptable, the desirable, path in the quest of the particular departicularized
grail.

In writers of this tradition—in a John of the Cross, for example—

> the name of God constantly reintroduces something other around
> the borders of every system of knowledge and every pleasure. It is
> a mechanism of exteriority, an "open sesame" working inside mean-
> ing, moving outward in relation to all cognitive or affective states. It
> is a principle of travel. . . . The *Ascent of Mount Carmel* sends the
> hierarchical order of systems of knowledge and pleasures on an
> endless voyage, entirely by the force of a "something else again." . .
> . "God" is a tool of dissuasion in every place, a *password*. It makes
> things pass. It dis-places; . . . it is an operative signifier, a part
> functioning as the *lapsus* or *raptus* the *Cloud of Unknowing* recom-
> mends for use. (de Certeau 1986, 111)

But beyond the ecstatic state, the diurnal necessities and questions return,
and in the engagement with these questions arises the border condition of
aporia. The stories to which de Certeau refers in his account of the time of

Ignatius of Loyola are what might be termed "significant" narratives, for a time. Commenting on the work of Edith Wyschogrod, H. Frederick Felice notes that "a form of hagiographic narrative makes possible the creation of a space in which modern dichotomies and postmodern aporias can be overcome and the voice of the Other can resound" (Tilley 1995, 70). And, because Wyschogrod demands a radical altruism from her saints, and one may always slip from this ideal while still living, it is "only in narratives, complete narratives . . . [that] saintliness [can] truly appear" (1995, 75). Furthermore, building on Levinas's writings, both Wyschogrod and Felice note that "only if the other remains an other (who is not taken as a mirror of oneself) can one respond to another and be called out of oneself" (72).

Narratology would suggest that storytelling requires a different sort of thinking, a rationality that speaks through emotions. David Klemm, while regretting the loss of a theological framework, suspects as much:

> This situation leads back to literature because the first step in moving beyond the impasse of the loss of a framework becomes that of telling the *story* of the loss of framework. Many suppose that constructing the narrative of the demise of theology's framework itself can orientate our questions concerning the task of theology. Habermas, as well as Charles Taylor, Alasdair MacIntyre and others, proceed in that way. Such a method leads us back to literature, in the sense that theologians therewith become more aware of the narrative form their presuppositions must take in the absence of a solid framework. (1993, 180)

And thus, in seeking such a narrative form, we seek out the stories of others. The chapters by Ned Hayes, Sam McBride and Ed Madden introduce questions of gender as central to these individual experiences of alterity. Hayes recurs to Julia Kristeva and Hélène Cixous to cast his discussion of Mark Taylor's theology in feminist terms; in a somewhat similar strategy Sam McBride quotes Luce Irigaray to "feminize" God by removing the need for a master, or master's narrative. Ed Madden uses Havelock Ellis's 1897 study of homosexuality, *Sexual Inversion*, and Radclyffe Hall's 1928 lesbian novel, *The Well of Loneliness*, to exemplify the discussion of "minor literature" carried out by Gilles Deleuze and Félix Guattari, and asks when such a literature may claim authority (see also, Laurel Schneider).

Gilles Deleuze notes that "a minor literature doesn't come from a minor language; it is rather that which a minority constructs within a major language" (Deleuze and Guattari 1986, 16-27; Deleuze and Parnet 1987, 4). In our own age the importance of "minor literatures" can conceivably function in the broader society much as mystical writings did in the six-teenth century, as goads to imagination. However, speaking on behalf of many such "subaltern" individuals and groups, feminist writer Rebecca Chopp notes that "questions about the contours of modern theory can be charted from many places, with the resulting sense that modern theory was displaced from all sides at once. African Americans, Hispanic Americans, lesbians, and others who could not or would not occupy the 'subject' position of modern theory asked whose interests modern truth and power served. Those not represented in the dominant center questioned how their otherness had been constructed or rendered invisible" (Chopp and Davaney 1997, 218). Maggie Kim describes the resulting task as dual. "As feminist theologians," she writes, "we face the 'double task' of deconstructing the terms that allow for meaning in patriarchy and of dis-covering new terms that would give rise to a more just society" (Kim et al. 1993, 7).

In Winquist's words, "[T]he need for a minor literature is to resist the repressive totalizing tendencies of the dominant discourse that seeks to stabilize itself in the midst of its incompleteness" (1995, 128). Apart from any questions of justice that may demand such tolerance, the practical need embodied for society by such openness is our ongoing desire to break out of entropic totalization. Winquist, in fact, looks upon theology itself as a minor literature, one that provides a "tactical implementation of the mul-tiple strategies of acoluthetic reason,[16] erring, deconstructive and herme-neutical tropologies, bricolage, radical criticism, parabolic and paradoxical narratives in the context of a dominant discourse of commodification." Theology thereby fulfills its contemporary role by becoming a *contami-nant.* "A minor literature is made of texts that are unsafe and are a conta-gion that makes all texts unsafe" (1995, 128–29). Such "contamination" becomes a liberatory battle cry in recent influential theological works that integrate queer theory, feminism, and cultural studies into their methods. These writers often enough identify the Other, despised by the dominant religious tradition, with the Divine Other itself.

Robert Goss's queer study of Christian violence toward lesbians and gays, for example, takes an approach that would have tickled Bataille: "On Easter . . . Jesus 'came out of the closet' and became the 'queer' Christ. Jesus the Christ becomes actively queer through his solidarity with our struggles for liberation" (Goss 1993, 84). Echoing the work of Sallie McFague, in which the erotics of the divine are called forth (McFague 1987, 130), Goss broadens his argument:

God has been used as a heterosexist and homophobic weapon to repress women, gay men and lesbian women, and other minorites. The apathetic God has rendered them socially and politically invisible. God is neither a homophobic oppressor nor an ecclesial superego, constraining us from integrating our own gay/lesbian sexual identities. This imaging God as passionless is ecclesial idolatry. It is biblical heterosexism and homophobia that culturally constructs God as apathetic, failing to understand the Hebrew theological statement that we, female and male, lesbian and gay, bisexual, transsexual, and heterosexual, were created in the image of God. The biblical God is a God of erotic and human diversity. . . . *Agape, eros,* and *philia* are unified in love and are part of God's relating to us. To eclipse one aspect of love in God is to eclipse the image of God. (1993, 163–64)

Goss's concern to envision "socially involved and erotic metaphors of God" (162) reverberates in much feminist theology. Anne Gilson, for example, suggests that "eros is a yearning for embodied connection with one another, a movement toward embodied justice. . . . [Therefore,] finding ways to de-alienate and reconnect an alienated and dis-connected eros is precisely the agenda for feminist liberation theo-ethics" (1995, 109). For Carter Heyward "God is our power in mutual relations." She writes that "the erotic is not only movement toward mutuality. It involves a yearning or longing for mutuality. 'Yearning' implies a desire for something we don't yet have, don't quite know how to participate in, or don't experience fully as ours" (1989, 105). Along these lines, Robert Manning takes his inspiration from Levinas, who posits that "the erotic relationship differs from the relationship of knowledge or power, in which the subject obtains what it seeks and is satiated. There is no satiation in love, however, because the subject seeks what shows itself as unobtainable. . . . The beloved is always revealed/concealed as an absent presence and a present absence" (1993, 76). Maggie Kim looks with hope to Julia Kristeva's work, suggesting that her "concern with the process of meaning coming to be rather than with particular meanings already given offers us a new way to think about the practice of theology" (Kim et al. 1993, 7). Elizabeth Grosz turns to the work of Luce Irigaray and writes that for Irigaray

God is the term necessary for positioning one's finite being in both the context of other finitudes (sexual, social, terrestrial) and in the context of the infinite. God provides the genre, the context, the milieu and limit of the subject, and the horizon of being against which subjectivity positions itself. . . . The divine is not simply the reward for earthly virtue, all wishes come true; it is rather the field

of creativity, fertility, production, an always uncertain and
unpreempted field. It is the field or domain of what is new, what
has not existed before, a mode of transcendence, a projection of the
past into a future that gives the present new meaning and direction.
The divine is a movement, a movement of and within history, a
movement of becoming without *telos*, a movement of love in its
Empedoclean sense. (Grosz, quoted in Kim et al. 1993, 208, 210)

Ed Madden's discussion of "gospels of inversion," therefore, serves
as a transition to this volume's second section, which focuses on specific
examples of "alienated" narration. What is being invoked in these chapters
is the potential for another way of seeing, another way of opening a window on the divine aporia. Recalling James Olthuis's question about the
possibility for a nonphilosophical/nontheological "gift" of an encounter, Susan Petit introduces readers to the remarkable French novelist Françoise
Mallet-Joris, in whose disturbing 1991 novel, *Divine*, a high-school science teacher in contemporary Paris retraces the classic path of many mystics but does so in the context of historical parody and mixed genres.
Through bulimia the protagonist finds herself in the dark night of the senses,
has a mystical experience in a supermarket, experiences the dark night of
the soul partly in the form of seemingly unrequited love, and finally, following a deeper mystical experience while defrosting her refrigerator, makes
an attempt to balance mysticism with practicality. This effort is cut short
when she is murdered by a former lover. Petit's essay ponders seemingly
uninvited encounters with "the other," whether from within or without,
and her account is surely defamiliarizing.

Bradley Monsma's suggestive discussion of the "intersection" of mythic
worlds asks us to consider trickster texts as invitations to liminality which
cause us continually to interrogate the knowledge and motivations we bring
to texts, and to ask, as well, what it is that we wish to take from them (on
this point, see Bron Taylor's discussion of the appropriation of Native
American spiritualities [1997]). The attention Monsma directs to Native
American thinking and engagement with the physical world alerts us to
David Griffin's caveat that "'others' should not be understood as limited to
other human beings, but as including God and nature as well" (Griffin
1973, 241). And, as Herbert Grabes notes, "[A]n even more rigorous
demand to respect alterity can be found in another strain of more recent
ethical thought, in ecological ethics. . . . The question of what man should
do in this context is no longer humanly self-determined, but determined by
the radically other, by what nature can endure" (1996, 22). This is a concern that engages Carol Adams in her essay in this section.

Charlene Spretnak underscores that "nonmodern cultures have never lost sight of [the fact that] all human endeavors are situated in *eco*social, or *cosmic*-social, construction" (1997, 184). In Spretnak's view, the most interesting work in the last decade by those who are grappling with the problematic assumptions inherent in objectivism is, from the vantage of ecological postmodernism, "experientialist," finding metaphors for conceptual and abstract thought that "derive from *bodily experience in the world*" (1997, 75) and, specifically, "acts of *participation in nature*." For Spretnak, this problem (and its potential solution) takes on a feminist slant:

> In patriarchal societies the fundamental orientation toward the two primal power-mysteries—nature and the elemental power of the female—is fear because those powers are conceived of as power-over and threatening, rather than as cosmic presence, a dynamic and transformative power in which males participate. This fundamental response infuses all social constructions. For patriarchal men in particular, who have traditionally shaped Western culture, all relationships, and even the very nature of relationship, are potentially dangerous. Safety lies in guarding one's autonomy and dominating others whenever possible. (1991, 121)

Rosemary Ruether (1992), Sallie McFague (1987, 1993), David Levin (1988), John Llewellyn (1991), and others generally concur with Spretnak's reading of the situation and her suggestions of a possible alternative, but they do draw the criticism of others.[17]

Ethical Maps on Shifting Grounds

"The problem of how to deal with alterity," writes Herbert Grabes, "is more acute in the domain of ethics than in any other," and he offers a summary of how it has been addressed. In his view, "The central objective in the tradition of ethical thought has . . . been mediation" (1996, 19). Some of our discussion to this point might overvalorize an implicit mystical, intuitive, privatizing of religious phenomena that continues to associate theological activity with antirationalism. However, as Gerhard Hoffmann and many others have noted, there is a "new interest in an ethical component of aesthetic structures which for short might be called 'the moral turn of postmodernism.'" He goes on to explain why this is so:

> Since its inception in the 1960s, postmodernism has been associ-

ated with decorative, nonfunctional and playful practices. Its initial
assumption of a breakdown of the distinction between fact and
fiction and the negation of an extralinguistic reality have given way
to a renewed interest in the outside world. The changed conditions
of the 1980s, most visible in the debate about race, class, gender and
creed, the practice of multiculturalism, and the fervor of political
correctness in the United States, or the postcolonial concerns world-
wide, have brought about a form of what Salman Rushdie terms the
"emancipatory postmodernism" intent on expanding and enhancing
our notions of reality guided by a moral impetus. (Hoffmann and
Hornung 1996, v)

The book's third section, therefore, addresses the possibilities and responsibilities that alterity occasions. We do not immediately say alterity
demands this engagement, but only that it occasions it. As John Milbank
notes, "[T]he Christian paradigm for a virtuous act is a spontaneously creative act, which does not fundamentally assume a prior evil to be contained" (1997, 4). This emphasis on creative energy rather than onerous
burdens opens the subject to a far less economic and rational exchange
with "the other."
     In discussing Levinas's thought, Krzysztof Ziarek puts the problem
clearly:

> There is no possibility of establishing a relation with what makes
> the other other . . . [because] [d]ialogue is predicated upon a com-
> mon frame of reference, that is subjectivity, which reduces the oth-
> erness of the other to another subject. The other becomes then like
> myself, an/other me, whom I can understand on its own terms. . . .
> For Levinas, [this] intersubjectivity then continues, under the guise
> of a mutually respectful dialogue with the other, the domination of
> the Same in Western philosophy. (Ziarek 1990, 95)

Levinas uses the story of Abraham as a better model for "relating" to the
other, since Abraham went out from his fatherland forever into an unknown land, from which return was forever prohibited—in Ziarek's words,
"the other's alterity remains inaccessible to thought and makes impossible
its return to itself and self-reflection" (95). Again, as in much of the writing on this topic, there is established that *zwischenraum* (an in-between
space) that, if allowed to remain foreign, preserves the otherness and resists "colonization," rationalization, or familiarization. "The relation to or
non-indifference toward the other," writes Levinas, "does not consist, for
the Other, in being converted into the Same" (Levinas 1996b, 159), where

the Other is defined as that which resists or refuses the ego's powers of conceptualization and thematization. What that Other is seeking is a "*spiritual intrigue wholly other than* gnosis" (154).]

Sharon Welch's Foucauldian-inspired work, while acknowledging the failure of liberal theology to speak convincingly of its referent (God), advances a liberationist praxis that evokes a different set of cultural practices aimed at transforming society. She notes that some theologians, uncomfortable with ambiguity, "claim that . . . endless changes in theological discourse can be avoided. They find a secure home for theological discourse in ahistorical or supernatural authorities, either in revelation as found in scripture and doctrine or in the weight and wisdom of tradition. Both authorities are valued and used without acknowledgement that they are characterized by the same tenuousness, contingency, and partiality as the discourse they are presumed to ground" (1985, 32; see also Hawley, 1994). But, Welch suggests, resisting this spurious uniformity results in new forms of community which share much in common with the marginalized groups discussed in this collection's second group of essays:

> To state that liberation theology is an insurrection of subjugated knowledges means that the discourse of liberation theology represents the resurgence of knowledges suppressed by a dominant theology and a dominant culture. Further analysis involves three elements of genealogy: the preservation and communication of memories of conflict and exclusion; the discovery and exposition of excluded contents and meanings; and the strategic struggle between the subjugated and dominant knowledges. (1985, 35; see also Foucault 1980, 81–83)

This "vision is not based on anthropology but emerges from communal struggles for a particular kind of humanity. . . . It is to be achieved, not merely recognized" and, in the process, "concepts of faith and of God are correspondingly relativized" and realized in praxis (1985, 66).

One thing that is striking about many of the movements in theology, philosophy, cultural studies, etc., is this renewed emphasis on experience and upon the body. Edith Wyschogrod's reading of Levinas certainly takes note of this aspect of being, recognizing that "the passivity, the vulnerability of the body-subject is preparatory. It is the vulnerability of the other that challenges the structure of the self as an egology" [*sic*] (1996, 66). It results in a recognition of responsibility in quite practical terms: "In sum, the body as a whole, construed in a preliminary way by a number of traditional philosophers (Aristotle, Condillac et al.) as a field of tactility, can now be seen in its dual function as a proscription against harming the other and as placing oneself at the disposal of the other. No longer an isolated consciousness nor even a being in the world, the body of the body-subject has become the body of ethics" (1996, 67). She is building upon Levinas, who considers the issue as follows:

> [H]aving set its sovereignty aside, [the *I*] makes itself responsible for freedoms foreign to its own, as non-indifferent to others, and, precisely thus, as absolutely different. An existence relative indeed, of one-for-the-other. . . . An excessive expenditure if there ever was one, in the responsibility of the *one* reduced to the condition—or incondition—of hostage to all the *others*. . . . But the significance and indisputable obligations that can be called religious (even if this term remains intolerable to certain people because of the puerilities it evokes)—significance and obligations that give meaning to an entire group of human beings who are responsible for others—may not adhere to the revolving, englobing movement of Greek philosophy. And the end of that philosophy, the escape from that encirclement, is not the end of the meaningful that a non-disseminated language, not encrusting its meaning in its syntax, might be able to say. (1996a, 88–89)[18]

The essays in this third section, therefore, attempt to consider some of the ethical issues suggested by postmodern considerations of alterity. Jennifer Leader offers an interesting account of the implied debate between Sigmund Freud and Romain Rolland on the possibilities of loving, and uses contemporary discussions of mysticism and "interpathy" as accessible agents for dialogue. Susan Handelman begins her illuminative essay by considering the various interpretations that philosophers have offered for the central term in our discussion, that is, "the other," and then moves on to the writings of Levinas because he "is one of the few writers who is able to restore *ethical binding* in the face of the ruptures enacted in postmodern thought. His aim," she writes, "is to deconstruct the subject but retain it as responsible, lucid, awake, obligated." She then demonstrates how his thought has connections with such writers as Chaim Perelman and Franz Rosenzweig. Robert Manning looks to the late writings of Levinas to consider not only the obligations one has to an other, but also the obligations implied by "the third." Kenneth Reinhard's article contrasts Jacques Lacan's "other love" with Levinas's "intertextual neighboring," and notes how they both deal with the Holocaust "as trauma, as that which cannot be symbolized." The concatenation among these chapters is often surprising, with cascading levels of allusion and interplay. At the same time, though, the complexities of our discussion leave little room to doubt the accuracy of Charles Winquist's gloomy assessment of the state of human knowledge: "The death of God," he writes, "and the disappearance of a unified and single subject as legacies of the nineteenth century are perhaps the most vivid of our losses, although they entail other losses, such as the end of the meaning of history and the closure of the book as a source of wisdom" (1995, 7).

And yet, in the face of rational analysis and the debate between philosophers and theologians, it does not take long before the charm of narrative reasserts itself. As Jack Miles notes regarding the Tanakh,

> God maintains his peculiar power as a literary character because in him—around and through whatever fusion of ancient Semitic divinities he represents—that which is most radically, unanswerably terrifying in human existence is endowed with voice and intention as well as with caprice and silence. In the confrontation between Job and the Voice from the Whirlwind, the process by which that inescapable condition becomes this overpowering character comes to a climax. (1995, 327)

We live with as much fear as hope that the silence may be shattered, that the Voice from the Whirlwind may make its "othered" self terrifyingly present—in a whisper. Our fears may simply center on a concern that the God about whom we continue to tell stories is as confused, vindictive, and bumbling as we. On the other hand, the fears may be our less familiar, occasional glimpses into a tabernacle *beyond* our imagining—but, finally, no less terrifying.

"As the years pass," writes Harold Bloom, "I develop an ever greater horror of solitude, of finding myself having to confront sleepless nights and baffled days in which the self ceases to know how to talk to itself" (989, 131). He turns, he says, to Wordsworth and to Freud to learn how to continue the internal conversation. But there are limitations to the lessons they may teach. "Otherness," Bloom writes,

> is the overt teaching of Wordsworth and of Freud, whether the other be the object of the heart's affections or the object of the drives. Yet there is something equivocal in that otherness, whether Freudian or Wordsworthian, because tropologically such otherness itself is a kind of death, a figuration for one's own death. (1989, 132)

What is needed—what, some believe, remains—is a stark otherness, beyond this internal conversation. The contributors to this collection hope to show how reasonable it is for Catherine Bell to assert that "no single 'trope' has been more important to modernists and postmodernists alike than the identification of a theological other." And in that search, the "presence" of this aporia takes center stage:

> While many have attempted to reintegrate what modernism and postmodernism have differentiated and polarized, no particular formulation of integration can ever hold. It is the *gaps* that enable us to do what we have been doing as scholars, explaining religion and interpreting the "culturally other." . . . For the most part, we proceed with a language of cultural symbols that allows us . . . to play cultural differences off against sufficient structural commonality to legitimate *our* discourse on *their* codes. However, . . . we have to understand more clearly how "culture" in all its forms becomes the "other" of explanation and research, and how this opposition is itself dependent on the "othering" that postmodernism both critiques and promotes. (Bell 1996, 187–88)

An "early" Mark Taylor may offer cold comfort: "The death of the transcendent Father," he writes, "need not be the complete disappearance of God, but can be seen as the birth of the divine, which now is grasped as an immanent and eternal process of dialectical development. The death of solitary selfhood need not be the total disappearance of self, but it can be seen as the birth of universal selfhood in which each becomes itself by relation to all" (1982, 102). But one can further hope that James Olthuis is correct in his estimate of the context of our discussions here and in ongoing investigations: "Because God as love (and love as God) is an overflowing, an excess, an emptying going beyond its own limits, a letting go, life and discourse can be connective, celebrative, communicative" (1997, 244). Lest this be seen as simply an act of the will, perhaps the last word should be given to John Milbank. Making no bones about his own commitment as a British Christian, he asserts that Jesus ("essentially a linguistic and poetic reality") is the only answer to the nihilistic abyss that these various philosophical and theological aporias seem to open up. Obviously, not everyone involved in the discussion has come to this conclusion nor, perhaps, is likely to. But his hopeful rationale for the work in which he is engaged may suggest a new way of thinking that others may translate for themselves in helpful ways. He seeks, he says, to disinter a spirit within British tradition which runs counter to the myth of British identity to which it has nonetheless surrendered: that it is empiricist, philistine, and basely pragmatic. For there is an alternative vatic, "Platonic" tradition within British culture which construes empiricism as openness to the strange and unclassifiable, and pragmatism as surrender to the surprise of that which is mediated to us through language, from a transcendent source. (1997, 2)

Notes

1.   "In contemporary thought aporia represents a dead-end to a line of thought which calls for the mediation of new ideas or perhaps the reformulation of the questions asked. For example, in *Hermeneutics and the Human Sciences* (1981) Paul Ricoeur refers to an internal aporia of hermeneutical reflection which calls for a reorientation of hermeneutics through semiotics. The hermeneutical inquiry after Martin Heidegger and Hans-Georg Gadamer has overcome the aporia of subject/object through the concept of Being-in-the-world as linguistically constituted, but the aporia has been displaced and not eliminated. Heidegger has displaced the arena from 'how do I know the other' (epistemology) to 'the primacy of belonging in language' (ontology). After Gadamer the aporia becomes how does my world fuse with the text's world? The mediation of the textual sciences offers a possibility of shared meaning not only within language but also within textual analysis" (Makaryk 1993, 507).

2.   Bell calls Talal Asad's *Genealogies of Religion* (1993) "the most intelligent and nuanced postmodernist challenge to the field [of religious studies] to date. For Asad . . . the modernist model of religion and the academic study of religion legitimate a certain narrative understanding of history that culminates in the dominance of secular institutions over religion on the one hand, while, on the other, they authorize scholars of religion to subordinate a multitude of cultural experiences to the status of mere examples of a reality that scholars alone can articulate" (1996, 184–85).

3.   Craig Westman similarly notes that "Griffin's vision defines itself over against the modern individualistic dualism that allows humans to exploit nature mechanistically through setting the exploiting self apart from exploitable nature" (Tilley 1995, 17), and he aligns his theology with the ecological movement (see also MacKinnon and McIntyre 1995). Graham Ward also describes David Griffin's theology as "animistic theism . . . developed through an examination of quantum mechanics and process philosophy" (1997, xl).

4.   Phillip Blond writes, "Theology is the discourse about the origin of being. For this reason ontology cannot account for theology; ontology can offer no

discourse as to its own origin. . . . If ontology is the discourse of being *qua* being, an investigation of being in its most general and universal form, then without God, I would suggest, it is a discourse that cannot grasp its own essence. The undoubted profundity and weight of a secular ontology will consist only in its perpetual marking of aporias and paradoxes. For only theology can give an account of these disjunctures that allows thinking to move beyond them" (Blond 1998, 12). Does this echo Newman? Does it require faith, which then seeks understanding? Where is this "beyond"?

5.   Kevin Hart makes the point that "negative theology cannot lead us silently into the immediate presence of a deity regarded as *res cogitans*. Its function is otherwise: it reminds us that God escapes all programmes, even the many subtle ones developed by philosophers and theologians. God is possible, says the positive theologian, meaning that the divine is revealed if only we would see (and the terms of seeing are then spelt out). God is impossible, says the negative theologian, meaning that God always exceeds the concept of God. Each theology claims priority: without negative theology God talk would decay into idolatry, yet without positive theology there would be no God talk in the first place. It is a permanent task of religious thought to keep the negative and the positive in play, to demonstrate that the impossible is not in contradiction with the possible. What Derrida helps bring into focus is that the possible and the impossible are not to be resolved dialectically or logically: they arrange and rearrange themselves in the negative form of an aporia. Religious experience pulls a person in different directions at the same time, demanding we attend both to the possible and the impossible; and in negotiating this aporia one's conscience is never satisfied. This experience of desire, dissatisfaction, insufficiency and uncertainty is a part of the God effect" (1998, 278). One must be cautious, of course, in merging Derrida with negative theology and believing that there is necessarily something divine or religious in facing the limits of epistemology; see, for example, Derrida 1993.

6.   Marion notes the conversation from which his writing arises: "Written at the border between philosophy and theology, this essay [*God Without Being*] remains deeply marked by the spiritual and cultural crisis in which it is thought and written. That crisis, shared by an entire generation (at least), had a time and a stake. The time: the test of nihilism which, in France, marked the years dominated by 1968. A stake: the obscuring of God in the indistinct haze of the 'human sciences,' which at the time were elevated by 'structuralism' to the rank of dominant doctrine. Later I shall have to say what this field of passions, discoveries, strife, and work actually was—this field in which I struggled like so many others, having as close teachers [Jean] Beaufret, [Jacques] Derrida, but also [Louis] Althusser; as masters, [F.] Alquie and [E.] Levinas, but also [Etienne] Gilson, [Jean] Danielou, and [Hans Urs] von Balthasar" (Marion 1991, xix).

7.   Krzysztof Ziarek notes Jean-Luc Marion's interest in the icon as an object that seems to gaze at the subject: "the other as the icon makes impossible the closure of the I in the field of visibility produced by its own gaze" (Ziarek

1990, 99–100).

8.   H. D. Harootunian notes that Foucault, whom he describes as the "historian of alterity," "problematized the relationship between ourselves and the Other and, in fact, recentered the question of otherness altogether, asserting what Bakhtin elsewhere called 'exotopy,' the affirmation of the Other's exteriority which requires acknowledging its subjectivity" (1988, 111–112).

9.   Winquist defines the concept this way:

[Descartes's] concept of God is of an infinite substance, eternal, immutable, independent, omniscient, omnipotent, and the creator of all things. Descartes claimed that the more attentively I considered the attributes of this concept of God, "the less I can persuade myself that I could have derived them from my own nature." [But] it would seem to a reader in the twentieth century that this argument is less a proof for the existence of God than the use of the concept of God to trope the discourse of subjectivity and transgress its domain. . . . [T]his theological crack in subjectivity does not give any immediate access to an objective world. Consciousness is still phenomenal consciousness. (1995, 35)

10.   See, also, John Caputo:

Everything that Derrida has to say, especially in the most recent work, about the invention of the wholly other, about the passion for the impossible, about a hospitality toward something to come that explodes our horizons of expectation, about the promise, the yes, yes, the gift, about *croire sans voir, sans avoir, sans savoir*, about the justice to come—all that is charged with a religious and messianic force, like a certain Judaism without rabbis and religion, transparently and audibly so, I would say. On this accounting, deconstruction is a certain religion without religion, a non-dogmatic doublet of Judaism, affirming a doublet of a Messiah whom we will never live to see. We long, we live to see the Messiah, but we will never live to see him. (*Deo gratias.*). (1997, 195)

11.   In assessing his work, for example, Jean-Paul Sartre wrote:

These are not the scruples of an agnostic suspended between atheism and faith; a mystic is talking, a mystic who has seen God and who rejects the overly human language of people who have not. . . . I know that I am unable to help him and that he cannot help me; he is a madman in my eyes, and I know he thinks I am crazy too. What horrifies me is not what he says, but what he *is*. . . . He no doubt belongs to the spiritual family whose members are partial to the exhausting and acid charm of fruitless endeavors. . . . I do not deny that our author might be familiar with some ineffable states of anguish and masochistic joy. I only wish to point out that he fails in his attempt to furnish us with a method which would enable us to achieve the same result. . . . Who wants to know about the author of these pages, about his "sumptuous and bitter" soul, his pathological pride, his self-disgust, his eroticism, his frequently magnificent eloquence, the rigorous logic which masks his incoherent thoughts, his passionate bad faith, or his vain quest for an impossible escape? Literary criticism stops here. The rest is a matter for psychoanalysis. (1947, 21)

And Bataille himself conceded that "[in 1927] I was not insane but I made too much of the necessity of leaving, in one way or another, the limits of our human experience, and I adapted myself in a fairly disordered way so that the most improbable thing in the world (the most overwhelming as well, something like foam on the lips) would at the same time appear to me to be necessary" (1985, 74–75).

12.   An anonymous reviewer for the *Times Literary Supplement* noted in 1972 that "Bataille . . . would have no time at all for the guiltless sex now glibly recommended to us as a 'natural' ambition; for him this was pure self-deception. Not that the source of anguish in his own version was guilt in quite the normal sense, since the feeling in question is ontological rather than social. But there can be no doubt that Bataille's eroticism would be an easier accomplishment for a tormented Christian than for an easy-going secularist. Eroticism for him was a 'sexualite honteuse'" (234).

13.   Bataille is a master of such ambivalence: "It is not self-evident that the noble parts of a human being (his dignity, the nobility that characterizes his face), instead of allowing only a sublime and measured flow of profound and tumultuous impulses, brusquely cease to set up the least barrier against a sudden, bursting eruption, as provocative and as dissolute as the one that inflates the anal protuberance of an ape" (1985, 78).

14.   Hart contends that

   most attempts to develop a non-metaphysical theology are destined to fail before they begin. In my view the strongest attempts are made by the mystics, especially those who develop negative theologies, such as Pseudo-Dionysius. Contrary to the Thomist tradition, I argue that negative theology does not merely correct positive (or metaphysical) theology but supplements it at its ground and origin. Deconstruction may not be a negative theology, as Derrida repeatedly and rightly insists, but negative theology may deconstruct positive theology. In general terms, deconstruction helps to clarify the concept "non-metaphysical theology," while its strategy of using language "under erasure" illuminates particular moves and attitudes in mystical texts. (1989, xi)

15.   The objects of the mystics' discourse have the status of symptoms; essentially, they are prayer (in the form of communal exchanges and "spiritual guidance"). "Communication" (communications from God or those established among the saints) is everywhere a void to be filled, and forms the focal point of this lack. The rupture, ambiguity, and falsity that plurality spreads throughout the world creates the need to restore a *dialogue*. This *colloquium* would take place under the sign of the *Spirit* ("*el que habla*," the speaker, as St. John of the Cross phrases it), since the "letter" no longer allows it. How can one *hear*, through signs transformed into things, that which flows from a unique and divine *will to speak*? How can this desire in search of a *thou* cross through a language that betrays it by sending the addressee a different message, or by replacing the statement of an idea with

utterance by an "I"? (88)

    [In] "the distancing that constitutes the no-place of allocution on the margins of objective contents [the question is] if one can: address *to* God . . . the statements that concern Him; be in intercourse . . . *from thee* to *me*, with the Other or with others; hear and understand . . . those statements considered inspired" (89). "Do we exist to speak to the other, or be spoken by him?" (91).

16.   Acoluthetic reason is defined by Robert P. Scharlemann as implying that "subjectivity in one person is capable of encountering not only an analogy of its own inwardness in the person of the other, but also the identity of its own I in the other" (1991, 139).

17.   Steven Connor, for example, claims that this "dream of a healing saturation of intellect in the body, an achieved corporeal innocence that in claiming to go beyond, or get back to a condition before the dismembering dualisms of Western metaphysics, is itself an extension and effect of the tradition it wishes simply to surpass" (1996, 7).

18.   Caputo says Levinas was wrong in his "too assimilative attempt to cast the God of the prophets in the language of Greek philosophy, to give Greek thought the 'last word,' a tendency that has earned him some well-earned criticism from strictly Jewish quarters" (1997, 337).

Works Cited

Altizer, Thomas J. J., et al. 1982. *Deconstruction and Theology*. New York: Crossroad.

Anon. 1972. "Taboos and Transgressions." *Times Literary Supplement*. No. 3653 (March 3):233–34.

"Aporia." 1994. *Encyclopedia of Contemporary Literary Theory: Approaches, Scholars, Terms*. Ed. Irena R. Makaryk. Toronto: University of Toronto Press.

Arac, Jonathan, ed. 1988. *After Foucault: Humanistic Knowledge, Postmodern Challenges*. New Brunswick, NJ: Rutgers University Press.

Asad, Talal. 1993. *Genealogies of Religion: Discipline and Reasons of Power in Christianity and Islam*. Baltimore: Johns Hopkins University Press.

Bataille, Georges. 1943. *Expérience Intérieure*. Paris: J. J. Pauvert. [1988]. *Inner Experience*. Trans. Leslie Anne Boldt. Albany, NY: State University of New York Press.

———. 1985. *Visions of Excess: Selected Writings, 1927–1939*. Ed. and trans. Allan Stoekl. Minneapolis: University of Minnesota Press.

———. 1992. *On Nietzsche*. Trans. Bruce Boone. New York: Paragon House.

Bauman, Zygmunt. 1992. *Intimations of Postmodernity*. London: Routledge.

———. 1993. *Postmodern Ethics*. Oxford: Blackwell.

Beaujour, Michel. 1971. "Eros and Nonsense: Georges Bataille." *Modern French Criticism: From Proust and Valery to Structuralism*. Ed. John K. Simon. Chicago: University of Chicago Press. 149–73.

Bell, Catherine. 1996. "Modernism and Postmodernism in the Study of Religion." *Religious Studies Review* 22 (3):179–90.

Berry, Philippa and Andrew Wernick, eds. 1992. *Shadow of Spirit: Postmodernism and Religion*. London and New York: Routledge.

Blond, Phillip, ed. 1998. *Post-Secular Philosophy: Between Philosophy and Theology*. New York: Routledge.

Bloom, Harold. 1989. *Ruin the Sacred Truths: Poetry and Belief from the Bible to the Present*. Cambridge: Harvard University Press.

Botting, Fred and Scott Wilson, eds. 1998. *Bataille: A Critical Reader*. Oxford: Blackwell.

Caputo, John D. 1997. *The Prayers and Tears of Jacques Derrida: Religion Without Religion*. Bloomington: Indiana University Press.

Caputo, John D. and Michael J. Scanlon, eds. 1999. *God, the Gift, and Postmodernism*. Bloomington: Indiana University Press.

Carlson, Thomas A. 1998. "The Poverty and Poetry of Indiscretion: Negative Theology and Negative Anthropology in Contemporary and Historical Perspective." *Christianity and Literature* 47 (2):167–94.

Chopp, Rebecca S. and Sheila Greeve Davaney, eds. 1997. *Horizons in Feminist Theology: Identity, Tradition, and Norms*. Minneapolis: Fortress.

Cloud of Unknowing, The, 1981. Ed. James Walsh, S.J. New York: Paulist.

Connor, Steven. 1996. "After Cultural Value: Ecology, Ethics, Aesthetics." In Hoffmann and Hornung, 1–12.

Coward, Harold and Toby Foshay, eds. 1992. *Derrida and Negative Theology*. Albany: State University of New York Press.

Daly, Mary. 1978. *Gyn/Ecology: The Metaethics of Radical Feminism*. Boston: Beacon.

de Certeau, Michel. 1986. *Heterologies: Discourse on the Other*. Trans. Brian Massumi. Minneapolis: University of Minnesota Press.

Deleuze, Gilles and Felix Guattari. 1986. *Kafka: Toward a Minor Literature*. Trans. Dana Polan. Minneapolis: University of Minnesota Press.

Deleuze, Gilles and Claire Parnet. 1987. *Dialogues*. Trans. Hugh Tomlinson and Barbara Habberjam. New York: Columbia University Press.

Derrida, Jacques. 1993. *Aporias*. Stanford, CA: Stanford University Press.

Dupré, Louis. 1998. *Religious Mystery and Rational Reflection: Excursions in the Phenomenology of Religion*. Grand Rapids: Eerdmans.

Ebert, Teresa L. 1996. *Ludic Feminism and After: Postmodernism, Desire, and Labor in Late Capitalism*. Ann Arbor: University of Michigan Press.

Farley, Wendy. 1996. *Eros for the Other*. University Park: Pennsylvania State University Press.

Foucault, Michel. 1980. *Power/Knowledge: Selected Interviews and Other Writings, 1972–1977*. New York: Pantheon.

———. 1998. "A Preface to Transgression."Iin Botting and Wilson, 24–40.

Friel, Brian. 1990. *Dancing at Lughnasa*. London: Faber and Faber.

Fulkerson, Mary McClintock. 1997. "Contesting the Gendered Subject: A Feminist Account of the Imago Dei." In Chopp and Davaney, 99–115.

Gans, Steven. 1972. "Ethics or Ontology: Levinas and Heidegger." *Philosophy Today* 16 (2):117–21.

Gilson, Anne Bathurst. 1995. *Eros Breaking Free: Interpreting Sexual Theo-Ethics*. Cleveland: Pilgrim.

Goss, Robert. 1993. *Jesus Acted Up: A Gay and Lesbian Manifesto*. San Francisco: HarperCollins.

Grabes, Herbert. 1996. "Ethics, Aesthetics, and Alterity." In Hoffmann and Hornung, 13–28.

Griffin, David Ray. 1973. *A Process Christology*. Philadelphia: Westminster.

———. 1989. *God and Religion in the Postmodern World: Essays in Postmodern Theology*. Albany: State University of New York Press.

———. 1990. *Archetypal Process: Self and Divine in Whitehead, Jung, and Hillman*. Evanston, IL: Northwestern University Press.

Griffin, David R. et al., eds. 1989. *Varieties of Postmodern Theology*. Albany: State University of New York Press.

Habermas, Jürgen. 1998. "The French Path to Postmodernity: Bataille Between Eroticism and General Economics." In Botting and Wilson, 167–90.

Harootunian, H. D. 1988. "Foucault, Genealogy, History: The Pursuit of Otherness." In Arac, 110–137.

Hart, Kevin. 1989. *The Trespass of the Sign: Deconstruction, Theology, and Philosophy*. Cambridge: Cambridge University Press.

———. 1998. "Jacques Derrida: The God Effect." In Blond, 259–80.

Hawley, John C. 1994. "Literature and the Evolution of Religious Discourse." In *Reform and Counterreform: Dialectics of the Word in Western Christianity since Luther*. Ed. John C. Hawley. Berlin: Mouton de Gruyter. 225–40.

Heyward, Carter. 1989. *Touching Our Strength: The Erotic as Power and the Love of God*. San Francisco: Harper and Row.

Hoffmann, Gerhard and Alfred Hornung, eds. 1996. *Ethics and Aesthetics: The Moral*

Turn of Postmodernism. Heidelberg: Universitatsverlag C. Winter.

Ionesco, Eugene. 1958. *Four Plays: The Bald Soprano, The Lesson, Jack or the Submission, The Chairs.* Trans. Donald M. Allen. New York: Grove.

Jasper, David, ed. 1993. *Postmodernism, Literature and the Future of Theology.* London: Macmillan.

Kierkegaard, Soren. 1944. "The Instant," No. 5. *Kierkegaard's Attack upon Christendom 1854–1855.* Trans. Walter Lowrie. Boston: Beacon.

Kim, C. W. Maggie, Susan M. St. Ville and Susan M. Simonaitis, eds. 1993. *Transfigurations: Theology and the French Feminists.* Minneapolis: Fortress.

Klemm, David E. 1993. "Back to Literature—and Theology?" In Jasper, 180–90.

Lakeland, Paul. 1997. *Postmodernity: Christian Identity in a Fragmented Age.* Minneapolis: Fortress.

Levin, David Michael. 1988. *The Opening of Vision: Nihilism and the Postmodern Situation.* New York: Routledge.

Levinas, Emmanuel. 1979. *Totality and Infinity.* Trans. Alphonso Lingis. The Hague: Nijhoff.

———. 1996a. *Proper Names.* Trans. Michael B. Smith. Stanford, CA: Stanford University Press.

———. 1996b. *Emmanuel Levinas: Basic Philosophical Writings.* Ed. Adriaan T. Peperzak, Simon Critchley, and Robert Bernasconi. Bloomington: Indiana University Press.

Lichtman, Maria. 1998. "Negative Theology in Marguerite Porete and Jacques Derrida." *Christianity and Literature* 47 (2):213–27.

Lindbeck, George A. 1984. *The Nature of Doctrine.* Philadelphia: Westminster.

Llewellyn, John. 1991. *The Middle Voice of Ecological Conscience.* New York: St. Martin's.

MacKinnon, Mary Heather and Moni McIntyre, eds. 1995. *Readings in Ecology and Feminist Theology.* Kansas City: Sheed and Ward.

Makaryk, Irena R., ed. 1993. *Encyclopedia of Contemporary Literary Theory.* Toronto: University of Toronto Press.

Malevich, Kazimir S. 1982. "Suprematism. 34 Drawings." In *Malevich: Suprematism and Revolution in Russian Art, 1910–1930,* by Larissa A. Zhadova. Trans. Alexander Lieven. New York: Thames and Hudson. 284–87.

Manning, Robert John Sheffler. 1993. *Interpreting Otherwise than Heidegger: Emmanuel Levinas's Ethics as First Philosophy.* Pittsburgh: Duquesne University Press.

Marion, Jean-Luc. 1991. *God Without Being: Hors-Texte.* Trans. Thomas A. Carlson. Chicago and London: University of Chicago Press.

Mason, Peter. 1990. *Deconstructing America: Representations of the Other.* London and New York: Routledge.

McFague, Sallie. 1987. *Models of God: Theology for an Ecological, Nuclear Age.* Philadelphia: Fortress.

———. 1993. *The Body of God: An Ecological Theology.* Minneapolis: Fortress.

Metz, Johann. 1980. *Faith in History and Society: Toward a Practical Fundamental Theology.* New York: Seabury.

Milbank, John. 1990. *Theology and Social Theory: Beyond Secular Reason.* Cambridge: Blackwell.

———. 1997. *The Word Made Strange: Theology, Language, Culture.* Cambridge,

MA: Blackwell.

Miles, Jack. 1995. *God: A Biography*. New York: Knopf.

Olthuis, James H., ed. 1997. *Knowing Other-Wise: Philosophy at the Threshold of Spirituality*. New York: Fordham University Press.

Peirce, Charles Sanders. 1960. *Collected Papers*. Ed. Charles Hartshorne and Paul Weiss. Cambridge: Belknap Press of Harvard University Press.

Peperzak, Adriaan T., ed. 1995. *Ethics as First Philosophy: The Significance of Emmanuel Levinas for Philosophy, Literature and Religion*. New York: Routledge.

Raschke, Carl. 1979. *The Alchemy of the Word: Language and the End of Theology*. Missoula, MT: Scholars.

———. 1989. *Theological Thinking*. Missoula, MT: Scholars.

———. 1992. "Fire and Roses, or The Problem of Postmodern Religious Thinking." In Berry and Wernick, 93–108.

Rose, Gillian. 1992. *The Broken Middle*. Oxford: Blackwell.

Ruether, Rosemary Radford. 1992. *Gaia and God: An Ecofeminist Theology of Earth Healing*. San Francisco: HarperCollins.

Salomon, David A. 1998. "Forging a New Identity: Narcissism and Imagination in the Mysticism of Ignatius Loyola." *Christianity and Literature* 47 (2):195–212.

Sartre, Jean-Paul. 1947. "Un nouveau mystique." Rev. of Bataille (1943). [*Cahiers du Sud*, 260 (October 1943): 782–90]. Reprinted in *Situations I*. Paris: Librarie Gallimard. 3–34.

Scharlemann, Robert P. 1991. *The Reason of Following: Christology and the Exstatic I*. Chicago: University of Chicago Press.

Schneider, Laurel. 2000. "Homosexuality, Queer Theory, and Christian Theology." *Religious Studies Review* 26.1:3–10.

Shaffer, Peter. 1964. *The Royal Hunt of the Sun*. New York: Ballantine.

Spretnak, Charlene, ed. 1982. *The Politics of Women's Spirituality: Essays on the Rise of Spiritual Power Within the Feminist Movement*. Garden City, NY: Anchor Doubleday.

———. 1991. *States of Grace: The Recovery of Meaning in the Postmodern Age*. San Francisco: HarperCollins.

———. 1997. *The Resurgence of the Real: Body, Nature, and Place in a Hypermodern World*. Reading, MA: Addison-Wesley.

Taylor, Bron. 1997. "Earthen Spirituality or Cultural Genocide? Radical Environmentalism's Appropriation of Native American Spirituality." *Religion* 27:183–215.

Taylor, Mark C. 1982. *Deconstructing Theology*. New York: Crossroad.

———. 1984. *Erring: A Postmodern A/theology*. Chicago: University of Chicago Press.

———. 1990. *Altarity*. Albany: State University of New York Press.

———. 1993. *Nots*. Chicago: University of Chicago Press.

———. 1994. "Denegating God." *Critical Inquiry* 20 (4):592–610.

Tilley, Terrence W., ed. 1995. *Postmodern Theologies: The Challenge of Religious Diversity*. Maryknoll, NY: Orbis.

Todorov, Tzvetan. 1984. *The Conquest of America: The Question of the Other*. Trans. Richard Howard. New York: Harper and Row.

Tracy, David. 1987. *Plurality and Ambiguity*. San Francisco: Harper and Row.

Ward, Graham. 1996. *Theology and Contemporary Critical Theory*. London: Macmillan.
———, ed. 1997. *The Postmodern God: A Theological Reader*. Oxford: Blackwell.
Welch, Sharon D. 1985. *Communities of Resistance and Solidarity: A Feminist Theology of Liberation*. Maryknoll, NY: Orbis.
Westphal, Merold, ed. 1999. *Postmodern Philosophy and Christian Thought*. Bloomington: Indiana University Press.
Winquist, Charles E. 1995. *Desiring Theology*. Chicago and London: University of Chicago Press.
Wyschogrod, Edith. 1974. *Emmanuel Levinas: The Problem of Ethical Metaphysics*. The Hague: Nijhoff.
———. 1988. "On Deconstructing Theology: A Symposium on *Erring: A Postmodern A/theology*." *Journal of the American Academy of Religion* 54 (3):523–57.
———. 1990. *Saints and Postmodernism: Revisioning Moral Philosophy*. Chicago: University of Chicago Press.
———. 1996. "Towards a Postmodern Ethics: Corporeality and Alterity." In Hoffmann: and Hornung, 53–68.
Wyschogrod, Edith, Carl Raschke and David Crownfield, eds. 1989. *Lacan and Religious Discourse*. Albany: State University of New York Press.
Ziarek, Krzysztof. 1990. "The Language of Praise: Levinas and Marion." *Religion and Literature* 22 (2–3): 93–108.
Zornado, Joseph. 1998. "Free Play: Christian Hierarchies, the Child, and a Negative Way." *Christianity and Literature* 47 (2): 133–66.

QUESTIONS AND APPROACHES

Man has learnt to deal with himself in all questions of importance without recourse to the "working hypothesis" called "God."
—Dietrich Bonhoeffer, *Letters and Papers from Prison*

The end of the age of the sign, disclosed in the *differend*, in the silence, is at the same time an overture to what is genuinely postmodern, understood at last as a total presence, an eschatological fullness, a *parousia*—after the fashion of Heidegger—of the very sign-universe.
—Carl Raschke, "Fire and Roses"

2

Is the Holy Wholly Other, and Is the Wholly Other Really Holy? Reflections on the Postmodern Doctrine of God

Paul Lakeland

I

When the question of "the other" is raised in Christian theology, it refers most usually to one or other of two related but distinct issues. There is first and of most immediate practical concern, the so-called problem of other religions and the project of a "theology of religions." This is the distinctively religious face of the otherness debate in general. The other, as we know, is erased by metanarrative. The one who possesses the metanarrative, be it one of white supremacy, patriarchy, or Christian imperialism encounters others only through their inevitably subjugated place in the metanarrative. Thus, they are not met as other, only as comprehended. They may not speak on their own terms, because the metanarrative has spoken for them. They are present in the world of the metanarrative, but voiceless, situated, put in "their" place, which is of course anything but their place.

"Other" religions are an intractable problem for Christianity. All the options for dealing with them create difficulties. A sheer Christian exclusivism simply eradicates the other as worthy of attention. The once popular inclusivism, which saw other religions as "preparatory to" or imperfect vehicles of the Christian revelation, is no less imperialistic in its implications. The otherness of the other religion is where it errs, while that which it has in common with Christianity is where the Spirit is leading it *toward* the fullness of truth. And the pluralism beloved of enlightened liberal religion, in which all religions are specific cultural manifestations of a universal search for truth, raises equally problematic questions. While the abandonment of the Christian metanarrative releases the other to be other, the liberal metanarrative of pluralism which takes over promotes a vision that differences don't, in the end, really matter all that much. Such a view, of course, erases otherness equally effectively, and may be particularly alien to other religious traditions that find themselves unable to accept the discourse of pluralism.

Theologically, what is at issue for Christians in the debate over other religions is the role of Christ as savior. In philosophical terms the focus must be on the status of Christian truth-claims. The thrust of the inquiry here can be stated quite baldly, even naively: what is the relationship between the Christian claim that Jesus Christ is the cosmic savior and the understandings of salvation and liberation expressed by non-Christian and nontheistic religious traditions? Is Christ cosmic or parochial? If the former, then are non-Christians saved despite themselves? If the latter, then what is the relationship between, say, the salvation offered in Christ and the liberative teaching of the Buddha?

The second dimension of the question of otherness in Christian theology has to do with the nature of the relationship between God and creation or God and the world, as it has traditionally been presented. On the one hand, the transcendent creator-Lord of the universe, the "wholly Other," the free creator of a free creation, seems from a philosophical perspective to be in a one-sided relation to the world. While the world is dependent on God, God is not dependent on the world. To put God in any dependent relationship to the world would seem to compromise that transcendence. This, of course, is the deistic point of view. On the other hand, from the perspective of Hebrew and Christian theology, God is anything but indifferent to creation. It is God's initiative to establish a covenant with Israel, God's providence that leads to God becoming incarnate in history and suffering death, God's gift of the spirit to be with the Christian church for all time. The theological problem here is the reconciliation of the caring God of the Bible with the transcendent Lord of history. How can God at one and the same time be so utterly other, and yet be so evidently in relation to the world? And how can that reciprocal relation that God enables in the covenant and expands upon according to Christians in the gift of Christ and the Spirit be possible, if indeed God is other? Pneumatology must turn for help to philosophy, and has tended to do so most frequently by looking to metaphysics or ontology for a reconciliation of the total otherness of the infinite with the God who is relatedness.

This dimension of the question of otherness has become radicalized, at least in contemporary theological reflection in the West, in a philosophical challenge to the entire onto-theo-logical project. Is it actually bankrupt, even pernicious? Have metaphysics and ontology led us far away from the God who gives self in and through revelation? Are philosophical categories of themselves necessarily misleading in attending to "the doctrine of God"? Is God so utterly other that even ontological difference does not capture the quality of the gap between creator and created reality?

In what follows here I would like in the main to focus on the radicalization of this second dimension of otherness. To do so, I wish first to examine some aspects of the debate between Jean-Luc Marion and John Milbank on the question of whether a Christian God stands outside any metaphysical or ontological framework. Second, I shall try to show that Marion's insistence on "God without Being" and Milbank's urging the retention of a trinitarian metaphysics both are necessary and do not contradict one another. Third and finally, I will make some remarks on the implications of these conclusions for the status of models of the God–world relationship, and for the project of a theology of religions, if only to show and to insist upon the fact that the most apparently arcane theological speculation can have surprisingly practical consequences.

II

One of the more reliable readings of the term *postmodern* is as a label for intellectual and cultural currents that challenge, explicitly or otherwise, the Enlightenment legacy of modernity. Such a usage of the term makes it possible to shed light on the bewildering variety of phenomena included within the rubric "postmodern." The critique of modernity, after all, may be in the name of a nostalgic recovery of the premodern. It may equally well be inspired by a reformist accommodation of the modern commitment to reason to the twentieth-century demise of transcendental subjectivity. Or it may reflect a playful fin-de-siècle insouciance in the face of environmental and moral collapse. Postmodern religious reflection is similarly explicable as a reaction to modern or liberal theology, and reflects the tripartite division of agendas or motivations operative in postmodern thought and culture as a whole. There are postliberals (Frei, Lindbeck, Thiemann and the "Yale school") whose neo-Barthianism is driven by a reaction to the Enlightenment's privatizing of religion and liberal theology's capitulation to a foundationalist or correlationist methodology. There are critical or late moderns (Metz, Tracy, Kaufman) whose revisionist agenda keeps them warily attentive to fideism and fundamentalism on the one side, and to deconstruction and methodological atheism on the other. And there are the young (and not so young) Turks of the death of God (Altizer, Taylor, Winquist), looking to the release of a new spirit and consciousness in the demise of traditional theism.

The discussion of God and otherness is pursued in most interesting fashion, however, in the emerging debate between two theologians who escape these categorizations, while being discernibly postmodern. Jean-

Luc Marion, best known for his work on Descartes, has sought in his 1991 publication, *God Without Being*, to argue for an understanding of God which stands beyond all metaphysical categorizations, in which the self of God is encountered in God's self-revelation as gift. Like Marion, John Milbank brilliantly wields a postmodern vocabulary in the service of what turns out to be a theologically conservative set of conclusions. Whereas Marion's work is taken up with the concept of God, Milbank's tour de force, *Theology and Social Theory*, is ecclesiological in focus. Insisting that the saeculum is a remainder-concept, comprehensible only in the context of the originally theological world out of which it emerged, Milbank mounts a defense of an Augustinian vision of Christianity as the "peaceable kingdom." In a 1995 article, however, he enters into the debate on the relationship between God and Being. In "Can a Gift Be Given? Prolegomena to a Future Trinitarian Metaphysics," Milbank directly challenges Marion's philosophical conclusions. Where Marion argues that God as gift precedes Being, Milbank contends that Being, as that which is there to be given, precedes the gift. For Marion's "post-ontological" model (Milbank's characterization), the otherness of God must be complete. But in Milbank's reclamation of metaphysical speculation, absolute otherness would, of course, only leave us with the "bad infinite" that Hegel so devastatingly analyzed.

Marion's central concern with the distinction between onto-theo-logy and revelation is most clearly illustrated in the contrast he draws between "the idol" and "the icon." In an essentially Feuerbachian analysis, Marion sees the philosophical concept of God as inevitably idolatrous. Locked within human cognition, the God-concept—like any other idol—is a mirror in which we see ourselves reflected. Inevitably, therefore, ontotheology erases otherness. However much we may declare God is other, it is we who are doing the declaring, and this other cannot be the genuinely other, which must come from beyond. We must, rather, await the icon, that through which the invisible gazes upon us, and through which the other reveals self to us. In self-communication through the icon, God erases the distance from the creature while preserving otherness. But the icon can "proceed" conceptually, provided that "the concept renounce comprehending the incomprehensible, to attempt to conceive it, hence also to receive it, in its own excessiveness" (Marion 1991, 22).

Marion's distinction between the idol and the icon is a way of privileging phenomenological method over metaphysical speculation. He seems to be saying that the icon, that through which God is manifest, must be awaited, attended upon, even passively received, so that whatever then appears and is shown through the icon *is* the appearing of God. For Marion, this appearing is gift, or better, "giving," without content, without Being. The otherness of God as contentless giving is beyond ontological difference. Metaphysical speculation, on the contrary, will always be proactive, seeking comprehension—and thus entrapment—of the concept, and more often than not its subsequent placing within a metaphysical system. Metaphysics, then, will be a form of metanarrative, itself inevitably always a controlling device. And it would seem to follow, though Marion never says this quite explicitly, that only phenomenological method can let the other be the other. The reaching out to comprehend, which is metaphysical or ontological speculation, can only encounter the idol.

Marion's case is made very clearly in an article entitled "Metaphysics and Phenomenology: A Relief for Theology." Seeking an adequate definition of metaphysics, he rejects the arbitrariness of the scholastic formulation, that metaphysics is the science of being in general and of being *par excellence*. No logic for the subsumption of two such different inquiries under one rubric is forthcoming. Marion prefers the ontotheological formulation of Heidegger, which establishes a reciprocity between Being and beings—"Being grounds beings, and beings, as what *is* most of all, cause Being" (1994, 576). However, Marion also recognizes the cogency of Nietzsche's negative anticipation of the Heideggerian formulation. For Nietzsche, nothing needs to be grounded, and therefore there is no need to invoke the *causa sui*. Thus, the end of metaphysics lies in its lack of necessity.

While one could easily pass from Marion's position on the end of metaphysics to a privileging of the "God of revelation" over that "of the philosophers," Marion prefers to make a somewhat different point. Why, he asks, should we assume that the God of metaphysics, God as ground or cause, is the only or even the best way of thinking the thought of God in philosophy? "Do 'causa sui,' 'sufficient Reason,' 'purus actus,' or *energeia* offer a name that is sufficiently divine to make God appear?" (579) ponders Marion. If there is any doubt at all, he thinks, and then there is something lacking in this appearance of God, then it is not God, but "God" (that is, the idol) that is at issue.

Marion's solution is to replace metaphysics with phenomenology, which substitutes "donation" for a priori principle. Indeed, the "principle of principles" of phenomenology, which states that understanding is ultimately seeing ("what you see is what you get, and if you don't see it, you don't get it"), is a way of saying that there is no principle, that there is nothing a priori but donation, which is in itself process rather than content. The "originary impression"—given in intuition—precedes consciousness. Intuition "gives" the phenomenon, consciousness receives it. Because "intuition as donation always precedes the consciousness of it that we receive as after the fact" (582), the only "legitimate a priori" turns out to be the a posteriori itself.

The priority of the a posteriori entails two theses. First, phenomena appear without the need for recourse to any category or concept of Being. So, possibility is prior to actuality, certitude is replaced by donation, and the being of beings is seen to be a being-given, not the "possessing of its own funds" implied in the etymology of *ousia*. Second, the need for Being as ground or cause of beings is removed by their essential appearing as "being-given." But this is not simply the demolition of special metaphysics; rather, it is the "relief" of philosophy through the substitution of being-given for being, and the potential relief of theology through the reception of God not as the giver (which would restore metaphysics), but as "the being-given par excellence":

> If the world can be defined as what appears as the being-given in its totality, if the "I/me" can be designated as what appears as the closest being-given, then "God" would be determined as the being-given par excellence. That excellence indicates neither sufficiency, nor efficiency, nor principality, but the fact that he gives himself and allows to be given more than any other being-given. In short, with "God" it is a question of the being-abandoned. (588)

God as the being-given par excellence is given without reserve, thus saturates every horizon. But such a saturation means that God cannot be present as an object, which has limits, but may be present as absence, and so "donation can thus pass for abandon."

Phenomenology, of course, though it is not metaphysics, remains philosophy, and so can only testify to the possibility of "the saturated phenomenon of the being-given par excellence." The real experience of the donation falls into the domain of theology, where possibility passes over into historicity. In theology, the donation is encountered in a face, and that face turns out to be a face of charity. Here, phenomenology yields to revealed theology, but it has given "a certain coherence" to the rational thought of God, one that escapes metaphysical modes of thought. One would, it seems, have to designate the theologian's turn to phenomenology as an instance of *fides quaerens intellectum*, not as a search for a channel through which to mediate theological truth.

John Milbank most trenchantly takes issue with Marion's attempt to overstep the metaphysical. In his 1995 article "Can a Gift Be Given? Prolegomena to a Future Trinitarian Metaphysics," Milbank first challenges what he calls the "purism" of modern understandings of what a gift is, in which a totally disinterested unilateral giving is promoted. He tries to show that there is no such thing as a purely unilateral generosity and, secondly, that such purism emerges out of a misunderstanding of Christian agape. In completely dissociating agape from the giver's own well-being and from eros, it leads to "a suicidally sacrificial will against oneself" (something once described more colorfully by Dorothee Sölle as "Christian masochism"). Moreover, delay in returning the gift and "non-identical repetition" (that is, we don't give exactly the same thing back) need not be seen as tactical maneuvers with a self-serving agenda—one of Derrida's points in denying the very possibility of a gift. They could be seen rather as manifestations of attention to the other, of self-expression and of connectedness.

Milbank criticizes Marion on precisely these two grounds. In Marion's phenomenology of the divine gift, the gift is marked by distance. God gives gratuitously but remains at a distance, giving an empty gift marked in no way by the specificity of the giver. It is thus thoroughly impersonal and—as we can see in Marion's notion of the icon—inevitably unilateral. Milbank insists on reciprocity. Since God gives to no one, but just gives, the very being of the recipient "resides in its reception of itself as a gift" (1995, 135). So, for the creature to be as gift, is "the gift of a return." Moreover, Marion's insistence on the passivity of the recipient of the gift inevitably collapses the distinction into mere ontic difference, continues Milbank, in which God and revelation are objects we experience in an immediate fashion.

In contrast to what he considers to be Marion's imprisonment within Cartesian understandings of the given, Milbank himself proposes attention to a metaphysics of eros. This would respect the gift-exchange character of the divine gift, and would allow for the primacy of subjective desire over knowledge in the reception of Being "correctly in its alterity." If Being is equated with knowledge, then of course love exceeds the ontological, but an understanding of Being as encompassing eros retains gift-exchange within ontology and respects the character of Christian revelation as more than overwhelming knowledge, indeed, as "self-expression in generosity" (144).

Had Milbank attended to one modification in particular that Marion made to his proposals in the 1994 article, and not concentrated so much on *God Without Being*, much of his critique would have had to be recast.[1] As we saw earlier, while in *God Without Being* Marion uses the language of God as contentless gift or giving, in "Metaphysics and Phenomenology" he prefers to describe beings as "being-given" and God as "being-given par excellence," as the one who gives and allows to be given most fully. This reformulation remains "without Being," but seems perhaps to portend the overcoming of otherness in what may after all only be a difference of degree between "being-given" and "being-given par excellence." On the other hand, it might be that the being-given of God is a self-giving, while that of beings is a discovery of themselves in their total gratuity, so being-given by another, by God. In this case, while beyond or without Being, the relationship envisaged is not all that different from the Heideggerian onto-logical difference between Being and beings. Except, and here perhaps we have to continue partially to side with Milbank, that there is no evident reciprocity. While the being-given par excellence is the one who gives self, gives the world as the totality of being-given and thus gives individuals as "beings-given," the enabling relationship is not reciprocal. To argue that there is reciprocity in the fact that the givenness of the beings-given com-pletes the project of the being-given par excellence seems to me a trivial and somewhat sophistical observation.

III

In theistic religious traditions, otherness achieves a foundational char-acter that far exceeds the depth of otherness questions in nontheistic reli-gion or in philosophical reflection. In Christianity, to which the current inquiry is confined, God's self-revelation is highly ambiguous. Scripture portrays a God who is transcendent creator, and the New Testament adds that this God "is love." The doctrine of the Trinity is Christianity's attempt to finesse the aporia of a wholly other who is yet in relation to the world and human beings. The trinitarian processions establish a relationship be-tween the wholly other Lord of creation and the "Son" and "Spirit" within that creation. But by positing the economic interrelations as a real reflec-tion of the "inner life of the Trinity" the aporia is placed beyond human investigation. So a radical otherness which is yet overcome by divine initiative, while remaining a real "moment" in God, is encountered at the heart of Christianity. To anticipate a little, such a character should render Christianity in the end sympathetic to the merely ontic difference it en-counters beyond its own tradition.

Both Marion and Milbank offer resources for examination of the depth of otherness in God, but each needs first to be qualified by the strengths of the other's position. To begin with Marion, he is very persuasive in prof-fering phenomenology as the "relief" of theology, in opposition to the apo-rias into which metaphysics leads it. A religion of revelation needs the capacity to present that revelation as genuinely the *self*-revelation of the divine, and the phenomenological fit with Christ as the icon of God is invaluable. However, since it is scripture that is the primary vehicle for the communication of God's self-revelation, the gift without being is given expression in human conceptualities and images. Marion allows for the concept, provided that it in turn envisages the ultimately incomprehensible as its content. But while the "wholly other" or gift itself might be manageable in this way, "God is love" is a distinctly greater challenge.

Marion certainly understands his position to be capable of explicating the logic of "God is love" in terms of contentless gift. As he writes in "Metaphysics and Phenomenology," God as "being-given par excellence" is so totally poured out that gift itself can appear as abandonment. Thus the absence of God is the ultimate sign of God's presence. God is encountered as love in that absence of God which proves God's reality to lie in total agapic self-surrender. The problem with this, as Milbank went to such pains to demonstrate, is that such a conception of agape is nonreciprocal, amounts to a masochistic self-annihilation, and so represents a poor model, in passing, for human loving. In addition, and this is something Milbank does not point out, while Jesus Christ abandons himself totally in love, he certainly gets something out of it. There is reciprocity. But if he is, as Marion argues, the icon of God, then how can the God manifest through him be one of totally nonreciprocal abandonment?

Milbank's proposal is to create a metaphysics of desire so that the gift (of love) can be located within Being, and the priority of Being then means that there is something there to be given. This picture is much more reflective of Heidegger's ontological difference, in the reciprocity of Being and beings. Divine and human loving move closer to one another. God is freed from the urge to self-destruction, and the words of John make sense: "if God so loved us, we also must love one another." On the other hand, this is undeniably a metaphysics of presence. The gift/presents is a gift of presence. Milbank, unlike Marion, simply cannot account for the experience of God's absence. While for Marion the experience of God's absence is fruit of God's overwhelming presence, for Milbank it would be proof of spiritual blindness and lack of being.

The larger question behind all this is that of the identity or nonidentity of the God of Christianity with the philosophical *causa sui*. In other words, is the holy wholly other, and is the wholly other really holy? While the origins of ontotheology lie in an extension of the project of natural theology, and would therefore have to be considered in traditional terms as mere thought-experiments always finally placed under the authority of revelation, post-Enlightenment religious reflection saw it rather differently. The classic reversal of that premodern relationship lies in Hegel, where religion is the representation in symbols and images of a truth that has full and definitive expression only in philosophy. If putting religion in its place was the distinctive move of modern thought, however, latenineteenth and twentieth century currents show clear evidence of attempting to reverse that process. Here is where Milbank and Marion must finally be located, united in their suspicion of theological modernity, but parting to some degree in their remedy for it.

In the work of Milbank and Marion, while they differ on the role of special metaphysics, there is a common deferral to the positivity of Christian revelation. In Marion's terms, the formal representation in phenomenological terms of God as gift or "being-given par excellence" only presents a possibility, which revelation specifies in the "face" of charity. For Milbank, the "metaphysics of desire" that operates "within" being is only significant because God is revealed as love. The God of revelation, then, cannot be the wholly other, at least in the sense that a relation is established, even if one-sided, in God's giving. However, prior to the recourse to revelation, Milbank's God reveals Godself to be Being as loving, whereas Marion's God loves as the unknown giver who is apprehended, if at all, only indirectly through the appreciation of the very givenness of human being. Thus, Marion's is closer to the wholly other.

We are left, finally, clutching two conceptions of holiness, one of pure and perhaps purist agape, the other incorporating the erotic. The equation of holiness and wholly otherness will depend on which understanding of holiness we elect. Marion's God of pure gift, of agapic self-surrender into abandonment, "without" Being, is untouched by "beings-given." Here the holy truly is the wholly other. But when desire is included within being, so that the gift that is given in love is Being's enabling gift of being, and Being is only known through the reciprocal love of enabled beings, then absolute otherness is rejected for the false infinite that it is. The utter self-abandonment of God in which absence equals presence equals absence is an epistemological "night in which all cows are black." It also renders particularly problematic the scandal of particularity in *Christ*'s historical self-surrender.

IV

The implications of where we fall on the otherness spectrum, with Marion or Milbank, are enormous, and never more so than in examining the issue of "other" religions. Placing God "without Being" renders natural knowledge of God impossible, and the philosophical subordination of metaphysics and ontology to phenomenological contemplation of Christ as the icon of God raises the specters of Quietism, Jansenism, and perhaps most of all the extremist version of Jansen's thought propounded by Quesnel. If humble submission to revelation and an intense focus on eucharistic piety are *the* channels of God's gift, then it is hard to escape the conclusion that "other" religions and unbelief stand outside the grace of God. In the language of the theology of religions, Marion's position exhibits distinct characteristics of old-style Christian exclusivism. If God is as wholly other as Marion's theological vision suggests, and if phenomenology only demonstrates the possibility of God's self-communication that revelation confirms and makes specific, and if the God-concept is empty in philosophical terms, filled out and enriched only in Christ as the icon of God, then no other conclusion is possible.

In the case of John Milbank, the situation is a little more complicated. In brief, while his muting of the wholly otherness of God implied in the proposed metaphysics of desire ought to lead to a more generous theology of religions, he does not seem to take this path. In *Theology and Social Theory*, indeed, the Christian metanarrative of history is to be understood as "a gigantic claim to be able to read, criticize, say what is going on in other human societies." One historical implication of such a claim, says Milbank, was that "other religions and social groupings, however virtuous-seeming, were finally on the path of damnation" (1990a, 388). At the same time, there are resources in Milbank's thought for some correction, most notably in his preference for a God who includes all difference over "the unity of a bare simplicity, a naked will" (429), which he rightly associates with the neo-Platonic One.

Milbank's God is known "both as the 'speaking' of created difference, and as an inexhaustible plenitude of otherness" (430). That is to say, the narrative of revelation and ontology "reinforce each other in an ontology of difference." And for Milbank this is nicely captured in the words of Scripture, "I am before the creation of the world." Thus God is "infinite Being . . . difference in harmony." Now, in such a radically different picture of God, in which wholly otherness has been replaced by the inclusion of all difference, the world becomes "the serial occurrence of differential reality in time." The harmonious reconciliation of difference is revealed as the meaning of the church and the project for the world.

Milbank directly addresses the theology of religions in his essay, "The End of Dialogue." Here he argues that the pluralist position on other religions is in fact the privileging of Western liberal assumptions about toleration, dialogue, social justice, and so on, that in their own way represent the obliteration of difference. Simply because Western liberals seek to overcome difference in this way, it does not mean that their views are shared by the traditions with which they seek to enter into this kind of dialogue. In fact, thinks Milbank, by returning to Western religious thought, and eschewing political liberalism, we can uncover in the Christian (and possibly in the Jewish) tradition the sole resource for truly encountering the other, and respecting its different contribution to Being. In the Christian vision of the Trinity, difference is held within nonviolent consensus, and Christian life is constrained to participate in just such trinitarian dynamics. In Milbank's theology of religions, then, since God is not wholly other and since difference is contained within God in nonagonistic patterns, the metanarrative is revealed as one that recognizes the incommensurability of religious traditions. However, it also sees that each religion is not so much a contributor to the understanding of Being as an account of Being, the "way things are," which must inevitably "reclassify" other accounts when it encounters them. So, concludes Milbank, in dialogue we should pursue "the ecclesial project of securing harmony through difference," and "we should indeed expect to constantly receive Christ again, from the unique spiritual responses of other cultures." "But," he adds, "I do not pretend that this proposal means anything other than continuing the work of conversion" (1990b, 190).

Notes

1.   Milbank's article reveals no awareness of the 1994 article by Marion, but given the vagaries of publication schedules, this should not be held against him.

Works Cited

Marion, Jean-Luc. 1991. *God Without Being.* Trans. Thomas A. Carlson. Chicago: University of Chicago Press.

——. 1994. "Metaphysics and Phenomenology: A Relief for Theology." Trans. Thomas A. Carlson. *Critical Inquiry* 20:572–91.

Milbank, John. 1990a. *Theology and Social Theory: Beyond Secular Reason.* Oxford: Blackwell.

——. 1990b. "The End of Dialogue." In *Christian Uniqueness Reconsidered: The Myth of a Pluralistic Theology of Religions.* Maryknoll, NY: Orbis. 174–91.

——. 1995. "Can a Gift Be Given? Prolegomena to a Future Trinitarian Metaphysics." *Modern Theology* 11:119–61.

3

Balthasar's Theatrical Aesthetic of Transcendence, and Otherness

Ed Block, Jr.

It is almost a truism; organized religion seems on the wane, and along with it traditional talk of God. But religious experience, the numinous and the fascination of otherness, persists as long as human beings find themselves confronted with mystery and the unknown. Postmodernism has resolutely sought to transform radically—when it has not tried to put behind it utterly—the language and the forms of thought associated with traditional religious discourse. In the process, however, postmodernism has sometimes overlooked earlier thinkers whose ideas can contribute to the rethinking of religious experience and its bearing upon culture.[1] One such figure was the late theologian and humanist Hans Urs von Balthasar, simplistically categorized as a conservative.[2] Rooting his *Theodrama* in a thoughtful rethinking of Western drama that derives new insight from its source in myth and ritual, Balthasar provides a perspective on the nature of drama that preserves its event-character and its antifoundationalist confrontation with otherness and mystery. Balthasar's view of theology within the history of Western culture is as a dynamic, even expansive enterprise, capable of assimilating the best of not only classical but modern and postmodern trends in such allied disciplines as philosophy, literary criticism, and theory.

Though Balthasar's theology derives from the Greek and Latin Fathers, a strong admixture of Kierkegaard, Hegel, and Romanticism—as well as familiarity with Foucault (TD I, 107)—makes much of what he says explicable in postmodern terms. His agreement with Karl Barth on the absolute transcendence of whatever it is we mean when we refer to God also makes Balthasar's thought resolutely tentative about what and how human beings can know the transcendent. To anticipate other objections; neither Balthasar's philosophy nor his theology can be reduced to essentialist or foundationalist dimensions. Early in the *Prolegomena* to *Theodrama I* and again in *Theodrama II*, he rejects essentialist thinking and urges the need for a theodramatic approach that understands man's relation to the divine as event-like in character (TD I, 26; TD II, 12).

After a brief look at some crucial aspects of Balthasar's philosophical and theological position, I shall turn my attention to the *Theodrama* that offers new insights into the event-nature of drama. These insights help restore to our understanding of drama, the theater, and life a sense of the mystery and otherness without which both art and life become monotonous and repetitive parody. Such a world would become the very puppet theater of existence that Balthasar had claimed earlier eras used as a symbol of human freedom lost.[3]

Balthasar was addressing postmodern issues long before postmodernism had a name. His early discussions of the problem now sound dated, but even such early articulations of the situation accurately gauge the seriousness of the changes taking place. In *Science, Religion, and Christianity* (1959) Balthasar had invoked Nietzsche on the "death of God" (SRC, 36, 61) and had squarely faced the experience of God's absence, quoting from Karl Rahner: "Men are frightened at the absence of God from the world, they feel that they can no longer realize the Divine, they are terrified at God's silence" ("Wissenschaft als Konfession?" quoted in SRC, 95). From this Balthasar had concluded: "Today, as never before in the history of mankind, the sanctuary appears defiled; the old reverence has been replaced by a cynicism of incredible dimensions, and the truly 'natural' religion by a brazen irreligion that pretends to be just as natural" (SRC, 71). Summing up in a fashion similar to the Heidegger of "The Question Concerning Technology," Balthasar sees God's absence as the result of human dominance and manipulation of the world.

Proclaiming that "Man has attained a new stage of his religious consciousness" (SRC 72), Balthasar issues a warning that, having attained this new stage, "all three, God, man and the world, must lose something of their intelligibility" (SRC, 73). Though human beings may still have a "nature," that nature can only be understood as "something that is open and will receive a form that may differ according as God calls and disposes" (SRC, 73). Even what we commonly call "nature " must be "hidden together with him [God] under the veil of invisibility and unintelligibility (SRC, 74). Elaborated on in *Theodrama*, the significance of this openness finds its ongoing explanation for Balthasar in theater and drama. Though Balthasar uses the term "God," it should be clear that the situation that he describes resembles what we now call the postmodern. In another particularly postmodern statement, Balthasar says:

> Hence it is not enough to say that man has lost his sense of direction in modern nature, which has become unintelligible with its giant dimensions; that the house of the world has broken down and the wind of nothingness and "homelessness" blows through the ruins. We must also state the complementary truth: the dawn of the mod-

> ern age is characterized by its own specific form of the spiritual and
> intellectual consciousness of mankind in general as well as of the
> individual. (SRC, 74)

Lost and homeless, but also having "its own specific form of the spiritual
and intellectual consciousness of mankind," the modern world Balthasar
describes reflects the mood of the present era as well, when we feel both
homeless and bereft of any sense that transcendence—if it exists—is "an
image of the divine Spirit."

Though his ultimate project in *Theodrama* is theological, Balthasar is
sensitive to a post-Christian, postmodern world's impatience with God talk
and an uncomplicated metaphysics of presence. He is most aware of how
difficult it is to understand correctly the concept of Otherness as it con-
fronts us in the postmodern world. As a renewal for thought and action,
he points to a social form of experience, founded upon dialogue, whose
whole history brings "down to earth" a meeting between the explicable and
the inexplicable, the human and the transcendent Other—whether that Other
be imagined in mythic, traditionally religious, or more starkly postmodern
terms. That social form of experience is drama or the theater.

To understand the link between drama and life we can trace the significance of dialogue in Balthasar's thinking. In "A résumé of my thought"
Balthasar locates the origin of human consciousness in the relationship of
mother and child. Its formulation resembles that of some contemporary
psycholinguists: "The infant is brought to consciousness of himself only
by love, by the smile of his mother. In that encounter the horizon of all
unlimited being opens itself for him" (Résumé, 470). From this experience
of gratuitous love (deprivation of which is not refutation of its normative
character) derives the dialogic principle upon which Balthasar bases much
of his thinking and his theodramatic theory (TD I, 626–48). Seeing in this
primal experience an intimation of the religious, he also sees a dimension of
otherness. Analogizing the religious character as "this eros toward God
which is the deepest thing in man" (SRC, 52), Balthasar goes on to see in
this love the source of our deepest strivings. Stirred by even inchoate
awareness of such love, one may be moved to acknowledge a person, a
cause, or even an aesthetic object, "giving oneself" to the experience in
rapture and submission (LA, 44). In many cases the very "otherness" of
the beloved is a further reason for the self-giving. The ultimate form of
such surrender is dispossession, which Balthasar describes as joy even in
desolation (TIS, 154–55, 157–59).

Balthasar may have derived the terms and description of this phenomenon from late nineteenth century sources, but there is no denying the

potentially anarchic nature of such submission and surrender; it is clearly an ambiguous—but also notably postmodern—experience. Described as Balthasar does so, this phenomenon also lends support to postmodern claims for the loss of the subject. That is, individuals may be so dispossessed that they lose whatever autonomy they may have had and fall under the control of others.[4] But the power of the "call" and the totality of the self-surrender are precisely indications of a kind of transcendence. While ecstatic, however, such self-surrender and dispossession can also yield a profound sense of absence. Analyzing it in not only its theological but its dramatic context, Balthasar finds the experience of absence a further useful parallel. The godforsakenness of Christ in Gethsemane and on the cross, and the lesser example of a character like Bernard Shaw's Major Barbara, are both instances for Balthasar of individuals realizing the sense of absence that follows upon dispossession.

In the second volume of *Theodrama* Balthasar acknowledges that "right at the center of our existence in the world, there is the ugly, the grotesque, the demonic . . . all that makes it hard and often impossible for man to believe that the world has a total meaning" (TD II, 27). Referring to the terrible angels of R. M. Rilke's *Duino Elegies*, Balthasar says:

> Does the angel stand for the *shekinah*, the hidden, consuming glory of the Absolute; or is it the personified face of what is ultimately meaningless (as the disconsolate final Elegy suggests)? In pre-Christian times, the boundaries between the two can be very close, as we can see from the grotesque, imposing grimaces on the faces of Chinese or Aztec gods and demons, which suggest that the meaning at the heart of the world is a *mysterium horrendum* and *adorandum*. (TD II, 27)[5]

In an age so full of "the ugly, the grotesque, the demonic"—in such forms as racism, genocide, and terrorism—it is little wonder that many are unable to discern either love or meaning. In this state have we not come, in fact, to an impasse, an aporia anticipated when Balthasar had observed: "That the single person can possess eternal and irreplaceable value cannot be philosophically grounded, neither in pre-Christian philosophy nor in post-Christian idealism, not to mention materialism and biological evolutionism" (SC, 275–76). Observing that any such framework ultimately denigrates the person, Balthasar diagnoses why so many (often puzzlingly contradictory) efforts to explain the worth of the human person have failed to gain a consensus that will be socially and politically effective.

It is also easy to see why postmodern anthropology is often so directionless. According to Balthasar it is in the genuine I–Thou relationship that the worth of the person and the foundation of anthropology are to be found. For Balthasar this secular fact also mirrors theological "fact."[6] And it is precisely in the connection between dialogism and the worth of the person that the further significance of drama and theater become apparent for his project—and for our ability to see Balthasar as a significant contributor to postmodern theory.

For Balthasar it is precisely drama, produced and enacted before and for an audience, that analogizes the dialogic experience out of which arise our value as persons and the possibility of our finding meaning in the drama of life and history. What the playwright creates, the director directs, and the actors enact—what they raise to the reality of event—is fundamentally an action within which the revelation of self-surrender that calls forth personhood takes place. Persons responding to appeals and reacting to the actions of others show us to ourselves in what Balthasar says is neither reality nor illusion, but (in the words of Georg Simmel) "a mystery of real presence" (quoted in TD I, 281).[7] In drama as presented in the theater, a transcendent dimension opens up that is event itself. Difficult of analysis, it inheres in the assertions, questions, and challenges that, emerging in the dialogue, create the event at the same time it calls into question (TD I, 21). When the dramatic experience thematizes otherness, dispossession, or absence—by giving voice to the unheard and the marginalized—it doubly affects us. Both the character of dramatic experience and the content of the particular play, mediated by the cooperation of all participants, conspires to hold ready a sense of the transcendent.

In his analysis of drama, particularly the theatrical experience, Balthasar shows that the structure of love, dispossession, and absence runs through drama, both diachronically and synchronically. It is there diachronically from its origins in mythic stories of sacrifice like *Oedipus* to *St. Joan* and Shaffer's *Equus*. It is there synchronically, from drama's creation by the playwright to its enactment by actors, and its reception by the audience. Seen from the synchronic perspective, the dialogic nature of enacted drama places all the participants in question. Enactment and reception derive from the event-nature of the play. This is not simple representation. According to Balthasar such events also manifest an aspiration if not an explicable achievement of transcendence, a perspective that allows the participants a revelation, a glimpse of meanin —for self, life, and events in the world.

The dramatist loves his creatures so thoroughly as to give them a life of their own and so much as to give away his work (TD I, 271). The actors throw themselves into their roles, giving up their sense of self (perhaps in some instances fleeing it for a better—or at least "other"—self), embodying the role and transforming it in a disciplined ecstasy of technique. The earlier discussion of dispossession seems apt here. Actors in a company become vulnerable as they begin rehearsals, as they "give themselves" to a part. Like a midwife, the director (except in "directors' theater) gives herself—or himself—to both playwright and actors, delivering an event out of the actors, by the playwright.

Successfully produced and enacted, the play evokes a similar dispossession on the part of the audience. They see and judge themselves; they recognize and acknowledge a transcendent dimension of their lives and actions, perhaps seeing for the first time either the nobility or the depravity, the paltriness or the magnificence of their existences. Even in the plays of Beckett, Pinter, and Stoppard the *dramatis personae* realize, even as they question the "identity" of, the persons performing before the audience. Appearing on the stage, characters transform into compelling event the confrontation of human actions, a contested past with an inexplicable present and future. As Balthasar says in the preface to his *Prolegomena* to *Theodrama I* :

> In the theatre man attempts to a kind of transcendence, endeavoring both to observe and to judge his own truth, in virtue of a transformation—through the dialectic of the concealing-revealing mask—by which he tries to gain clarity about himself. Man himself beckons, invites the approach of a revelation about himself. (TD I, 12)

Oedipus recognizing his guilt, Lear lost in his loneliness, or Prior dying alone of AIDS in Tony Kushner's *Angels in America:* all seem totally bereft because, as a result of their complex and often ambivalent surrenders to other forces or other human beings, they find nothing of meaning left in life or are thrown totally upon themselves. Such plays complexly signify an absence of beauty, reason, and meaning, yet in them we discern "the spirit playing on the surface of the world" (Taylor 1992, 17), a distinctly postmodern experience.

In postmodern reflexive drama, the thematizing of the author/actor/audience relation is further proof that Balthasar anticipates postmodernism. What Balthasar has found in Pirandello and Wilder prepares for what we find in playwrights like Athol Fugard and Peter Shaffer. Because of the demands of their *métier*—which *Theodrama* carefully analyzes—dramatists are dimly aware of a transcendent dimension upon which drama itself is founded: the tension between unique and particular actions on the one hand and the openness of meaning on the other; between determined text and undetermined, almost limitless effect. In the ecstasy of dispossession all the participants may simultaneously see a potential for meaning as values are undermined or transvalued. What was the case in earlier expressionist, Dadaist, surrealist, and absurdist drama continues true today. Feminist drama, or any drama that takes the rights of the oppressed seriously, offers a challenge to accepted values, making possible a transformation of the audience's perspective and beliefs. Drama also awakens the audience to the otherness of the world. Peter Shaffer's Salieri, the gay world of *Angels in America*, or the plight of South Africans and the relations of black and white in the dramas of Athol Fugard: all trade on a postmodern fascination with what beckons from the experience of otherness.

Balthasar's *Theodrama* demonstrates that particular plays need not have religious themes to reflect the structure and awaken a sense of otherness and transcendence.[8] Even in postmodern drama we find love, dispossession, and absence at work. These themes run through drama from its most secular to its most hieratic forms. And even when we view drama from a postmodern perspective, taking the actions at face value, attending to the "surface" as a play of difference, otherness, absence, and desolation, the effect is no less powerful for its apparent vacuity.

A play like Athol Fugard's 1972 *Sizwe Bansi Is Dead*, for instance, depicts a starkly secular encounter with otherness and dispossession. Sizwe Bansi is a black South African worker forced to relinquish his identity in order to provide for his family. Premised on conditions that no longer apply to the same degree that they did when Fugard wrote the work, the play nevertheless dramatizes the transformation that results from dispossession. In many ways the play is postmodernism itself. Dispossession for the audience first occurs as thwarted expectations, *mise en abyme*, distorted theatrical conventions, and other techniques that "distance" the audience—most notably from its own values and preconceptions. Dispossession also takes place when real and fictional characters blend. It is also apparent in the dislocation—temporal, spatial, and otherwise—that is part of the play's structure. Originating from Fugard's collaboration with two black South Africans, John Kani and Winston Ntshona, *Sizwe Bansi* affronts our theatrical conceptions from the start. Told in the form of flashbacks, Sizwe Bansi's story is at one and the same time familiar and marked by the otherness of the oppressed. An illiterate emigrant worker from the country, Sizwe Bansi learns he can no longer stay in Port Elizabeth because the Labour Bureau has stamped his passbook (that infamous instrument of apartheid oppression) "for the purpose of repatriation to home district." Yet he *must* work to support wife and family back in the "location."

Sizwe Bansi turns for help to Buntu, an urban wheeler-dealer. After an evening on the town, Sizwe and Buntu find the body of another black worker, apparently a murder victim. Sizwe Bansi wants to tell the authorities until Buntu warns him that the authorities will accuse *them* of the murder. Bansi suggests they find the man's next of kin, but when they search the body for information, they learn that the dead man, whose passbook identifies him as Robert Zwelinzima, is also a "migrant" worker who lives in one of the worst parts of Port Elizabeth. Buntu's description illustrates the alien setting of the play: "You know what Single Men's Quarters is? Big bloody concentration camp with rows of things that look like train carriages. Six doors to each! Twelve people behind each door!" Buntu's counterproposal is equally shocking. Take the man's passbook, which indicates that Robert Zwelinzima has a permit to work in Port Elizabeth, and assume Robert's identity. Buntu will help with the transformation by getting Sizwe a job. But Bansi is worried about his family, and he complains: "I don't want to lose my name." Buntu's response is harsh but to the point: "Are you really worried about your children, friend, or are you just worried about yourself and your bloody name? Wake up, man! Use that book and with your pay on Friday you'll have a real chance to do something for them."

Buntu presents the stark alternatives: personal identity, poverty, and probable death for self and family. Or dispossession, security however tenuous, and the chance to support wife and children. Sizwe Bansi accepts dispossession and is transformed. Sizwe Bansi is dead, but in his place a man with the passbook of Robert Zwelinzima can continue to live. Though unaware of all the consequences of his choice, Sizwe Bansi can come to figure for the receptive audience something like the total self-surrender that Balthasar describes as the transcendent goal of love. It is a rather mundane sense of duty and responsibility to his family that makes Sizwe accept dispossession and loss of self. Yet in the way he is depicted at the end of the play, particularly in his interaction with the narrator, Styles, Sizwe Bansi manifests something of that ecstasy of dispossession whose distinctly postmodern quality another writer, Milan Kundera, articulates in *The Unbearable Lightness of Being*. From the dramatization of Bansi's ghost-like existence, the audience evinces something of the day-to-day irreality which the oppressed and dispossessed endure. At the end of the play it is the sense of absence that hangs palpably in the air.

Perhaps the most powerful example of an encounter with otherness, because it explicitly involves the otherness of religious experience, is Peter Shaffer's play, *Equus*.[9] Ostensibly the play concerns the ordeal of Martin Dysart, a child psychiatrist in a rural English mental hospital, who is disil-

lusioned with himself and his role as professional care-giver. Confronted
with the otherness of a young man, Alan Strang, whose violent acts and
aberrant religiosity are a challenge to comprehension, Dysart experiences
disorientation and dispossession. His response resembles that of many
who have come face to face with the violence of serial killers, terrorists, or
news stories of "ethnic cleansing" in the Balkan war.

   In *Equus* dispossession for the audience begins with the use of the
masks and the ritualized acting. Dispossession is compounded by the dic-
tion of madness, the thought forms of psychiatry, and the wholesale appropriation of religious and commercial language. Love as sexual ecstasy,
ambivalent as to object or gender, further intimates a strange transcendence. The characters dramatize or acknowledge multiple self-emptyings
and dispossessions. In an almost classic dramatic struggle, the doctor
tries to understand why Alan blinded six horses in the stable where he
worked. In time Dysart pieces together the story of Alan's strange religious rituals, compounded of Biblical phrases, parental prohibitions and
phobias, and sado-masochistic sexual practices. It is tempting to say that
the deprivation of maternal and paternal love is part of what turn Strang to
distorted religious love and finally obsession with horses. Alan's eclectic-
syncretic cult analogizes a myriad of obsessions in the postmodern world,
and does so in an almost universal fashion.

   Disillusioned by the emptiness of his own life and marriage, Dysart
grudgingly acknowledges that Alan's intensity is a kind of worship, and an
acknowledgment—however ambiguous—of transcendence. And worship
is essential. Dysart states flatly: "Without worship you shrink, it's as brutal
as that." Alan ultimately submits to the therapeutic control that Dysart will
impose. Here, too, is a form of surrender—and potential destruction—
which Dysart himself acknowledges and about which he feels guilt. But
struggling to help Strang, Dysart ends by realizing his own blindness. Having determined to cure Alan, even if it means taking away his aberrant
worship, Dysart himself is left in the dark. The play ends with an ambiguous image of Dysart, lost and empty, but hoping for, if not yet capable of
transformation: "I need—more desperately than my children need me—a
way of seeing in the dark. What way is this? . . . *What dark is this?* I
cannot call it ordained of God: I can't get that far. I will however pay it so
much homage." To those receptive to the relation of otherness and transcendence, Dysart's state seems like a "dark night of the soul" preliminary
to a leap of faith. To those for whom the postmodern world is merely—in
Heidegger's terms—"undisclosure," Dysart's state may seem emblematic
of the postmodern, post-Christian world, a place that offers at most a dim
and lean hope of finding some transformative power in otherness.

It is finally Dysart who is most reflective and capable of acknowledging (and suffering) the pain of absence. As he was at the start of Act II, so Dysart at the end of the play is again staring into the darkness, a Plato's cave in which there seems little hope of deriving insight. Yet he continues to look. Unlike Strang, who can only stutter his acknowledgment of mystery, Dysart's articulation of absence speaks eloquently of what he has not yet (re)gained. It is, in the end, with this anguish of absence—this evacuation of the signs, the signifieds, and the very agency upon which theater depends—that the play leaves us. Only the (empty) image of the horse, and the nearly stuttered syllables—"ek, ek, Equus"—remain to point beyond, intimating the perennial power of the dramatic experience.

With this brief look at two exemplary plays it is only possible to suggest what Hans Urs von Balthasar's model of theatrical experience contributes to our understanding of religion's encounter with otherness in postmodern literature—and the world that has given it rise. A thorough test of Balthasar's insights will require other, more painstaking analyses of his work on drama and the relation of transcendence and otherness. From even such a short sketch, however, it should be possible to see that Balthasar's work suggests the complex relation between the often overpowering claim of otherness and the transcendent experiences of beauty and love. To comprehend this relation fully, subsequent critics will need to bring to bear a dynamic and flexible approach to theology and literary criticism, one informed by the best current insights in not only theology and critical theory, but philosophy and other disciplines as well.

Notes

1.   If postmodernism opts for a purely immanent theology, it will likely end in the atheology to which such emphasis on immanence led J. Hillis Miller in the 1960s. See "Interview with Nathan A. Scott, Jr., *Christianity and Literature* 43.2 (1994): 221.

2.   Louis Dupré's *Passage to Modernity* implicitly acknowledges Balthasar's relevance to postmodern thinking, attributing to him a number of the seminal ideas in Dupre's own work.

3.   It comes as no surprise that Balthasar returns to the same sources as Thomas Mann in *Dr. Faustus*, referring to Heinrich von Kleist's *Die Marrionettentheater* as a source of the Romantic era's critique of lost human freedom. See *Dr. Faustus*, chapter 30.

4.   It is almost equally common to hear theorists extol the strength of individuals who, even in their submission to a cause or ideal, retain sufficient balance and control to transform themselves, however temporarily. Balthasar's earlier

study of the Promethean tendency in German literature makes him a perceptive commentator on this phenomenon. See *Prometheus*.

5.   But as Balthasar's life work means to assert: subsequent to the Incarnation,
the situation is somewhat different: "But after the event of Christ's Cross,
man is presented with a choice: hearing the cry of dereliction, he must 'discern' either hidden love (shown in the Father's surrender of the Son) or the
meaningless void" (TD II, 27).

6.   For Balthasar, on the other hand, the explanation is so simple and "imper-
ceptible" that it is easy to overlook philosophically. "That one person, Jesus
Christ, takes me so much as a spiritual person that he dies for my eternal
salvation and, dying, buries my lack of salvation with himself in hell is what
first arouses me to be a person" (SC, 276). See also Oakes 1994, 220.

7.   Szondi, Pfister, and others support the fact if not the phrase. For them what
is enacted on the stage becomes real action largely because human beings
enact it (Szondi 1987, 7–10; Pfister 1988, 6–7, 199–201).

8.   Paradoxically Balthasar says they remain a gloss on the Christian story (TD
I, 321).

9.   Quotations are from *Equus* (Shaffer 1974), an edition that includes section
numbers in addition to a two-act division. A subsequent Penguin edition
eliminates section numbers, retaining only the two-act division.

Works Cited

Balthasar, Hans Urs von. 1947. *Prometheus: Studien zur Geschichte des deutschen Idealismus.* Heidelberg: Kerle.

———. 1959. *Science, Religion and Christianity.* Westminster, MA: Newman. Cited in the text as SRC.

———. 1967. *Spiritus Creator.* Einsiedeln: Johannes Verlag. Cited in the text as SC.

———. 1969. *Love Alone.* New York: Herder and Herder. Cited in the text as LA.

———. 1979. *Heart of the World.* San Francisco: Ignatius.

———. 1983. *Theodrama, Theological Dramatic Theory I: Prolegomena.* San Francisco: Ignatius. Cited in the text as TD I.

———. 1987. *Truth Is Symphonic.* San Francisco: Ignatius. Cited in the text as TIS.

———. 1989. *Explorations in Theology, I: Word Made Flesh.* San Francisco: Ignatius. Cited in the text as TS.

———. 1990. *Theodrama, Theological Dramatic Theory, II .* San Francisco: Ignatius Press. Cited in the text as TD II.

Dupré, Louis. 1993. *Passage to Modernity.* New Haven: Yale University Press.

Fugard, Athol. 1976. *Sizwe Bansi Is Dead, and The Island.* New York: Viking.

Oakes, Edward T. 1994. *Pattern of Redemption: The Theology of Hans Urs von Balthasar.* New York: Continuum.

Pfister, Manfred. 1988. *The Theory and Analysis of Drama.* European Studies in English Literature. Cambridge: Cambridge University Press. Originally published in German as *Das Drama* (1977). Munich: Wilhelm Fink Verlag.

Shaffer, Peter. 1974. *Equus.* New York: Avon.

Szondi, Peter. 1987. *Theory of the Modern Drama: A Critical Edition.* Ed. and Trans. Michael Hays, Foreword by Jochen Schulte-Sasse. *Theory and History of Literature,* Vol. 29. Minneapolis: University of Minnesota Press. Originally published in German as *Theorie des modernen Dramas* (1965). Szondi, Germany: Suhrkamp Verlag.

Taylor, Mark. 1992. "Reframing Postmodernisms." In *Shadow of Spirit: Postmodernism and Religion.* Ed. Philippa Berry and Andrew Wernick. New York and London: Routledge. 11–29.

4

Uncanny Christianity:
René Girard's Mimetic Theory

Andrew McKenna

Freud notoriously described the uncanny as something strange and familiar, outlandish and ordinary. It is, perhaps, in just such paradoxical terms that we need to approach the mimetic theory of René Girard as it raises anew the question: is it possible to think as a believing Christian without surrendering any of one's rationality? For the author of *The Future of an Illusion*, the answer is emphatically negative. But psychoanalysis, which solicits our belief in unconscious forces as autonomous and irrational as any mythical divinity, has not displayed the explanatory virtues promised by its inventor, so the question remains before us.

What is uncanny or paradoxical about mimetic theory in its fullest elaboration is its scholarly and critical recourse to data across virtually all the human sciences—literary criticism, history, philosophy, anthropology, psychology, sociology—to establish its empirical and rational foundations, while on the other hand it locates the impetus of its scientific claims in the canonical texts of Judaeo-Christian tradition. The theory and the research undertaken around it (see *Bulletin* and *Contagion*) take on the special urgency of its centrally explosive topic, human violence and the means employed by culture to control it but also to misrepresent it. While focused on concrete human concerns, the debate fomented around Girard's ideas injects renewed vigor into the faith/reason conundrum as articulated earlier by Anselm and Aquinas, before it was recast in archly skeptical terms by Enlightenment philosophers. For Nietzsche it was the defining controversy of Western culture (see *On the Genealogy of Morals*, III, 27), a view corroborated by Leszek Kolakowski, who follows Nietzsche in reading the Enlightenment as Christianity turned against itself, and who, after Adorno and many a self-styled postmodern thinker, reads our present intellectual crisis as the Enlightenment turned against itself. The result is our epistemological nihilism (Kolakowski 1990, 29), for which, under various labels and slogans, our institutions of higher learning are under vigorous attack, and very often in the name of religious values.

As an anthropological inquiry into the violent origins of culture, mimetic theory turns a decisive corner on this debate; it performs a critique of religion as originating in sacrificial practices we all repudiate and continue nonetheless to engage in. While doing so, it restores to our literary and biblical canons a cognitive and interpretive authority that is rarely accorded them, at least these days, where excessive modesty about truth claims of any sort are the rule among scholars.

If we are to understand what happens among humans so as to improve relations among us, we have to distinguish, as philosophers rarely do, between the logic of thinking and the logic of desire. The logic of thinking is unitary: if we think the same thing, we will agree, and there will be harmony among us. The logic of desire works just the other way; it is essentially divisive, conflictual: if we desire the same thing, conflict will arise among us over its possession. Amidst varying degrees of violence, we observe this all the time in the rivalry of nations for territory, of political parties for power, but no less so in the behavior of children in a nursery, where each child typically wants the toy that another has. The latter's hold on it makes it interesting, appealing, in a way displayed by no other toy strewn about the nursery floor. Sooner or later an adult, familiar proxy of the law, will have to separate the children from each other and both from the toy, doubtless with some unwelcome advice about sharing or taking turns. There is an even chance, too, that the adult will yell at the children, ensuring that a certain violence will attach to the empirical apprenticeship of possession.

This is an example of mimetic desire at its most rudimentary level: the second child's desire imitates the apparent desire of the first one. But the word mimesis is preferable to imitation, which has connotations of deliberate conscious choice, whereas we are observing a mechanism in which no deliberation is necessarily at work. We easily imagine or recall other instances of this behavior in the life of adults, and entire groups of adults, whose conduct testifies to the single organizing principle of mimetic theory, upon which the entire advertising industry that drives our consumer culture in predicated: desire is contagious; it is not conceived immaculately from the mind of the subject, nor does it radiate from an intrinsically valuable object.

The postulate that value originates in the object may be described as the classical view, as it is formulated at least as far back as Plato. It argues that we develop and purify our knowledge of objects so as to pursue only those deemed worthy of desire. The alternative postulate, that value originates in the desiring subject, corresponds to a romantic view, which has been especially legible in our literature and culture since the late eighteenth century. It represents the subject, the self, as sole agent and arbiter of value, whose objects are but an extension or an expression of the subject's identity and autonomy. Cast in terms of personal fulfillment, this postulate flourishes still, though it is hotly contested by a version of the classic view that sees itself defending social stability in terms of traditional values that are held up as incontrovertible.

Mimetic theory surmounts this subject/object dualism by defining desire as a relation between subjects who imitate each other, often as unwittingly as children, in their pursuit of objects whose value derives from that rivalry alone. Girard's word for this other-centered or one-anotherness is "interdividuality" (1987b, *Things Hidden*, part III: "Interdividual Psychology"), coined in preference to "intersubjectivity," which implies more integrity to an individuated subject than mimetic theory finds evidence for. Human relations are first and foremost desire relations, and this from the very beginning of culture. For the theory includes a genetic hypothesis of human origins whose fundamental structure continues discernibly to govern human interaction among us. It is a properly evolutionary theory as it argues continuity between human and other animate forms. Motor mimicry and matching behavior have been monitored up and down the ladder of animal life, but in humans it undergoes a qualitative leap, whereby symbols or signs represent and substitute for things and for other signs, generating what we call culture, which we may define minimally as a system of representations. This first substitution takes place with the victim; it takes place in what the victim takes the place of, which is mimetic violence.

According to this hypothetical scenario, protohuman mimesis increased with brain size to a point where instinctual brakes on violence, which inform dominance patterns among other animals, were eroded beyond repair. At this point we have a creature, as Eric Gans quipped, who is "too mimetic to remain animal" (1993, 8), in that internecine violence prevents such ordered social gathering as is necessary to the collective survival of the species. Mimetic conflict here realizes Hobbes's image of the violence of all against all, but with no prospect of a contract that assumes linguistic origins prior to social organization. What is envisaged instead is a radical structural transformation whose possibility nonetheless inheres in the very disorder it terminates: the violence of all against all is convertible at any point to the violence of all against one, whose vulnerability for instance would single it out for destruction. When unanimous violence is concentrated on a single victim, it ends with the victim's destruction, and a moment of calm, of "non-instinctual attention" (Girard 1987b, 99–100) ensues for which the victim appears responsible, and in which symbolization is possible.

According to Gans, who has refined adroitly on Girard's hypothesis, this attention is structurally inevitable. Any gesture to seize the victim will find its imitators all around it, whereby the very same gesture aborts, signaling the victim as inappropriable, as dangerous to seize lest any one fall prey in turn to the violence that produced the victim in the first place. Everyone surrounding the victim is at once a model and an obstacle to everyone else in this structure, the prototype of all human social structure and the triangular forces of desire, of simultaneous attraction and repulsion, that hold it in place.

The structure is a circle composed of a hallowed, inappropriable center and mimetically gesticulating predators or appropriators surrounding it. The double bind of mimetic desire—take/do not take—issues from the band of mimetic doubles convened ecstatically by the inappropriable and accordingly sacralized victim. This double bind is the necessary and sufficient condition for the noninstinctual attention postulated by Girard, necessary, that is, for the passage from reflex action to reflection. The victim is taboo just because it is desirable, everyone in the circle mimetically performing their desire for it by their aborted gestures of seizing it. Properly human desire, defined at this and every subsequent stage of human culture as deferred or imaginary possession, is born of this structure, replete with its essential paradox, namely, that it imitates other desires and therefore finds in them both a model and an obstacle to its gratification. Language, too, is born of this structure, as the expression of desire, the first sign being any word that necessarily echoes throughout the newborn community as it represents the victim as alluring and dangerous to appropriate, as taboo and desirable at once, the one because the other. And so is divinity, in the form of the untouchable victim whose destruction produced unwonted harmony and whose representation can ritually convene nonviolent communal presence.

The sacred requires sacrifice, ritualized killing, because social foundations need to be periodically renewed in the form of a victim to which the community rightly and wrongly supposes it owes its foundation: rightly because it owes its origin to the designation of the victim; wrongly because it is to representation, deferred possession, desire, that it owes its origin, not to violence.

In sum, language and desire are born of each other in the same moment as the sacred, which we define as the violence that the community expels from its midst in the form of the victim it destroys and worships as the foundation of its newly structured assembly. Human culture begins as a circle of proto-consumers who can exchange signs to convene nonviolently and who, with a gradual lowering of anxiety, can exchange goods and services among themselves *ad infinitum*, as long as they defer to a sacred center monopolizing violence. As culture evolves and complexifies, other objects can substitute for this first one, itself a substitute for mimetic violence, and they will always be more or less tainted with the sacred, the latter being defined as anything desired so intensely and collectively that none dare appropriate it, being defined, in other contexts, as violence itself. We have seen this pathology driving the nuclear arms race. Because desire sacralizes its every object in inverse proportion to its access or attainability, violence is a signifier of the sacred (Girard 1978b, 148, 151).

When we define human culture as a system or a hierarchy of representations (*fas/nefas*, sacred/profane, pure/impure, etc.), what we mean primarily and ultimately are representations of desire. Desire originates in representation, representation originates in desire. From whence comes Girard's anthropological estimation of great literature in terms of works that, with Shakespeare, for instance (1991, *A Theater of Envy*), or Cervantes and Proust (1965, *Deceit, Desire and the Novel*), offer true representations of desire as mimetic and mediated, as opposed to the romantic lie that represents desire as spontaneous, originary.

This hypothetical scenario is one of the most controversial dimensions of mimetic theory. The other, at the opposite end of the disciplinary spectrum, is Girard's claim for Judaeo-Christian Scripture as the origin of our critique of sacrificial violence. This claim applies not only to our most basic ethical stance against scapegoating but also to the relentlessly truth-seeking impulse of our scientific rationality. For Girard, the Bible ranks first as an active agent rather than the passive object of anthropological inquiry. It inaugurates an unparalleled discovery procedure from a perspective totally alien to mythologies with which we blithely confuse it, namely, the perspective of the victim. There is something like an epistemological revolution here, standing much biblical scholarship on its head.

In *The Future of an Illusion*, Freud lends a telling metaphor to his imaginary interlocutor defending religion that handily portrays scientific progress as undermining the very foundations that one seeks to establish. It aptly depicts some of the devastation wrought by scholarly research in scriptural and doctrinal studies as well:

> Archaeological interests are no doubt most praiseworthy, but no one undertakes an excavation if by doing so he is going to undermine the habitations of the living so that they collapse and bury people under their ruins. (1964, 56)

This is a pretty good description of what has happened in the Western study of religion, not to mention our other institutions riven by self-criticism. It is a process in which both believers and nonbelievers, debunkers and disciples, have been complicit in their fidelity to a cognitive ideal that Nietzsche caricaturized as "intellectual cleanliness at any price." It is not uncommon to find former students of religion who have more or less talked themselves out of a job, their efforts to consolidate the foundations of their faith having had the opposite result of pulverizing their underpinnings into myriad uncertainties. According to Richard Rorty (1979, esp. chap. VIII), a similar fate has befallen philosophy, whose centuries-long efforts to polish the mirror it holds up to nature have virtually shattered any attempt at a unified perspective on reality. In the absence of any transcendent notion of truth, Rorty bequeaths to anthropologists, journalists, and novelists the task of chaperoning our moral concerns, in which religion has no discernible role (1989, xvi). For Girard, at once more interdisciplinary and more monist, a great novelist or playwright like Stendhal or Molière is a collaborator in the "fundamental anthropology" (Girard 1987b, part I) animated by Scripture.

As Kolakowski has reminded us, a sense of incompleteness and unestablished identity is the hallmark of Western culture, doubt and uncertainty about our own beliefs and institutions being the defining feature of a culture that accordingly values mobility and flexibility. This is a recipe for adaptability and change that our culture eventually enshrined as the doctrine of progress, about which the only thoughtful disputes since the French Revolution have concerned rates and regulations. Our indubitable success in this relentless experimentation is discernible in the apparently irreversible Westernization of the globe, a prospect that delights consumer marketers as much as it horrifies anticolonialists and culture critics among us. However, one need not affirm capitalism as God's will or history's Manifest Destiny for our species in order to acknowledge the global triumph of the market society, which Eric Gans (1993, chap. 10) has persuasively shown to be anthropologically sound and rationally consistent for a species born of a substitution mechanism. The exchange of symbols for violence and subsequently of words for things logically evolved to the exchange of goods and services as a limitlessly productive and resourceful substitute for their violent appropriation, which remains nonetheless the essential human dilemma confronting us still.

The vertiginous rate of change in our century only accentuates the violence convulsing our globe as our central and abiding anthropological concern. An originary hypothesis that traces cultural origins to the sacrificial control of a violence unique to our species merits serious consideration if the increase of violence among us can be linked to the decline of hieratic institutions that developed to regulate its exercise. Scapegoating persists, but without the limiting framework of ritualized forms. In this leveling process, competition, emulation, envy spread contagiously, being uninhibited by hierarchizing social institutions. These have gone the way of extinction prescribed for them by our persistent spirit of self-criticism that questions every institutional prerogative requiring victims. It is the spirit that, in principle if not in fact, weighs the value of social stability in favor of the unexchangeable value of the human person.

It is this self-critical attitude that, as Kolakowski reminds us, gave birth to Anthropology as the European science par excellence (Kolakowski 1990, 19). While sometimes attacked for being imperialistic, anthropology is cardinally pacific in its impulse to get us to see ourselves at a distance, critically, through the eyes of others. This is an attitude, he states, that favors tolerance in public life and skepticism in intellectual work (1990, 22). It also tends to repudiate the exercise of force, as if such an exercise were evidence of an absence of rationality, of unsound and ethically irresponsible motivation, of prerogatives, in short, awarded to a divine power that by definition transcends our reasoning and needn't answer to it. When violence is in question, so always is the sacred, if only in the form of an object desired so intensely as to provoke violence amidst those disputing its possession.

Kolakowski ascribes our questioning disposition chiefly to Christianity, whose theology oscillates irresolutely and dynamically between an image of a finite world created by God and a counterimage of the world as a negation of God (1990, 27, 28). While this tension is visible in the disputes and divisions of the churches, Girard is far more specific and concrete when he traces our anthropological disposition to the biblical impetus to see the world through the eyes of the victim of persecutions. He argues that the organic solidarity and cohesiveness of a culture is rendered suspect for us when it is achieved at the expense of even one of its members, and that this suspicion originates in Hebrew Scripture.

Self-doubt is poison to cultural cohesiveness, but it is also a remedy to stagnation; it destabilizes, but it also mobilizes for other, wider possibilities, of which our really astonishing cultural and technological virtuosity is the historical consequence. Today we do well to look for the source of plagues in microbes rather than in magic spells. We need to see our faith in scientific progress, which is real, as the dividend of the faith in alternatives to violent reciprocity and sacrificial mystifications that only momentarily resolve them (Girard 1986, 204–5). People could not envisage scientific solutions to society's dilemmas before the socius was desacralized and this, as Nietzsche was among the first to recognize, is the work of Christianity. And one should note that everywhere, here and abroad, that a social order is resacralized is evidence of movement away from our uniquely antifoundational tradition. The rhetorical and real violence that accompanies such movement confirms the equation between violence and the sacred.

The victim perspective is what causes Ivan Karamazov to refuse membership in a creation that would beckon his assent to tormenting a child, however great the benefits to everyone else (see Le Guin and Jackson for variants of this bargain). For Girard, the modern novel at its most revelatory moments takes up the challenge to culture that issues from Hebrew Scripture and that is confirmed, ratified, fully thematized by the Gospel narratives in a way that binds the two traditions into one.

Among ancient cultures, it is fair to say that none reads itself as consistently and self-critically, as emphatically and thematically, from the point of view of the victim as does Israel. The victim of oppression is not the originator or agent of resentment, as averred by Nietzsche, but its primary target, as rival desires accumulate and concur in seeking scapegoats for their disappointments. This perspective is legible in Israel's hypothesis on the foundation of culture, as we are told that the blood of Abel, Cain's rival twin, cries out from the ground to his divine creator (contrast the fate of Remus, slain by divine sanction). The mark of Cain signifies explicitly the repudiation of vengeful reprisal that is always in question, though not always decisive, in Hebrew Scripture, which is described as a "text in travail" (Bailie 1995, chap. 7) as it alternates, no less than our own culture, between sacrificial modes of thought and their symmetrical reproof. The divine rescue of Isaac beneath his father's knife promulgates an end to human sacrifice, whose survival among the Hebrews is regularly denounced by the prophets. Israel's God statutorily reserves vengeance for himself, a monopoly that secular societies award in principle to the law. Advocates of consistently more punitive measures among us serve unwittingly to remind us that the law is heir to sacrifice, being an effort to rationalize vengeance to preserve a social order that must needs disintegrate amidst endless reprisals.

Mosaic law is throughout an effort to control violence, and the envy or covetousness that generates it within the community (see Williams 1991, chap. 3; Bailie 1995, 143–45). It is the victimary perspective that fuels the great prophetic denunciations of sacrifice, where ritual integrity is rebuked as an unacceptable substitute for the succor of widows, orphans, the poor and the downtrodden, a leitmotif governing many of the Psalms as well. The moral exhortations of this tradition are integral to its institutional self-critique; consequently, there are grounds here for refocusing on the anthropological foundations of our basic ethical concerns in ways that are unavailable to strictly philosophical rationality.

The story of Job takes on fresh significance in this light, which we often evade when we blame God for evil among us—"especially," as Girard quips, "if we don't believe in him" (Girard 1987a, 7). Job's novelty, his anomaly, is to hold out for his innocence against his interlocutors who urge him to consent to his sufferings as divine punishment. In asserting instead his confidence in a god of victims, Job, rather than Gilles Deleuze's manic-hysteric Dionysus, is the true anti-Oedipus (Girard 1987a, chap 6; for Deleuze, see Girard, "Delirium as a System" in 1978a, 85-120):

> Henceforth I have a witness in heaven,
> my defender is there in the height.
>
> (16:19)

For Theban piety and the order it sanctions to be restored, Oedipus too must consent to his expulsion, though Teresias's angry repartee, his violent mimesis (Girard 1978b, chap. 3) should raise doubts about the king's uniquely tragic flaw, his fiery temperament. Sophocles' play allows us to entertain these doubts only momentarily; the curtain closes on *Oedipus Tyrannos* with the unanimous expulsion of the monster-outlaw, and when it reopens in *Oedipus at Colonnus* he is on his way to becoming a protective divinity, a foundational victim, with Thebes and Athens rivaling for his return to the boundaries of their community. As Cesareo Bandera argues, the Greeks, and the Romans after them, shrank back from their own critique of sacrifice because their culture provided no hopeful alternative to scapegoating mechanisms and the ritual mystifications surrounding them.

Like the suffering servant in the later chapters of Isaiah (esp. 53), Job prefigures Jesus. His life and teachings challenge his own culture, which aims at being the most upright and morally scrupulous of its time, to dissociate its religion from the rites and mechanisms of violent expulsion, and to acknowledge the God of love embedded in its Law. The Sermon on the Mount not only blesses or beatifies the poor and the meek, the oppressed and the persecuted; it also prescribes remedies to the violence that produces them (see Alison 1994, 42–44). When Jesus urges that we turn the other cheek, that we surrender our cloak to the man who solicits our coat, it is essential that we assess the rigorous structural coherence of such hyperbole: we are being summoned to withdraw from the cycle of violent reciprocity and defensiveness that only breeds more of its kind.

According to such a reading, the prayer to the Father (Mt 6:9–13; Lk 11:2–4) that Jesus prescribes for his followers is essentially grounded in the same remedy to violent reciprocity. Asking forgiveness of God does not chiefly concern our moral shortcomings or imperfections; it replicates because it depends on forgiving one's "debtors," those whose offenses or "trespasses" ensnare us in the economy of resentment and reprisal, the *ratio* of retaliation, in ways we no longer distinguish from rationality itself. Our structural immersion in violence is opaque to us, as we see better the speck in another's eye than the lintel in our own.

It is essential to recognize the epistemic valence of forgiveness here, as confirmed by the words Jesus spoke from the cross: "Forgive them father for they know not what they do" (Lk 23:34). These words express not only the repudiation of revenge on the part of the victim of a veritable lynching, but also the rationale for that repudiation; for they enunciate the structuring principle of mob violence: they know not what they do in their mimetic participation in the lynching mechanism recorded and analyzed by the passion narratives (Girard 1986, 110–11). The utterance fairly broadcasts mimesis as the originating sin of a creature whose creator, on the other hand, desires mercy, not sacrifice (Mt 9:13, quoting Hos 6:6).

Forgiveness, then, is not only an ethical or moral principle among many, but the foundation of peaceful human interaction for a species lacking instinctual brakes to endless violent reaction. It is the virtually infinite (seventy or seventy-seven times seven in Mt 18:22) antidote to ubiquitously mimetic reciprocation. It is not a moral virtue, because it doesn't moralize at all. It is beyond good and evil as those terms designate various prescriptions and proscriptions, rules and codes of behavior, by which people judge themselves and especially one another. But the beyond it points to is not necessarily located in some mysterious hereafter. Jesus declared to his accuser Pilate that his kingdom is not of this world, by which he meant the world of principalities and powers, armies and revolutions, orders and overthrowers bringing still more violent orders in their wake, in sum, the world organized by mimetic violence, scapegoating, and sacrificial expulsions that we read about everyday in the popular and scholarly press. He told people the Kingdom was among them and within them, by which he is understood (see Hamerton-Kelly 1994, 106–8) as meaning a world of human relations no longer structured by resentments and reprisals that his words and deeds effectively deconstruct.

I use that word advisedly, a minimal definition of deconstruction being a critique of difference as ontological foundation. It is accordingly a critique of representations that collude with overtly or covertly violent differentiations, with hierarchies founded on various forms of exclusion, expulsion, occultation. It is as a critique of violence that deconstructive analyses of all sorts of difference (racial, cultural, sexual) gathered their ethical appeal among professors and students, however much a cocky skepticism outran moral insight among some, to whom certainty of any kind is so tainted by violence that epistemological nihilism is preferable to it (see Siebers 1988, 105).

Deconstruction is the work of many parables as they appeal to people's understanding of the law only to "subvert from within" (Alison 1996, 124) the social and moral boundaries assumed to be drawn by it (for Jesus' thorough immersion in the Law, see Derrett 1970). The good Samaritan story accordingly obliterates the cultural differences cherished by Jesus' hearers by obliging them to conceive of their neighbor from the perspective of the victim of a brutal mugging, a perspective the story makes their own (see McKenna 1992, 211–21). The prodigal son parable redefine's God's love as that of a father for a son who is lost and returned to him, while warning the faithful son against any resentful rivalry. The parable of the laborers who receive the same recompense regardless of when they came to work summons the image of an essentially giving divinity who is indifferent to the calculations of merit that humans make among themselves over against one another; indifferent, again, to the rational economy of deserts.

This is the core dynamic of the episode of the woman caught in adultery (see Girard 1994, 179-86). It is a situation that Derrett (1970, 167, 169-70), long before Girard, labels as a potential lynching, an outcome threatening Jesus along with the woman if he gives evidence of repudiating Mosaic law. What Jesus does by suggesting that anyone without sin cast the first stone is to decollectivize the enthusiasm for killing. His remark deconstructs the sacrificial circle, delegitimizing violence by restaging it as an individual choice on the part of any who has never lusted unlawfully. The sacrificial formula of "unanimity minus one" gives way to recognition of the anonymity of desire. The crowd disperses "one by one," the sacred circle collapses, implodes, with the nomadic circulation of its center. The mutual reinforcement of collective zeal has been punctured like a soap bubble whose vacuous solidarity depended on the total bonding of all its molecules.

It is because of his challenge to ritual practices and ethnic and social boundaries that Jesus is immolated to the cultural cohesiveness he questions, as expressed in the sacrificial principle par excellence enunciated by Caiphas: "It is better for one man to die for the people, than for the whole nation to be destroyed" (Jn 11:49–50). There is hardly any institution, from the inquisitions, witch hunts, and pogroms betokening epistemic despair of the churches, through our modern revolutionary tribunals, that does not enact this principle (for its structural or systemic ubiquity, see Dupuy 1992, chap. 4), and when we denounce persecutions undertaken by sacred or secular tribunals, it is the selfsame religious tradition that authorizes our censure.

Jesus reproves ritual insularity and ethnic closure, but only so as to universalize Israel's core ethic, the superb moral energy of his people, whose sacred texts regularly oppose the god of victims to the cultic image of a violent divinity. For this he is hanged, but his prescience about the fate that awaits him at the hands of officialdom is not drawn from a divine blueprint or contract, an idea that is preposterous to modern reason. His own predictions of his violent end flow from his discernment of all-too-human mechanisms requiring expulsion of anyone challenging the violent underpinnings of social order. His murder is proof of that very violence, which he denounces among the Pharisees for dissociating themselves from the violence of their fathers who murdered the prophets (Mt 23:29–32). To condemn the other's violence is to veil one's own participation in it, as evidenced by that very scapegoating accusation. For the essential aim of scapegoating "since the foundation of the world" is to burden another with our own guilt. This is still how we understand the word today and why we reprove every recourse to it as mendacious, fraudulent—especially in others. Hypocrisy didn't end with the Pharisees, whose denunciation by Jesus applies no less to the lamentable conduct of the churches claiming him as its founder. If Christendom repeats ten- or even twentyfold the crimes denounced by its scriptural tradition, we have reason to acknowledge the moral and epistemic preeminence of the latter rather than to tax it with the wrongs it condemns. When we fail to distinguish between the moral integrity of a tradition and the all-too-human institutions that betray it, we are indulging in the very scapegoating practices we reprove.

According to this reading of texts and events, the scriptural tradition culminating in the Gospel narratives survive every demystifying, demythifying, and debunking criticism because it is the originating principle of demystification itself. The Amerindian slave in Voltaire's *Candide* (chap. 19) who ironizes about his dismemberment at the hands of his very own relatives, as propagated by the biblical doctrine of descent from Adam, is effectively evoking the Word against the institutions of Christendom set up as its (unfaithful) guardians.

Anthropologically speaking, deconstruction in Scripture means displacing the difference between profane and sacred, which by definition defies interrogation, to the difference between victim and persecutor, which is the difference by which not only moral judgments are made among us, but truth claims as well. Do we believe that Dreyfus was guilty, that Jews poisoned the wells, or captured whole economies, or do we believe that their accusers define and structure their anxious and fragile identity over against the people they arbitrarily blame for their ills? According to mimetic theory, it is this kind of certainty, from which there is no retreating, that has guided our Western confidence in reason, of which our truly formidable economic and scientific enterprise are the beneficiaries. The victimary perspective is one that virtually every institution has to factor in to its operations today, to a point where it has been banalized and perverted: claiming victim status for oneself has become a license for all manner of scapegoating, from the excesses of moral blackmail (see Gans 1997, chap. 3) through outright terrorism, where violence fully discloses its sacrificial trajectory in the anonymity of its victims.

Mimetic theory helps articulate the apostle Paul's idea of Jesus bringing freedom from sin and from law, which exists to regulate sin. Anyone authentically imitating Jesus ("mimetai christou," 1 Cor 11:1) in reciprocating love of the Father is immune to the fascinating allure, the attraction-repulsion, or the scandal of mimetic models. "Skandalon," a ubiquitous word for "sin" and "offense" in the Gospels (see McCracken 1994), designates a "stumbling block" which effectively distracts us from rational or benevolent decisions affecting no less our own than our neighbor's welfare. It is true, then, as averred, that "the truth shall make you free" (Jn 8:32), if we understand truth as our unwitting participation in violence and understand freedom as release from mimetic compulsions, the binds and bonds controlling our behavior as we imitate our neighbor's desires and the violence fomented by their obstruction.

This notion of truth invested in Johannine logos is not reducible to our forensic notion of truth inherited from the Greek philosophy and Roman law: the secular, philosophical model determined strictly according to accusatory and polemical modes of determining guilt, fault, flaw, infraction, error. A negative valence obtains to the extent that error is measured by the exercise of violence. But it is outshone by a logos that is essentially expansive, performative, interactive, and conciliatory. We don't much know what a future like that would look like; our institutions, sacred and profane, are still mostly geared to a sacrificial rationality, to thinking over against a real or imagined rival. But, from an anthropological or social scientific point of view, there is nothing illusory about it. Faith remains a debatable option; it can only by definition be a free choice (Heb 11:1), but, as informed by the insights of mimetic theory, it no longer seems so irrational.

Works Cited

Alison, James. 1994. *Knowing Jesus*. Springfield, IL: Templegate.

——. 1996. *Raising Abel: The Recovery of the Eschatological Imagination*. New York: Crossroad.

Bailie, Gil. 1995. *Violence Unveiled: Humanity at the Crossroads*. New York: Crossroad.

Bandera, Cesareo. 1994. *The Sacred Game: The Role of the Sacred in the Genesis of Modern Literary Fiction*. University Park: Pennsylvania State University Press.

Bulletin of the Colloquium on Violence and Religion (COV&R). P.O. Box 925, Sonoma, CA 95476.

Contagion: Journal of Violence, Mimesis, and Culture. 1994–1998. 5 vols.

Derrett, J. Duncan. 1970. *Law in the New Testament*. London: Darton, Longman and Todd.

Dupuy, Jean-Pierre. 1992. *Le sacrifice et l'envie: Le libéralisme aux prises avec la justice sociale*. Paris: Calmann-Levy.

Freud, Sigmund. 1964. *The Future of an Illusion*. Trans. James Strachey. New York: Doubleday.

Gans, Eric. 1993. *Originary Thinking: Elements of Generative Anthropology*. Stanford, CA: Stanford University Press.

——. 1997. *Signs of Paradox: Irony, Resentment, and Other Mimetic Structures*. Stanford, CA: Stanford University Press.

Girard, René. 1965. *Deceit, Desire and the Novel: Self and Other in Literary Structure*. Trans. Yvonne Freccero. Baltimore: Johns Hopkins University Press.

——. 1978a. *"To Double Business Bound": Essays on Literature, Myth, Mimesis and Anthropology*. Baltimore: Johns Hopkins University Press.

——. 1978b. *Violence and the Sacred*. Trans. Patrick Gregory. Baltimore: Johns Hopkins University Press.

——. 1986. *The Scapegoat*. Trans. Yvonne Freccero. Baltimore: Johns Hopkins University Press.

——. 1987a. *Job: The Victim of His People*. Trans. Yvonne Freccero. Stanford, CA: Stanford University Press.

——. 1987b. *Things Hidden Since the Foundation of the World*. Trans. Stephen Bann and Michael Metteer. Stanford, CA: Stanford University Press.

——. 1991. *A Theater of Envy: William Shakespeare*. New York: Oxford University Press.

——. 1994. *Quand ces choses commenceront: Entretien avec Michel Treguer*. Paris: Arléa.

Hamerton-Kelly, Robert. 1994. *The Gospel and the Sacred: Poetics of Violence in Mark*. Minneapolis: Fortress.

Jackson, Shirley. 1966. "The Lottery." *Points of View: An Anthology of Short Stories*. Ed. J. Moffett and K. McElheny. New York: NAL.

Kolakowski, Leszek. 1990. *Modernity on Endless Trial*. Chicago: University of Chicago Press.

Le Guin, Ursula. 1975. "The Ones Who Walk Away from Omelos." In *The World's Twelve Quarters: Short Stories by Ursula Le Guin*. New York: Harper and

Row.

McCracken, David. 1994. *The Scandal of the Gospel: Jesus, Story, and Offense*. New York: Oxford University Press.

McKenna, Andrew. 1992. *Violence and Difference: Girard, Derrida, and Deconstruction*. Urbana: University of Illinois Press.

Nietzsche, Friedrich. 1967. *On the Genealogy of Morals*. Trans. Walter Kaufmann. New York: Vintage.

Rorty, Richard. 1979. *Philosophy and the Mirror of Nature*. Princeton: Princeton University Press.

———. 1989. *Contingency, Irony, and Solidarity*. New York: Cambridge University Press.

Siebers, Tobin. 1988. *The Ethics of Criticism*. Ithaca: Cornell University Press.

Williams, James. 1991. *The Bible, Violence, and the Sacred: Liberation from the Myth of Sanctioned Violence*. San Francisco: Harper.

5

Midrash and Intertextuality:
Ancient Rabbinic Exegesis and
Postmodern Reading of the Bible

T. R. Wright

Midrash, as David Stern somewhat skeptically comments, became something of a "hot topic" during the deconstructive, interdisciplinary eighties. Its "predilection for multiple interpretations" and blurring of boundaries between literature and commentary were seized upon with some excitement as offering an alternative to the Greco-Christian logocentric literary tradition. Stern compares the interdisciplinary excitement generated by literary and theoretical interest in midrash with the "Bible as Literature" movement of the previous decade, another attempt to preserve the Bible from neglect by the secular and fragmentation at the hands of historians (Stern 1996, 3–10). Stern, while rightly emphasizing the need for a proper understanding of midrashic practice within its original rabbinic context, fails fully to do justice to what it is about midrash which continues to appeal to postmodern critics beset with similar problems to those of the ancient rabbis: how to make sense in their own time of their traditional sacred texts, how to read the Bible.

Both the excitement and the difficulties to which Stern points are illustrated by a curious anthology which appeared recently entitled *Modern Poems on the Bible* (Curzon 1994). This prints a wide range of modern poetry on a variety of subjects taken from the Hebrew Bible opposite the relevant scriptural verses (the intertexts). David Curzon, the editor, claims, "Whether the poets knew it or not, and some of them did, they were writing midrash" (1994, 3). He proceeds to describe the basic characteristics of a typical midrash as "a response to a specific and very short biblical text" which is "imaginative, and . . . makes a point" (1994, 4–5). Rabbinic midrashic exegesis of the early centuries of the Christian era, as Curzon explains, used other verses from Scripture as proof-texts with which to open up the meaning of the primary biblical passage under consideration. In these "twentieth-century midrashic poems," however, according to Curzon, "such implicit proof-texts are drawn from virtually all domains of knowledge," including science, history, and other religious traditions (1994, 4–5). In order to illustrate what he means by modern midrash, Curzon reproduces a poem by the Italian holocaust survivor Primo Levi, "In the Beginning," the title taken from the very first words of the Hebrew Bible, as if it were a rabbinic midrash, with the standard formulas:

> Another interpretation of IN THE BEGINNING GOD CREATED THE HEAVENS AND THE EARTH (Gen. 1:1). Primo Levi opened his discourse: this is to be understood in terms of the current scientific theory of the creation of the universe, which assumes that "Twenty billion years before now,/ Brilliant, soaring in space and time,/ There was a ball of flame, solitary, eternal,/ Our common father and our executioner." (Curzon 1994, 14)

There are, of course, a few problems about this, not the least of them theological. Primo Levi writes, unlike the rabbis, from outside any believing community. But the example raises interesting questions about how we (late twentieth century survivors of the horrors of recent history) read the Bible, given the fact, as Harold Bloom puts it in *Kabbalah and Criticism*, that "every act of reading is an exercise in belatedness" (Bloom 1975a, 97). In what follows I want to consider why the model of rabbinic midrash is such an attractive way of approaching what literary critics refer to as intertextuality. These critics, by the way, include not only the Jewish Harold Bloom and Jacques Derrida, both familiar with midrash, but the Russian Orthodox Mikhail Bakhtin and the agnostic Julia Kristeva, neither of whom, as far as I know, were particularly well informed about Jewish exegetical practices. All of them, however, explore the difficulties of relating to a religious tradition, of mediating between ancient and modern cultures, of reading the Bible.

"Defining Midrash," as Gary Porton has shown, in his article of that title, is no easy matter, and attempts to do so range from the narrow to the broad. The Harper Bible Dictionary goes from one end of the spectrum to the other in one paragraph: having defined it as "the type of biblical interpretation found in rabbinic literature" which "pays close attention to the meanings of individual words . . . , elucidates one verse by another verse, and relates the teachings of rabbinic Judaism to the biblical text," it acknowledges that "in a wider sense, the word midrash is used for any interpretation which . . . assumes that the biblical text has an inexhaustible fund of meaning that is relevant to and adequate for every question and situation" (635). The entry under "Midrash" ends with that instruction so beloved of all dictionaries, "see also Haggadah," which is in turn defined negatively (as it normally is) as "the interpretation of the historical and religious passages of Jewish Scripture that are not legal in character" but "often supplement the biblical narrative" in a "rich variety of Jewish 'retelling' of the tradition" (366). When Jacob Neusner attempts to answer the question, *What Is Midrash?* (1987), he refers approvingly to Porton's definition, which also emphasizes that "midrash is a term given to a Jewish activity which finds its locus in the religious life of the Jewish community." Neusner appends a footnote to the effect that he distinguishes "between 'midrash' and 'exegesis' only by assigning the former word to activity within the Israelite community." He admits, however, that "there may be extensive parallels between midrash which occurs within an Israelite context and exegesis which occurs in other religious and cultural systems" (Porton 1981, 10). It is clearly debatable whether or not one can use the term *midrash* in this analogous sense, but it is this kind of exegesis, to some extent modeled upon midrash, that I want to explore.

Geoffrey Hartman and Sanford Budick, in their highly influential study *Midrash and Literature*, make very large, some would say extravagant, claims for the extent to which Western modes of reading and writing have historically been modeled upon midrash. While the "authorized interpreters—in church and university— . . . remained oblivious to its influence, ignoring midrash as a subject and misconceiving or misappropriating the Hebraic elements in our culture," they claim, "the great poets who wrote out of the western tradition somehow evidenced its existence in our collective literary imagination" (Hartman and Budick 1986, x). The "somehow" here worries me, as do the Jungian connotations of the "collective . . . imagination." In some cases, such as that of Milton, it is fairly clear to which Latin editions of midrash he was referring, but for some of the modern poets represented in Curzon's volume to have absorbed midrash unconsciously would have involved quite a feat of collective memory.

Hartman and Budick are similarly unconvincing when they claim, "For some time now, it has been understood [note the passive construction, always useful in glossing over the question "by whom"] that many profoundly ingrained habits of western reading . . . are historical derivatives of midrash" (1986, x). This, of course, would be extremely difficult to prove. They are more cautious in noting "resemblances" between midrash and contemporary literary theories of intertextuality and they are clearly joking when they refer to Reb Derrida and Reb Kermode (not to mention Reb Milton and Reb Borges). But their point, like the kind of literary and critical "play" they advocate, is a serious one, that this mode of interpretation, "long lost to literary study" and neglected even by "students of Judaica," needs to be recovered because "it quickens our understanding of textual production" both in reading and in writing. It also addresses our postmodern predicament, our precarious relationship to religious and literary traditions:

> The canon is transmitted and even extended by an intertextual re-
> flection that has accepted the task of memory and preservation
> while adding a spacious supplement that derives from its primary
> source a strength and daring which is anything but secondary—
> which is, indeed, "literary" in the modern sense. (Hartman and
> Budick 1986, xii)

I will argue in a moment that one of Derrida's main concerns is the nature
of the supplement precisely in terms of our postmodern relationship to
religious, philosophical, political and literary traditions.

Midrash, narrowly defined, may have had literary elements but most
students of the rabbinic material insist that its primary emphasis was theological rather than literary (Neusner 1987: 80). Harold Fisch, after exploring midrashic elements in *Robinson Crusoe* and *Joseph Andrews,* insists on
the difference: "Midrashim are not novels." The two types of writing shed
light on similar literary processes, "the way in which stories or hints of
stories are generated by the art of interpretation," for example (Fisch 1998,
228), but they are not the same. Midrash, however free and open, operates
under constraints related to its function within a believing community for
which the primary text has "unlimited authority" as revelation. Midrash
always comes back with a "joy of recognition" to its primary text, rather
than struggle, as Bloom would have it, to escape the anxiety of its influence
(231–32). Even this, however, is too clear-cut a generalization, for Judah
Goldin demonstrates in the same volume that there were tensions even in
the tannaite centuries between exegetical midrash and halakha on the one
hand and haggadah on the other while later rationalists such as Maimonides
were particularly dismissive of the freedom of interpretation enjoyed by the
more imaginative rabbis.

One of the attractive features of midrash for literary critics, as the
South African critic and novelist Dan Jacobson acknowledges, is its imaginative freedom, its ability seriously and creatively to play with truth. His
lecture on "Biblical Narratives and Novelists' Narratives" compares a passage from the *Midrash Rabbah* with material from Kierkegaard's *Fear and
Trembling* and Thomas Mann's *Joseph and His Brothers,* similarly based
upon biblical originals. All three passages share a profound respect for the
original text, a recognition of their own relative provisionality and a celebration of imaginative truth. Jacobson concludes,

> The spirit of imaginative speculation and self-projection, out of
> which all our richest fictions, in all ages, have emerged, is by no
> means as irreconcilable as it might seem to be with the biblical

writers' conception of their task as sacred historians. Precisely because they have such confidence in the indefeasible veracity of the larger, overarching story they are telling, they are able to grant an autonomy, a dramatic presence, a psychological inwardness and coherence, to all or any of the participants in their tales. (Jacobson 1989, 6)

Elsewhere, in his wide-ranging study of the Bible, *The Story of the Stories,* Jacobson discusses the way in which he discovered for himself, while writing his midrashic novel *The Rape of Tamar,* that "every phrase, virtually every word, in the relevant chapter of 2 Samuel was like a seed . . . capable of astonishing growth" (1982, 131).

The Bible itself, as Michael Fishbane and others have demonstrated, is full of midrashic material or "inner-biblical exegesis," accretions to the canon within the canon as a result of a continuing process of self-reflexive commentary. We can distinguish between this "intratextuality" within the canon and the more extensive "intertextuality" between the Bible and noncanonical texts. But the process is the same, allowing for the continual supplementation and renewal of the tradition. "Aggadic exegesis," in Fishbane's words, is not simply "content to supplement gaps in the *traditum* [the sacred text] but characteristically draws forth latent and unsuspected meanings from it . . . its fullness of potential meanings and applications" (Fishbane 1985:283). This, he explains in *The Garments of Torah,* is how "cultures renew themselves hermeneutically" (ix), retaining reverence for the text while subjecting it to "a daring reinflection of the traditional sense," often signalled in midrash by a phrase such as *kivyakhol,* "as it were," thus acknowledging its own boldness and daring along with its own limitations (28). Fishbane indicates the relevance of contemporary literary theory in referring as he does to "midrashic *differance*," the serious play of meaning characteristic of the mythopoetic theology to be found in midrash (22). Even Neusner, not exactly famous for his enthusiasm for contemporary literary theory, indicates why midrash is so attractive to literary critics, providing as it does "a paradigm of creative and profound response to the biblical record" (Neusner 1985a: ix), "a valuable alternative" to the dominant literalism that "enjoys the authority of true religion" (xiii). He celebrates in *The Midrash* a literature that writes not about Scripture but "*with* Scripture," by which he means that the Bible "formed an instrumentality for the expression of a writing bearing its own integrity and cogency, appealing to its own conventions of intelligibility, and, above all, making its own points" (x).

It is its practice of intertextuality rather than its independence that links midrash with modern literary theory. As Daniel Boyarin explains in *Intertextuality and the Reading of Midrash*, "The intertextual reading practice of the midrash," itself a development of "the intratextual interpretive strategies which the Bible itself manifests," involves the more complex notion of intertextuality elaborated by recent literary theorists, in which all reading is described as an actualization or completion of gaps in the text in accordance with their "own intertext—that is, the cultural codes which enable them to make meaning and find meaning" (Boyarin 1990, 16). He quotes Gerald Bruns in Alter and Kermode's *Literary Guide to the Bible*: "The Bible always addresses itself to the time of interpretation; one cannot understand it except by appropriating it anew" (1990, 627–28). And here is where the difficulties start, not simply because Bruns goes on to celebrate the "astonishing examples of midrashic extravagance" which can be found among rabbinic material, an extravagance which more sober critics such as Meir Sternberg deplore, but because the act of appropriation, as Bakhtin and Bloom have shown, is not an innocent one. In fact, it can be so violent as entirely to change the meaning of the original.

The term intertextuality, as M. H. Abrams explains in the fifth edition of *A Glossary of Literary Terms*,

> is used to signify the multiple ways in which any one literary text echoes, or is inseparably linked to, other texts, whether by open or covert citations and *allusions*, or by the formal and substantive features of an earlier text, or simply by participation in a common stock of literary and linguistic procedures and conventions. (1988, 247)

Abrams might seem to be hedging his bets here, moving from the specific relationship of one text to another to the broader process by which all texts within a particular period might be said to be related to each other. But, like midrash, the term is used both in a specific and in a broad sense. The helpful glossary in Danna Fewell's study *Reading Between Texts: Intertextuality and the Hebrew Bible* notices the way intertextuality overlaps with cognate (and more conventional) terms such as allusion, echo, and poetic influence as well as more radical and recent notions of the trace. The confusion is partly caused by old-fashioned critics attempting to dress conventional activity (such as tracing influence and allusion) in the new and exciting language of poststructuralism. There is, of course, a difference between source-spotting and intertextuality, a difference that I will try to bring out with reference to the principal theorists in this area: Julia Kristeva, Mikhail Bakhtin, Harold Bloom, and Jacques Derrida. The last two, as I indicated earlier, are conscious of the connections between intertextuality as they define it and traditional rabbinic interpretation. Kristeva and Bakhtin, however, are not; and it is their awareness of the break between the modern period and the traditions upon which it draws that is particularly relevant to my argument that modern midrash (of a self-consciously literary sort) represents a break with traditional midrash (but nevertheless deserves to be considered a type of that genre appropriate for our age).

Most expositions of intertextuality begin with Kristeva's seminal article "Word, Dialogue, and Novel," written in 1966, published in 1969, translated in 1980 in her book *Desire in Language* and reprinted in *The Kristeva Reader* (edited for Blackwell by Toril Moi, who introduces the essay by explaining that it brings Kristeva's structuralist linguistic and psycho-linguistic interests of the period into "active dialogue" with Bakhtin). It needs to be recognized that Kristeva's interpretation of Bakhtin is partial in both senses, drawing from a limited range of his work (which was not then all in print) and twisting it quite self-consciously in accordance with her own poststructuralist concerns (which is what she would say reading is anyway). What Kristeva celebrates in Bakhtin is his writing as much as his scholarship:

> Bakhtin was one of the first to replace the static hewing out of texts with a model where literary structure does not simply *exist* but is generated in relation to *another* structure. What allows a dynamic dimension to structuralism is his conception of the "literary word" as an *intersection of textual surfaces* rather than a *point* (a fixed meaning), as a dialogue among several writings: that of the writer, the addressee (or the character) and the contemporary or earlier cultural context. (Moi 1986, 35–36)

The point (to halt this fluid process just for a moment) is that none of the entities involved in the traditional model of communication (writer, text, reader) are stable; all are dynamic and interactive constructs of ideology. In particular, in Kristeva's words, "any text is constructed as a mosaic of quotations; any text is the absorption and transformation of another." Kristeva proceeds to introduce the new term (to the accompaniment of textual drums in the form of italics): "The notion of *intertextuality* replaces that of intersubjectivity" (Moi 1986, 37). It's important to grasp the context of this apocalyptic utterance, which is Paris of the late sixties, when Roland Barthes was declaring in an equally famous text of 1968, "The Death of the Author":

Literature (it would be better from now on to say *writing*) by refusing to assign a "secret," an ultimate meaning, to the text (and to the
world as Text), liberates what may be called an anti-theological
activity, an activity that is truly revolutionary since to refuse to fix
meaning is, in the end, to refuse God and his hypostases—reason,
science, law. (Barthes 1977, 147)

The linguistic terrorist Barthes, who cites Kristeva as one of his own
"intertexts," enjoys "kidnapping" her term and, as Still and Worton explain
in their helpful introduction to *Intertextuality*, "using the borrowed vocabulary with a certain slippage" (Worton and Still 1990, 18). To use the language of *Roland Barthes by* Roland Barthes,

Words are shifted, systems communicate, modernity is tried (the
way one tries all the push buttons on a radio one doesn't know how
to work), but the intertext thereby created is literally superficial:
one adheres *liberally*: the name (philosophic, psychoanalytic, political, scientific) retains with its original system a line which is not
cut but which remains: tenacious and floating. (Barthes 1977, 74)

Barthes is not specifically addressing the problem of religious continuity
but his argument seems to me to encapsulate the predicament exemplified
by many modern writers in relation to religious traditions, in particular their
use of vocabulary derived from the Bible. It might be unfair to portray
them as pushing the buttons of their bibles without understanding how it
works (or worked in the past). But literature is liberal with language in this
way: it takes words out of one context and transfers them to another. Any
reading, in fact, could be said to do this, with more or less consciousness
of the difference between the two historical moments (the context of the
text's production and that of its reception).

This is what Bakhtin is about. He does not, *pace* Kristeva, replace
intersubjectivity with intertextuality; he attempts to show how subjectivity
is intertextually constructed. There are, as Simon Dentith has shown,
similarities between *Bakhtinian Thought*, forged in reaction to Russian For-
malism in the late 1920s, and the Parisian reaction against the neo-formal-
ism of structuralism in the late 1960s, when Bakhtin's work was rediscovered and revised. But throughout his career he insisted upon writing and
reading as dialogical rather than monological, a matter of interpersonal dynamics within specific historical contexts. Any language, according to
Bakhtin in *The Dialogical Imagination*, contains "a multitude of bounded
verbal-ideologies and social belief-systems," including vestiges of past sys-

tems coexisting in contradiction with the present to form a complex heteroglossia (literally the words of others). All these coexisting "languages of heteroglossia," Bakhtin explains,

> are specific points of view on the world, forms for conceptualizing the world in words, specific world views, each characterized by its own objects, meanings and values. As such they . . . encounter one another and co-exist in the consciousness of real people– first and foremost, in the creative consciousness of people who write novels. (1981, 291–92)

None of these words are "neutral"; they carry with them the ideological baggage they acquire in historical use. They can be "re-accented" in different social and historical contexts so that they become "multi-accented": "Each word tastes of the context and contexts in which it has lived its socially charged life" (1981, 293). Appropriating another's language involves a dynamic tension:

> The word in language is half someone else's. It becomes "one's own" only when the speaker populates it with his own intention, his own accent. . . . And not all words for just anyone submit equally easily to this appropriation, to this seizure and transformation into private property: many words stubbornly resist, others remain alien, sound foreign in the one who appropriated them. (1981, 293-94)

Bakhtin's model of heteroglossia provides a much more satisfactory framework within which to discuss the way in which the Word is appropriated in modern literature, I would suggest, than the disembodied and decontextualized textuality of Barthes and Kristeva.

Bakhtin, as his biographers Holquist and Clark reveal, was deeply interested in religion and religious language; Russian Orthodox by upbringing, he was highly unorthodox by temperament. *Problems of Dostoevsky's Poetics* celebrates the kind of novel written by the great Russian author precisely because it is dialogical, allowing for "a plurality of independent and unmerged voices and consciousnesses, a genuine polyphony of fully valid voices" as opposed to the work of Tolstoy, for example, which he found monological, attempting to submerge other voices in an authoritarian discourse which gave the final word to the narrator (Bakhtin 1984, 6). All monologic forms are suspect for this reason, whether in the shape of political or religious dogma, the epic, poetry, or the Bible. The point about

epic discourse, as Bakhtin explains in "Epic and Novel," the first of the
essays that make up *The Dialogical Imagination,* is that it is "given solely
as tradition, sacred and sacrosanct . . . demanding a pious attitude towards
itself":

> The epic past is locked into itself and walled off from all subsequent
> times by an impenetrable boundary, isolated . . . from personal
> experience, from any new insights, from any personal initiative in
> understanding and interpreting, from new points of view and evalu-
> ations. (1981, 16–17)

Whether this is a fair and accurate reflection of all epic is not the point;
what matters are the values of interaction and dialogue within a tradition,
its openness to reinterpretation and reevaluation.

The Bible too, in the second of the four essays in *The Dialogical Imagination,* "From the Prehistory of Novelistic Discourse," is seen as an authoritarian discourse which the Church attempted to impose upon the laity
in the Middle Ages but against which popular forms of resistance arose:

> The authoritative and sanctified word of the Bible . . . continually
> infiltrates the context of medieval literature and the speech of edu-
> cated men (clerics). But how does this infiltration occur, how does
> the receiving context relate to it, in what sort of intonational quota-
> tion marks is it enclosed? Here a whole spectrum of possible rela-
> tionships toward this word comes to light, beginning at one pole
> with the pious and inert quotation that is isolated and set off like an
> icon, and ending at the other pole with the most ambiguous, disre-
> spectful, parodic-travestying use of a quotation. (1981, 69)

The problem with poetry too, as Bakhtin conceives it in the fourth and final
essay of *The Dialogical Imagination,* "Discourse in the Novel," is that it
claims monological authority, forging a single voice, stripping words of the
accents of others and bathing them in Lethe, presuming "nothing beyond
the borders of its own context" and forgetting its own history (1981, 278,
297). The novelist, on the contrary, "does not acknowledge any unitary,
singular, naively (or conditionally) indisputable or sacrosanct language"
(1981, 332). He or she recognizes that there are many competing ideologies in circulation and that "the ideological becoming of a human being . . .
is the process of selectively assimilating the words of others" (1981, 341).

Bakhtin contrasts the "authoritative word," which is monological and
demands complete acceptance, with "internally persuasive discourse" char-

acteristic of the novel:

> The authoritative word demands that we acknowledge it, that we make it our own; it binds us, quite independent of any power it might have to persuade us internally. . . . The authoritative word is located in a distanced zone, organically connected with a past that is felt to be hierarchically higher. It is, so to speak, the word of the fathers. (1981, 342)

This monologic word, semantically "static and dead," comes to us "fully complete" with an authorized "single meaning," demanding not a "free appropriation and assimilation" but "unconditional allegiance":

> Authoritative discourse permits no play with the context framing it, no play with its borders, no gradual and flexible transitions, no spontaneously creative stylizing variants on it. It enters our verbal consciousness as a compact and indivisible mass; one must either totally affirm it, or totally reject it. (1981, 343)

Bakhtin holds it impossible for the authoritative word to be assimilated into "artistic representation":

> Its role in the novel is insignificant. It is by its very nature incapable of being double-voiced; it cannot enter into hybrid constructions . . . . it enters the artistic context as an alien body, there is no space around it to play in, no contradictory emotions. . . . For this reason images of official-authoritative truth . . . have never been successful in the novel. . . . The authoritative text always remains, in the novel, a dead quotation, something that falls out of the artistic context (for example, the evangelical texts in Tolstoy at the end of *Resurrection*). (1981, 344)

The translation is somewhat unidiomatic here, of course; what Bakhtin is referring to are the passages from the Gospels.

Internally persuasive discourse, on the contrary, "is affirmed through assimilation, tightly interwoven with 'one's own word'":

> Its creativity and productiveness consist precisely in the fact that such a word awakens new and independent words. . . . It is not so much interpreted by us as it is further, that is, freely, developed, applied to new material, new conditions; it enters into interanimating

relationships with new contexts. More than that, it enters into an intense interaction, a *struggle* with other internally persuasive discourses. (1981, 34–466)

The book ends with a celebration of "the process of re-accentuation" which is of such "great and seminal importance for the history of literature" and for the development of ideas. For, as the final words emphasize,

great novelistic images continue to grow and develop even after the moment of their creation; they are capable of being creatively transformed in different eras, far distant from the day and hour of their original birth. (1981, 422)

Some "Notes Made in 1970–71," published in *Speech Genres and Other Late Essays,* reaffirm both the positive and negative aspects of Bakhtin's understanding of the sacred word in relation to *The Dialogical Imagination.* "Modern man does not proclaim; he speaks. That is, he speaks with reservations," in contrast to the "priests, prophets, preachers, judges, leaders, patriarchal fathers, and so forth." Literature, according to these notes, "has been completely secularized," "expunging the sacred and authoritarian word," which "retards and freezes thought," removing itself from dialogue and displaying an "extremely limited ability to combine in general and especially with profane—not sacred—words" (1986, 132–33). I want to argue that, in spite of his own characterization of the Bible as "authoritative" in his pejorative sense, Bakhtin's model of creative transformation is particularly fruitful in considering what happens to biblical texts when they are assimilated and creatively transformed by modern writers. To do this, however, it will help to bring in the critic who has contributed perhaps more than any other writer to a recognition both of the literary power of certain parts of the Bible and of its creative assimilation by later writers, Harold Bloom.

Bloom's theoretical project began with a general de-idealization of poetic influence in terms of family romance. *The Anxiety of Influence* (1973) portrayed the relationship of poets to their precursors as one of struggle, a wrestling to avoid submission to the poetic father, the poet who first awakened creativity:

Poetic influence—when it involves two strong, authentic poets,— always proceeds by a misreading of the prior poet, an act of creative correction that is actually and necessarily a misinterpretation. The

history of poetic influence . . . is a history of anxiety and self-
serving caricature, of distortion, of perverse, wilful revisionism without which modern poetry as such could not exist. (Bloom 1973, 30)

After spelling out a variety of ways in which poets escaped the control of
the their precursor, whether by completion, repetition, swerving (the de-
tails of Bloom's arcane set of terms derived from Alexandrian gnostics
matter less than the general principle), Bloom proclaims "A manifesto for
Antithetical Criticism" which includes such aphorisms as:

> The meaning of a poem can only be another poem. . . . Every poem
> is a misinterpretation of a parent poem. . . . There are no interpreta-
> tions but only misinterpretations, and so all criticism is prose po-
> etry. (Bloom 1973, 94–95)

Bloom deliberately overstates the case in order to make his general point
that all writing is a form of reading and vice versa; in his view the most
powerful readings are creative and the most interesting criticism therefore
is to be found among the poets. Strength replaces accuracy as the prime
virtue.

Two books of 1975, *A Map of Misreading* and *Kabbalah and Criticism,* develop this general theory in relation to Jewish revisionism, the way
rabbinic and kabbalistic writers have reinterpreted and rewritten their sacred texts. Having spelt out the general principle of intertextuality, or "poetic influence," as he prefers to call it, "that there are *no* texts, but only
relationships *between* texts" and that all criticism involves the "misreading
or misprision, that one poet performs upon another" (1975b, 3), *A Map of
Misreading* takes Lurianic Kabbalism as "the ultimate model for Western
revisionism" in terms of

> its work of *interpretation*, of revisionary replacements of Scriptural
> meaning by techniques of *opening*. All Kabbalistic texts are inter-
> pretive, however wildly speculative, and what they interpret is a
> central text that perpetually possesses authority, priority, and
> strength. (Bloom 1975b, 4)

Isaac Luria's version of creation, a sixteenth century rewriting of *Genesis*,
involves three main stages, *Zimzum* ("the Creator's withdrawal or contrac-
tion so as to make possible a creation that is not himself "), *Shevirath
hakelim* (the breaking of the vessels of divine light, giving birth to base

matter, "a vision of creation as catastrophe"), and *Tikkun,* or redemption (the release of the imprisoned sparks of light by the action of righteous human beings), an unorthodox account of creation, fall, and redemption which Bloom finds attractive not only as theology but as "the best paradigm available for a study of the way poets war against one another" (1975b, 5). He explains that Kabbalah means literally "'tradition', that which has been received" and that tradition means etymologically "a carrying-over of influence." But *traditio,* Bloom argues, "is Latin only in language; the concept deeply derives from the Hebraic *Mishnah,* an oral handing-over, or transmission of oral precedents," and applies to the written and the literary as much as to the oral tradition (1975b, 31–32). *Midrash,* Bloom explains, which derives from *darash,* to seek and so to interpret, was originally oral but became written, a mode of seeking for the Torah, interpreting and developing it (1975b, 42). Bloom adds Kierkegaard's notion of repetition, a compulsion to recover the prestige of origins, the vision of the fathers, and Nietzsche's view of interpretation as the will to power to the Midrashic and Kabbalistic revision to create a model of relating creatively to tradition which goes well beyond the weak reading permitted by orthodox institutions.

    Kabbalah and Criticism goes even further into what Bloom recognizes as a modern form of gnosticism, abandoning the central platform of orthodox Judaism in which "a transcendent God allows Himself to be known by His people as an immediate Presence" (1975a, 20). In the *Zohar,* the acknowledged masterpiece of Kabbalism, God is presented as "totally unknowable, and beyond representation." The kabbalist turns self-consciously to the *Sefirot,* the expressions of God which Bloom likens to "poems, in that they are names implying complex commentaries that make them into texts" (1975a, 24–25). Kabbalah, the product of long periods of Jewish exile and suffering, attempts to reconcile that experience with the promises of the Bible; in Bloom's words, it "proposes to give suffering a meaning, by way of an interpretation of Scripture" (1975a, 51), which is why a writer such as Elie Wiesel found it so fruitful in his attempt to come to terms with the Holocaust. Kabbalah is also taken by Bloom not only as "a model for the processes of poetic influence" but a theory of writing, breaking down the boundaries so carefully preserved in the Talmud between text and commentary. "This line," to quote Bloom, "wavers and breaks in the Zohar" allowing for the creation of a magnificent poem which acted as "a collective, psychic defence . . . against exile and persecution" (1975a, 52–53). Bloom stresses both the literary and theological motives of the Kabbalists, who suffered "an overwhelming anxiety-of-influence" in response to Scripture as well as a need to reinterpret in the light of experience, which made Gnosis and Kabbalah "the first Modernisms" (1975a, 71, 79). Scripture, most notably at the end of the Book of Revelation, invokes a curse upon anyone who dares add to the canon (1975a, 99); the Kabbalists defy that curse and the control of normative institutions, producing a supplement to the canon which is both interpretive and creative.

The Breaking of the Vessels (1982) returns to Kabbalistic mythology in order to dramatize the process of poetic influence, the way in which individual writers and readers relate to their tradition. T. S. Eliot makes the process sound very benign in his famous essay on "tradition and the Individual Talent," which allows for the new work to be happily incorporated in the existing canon. Bloom points out that a less well known review, written only a few weeks before that essay and never subsequently reprinted, recognizes the ambivalence any poet feels toward a precursor, how "the awareness of our debt naturally leads us to hatred of the object imitated, a personal 'crisis' which changes our whole personality" (1982, 19–20). Bloom considers other followers of the path of Jacob, maimed as well as blessed by the angel with whom he wrestles: "Wrestling Waldo [Emerson], heroically confronting all the cultural past" and insisting that all products of the human intellect, including the Bible, are "revisable, corrigible, reversible" (1982, 35, 27), and "Wrestling Sigmund" (the title of chapter 2), whose agon with the past, especially the Yahwist, "is the largest and most intense of our century" (1982, 47). The "poetic tales of Yahweh and the Patriarchs," Bloom claims, are so strong, so strange and original, and so encrusted with traditional misreading that "we simply cannot read them" (1982, 50–51).

Both sacred and secular canons have occupied a large place in Bloom's work of the last decade. A number of the essays in *Poetics of Influence* (1988) develop Bloom's theory of influence with particular reference to poets and their relationship with the Bible. "The Covering Cherub" considers a triad of wrestling matches, between Jacob and Jehovah in Genesis 32, between Milton and Urizen in Blake's poem *Milton,* and between Blake and Milton, who for many an eighteenth century poet was "the Covering Cherub blocking a new voice from entering Paradise," a reference, of course, to the end of Genesis 3 (1988, 87). The Kabbalah is celebrated once more as "a massive misprision of both Bible and Talmud" in an "attempt to *restore* primal meanings to the Bible." "Martin Buber on the Bible," originally published as the introduction to a collection of essays, *On the Bible,* by Martin Buber, develops Bloom's critique of orthodox biblical scholarship as "inadequate" literary criticism, which fails to grasp the extraordinary power of a text such as that produced by J, the implied author of the earliest strand of writing in the pentateuch (1988, 325), described by Bloom as "a massively self-confident writer, fierce and primal in his approach to human personality and totally daring in his apprehension of divine realities" (1988, 329; in those days, notice, he was still male). Such was J's original-ity, especially in his portrait of an uncanny God beyond all conceptualization, Bloom argues, that he was inassimilable by "the entire tradition that he fostered, try though they did to tame and censor him (1988, 331–32). That tradition, of course, includes not only the normative voice of the Priestly Writer but the writers of the New (or rather, Belated) Testament, especially the author of John's gospel, who makes his Jesus blasphemously appropri-ate the words of Yahweh. "Before Abraham was, I am" (1988, 387–90).

Ruin the Sacred Truths (1989) continues Bloom's celebration of the literary strength of J in comparison with the revisionary and bowdlerizing writers who followed. "What are we to make," asks Bloom, of "texts that founded themselves upon a great original but which sought to absorb him into a final Scripture very different from his spirit and his procedures?" (1989, 9). The answer, of course, was a new edition of *The Book of J* (1991) which separated what Bloom regarded as the original document from its later encrustations. Much publicity was given to Bloom's pro-vocative speculation that J was in fact a woman, a "scholarly fiction" to account for the "astonishing differences between J and every other biblical writer" (1991, 9). More important, however, to Bloom's argument and mine is the "institutionalized misreading of J" by generations of Jews, Chris-tians, Muslims, and the secular culture of the West (11). "The Bible," as Emerson complained, "wears black cloth," which gives it an authority against which independent minds revolt. In Bloom's words, it is "hardly appropri-ate garb for that ironic and sophisticated lady (or enigmatic gentleman, if you would have it so)" (15).

Since Bloom doesn't believe in the possibility of correct reading, it's important to recognize that his argument is that a strong literary text has been subjected to weak institutionalized readings, a "long, sad enterprise of revising, censoring and mutilating J" (21), a process by which "an essen-tially literary work becomes a sacred text" so that its "reading becomes numbed by taboo and inhibition" (33). Bloom's fiction of an ancient Jane Austen, mistress of irony, is designed to stir us out of that numbing blind-ness into a recognition of the literary power of the text (33). Reading the Book of J up until now has been a matter of "scrubbing away at the varnish with which it is encrusted" (44), varnish that includes years of somber misogyny, "a long and dismal history of weak misreadings of the comic J, who exalts women throughout her work" (1991, 146). There is, of course, even in art history, a complex debate about the possibility of separating the original work from the history of its reception and encrustation. I would myself be less confident than Bloom about the startling originality of a separatable strand of the text of the pentateuch as traditionally conceived. But the point about the ways in which it can be misread, weakly or strongly, passively or imaginatively, still stands. To rewrite the Book of Genesis in the tradition of Luria, Milton, Blake, or Wiesel is not only a legitimate but an entirely necessary response to the imaginative power of the original text.

The final theorist to whom I want to turn is Bloom's Yale colleague, Jacques Derrida, the founder of deconstruction, which can be seen as a sophisticated theory of intertextuality. It's also an example of what Susan Handelman has called "the return of the Rabbinic repressed" (Handelman 1982, 166); both Bloom and Derrida (who are, of course, Jewish) are given chapters in her book *The Slayers of Moses,* subtitled "The Emergence of Rabbinic Interpretation in Modern Literary Theory," the chapter on Derrida being called "Reb Derrida's Scripture." As Bloom himself has noted, there are strong similarities between Derrida's understanding of writing and the "trace" and the kabbalistic *Sefirot,* both of which are a kind of archi-writing, mediating an absent center. The difference is, of course, that Derrida is not as confident about either canon, sacred or secular. His is a "religion of writing" (1982, 164) in a different sense. The joke is that in the seminal volume *Deconstruction and Criticism,* Bloom represents Criticism and Derrida, Hartman, de Man, and Hillis Miller, Deconstruction.

Deconstruction has been called boring from within (in more than one sense) because it is concerned with understanding (and to some extent dismantling) a tradition using terms and methods derived from that tradition. It is a very postmodern way of relating to that tradition. Just as in postmodern architecture there is an abundance of repetition and quotation from earlier traditions, whether ironically, cynically, or naively, so that old forms are given new meanings. This involves a reinterpretation of tradition which in Derrida's work can be interpreted as a wrestling with traditions, whether religious, philosophical, or literary. *The Specters of Marx,* for example, is an attempt to read Marx's will, to work out what remains of the spirit of Marx for his political heirs (which, according to Derrida, includes us all). Marx himself wanted men to make their own history, not so anxiously to "conjure up the spirits of the past" to justify their actions (108). Derrida sees that he tried to exorcise too many ghosts too quickly, spirits of the past that must be allowed to continue to speak (1994, 175–76), even if they are understood differently. Derrida has learned from Levinas the way repetition can bring out the alterity, the otherness to be found within traditional terms when they are repeated in new contexts.

For Derrida, of course, everything is textually mediated (which is what his famous phrase *Il n'y a pas de hors-texte* means: "There is not outside-text"). As Vincent Leitch explains it,

> Everything gets textualized. All contexts . . . become intertexts; that
> is, outside influences and forces undergo textualization. Instead of
> literature we have textuality; in place of tradition, intertextuality.
> (1983, 122)

The clear dividing line between what is inside and what is outside the text
has been broken down, since all signs contain traces of their other, opposites against which they are defined, differential traces that account for the
generation of meaning. *Dissemination* includes a discussion of *Numbers*,
by Philippe Sollers, which begins with three dots, a suspension of origins
which ensures that the reader is "immediately plunged into the consumption of another text that had already . . . set this text in motion" (Derrida
1981, 334). *Numbers*, Derrida continues, becomes

> a kind of cabal or cabala in which the blanks will never be anything
> but provisionally filled in . . . open to the play of permutations,
> blanks rarely glimpsed as blanks, (almost) pure spacing, going on
> forever and not in the expectation of Messianic fulfillment. . . .
> [T]here exists a whole interpretation of spacing, of textual genera-
> tion and polysemy, of course, revolving around the Torah. Polysemy
> is the possibility of a "new Torah" capable of arising out of the
> other. (1981, 334–35)

Derrida quotes a Hassidic Rabbi promising that God will eventually
"unveil the white in the Torah," the spaces between the letters. Here, on
the contrary, it is always possible for a text to become new, since the
blanks open up its structure to an indefinitely disseminated transformation
(1981, 344–45).

Derrida's works often dramatize the meanings generated by blanks, or
spacing, within or between texts. "The Double Session" and *Glas* place
literary and philosophical texts opposite each other, Plato opposite Mallarme,
Hegel opposite Genet, allowing the juxtaposition itself to create meaning.
"Living On/Border Lines" has a continuous footnote, rather like a Talmudic
commentary, supplementing the main text. The word "supplement," like
the concepts of the graft and the re-mark, brings out Derrida's concern
with citation and repetition (with difference) as a mode of generating meaning. As he explains in *Of Grammatology,* the supplement has two senses; it
both adds to and replaces, becomes a substitute for the original object
(whether in Rousseau's erotic imagination, the phantasy object standing in
for the missing mistress, or in the case of writing, a supplement to speech,
only brought in to replace the absent speaker but ending up by supplanting

it and producing surplus meaning). The graft in writing, as in horticulture, is a quotation introduced within a text, which generates new meaning: "A notch is marked there, one that again opens onto another text and practices another reading" (1981, 203–4). *Limited Inc* uses another botanical metaphor, dehiscence, referring to "the divided opening, in the growth of a plant," which "makes production, reproduction, development possible" (1988, 59). Dehiscence, like citation and iterability, makes pure repetition impossible, introducing the contamination of fresh growth, new interpretation. A mark or a sign can never be completely reproduced without difference since it always occurs in new contexts with different intertexts. Hence the notion of the re-mark, as explained by Rodolphe Gasché:

> The re-mark . . . is a form of the general law of supplementarity, which dislocates all presence, plenitude, or propriety. As the re-mark demonstrates, supplementation always consists of adding a mark to another mark. (1986, 217)

The word "re-mark" exemplifies what it represents, that repetition with difference characteristic of all signifying systems and all traditions. However hard institutions may try to control and regulate meaning, to delimit "proper" interpretation, all linguistic signs will open themselves to fresh meanings as they collide with different intertexts.

Derrida illustrates this kind of creative intertextuality in practice in *The Gift of Death*, which comes close to producing a postmodern form of midrash in its commentary upon Kierkegaard's comments upon the Akedah in *Fear and Trembling*. The title of Kierkegaard's book, of course, comes from St. Paul's letter to the Philippians, in which he exhorts them even in his absence to "work out your own salvation with fear and trembling" (Phil 2:12). Derrida points out that it is not only St. Paul who absents himself from his followers:

> God is himself absent, hidden and silent, separate, secret, at the moment he has to be obeyed. God doesn't give his reasons, he acts as he intends, he doesn't have to give his reasons or share anything with us. . . . Otherwise he would not be God, we would not be dealing with the Other as God or with God as *wholly other*. (1995, 57)

The mysterious, ungraspable otherness of God is particularly evident in the story from Genesis upon which Kierkegaard chooses to dwell, in which this "secret, hidden, separate, absent, or mysterious God . . . decides, without revealing his reasons, to demand of Abraham that most cruel, impossible, and untenable gesture: to offer his son Isaac as a sacrifice" (1995, 58).

Derrida is particularly intrigued by Abraham's truthful but (at the time) equivocal answer to Isaac's question where the sacrificial lamb is to be found: "God will provide a lamb for the holocaust" (Gn 22:8). This, as Derrida points out, is not exactly a lie but it is economical with the truth; not only does Abraham fail to tell his son anything about God's demand but he keeps his secret bargain from his wife, too (interestingly, in the Midrash Tanhuma, Satan tells Isaac what is going on in an attempt to destroy Abraham's secret).

Kierkegaard, who recognizes that Abraham's silence transgresses the ethical order, dwells on the extent to which it involves a huge burden of responsibility, relating it to Christ's command to hate one's family, offering them the same gift of death as the Father extends to the Son within Christian theology. Derrida picks up on the scandalous paradox of this command (and this theology), its deconstruction of logocentric assumptions about the possibility of complete, coherent truth: "Paradox, scandal, and aporia are themselves nothing other than sacrifice, the revelation of conceptual thinking at its limit, at its death and finitude" (1995, 68). He engages in his own supplementary midrashic additions to the biblical narrative, imagining what Abraham felt like, wanting to tell the whole truth to Sarah and Isaac and to comfort them, but fearing they will then demand he renegotiate with God (1995, 73–74). He also notices a secret (unacknowledged, unadvertized) citation of Matthew's gospel in Kierkegaard's reference to the way God "sees [all suffering] in secret" (Matt 6:4). The final chapter of *The Gift of Death* proceeds to discuss the Sermon on the Mount, within which this phrase is embedded, and its revaluation of justice, morality, and love. It is a curious subject for a supposedly nihilistic atheist but what is even more interesting is the way Derrida extends the midrashic reading of the Hebrew Bible to incorporate New Testament material and Christian theology.

Derrida's relationship to his religious tradition, particularly clear in the "Circumfession" he attaches as a running footnote to Geoffrey Bennington's book *Jacques Derrida*, is complex and problematic. He reads it in ways that run counter to the conventions of normative Judaism. Harold Bloom is similarly "beyond the pale" of orthodoxy. Bakhtin's relationship to the Russian Orthodox Church was also ambivalent, by all accounts. What I hope to have shown is that there is a peculiar blend of continuity and discontinuity in their readings of the respective traditions, a necessary ambivalence which is part of the postmodern condition, entailing both a modernist critique of the normative canon *and* a re-assertion or rereading of that tradition which retains at least some of its component elements. The kind of midrash available to us cannot find its place unproblematically within the believing community; neither, however, is it completely outside. Bloom, Derrida, and Bakhtin read the biblical texts so differently as to mark a break with tradition, producing a writing that both belongs to the tradition and is also significantly other.

Works Cited

Abrams, M. H. 1988. *A Glossary of Literary Terms*, 5th ed. New York: Holt, Rinehart and Winston.

Alter, Robert and Frank Kermode, eds. 1987. *The Literary Guide to the Bible*. London: Collins.

Bakhtin, Mikhail M. 1981. *The Dialogical Imagination: Four Essays*. Ed. Michael Holquist. Trans. Caryl Emerson and Michael Holquist. Austin: University of Texas Press.

———. 1984. *Problems of Dostoevsky's Poetics*. Ed. and trans. Caryl Emerson. Manchester: Manchester University Press.

———. 1986. *Speech Genres and Other Late Essays*. Trans. Vern W. McGee. Austin: University of Texas Press.

Barthes, Roland. 1977. *Roland Barthes*. New York: Hill and Wang.

Bloom, Harold. 1973. *The Anxiety of Influence*. Oxford: Oxford University Press.

———. 1975a. *Kabbalah and Criticism*. New York: Seabury.

———. 1975b. *A Map of Misreading*. Oxford: Oxford University Press.

———. 1982. *The Breaking of the Vessels*. Chicago and London: Chicago University Press.

———. 1988. *Poetics of Influence: New and Selected Criticism*. New Haven, CT: H. R. Schwab.

———. 1989. *Ruin the Sacred Truths: Poetry and Belief from the Bible to the Present*. Cambridge: Harvard University Press.

———. 1991. *The Book of J*. Trans. from the Hebrew by David Rosenberg. Interpreted by Harold Bloom. London: Faber and Faber.

Boyarin, Daniel. 1990. *Intertextuality and the Reading of Midrash*. Bloomington and Indianapolis: Indiana University Press.

Caputo, John D. 1997. *The Prayers and Tears of Jacques Derrida*. Bloomington: Indiana University Press.

Clark, Katerina and Michael Holquist. 1984. *Mikhail Bakhtin*. Cambridge: Harvard University Press.

Curzon, David. 1994. *Modern Poems on the Bible: An Anthology* . Philadelphia and Jerusalem: Jewish Publication Society.

Dentith, Simon. 1995. *Bakhtinian Thought: An Introductory Reader*. London: Routledge.

Derrida, Jacques. 1976. *Of Grammatology*. Trans. Gayatri Spivak. Baltimore and London: Johns Hopkins University Press.

———. 1979. "Living On/ Border Lines." In *Deconstruction and Criticism*. Ed. Harold Bloom et al. New York: Continuum.

———. 1981. *Dissemination*. Trans. Barbara Johnson. Chicago: University of Chicago Press.

———. 1986. *Glas*. Trans. J. P. Leavey, Jr., and Richard Rand. Lincoln: University of Nebraska Press.

———. 1988. *Limited Inc*. Ed. Gerald Graff. Evanston, IL: Northwestern University Press.

———. 1993. "Circumfession." In *Jacques Derrida*. Ed. Geoffrey Bennington and Jacques Derrida. Chicago: Chicago University Press.

———. 1994. *The Specters of Marx: The State of the Debt, the Work of Mourning, and the New International.* New York: Routledge.

———. 1995. *The Gift of Death.* Trans. David Wills. Chicago: University of Chicago Press.

Fewell, Danna, ed. 1992. *Reading Between Texts: Intertextuality and the Hebrew Bible.* Louisville, KY: Westminster.

Fisch, Harold. 1998. *New Stories for Old: Biblical Patterns in the Novel.* New York: St. Martin.

Fishbane, Michael. 1985. *Biblical Interpretation in Ancient Israel.* Oxford: Oxford University Press.

———. 1989. *The Garments of Torah: Essays in Biblical Hermeneutics.* Bloomington and Indianapolis: Indiana University Press.

Gasché, Rodolphe. 1986. *The Tain of the Mirror: Derrida and the Philosophy of Reflection.* Cambridge: Harvard University Press.

Haas, Peter. 1988. *Morality After Auschwitz: The Radical Challenge of the Nazi Ethic.* Philadelphia: Fortress.

Handelman, Susan A. 1982. *The Slayers of Moses: The Emergence of Rabbinic Interpretation in Modern Literary Theory.* Albany: State University of New York Press.

Hartman, Geoffrey H. and Sanford Budick, eds. 1986. *Midrash and Literature.* New Haven and London: Yale University Press.

Jacobson, Dan. 1970. *The Rape of Tamar.* London: Weidenfeld and Nicolson.

———. 1982. *The Story of the Stories: The Chosen People and Its God.* New York: Harper and Row.

———. 1989. *Biblical Narratives and Novelists' Narratives.* The Ethel M.Wood Lecture, 1989. London: University of London.

Leitch, Vincent B. 1983. *Deconstructive Criticism: An Advanced Introduction.* London: Hutchinson.

Moi, Toril, ed. 1986. *The Kristeva Reader.* Oxford: Blackwell.

Neusner, Jacob, editor. 1983. *Midrash in Context: Exegesis in Formative Judaism.* Philadelphia: Fortress.

———. 1985a. *Genesis and Judaism: The Perspective of Genesis Rabbah: An Analytical Anthology.* Atlanta,Georgia: Scholars.

———, trans. 1985b. *Genesis Rabbah: The Judaic Commentary to the Book of Genesis.* A New American Translation, 3 vols. Atlanta, GA: Scholars.

———. 1987. *What Is Midrash?* Philadelphia: Fortress.

———. 1990. *The Midrash: An Introduction.* Northvale, NJ: Aronson.

Porton, Gary. 1981. "Defining Midrash." In *The Study of Ancient Judaism.* Ed. Jacob Neusner. New York: Ktav.

Stern, David. 1996. *Midrash and Theory.* Evanston, IL: Northwestern University Press.

Worton, Michael and Judith Still, eds. 1990. *Intertextuality: Theories and Practices.* New York: Manchester University Press.

VOICES FROM THE MARGIN

As we degenerate, the contrast between us and our house is more evident. We are as much strangers in nature, as we are aliens from God.

—Ralph Waldo Emerson, *Nature*

Orator. . . . "He, mme, mm, mm. Ju, gou, hou, hou. Heu, heu, gu gou, gueue." [Helpless, he lets his arms fall down alongside his body; suddenly, his face lights up, he has an idea, he turns toward the blackboard, he takes a piece of chalk out of his pocket, and writes, in large capitals: ANGELFOOD, then NNAA NNM NWNWNW V]

—Eugene Ionesco, *The Chairs*

6

Gospels of Inversion:
Literature, Scripture, Sexology

Ed Madden

"A minor literature doesn't come from a minor language; it is rather that which a minority constructs within a major language."
—Gilles Deleuze and Félix Guattari, "What Is a Minority Literature?"

"The practice of homosexuality is incompatible with Christian teaching."
—1992 resolution by the American Baptist Church

"I have begun to assemble and name as my Scripture a small body of literature in which I find myself accepted for who I am."
—Gary David Comstock, *Gay Theology Without Apology*

In 1994 at Yale University Divinity School a debate about homosexuality and theology arose when a dean at the divinity school signed a public statement condemning homosexuality. The act, of course, angered a number of students, and a gay rights coalition questioned the relation between such a statement and the school's nondiscrimination policy, which prohibits discrimination based on sexual orientation. There were vigils, meetings, numerous letters and public forums, and two scholarly panels on the theological issues. "Despite the lengthy debate," wrote journalist Carolyn Mooney of the incident, "many observers say that, in the end, the two sides' positions are probably irreconcilable." She added, "On a poster announcing one of the two scholarly panels, someone scratched out the words 'homosexuality and morality' and wrote 'oil and water' instead" (Mooney 1994, A38).

Barbara Johnson, who runs an evangelical Christian ministry for parents of gay men and lesbians, describes discovering her son's homosexuality as a kind of cognitive—and textual—dissonance. She finds gay pornography next to Christian youth materials in his dresser. When she tries to tell her husband that their son is gay, he responds, "He CAN'T be; he's a Christian!" Johnson then tells her sister, who "sputtered, 'He CAN'T be; he's a Christian.'" Then the brother-in-law: "Why, he CAN'T be; he's a Christian!" (Johnson 1990, 41–42).[1] For Johnson and her family, as for many religious believers, one cannot be gay and Christian. In Jeanette Winterson's 1985 novel, *Oranges Are Not the Only Fruit*, the young protagonist Jeanette tells her girlfriend Melanie on their way to church one morning, "I love you almost as much as I love the Lord." But once in church, a service for the exorcism of "Unnatural Passions" begun, Jeanette is forced to confront the seeming incompatibility of those two loves. As the elders lead Melanie away, shaken and trembling, Jeanette tells the pastor, "I love her." "Then you do not love the Lord," he tells her. "Yes," she replies, "I love both of them." His final and unequivocal response: "You cannot" (Winterson 1987, 105).[2]

Homosexuality and Christianity are, it seems, "irreconcilable" categories, whether we think of them as issues, cultures, discourses, or people. Admittedly, there are many nuances in this debate. For example, many Christians admit that people may have a homosexual orientation, but insist that homosexual acts are immoral—an orientation/activity distinction.[3] Moreover, some Christian churches and some Christians now accept gays and lesbians as part of their spiritual communities, and for many years gays and lesbians have made places for themselves—however quietly, through whatever cognitive dissonance, silence, or subterfuge—at the tables of some traditions. John Boswell has traced, at length, the tolerance of homosexuality in the early church, and Joanne Glasgow has demonstrated more specifically Catholicism's blindness to lesbianism in the late nineteenth and early twentieth centuries.

But despite these qualifications, it is surely no mistake to state that many, perhaps most, Christian churches do not accept openly gay and lesbian people, and that the history of Christianity's response to the issue of homosexuality has been, for the most part, one of intolerance and condemnation, if not overt hatred and persecution. Christian tradition and scripture have been and continue to be invoked to justify the legal criminalization and social disapprobation of same-sex sexuality, and to validate both social and institutional discrimination against gay men and lesbians. The Bible itself is repeatedly used in antihomosexual discourse. Christian teaching and the world view of Christianity are often simply and uncritically assumed to be anti-gay. As Mooney began her article on the Yale debate, "Religious views and gay rights collided." Despite the exceptions, despite the scholarly debates, Christianity and homosexuality are usually seen as incompatible categories, if not irreconcilable enemies, and this categorical assumption extends to world views, to people, to languages, to cultures. The history and psychology of sexuality and the languages of Scripture seem historically and theologically incompatible. And "gay Christian" seems an oxymoron. Oil and water.

What is at stake in this repeated opposition of the gay or lesbian and the Christian, an opposition that seems to be discursive, ontological, and categorically programmatic? Is it possible to move past this either/or logic into a logic of both/and? Why is it impossible to be both gay/lesbian and Christian? What if one attempted to not only reconcile but to justify homosexuality in relation to Christianity? When does the voice of the sexual "other" have value in Christian discourse? When can it claim authority? What happens when the "other" of homosexuality attempts not only to speak (for) itself, but to claim a religious or spiritual right to existence as well? What happens to the regime of truth, to the discursive and "religious" production of stigmatized identities, and to the descriptive normalization of family and church when the gay and lesbian "other" finds voice in the languages that would condemn and stigmatize? What happens when the classification of sin is disrupted by a gospel of inversion?

In an attempt to historicize if not address these questions, I return in this essay to two critical moments in the historical and rhetorical development of arguments about homosexuality and morality. I focus on two texts from the beginning of this century, two texts that attempted to reconcile the new understandings of homosexuality suggested by late nineteenth century studies of sexual psychology with the traditional moral teachings of Western Christian culture. I examine two brief passages, one from Havelock Ellis's 1897 study of homosexuality, *Sexual Inversion*, and one from Radclyffe Hall's 1928 lesbian novel, *The Well of Loneliness*, for which Ellis wrote an introduction. One is a landmark nineteenth century text of sexology, a psychosexual science that would later be supplanted by Freud and psychoanalysis, but which nonetheless was profoundly important to the culture of late nineteenth and early twentieth century England, and which set the terms for our understanding of homosexuality. The other is a classic lesbian novel.

Both Ellis and Hall appropriate scriptural discourse in their arguments for the acceptance of homosexuality—Ellis only in a brief (albeit paradigmatic) figure, Hall in a number of allusions throughout the text. Ellis rather subtly uses a metaphor from Scripture within the very text of sexology, and Hall collapses sexology and Scripture into a literary narrative. In the specific passages I examine, both authors utilize sayings of Jesus from the Gospels. Ellis briefly alludes to the parable of the sower, a self-reflexive parable about the Gospel, about conversion, reception, and predisposition.

In Ellis's text, this Gospel parable becomes an allegorical intervention into the nascent nature versus nurture argument, suggesting that regardless of the social contexts and precipitating causes, sexual inversion, like Christian conversion, can only occur when the person is in some way (biologically, he argues) predisposed. Along with a number of other biblical allusions—indeed, *The Well of Loneliness* is an incredibly biblical narrative—Radclyffe Hall specifically invokes Christ's image of the good father who when asked for sustenance (for bread) does not give a stone. This parable fragment provides a key image in the novel's melodramatic closing, a plea to the world for social acceptance and simultaneously a prayer to God for acknowledgment as a part of creation.

Since Christian and biblical discourses are and were so often used to condemn homosexuality, I cannot help but admire Ellis's and Hall's bold appropriations of biblical imagery and rhetoric. Not only do they use biblical language to defend homosexuality, but Hall attempts a quite Christian defense of same-sex sexuality, suggesting an early lesbian and gay liberationist project and an incipient theology of (sexual) liberation. These are early and strong re-readings of scriptural discourse, readings echoed in our contemporary hermeneutics of suspicion, but readings that attempted, at the beginning of this century, to use the scriptural language of authority to ground a minority identity, a minority politics, and a minority spirituality. Rather than to prove their arguments, the point of this essay is to demonstrate the rhetorical effects and strategies of these texts, and to examine a historical and textual moment when sexology annexed a gospel trope, and a moment when literature subsumed both sexology and Scripture into an apologetics for gay and lesbian identity. At a time when gay and lesbian rights and religious values are very much a part of public discourse (usually in categorical opposition), and when the Bible is still invoked in public debate about sexuality, these texts may reflect uncannily our own fin-de-siècle arguments about sexual identities.

Sowing the Seeds of Love:
Havelock Ellis and the Parable of the Sower

The intersection of Christianity with the social otherness of homosexual and lesbian identities has a long and complex history, but that encounter may be at its most fraught, most anxious, and yet perhaps most productive at the end of the nineteenth century, when sexologists prompted a serious reexamination of sexual mores and a conversation about sexual identities that continues today. Sexologists and psychologists at the time began to delineate a homosexual identity, and many began to argue that homosexuality—also known as "inversion" or "uranism"— was not a willful choice nor a category of criminal activity but a preconscious or even congenital condition. Karl Heinrich Ulrich's famous characterization of this identity was that of a female soul trapped in a man's body—a figure that Michel Foucault has characterized as "a kind of interior androgyny, a hermaphrodism of the soul." Foucault explains in his *History of Sexuality* that when the criminal act of sodomy was theoretically and medically transformed into a psychologized (and perhaps biological) condition, this "hermaphrodism of the soul," the homosexual became a type of naturally occurring life form: "The sodomite had been a temporary aberration" he writes. "[T]he homosexual was now a species" (Foucault 1978, 43).

If homosexuality, or "inversion," was indicative of a species or a type rather than simply a behavior or a category of activity, then the type, the "invert," deserved scientific examination. Sexologists such as Havelock Ellis began to catalog the psychological and physiological markers of homosexuality, trying to "read" the bodies of homosexuals and lesbians in an attempt to find biological or physiological markers for inversion. Paul Robinson insists that Ellis made two important and fundamental contentions in his analysis in *Sexual Inversion*: that homosexuality is congenital, and that it is not a disease (Robinson 1976, 4–6). Although many sexologists sometimes lapsed into the language of disease, Ellis argued that since homosexuality was a naturally occurring condition, it was not categorically a disease, nor was it inherently criminal or immoral. Ellis wrote of inversion as an "abnormality," a word suggesting anomaly rather than pathology; he calls inversion a "sport" or a variation of nature. Drawing on the work of John Addington Symonds, he compared homosexuality to colorblindness, then later to "color-hearing," or the tendency to associate sounds with colors, the latter analogy suggesting a naturally occurring *difference* rather than an insufficiency in perception (or epistemology).

In Ellis's 1897 study, *Sexual Inversion*, there are a number of epistemic and paradigmatic images he uses for sexual desire, many of them, like "color-hearing," suggesting the natural or biological nature of sexual development. One of the primary images he uses, for example, is of streams. He speaks of desire running in channels. He writes, "Pathology is but physiology working under new conditions. The stream of Nature still flows into the bent channel of sexual inversion, and still runs according to law" (1897, 159). Desire is thus a natural force—like flowing water, or steam— which must find a channel (albeit in this case a "bent" one, not a "straight" one).[4] Furthermore, desires or drives move, by natural "law," even when they are inverted.

In the fifth chapter of his study, titled "The Nature of Sexual Inversion," Ellis introduces another paradigmatic metaphor, one that suggests that the "nature" of sexual inversion is, in fact, quite natural. He uses the image of a seed growing in proper soil and under the right conditions—a metaphor that suggests the developmental and yet organic state of sexual desire. In the chapter, Ellis summarizes a number of theories of the etiology of homosexuality, among them the inherited nature of nervous disease, the female soul trapped in a male body, masturbation as an origin for sexual inversion, and the role of causal events—causal explanations, other than masturbation, include disappointment in "normal" love, seduction by an older person, and the same-sex communities of the boarding school system. Each of the theories Ellis examines he finds to be, at some level, inadequate. Dismissing especially the idea that events can be causal, Ellis notes repeatedly that in each case history he discusses there seems to be "a well-marked predisposition" (1897, 109).

Dismissing specifically the idea that sexual suggestion (such as seeing male genitals or sleeping with a man) can be causal, Ellis writes, "The seed of suggestion can only develop when it falls on a suitable soil" (1897, 110). For example, he notes the case of a young boy who "caress[ed]" the genitals of a boy twice his age (an illustration that collapses theories of adult seduction and same-sex play into one incident); the boy "grew up without ever manifesting any homosexual instinct" (1897, 110). The person must be constitutively receptive, biologically predisposed, or, in the words of John Addington Symonds, whom Ellis quotes, "previously constituted to receive the suggestion" (1897, 109). The body and/or psyche is "suitable" soil, the "suggestion" of sexual desire (whether that be defined as seduction by someone else, sexual play, or the "normal" fascination with the sight of genitalia) is a seed, and sexual development is the natural growth of one in the context of the other.

In the sixth chapter, "The Theory of Sexual Inversion," Ellis again summarizes theories of homosexuality, and he returns to and develops the metaphor of the seed in an analogy that echoes Christ's parable of the sower. He divides theories of homosexuality into two major categories: those emphasizing the congenital nature of sexuality, and those stressing its acquired nature—categories that roughly replicate the contemporary arguments of nature versus nurture. Ellis argues, however, that "we must regard sexual inversion as largely a congenital phenomenon, or, to speak more accurately, as a phenomenon which is based on congenital conditions." He insists, "This, I think, lies at the root of the right comprehension of the matter" (1897, 129). His own rhetoric—"the root"—returns to the biological metaphor of growth, his own paradigmatic metaphor for sexual development. Self-reflexively, the phrase suggests the earlier metaphor;

the idea of congenital homosexuality, which has been imagined as a seed growing in proper soil, is here figured as the "root" of any argument about sexuality. He adds that there are "two streams of tendency in the views regarding sexual inversion," a phrase that returns, again almost self-reflexively, to the epistemic metaphor of streams and channels—two streams, two theories, two tendencies, two sexualities (one normative and straight, the other bent). But this rhetorical return to one metaphor is preceded by the discursive emphasis on the other: "the root of . . . right comprehension" (1897, 129). There may be "two streams" of thought, but there is only one "root" of comprehension.

Ellis then develops his argument, and his metaphor of "suitable soil," in a passage that surely suggests Christ's parable of the sower. He writes:

> The rational way of regarding the normal sexual impulse is as an inborn organic impulse, developing about the time of puberty. At this period suggestion and association may come in to play a part in defining the object of the emotion; the soil is now ready, but the variety of seeds likely to thrive in it is limited. That there is a greater indefiniteness in the aim of the sexual impulse at this period we may well believe. This is shown not only by occasional tentative signs of sexual emotion directed towards the same sex, but by the usually vague and non-sexual character of the normal passion at puberty. But the channel of sexual emotion is not thereby turned into an utterly abnormal path. Whenever this permanently happens we are, I think, bound to believe—and we have many grounds for believing—that we are dealing with an organism which from the beginning is abnormal. The same seed of suggestion is sown in various soils; in the many it dies out, in the few it flourishes. The cause can only be a difference in the soil. (1897, 130–31)

Ellis here describes homosexuality as "abnormal" as well as "organic"— echoed in his subsequent characterization of homosexuality as "a 'sport' or variation, one of those organic aberrations which we see throughout living nature, in plants and animals" (1897, 133). He suggests—as Freud will later—that sexuality in childhood is relatively undifferentiated, but he does not imagine homosexuality as a phase children go through or as the result of failed object orientation (or, as contemporary anti-gay psychologists now insist, failed gender identification). Rather, the "organism" is "from the beginning" "abnormal." Although the language of science ("organism") and the later reference to organic "variation" might suggest an evolutionary explanation (which causal theories uncannily echo—ontogeny recapitulates phylogeny), Ellis argues not for a Darwinian sexology, or for homosexuality as an early aspect of undifferentiated childhood sexuality, but for an essential, biological type, a type figured elementally as soil.

Admittedly, Ellis briefly returns to the metaphor of "the channel of sexual emotion" which may be diverted or turned into an "abnormal path." But the foundational metaphor, both allegorically and rhetorically, is that of the seed and the soil—if earlier it was the "root" of his theory, here he finds "grounds for believing" the theory. He briefly shifts the emphasis of the metaphor from types of soil to "the variety of seeds" of suggestion. But he concludes: "The same seed of suggestion is sown in various soils; in the many it dies out, in the few it flourishes. The cause can only be a difference in the soil" (1897, 131). The images used surely echo Christ's parable of the sower. Alan Sinfield has argued that Foucault, in his analysis of the nineteenth century creation of the homosexual "type," emphasizes medical and legal discourses to the exclusion of others, creating the sense of a sudden epistemological shift and thus ignoring other discourses at work in the creation and regulation of sexuality (Sinfield 1994, 13). One discourse, that of the Bible, seems especially vulnerable to academic dismissal. Foucault finds the discourse of "sin and salvation" clearly supplanted by the scientific discourse of "bodies and life processes" (Foucault 1978, 64). Ellis's parable of the soil, however, suggests that biblical discourse, at least though metaphorical equivalence and through arguments of analogy, may itself be appropriated into an apologetics of inversion.

Christ's parable of the sower, found in three of the gospels (Mt 13, Mk 4, and Lk 8; KJV), is a parable about reception, and it self-reflexively indicts or blesses its own hearers. It is a parable about parables, a gospel about gospels, a metaparable. John Dominic Crossan has said of such metaparables, "They reveal not just the product but the process of interpretation" (Crossan 1980, 26); he describes the parable of the sower as a polyvalent parable, and "always a metaphor for its own hermeneutical task" (Crossan 1980, 54).[5] Christ himself asks his apostles, "Know ye not this parable? and how then will you know all parables?" (Mk 4:13). This parable seems to offer the key for reading *any* parable. In the parable, a sower goes out to sow seed, and the seed falls on a number of types of soil: the wayside, where birds devour it; the stony ground, where plants spring up but are scorched; the thorny ground, where the plants are choked; and the good soil, where the seed yields fruit. The parable is explained in the gospels as an allegory for receiving the gospel. Those at the wayside receive it, but Satan takes it away. Those represented by stony ground lack roots and become "offended" in the face of hardship (Mark), or fall away when tempted (Luke). The thorns represent "the cares of this world" (Mark) or the "cares and riches and pleasures of this life" (Luke) which choke out the gospel. "But he that received seed into the good ground," explains Christ in Matthew, "is he that heareth the word, and understandeth it; which also beareth fruit" (Mt 13:23). "The sower soweth the word" (Mk 4:14), and those who hear it profit from it according to their own attitude and receptivity. Jesus ends this parable, as he ends many, "Who hath ears to hear, let him hear" (Mt 13:9).

Using the metaphorical equivalence of soil as predisposition (to gospel calling *or* sexual suggestion), Ellis rewrites this parable as a discursive intervention into the argument about the origins of homosexuality, arguments inevitably used to ground further arguments about control and acceptance. In Ellis's parable, the child who is predisposed biologically to homosexuality—the "congenital invert"—is equated with the good ground of the parable. Thus, no matter what the social environment, no matter what causal suggestions exist, the gospel of inversion can only find good grounds for development in the biologically or psychologically (and dare one suggest, spiritually) receptive person. Only those with "ears to hear" (Mk 4:9) will be able to hear; only those with the properly receptive organs, the properly constituted psyches and bodies, will be receptive to this particular truth, this word.

In the Gospel of Mark, once the parable is explained to them, the apostles enter the hermeneutic circle of parabolic discourse. The writer adds, "And with many such parables spake he the word unto them, as they were able to hear it" (Mk 4:33), hearing meaning understanding. They are able to "hear" the other parables, once they are instructed in how to hear (this one about hearing). In both Matthew and Mark, this parable precedes all other parables (in Luke the parable of the two debtors appears only a few verses before this parable).[6] In fact, Jesus tells them that the language of the parables marks receptivity. Some will refuse to hear them or understand: "they seeing see not, and hearing they hear not" (Mt 13:13). Parables exclude those "that are without" (Mk 4:11), those who are outside the hermeneutic circle, outside the community of interpretation, and outside the circle of sympathy and understanding. This allegory of understanding may, then, not simply provide the figure for congenital receptivity in Ellis's text. Read against its origins in the Gospels, it seems to intertextually function as a rhetorical comment on Ellis's text: the only ones who will understand Ellis's moral argument about homosexuality will be those who understand the idea of the congenital invert, the type, the homosexual as an identity rather than an incidental behavior, an idea figured in the parable of soil. Only those who understand the allegory of good soil will bear the fruit of understanding.

The Gospel According to Radclyffe Hall:
The Good Father and the Sexual Other

Thirty years after the publication of Ellis's *Sexual Inversion*, in 1928, Radclyffe Hall upped the ante considerably in her appropriation of scriptural discourse in her novel *The Well of Loneliness*. The novel is, in many ways, a retold gospel that substitutes a lesbian writer as the martyred messiah of her people.[7] There are repeated biblical allusions from both Old and New Testaments in the novel, and the more specific Christological allusions map the story of the heroine, Stephen Gordon, against the life of Christ. Although the novel is in some ways a portrait of the artist as a young lesbian (Stephen the novelist seems a self-reflexive figure for Hall), it is also the tale of a lesbian messiah. The conclusion most clearly demonstrates the novel's polemical point, its defense of lesbian love. But that point works in the context of the messianic narrative; it is couched in the model of a prayer, and simultaneously in the language of Christ's story of God as the good father, who would give his child bread, not stone. Hall uses this parable fragment to figure a cry to God for communal deliverance. Although the world may be slow to understand homosexuality, Hall seems to suggest, there is hope for a spiritual vindication. Some feminist critics have dismissed Hall's otherworldly politics, her representation of lesbianism as a "stigma that the politics of heaven, not of earth, must first relieve" (Stimpson 1982, 248). Although there may be problems with Hall's representation of lesbianism as a biological (and masculinized) "stigma," I would like to reexamine her use of the language of religious justice in her sexual apologetics, her attempt to ground social liberation in religious validation.

Stephen Gordon, the young lesbian in the novel, is rejected by her mother, Anna, when she discovers a love letter Stephen had written to another woman. Anna asks her to leave the room (and eventually the house), she wishes Stephen "dead at my feet," and she describes her daughter's physical presence as nauseating—"my gorge rises" (Hall 1928, 200); she thus marks her daughter as the abject, in Julia Kristeva's terms, that which must be excluded (like a cadaver or vomited food), "what disturbs identity, system, order" (Kristeva 1982, 4).[8] Stephen moves from this physicalized maternal rejection, a rejection by family and community, into the study—a realm of spirit (her dead father) and textuality. While her father, Philip, was alive, Stephen repeatedly turned to him for counsel. She had even asked him at one point, "Father, is there anything strange about me?" (1928, 106), a question he refused to answer honestly. But, once rejected by her mother as something "unnatural" and "unspeakable" (1928,

200), Stephen wanders into her dead father's study, "as though drawn there by some strong *natal* instinct" (Hall 1928, 203, emphasis mine). In the study, she finds her true identity in her dead father's locked bookcase of sexological texts, where she recognizes her nature in the case histories of the sexologists. But she literally sees herself in these texts as well, for she finds that her father had written her name in his notes in the margins of these texts. Her father had already named her, written her in the margins of the history of sexuality. She realizes that her father had known all along her sexual nature, but was unable to tell her, out of pity (1928, 204). But she has been always already named as lesbian by her beneficent father, who is absent, but who does not reject her—the image of God she will seek in her final prayer.

This scene suggests an intersection of fathers and texts. Stephen's birth-father had written her name in the sexological tomes, but the writers of those tomes are themselves forefathers to this novel. (In fact, *The Well of Loneliness* seems an extrapolation itself of case history 166 from Krafft-Ebing's *Psychopathia Sexualis*; Krafft-Ebing is the only author mentioned in the scene.) Havelock Ellis wrote an introductory "Commentary" to Hall's novel, lending his own imprimatur of author-ity to her text, her corpus and story. The novel even opens with an image reminiscent of Ellis's "stream" or channel metaphor: "Not very far from Upton-on-Severn—between it, in fact, and the Malvern Hills—stands the country seat of the Gordons of Bramley; well-timbered, well-cottaged, well-fenced and well-watered, having, in this latter respect, a stream that forks in exactly the right position to feed two large lakes in the grounds" (Hall 1928, 11). Into this realm of order, Hall writes two streams, two equivalent sexualities. Elsewhere she echoes Ellis's channel metaphor, though it suggests as much the buried life of Matthew Arnold and the sewers of Paris as it does an epistemic metaphor of desire. When Stephen and her lover Mary join the salon of the lesbian Valerie Seymour, Hall writes: "So now they were launched up the stream that flows silent and deep through all great cities, gliding on between precipitous borders, away and away into no-man's land" (1928, 356). Yet this image is clearly an image of gay and lesbian subculture that develops in metropolitan areas, of the "silent" minority and culture outside (pardon the pun) the "mainstream."

But the other father present in this scene, other than her dead father who survives as a text, is God—another father who survives in textuality. Stephen cries to her father, "Oh, Father—and there are so many of us," a cry that bridges into an indictment of God's cruelty, "He let us get flawed in the making." Stephen immediately takes her father's "well-worn Bible," and demands a sign from heaven. Where the book falls open, she reads:

"And the Lord set a mark upon Cain." Hall thus imagines sexual orientation as the mark of Cain, an image that becomes echoed in later allusions to the "stigmata of the abnormal" who are "nailed to a cross" (1928, 246), and in the literal scarring of Stephen's face during her service as an ambulance driver in the Great War. Over the course of the novel, then, Hall metonymically and metaphorically connects lesbianism, the mark of the pariah on Cain, the historical scarring of Stephen Gordon in World War I, and the crucified Christ. Stephen, son of Philip, is in some way parallel to Jesus, son of God.

This equation—or more specifically the conflation of Christ and Cain in the body of Stephen—suggests a grounding liberationist theology for Hall's narrative, in that the pariah and the messiah are inextricable, and the lesbian author is their figure. The protagonist's name, Stephen, is also that of the first Christian martyr. And Stephen's father's name is Philip, the name of the evangelist in Acts who took care of the socially powerless (the widows in Acts 6), who planted a church among the racially despised (the Samaritans in Acts 8), and who baptized the racially and sexually other (the Ethiopian eunuch, also in Acts 8).[9] He was an evangelist to the economically, socially, racially, and sexually disenfranchised.

The narrative, in fact, is a Christological allegory of martyrdom concluding with a prayer for (or promise of) deliverance. Stephen sees herself as, in some way, called to proclaim the existence of her people, and in the end she sacrifices herself for her lover—who is named, significantly, Mary. (She denies her love for Mary so that she may live in the world of the heterosexual, dominant culture—admittedly, to modern queer sensibilities, a problematic and probably reprehensible move, despite the symbolism.) As Michael Baker, among other critics, has noticed, "the novel contains submerged but pointed parallels to the example of Christ. It is no accident that Stephen is born on Christmas Eve and that her decision to sacrifice herself for Mary's happiness is finally affirmed in front of the supplicant Christ figure above the altar of a little church in Montmartre" (1928, 214). As Stephen embarks on her literary career, Valerie Seymour tells her, in the words of the thief on the cross, "Remember me when you come into your kingdom" (1928, 408).

Stephen's literary career is a career of evangelism or apologetics, as this novel is self-reflexively about its own inspiration, and the novel itself repeatedly attempts to explain and defend lesbianism and homosexuality. Echoing Ellis's use of the parable of the sower, Hall uses the metaphor of soil and seed in *The Well of Loneliness* as a figure for this literary project. Hall uses the image of seed and soil to refer to Stephen's "deep" ambition to be a writer, an ambition her father wishes to nurture: "Sir Philip discovered a secret ambition had lain in the girl like a seed in deep soil; and he, the good gardener of her body and spirit, hoed the soil and watered this seed of ambition" (1928, 79). But that "seed" deep within is also her lesbianism, since Stephen's writing is marked by her sexuality; from the beginning she creates "queer compositions" (1928, 79)—"queer" having multiple resonances throughout the novel, including the marginal, the other, and the homosexual. Continuing the metaphorization, Stephen's first novel after leaving her home is titled *The Furrow*. The metaphor doesn't suggest the parable of the sower in the sense of a receptive soil, but it may more emphatically suggest a gospel calling, to write, to evangelize, to sow the seeds of understanding and love, especially since her "queer" writing is inextricably and preconsciously tied to her "queer" sexuality. Stephen's work, as she is told by the priest-like homosexual Adolphe Blanc, is a work of duty and courage; it is an "urgent and desperate mission" (1928, 389)— she is to write in order to awaken awareness, sympathy, and perhaps even justice for "queer" peoples.[10]

Stephen also finds herself a "stranger within the gates" when she returns to her mother's home (1928, 212), suggesting both Christ's return to Nazareth and his parable of hospitality—the tale of those who refuse to take in the stranger at their own gates (in Mt 25:34–43). (The image of the stranger at the gates is also used as the title of Mel White's recent biography, *Stranger at the Gates*, subtitled *To Be Gay and Christian in America*, echoing the idea of the sexual other being denied dignity and recognition within their own families and communities.) This image also echoes the story of Sodom and Gomorrah, another tale of strangers at the gates. It is not as a tale of sexual morality (surely an awkward idea when Lot offers his own daughters for rape, and then gets drunk and commits incest with them himself), but a tale of the mistreatment of the strangers at the gates, the alien and marginal others who had been welcomed by Abraham (Gn 18) but threatened with violence and rape by the people of Sodom (Gn 19). Interestingly enough, Stephen's first lover, Angela, an American actress trapped in a lonely marriage in the British countryside, invokes this phrase, "the stranger at the gates," too (1928, 140). Stephen, however, welcomes this American other to her own estate, telling this "stranger" that she "belongs" (1928, 144).

By using this allegory of human compassion and hospitality, Hall may suggest, for contemporary readers, the necessity for alliances within the larger project of liberationist politics and theology. She explicitly portrays the scapegoating of the sexual other. Alliance fails in the novel, for the "stranger" Angela betrays Stephen, and it is Angela's passing on of their private correspondence to a hostile man that precipitates Stephen's es-

trangement and banishment. In fact, people who otherwise hate each other
(or who are otherwise divided by social and economic bonds) find community in their common hatred for same-sex sexuality ("creatures who
hated each other . . . shamefully united in the bond of their deeper hatred of
Stephen" [1928, 184]). Just as Hall uses Christ's image of the alien at the
gates to figure the status of the sexual "other" in a hostile world, contemporary apologists turn to the parable of the good Samaritan, a parable about
human compassion that begins with the question, "Who is my neighbor?"
(Lk 10:29). To the audience Jesus addressed, the Samaritan, the figure of
hospitality and compassion in the novel, is actually a racially and socially
despised person. Virginia Mollenkott and Lethe Scanzoni use the parable to
argue for the acceptance of homosexuals in a hostile Christian church in *Is
the Homosexual My Neighbor?* (Scanzoni and Mollenkott 1978, 1-11).
Former Jesuit priest Robert Goss makes the connection and the analogy
more explicit: "In the first century, the term *good Samaritan* was as shocking
as the term *queer Christians* is to fundamentalist Christians" (Goss 1993,
73).[11]

Hall's novel features two other important aliens from biblical literature:
Ruth and Daniel. Stephen's maidservant Puddles uses language similar to
Ruth's pledge to Naomi when she vows to follow Stephen away from her
home and help her: "Where you go, I go, Stephen," she says (Hall 1928,
205). (See Ru 1:16.) Ruth, the Moabite, left her homeland to follow her
mother-in-law Naomi back to Bethlehem; consequently, this racial other
remarried, and became part of the genealogy of David, and thus of Christ.
The story of Ruth and Naomi is also a story of love and devotion between
two women, a story that many gay and lesbian critics have seen as a model
for lesbian devotion, despite the tale's ending in marriage. Raymond-Jean
Frontain calls it one of the "biblical authorizations of the homoerotic," noting its "particular resonance in lesbian writing" (Frontain 1995, 94, 97).

The other alien figure is Daniel, a Hebrew in Babylon, delivered by God
from both political enemies and a den of lions. In the novel, two African-
American singers, Henry and Lincoln (obviously a symbolically important
name), sing Negro spirituals, including a song that ended, "Didn't my Lord
deliver Daniel, Then why not every man?" Hall describes their singing:
"They seemed to be shouting a challenge to the world on behalf of themselves and of all the afflicted" (1928, 363). Stephen transforms their question in her mind; she hears it as "an eternal question, as yet unanswered,"
and she asks herself, "Why not? . . . Yes, but how long, O Lord, how
long?" (364, ellipsis hers). She makes their song into her own question, no
longer just a plea based on the image of Daniel in the lion's den, but an
emphatic expectation, even a demand. No longer *why not*, but *when*. "How

long, O Lord, how long?" she asks, repeating the psalmist cries for deliverance in Psalms 6 and 13.[12] Why shouldn't deliverance be offered to all those afflicted?; she asks. Why not every man and woman, including lesbians and gay men?

The novel ends with an oft-noted melodramatic prayer to God for "the right to our existence" (Hall 1928, 437), a prayer that incorporates Christ's promise of the good father's gifts, a prayer that pulls together the Christological allegory, the images of spiritual and textual fathers, and the promises of deliverance for the alien and marginalized. In a scene that suggests demonic possession, pregnancy, and sexual orgasm, Stephen is taken over by the spirits of gays and lesbians, those who have died, those who are living, and even of those yet to come:

> They possessed her. Her barren womb became fruitful—it ached with its fearful and sterile burden. It ached with the fierce yet helpless children who would clamour in vain for their right to salvation. They would turn first to God, and then to the world, and then to her. They would cry out accusing: "We have asked for bread; will you give us a stone? Answer us: will you give us a stone? You, God, in Whom we, the outcast, believe; you, world, into which we are pitilessly born; you, Stephen, who have drained our cup to the dregs—we have asked for bread; will you give us a stone? (Hall 1928, 437)

The reference is to Christ's promises concerning the good father, God. "What man is there of you," Christ asks in Matthew 7, "whom if his son ask bread, will he give him a stone? Or if he ask a fish, will he give him a serpent? If ye then, being evil, know how to give good gifts unto your children, how much more shall your Father which is in heaven give good things to them that ask him?" (Mt 7:9-11). The spirits demand bread or sustenance first from God, then from the world, then from Stephen, who has drained their cup of bitterness (rather than letting it pass from her lips, as Christ asked in the Garden of Gethsemane).

In the Gospels (Mt 7 and Lk 11), this parable fragment of promise is connected to the threefold promise, "Ask and it shall be given, seek, and ye shall find; knock, and it shall be opened" (Mt 7:7). Ask God, the gospel says, for he is a good father. The demand for bread, then, becomes Stephen's transformed into Stephen's *asking* in her prayer for acknowledgment:

> And now there was only one voice, one demand; her own voice into

which those millions had entered. A voice like the awful, deep
rolling of thunder; a demand like the gathering together of great
waters. A terrifying voice that made her ears throb, that made her
brain throb, that shook her very entrails, until she must stagger and
all but fall beneath this appalling burden of sound that strangled her
in its will to be uttered.

"God," she gasped, "we believe; we have told You we
believe. . . . We have not denied You, then rise up and defend us.
Acknowledge us, oh God, before the whole world. Give us also the
right to our existence!" (Hall 1928, 437, ellipses hers)

Just as she transformed the prayer in the song about Daniel from "why
not" to "when," here she transforms the promise of the good father's gifts
into a request for those very gifts. She asks: "Acknowledge us, oh God.
. . . Give us also the right to our existence." To not be acknowledged by
God is to find oneself without sustenance in an already hostile world. It is
to be offered a stone instead of bread, a serpent rather than a fish, scorpion
instead of egg. And this, according to the parable, is something God as
good father would not do. The invocation of the biblical promise—through
the repetition of Christ's own discourse—holds out the possibility of eventual deliverance, of God's "good gifts." In a world of social hatred, the
revised parable promises at least spiritual acceptance (acknowledgment),
which may provide the grounds for further spiritual and material liberation
projects (the right to existence, a civil not special right).

In both Matthew and Luke where the promise of the good father appears, it is followed by the healing of the demon-possessed (Mt 8, Lk 11),
and in Luke the demon-possessed are specifically the dumb; Christ's healing grants them the power to speak—surely an important intertextual reference to the conclusion of *The Well of Loneliness*, in which Stephen experiences the history and oppression of gays and lesbians not as a will to
power or a will to freedom but as a "will to be uttered" (Hall 1928, 437).
These spirits in the novel's conclusion cry, "our name is legion," an allusion to the demon-possessed man in Luke 8, who is called Legion "because
many devils were entered into him" (Lk 8:30). Once their voice breaks
free through the speech of Stephen—and through the novel itself—Stephen
cries: "We have not denied You, then rise up and defend us" (Hall 1928,
437). Asking God to rise up and defend echoes the cries for deliverance in
the Psalms, a final appropriation of biblical language in the face of both
religious disapprobation and social persecution.

In Hall's novel, this repetition and discursive appropriation of biblical
language functions as an interventionary rhetorical strategy. Hall uses biblical rhetoric to argue for social and religious—indeed, God's—acceptance.

The good Father's gifts, in this context, can only be the acknowledgment, understanding, and justification of homosexual and lesbian lives, and, in the words of the phrase that ends the novel, the "right to our existence." Hall, by using the language of scripture and the theories of sexology, offers hope for eventual deliverance, grounded on both spiritual principles and social understanding.

Hermeneutics and Hybridity:
E(a)rotic Parables and Queer Messiahs

Within a month of the novel's release in July 1928, James Douglas published a scathing review in the *Sunday Express* under the headline, "A Book That Must Be Suppressed." Within four months the novel was prosecuted in England for obscenity. Of course, primarily at stake was what Thomas Yingling has called "the battle for the scene of persuasion in which the text of homosexuality will be interpreted" (Yingling 1990, 23)—over what may be said about homosexuality and who may say it, and, in this case, what language may be used. The problem was this novel's theological and rhetorical hybridity, its yolking sexology and scripture together in a literary project that would validate, through both spiritual and social claims, lesbianism—the collapse of literature, Scripture, and sexology into a gospel of inversion. A reason this was a problem was the categorical opposition of Christianity and homosexuality as irreconcilable or incompatible categories, like the proverbial oil and water. The idea that one might indeed be both gay/lesbian and Christian was an unthinkable idea. Worse, that one might attempt not only to reconcile the two but to *justify* homosexuality through the language of Christian morality was untenable.

Douglas wrote of *The Well of Loneliness*, "This terrible doctrine [of sexual inversion] may commend itself to certain schools of pseudo-scientific thought, but it *cannot be reconciled* with the Christian religion. . . . Therefore it must be fought to the bitter end by the Christian Churches" (in Brittain 1968, 56, emphasis mine). Sexology and Scripture, homosexuality and Christianity cannot be reconciled. In the use of the vaguely religious word "doctrine," Douglas metonymically collapses the understandings of sexuality proposed by sexology into Hall's literary narrative, that novel as representative of any text that would attempt to encourage a sympathetic understanding of homosexuality. Douglas adds, apocalyptically, "If Christianity does not destroy this doctrine, then this doctrine will destroy it, together with the civilization which it has built" (in Brittain 1968, 56). The categorical opposition is not simply doctrinal, it is an apocalyptic battle for Western culture. Not only are the two "doctrines" incompatible, they are mortal enemies.

Such hyperbolic and apocalyptic rhetoric sounds all too familiar to contemporary readers. As Elaine Showalter has pointed out, religious and social polemicists now echo those at the end of the nineteenth century, who saw sexual decadence and women's rights as signs of the fall of civilization, and homosexuality in particular as the indicative sign of cultural ruin (Showalter 1990, 3–4, 169–72). Religious writer Tim LaHaye has written of the contemporary gay movement, "The battle lines are drawn as never before for the moral contest of the century," and he proposes that the "Anti-Christ" will be homosexual (LaHaye 1984, 178, 204). In *Sodom's Second Coming: What You Need to Know About the Deadly Homosexual Assault*, contemporary evangelical writer F. LaGard Smith writes in his "Call to Arms": "Gay rights is not just another political issue. Nor is it just another moral issue. Gay rights presents us with the ultimate issue of our time: Whether or not God will ever again be honored in our nation" (L. Smith 1993, 245). Like Douglas, and like so many polemicists before, Smith sees homosexuality as the evil other, sign of cultural ruin, and apocalyptic opponent of God.

Douglas continued of *The Well of Loneliness*: "It is a seductive and insidious piece of special pleading designed to display perverted decadence as a martyrdom inflicted upon these outcasts by a cruel society." Douglas rejects the arguments for social tolerance as "seductive" and "special pleading" (prefiguring contemporary arguments about "special" versus "civil" rights). He rejects, further, the arguments of Ellis and Hall that sexuality is a given identity, and Hall's insistence that lesbianism is part of God's creation; like contemporary anti-gay writers, he insists "they choose to be damned"—sexuality is a choice (in Brittain 1968, 56). His modern echo, Smith, also rejects such arguments, invoking the very parable fragment that Hall uses so effectively in her conclusion. Asking, "Did God really create homosexuals as homosexuals?" Smith answers an emphatic no, adding, "One thing you can count on: God does not give the 'gift' of homosexuality. Jesus himself explodes that theory: Which of you, if his son ask for bread, will give him a stone?" (L. Smith 1993, 140). Where Hall used the parable to demand the "gift" of acknowledgment in narrative of justification and (the hope of) liberation, Smith uses the parable to deny that sexual orientation is a given, in an attempt to stifle the very grounds of arguments such as Hall's.

Both Smith and Douglas find arguments for acceptance and understanding to be "seductive," and both demand protection from (and the silencing of) such rhetoric. Uncannily echoing Anita Bryant's "Save Our Children" campaign and those who, even now, would keep lesbian and gay literature and safe sex education out of schools, Douglas insists, "We must protect our children against their specious fallacies and sophistries." Although he perhaps alludes to the reprehensible stereotypes of gays and lesbians seducing the young, he clearly indicates that certain language should be kept away from the young. "We must banish their propaganda from our bookshops and our libraries," he writes, adding, melodramatically, "I would rather give a healthy boy or a healthy girl a phial of prussic acid than this novel" (in Brittain 1968, 56–57).

Smith writes, "In the gay-rights assault against the American culture, no citadel is more coveted than the church. Getting the church's imprimatur on the homosexual lifestyle would be the ultimate stamp of legitimacy." "But," Smith insists, "no matter how seductive that idea is for many mainstream churches—in keeping with the spirit of Christian tolerance and love—there is always that one last hurdle to cross: the Bible" (L. Smith 1993, 117). To Smith, homosexuals are outsiders (outside the "citadel" and the church, not part of the "mainstream"), and any appeal for understanding is an act of "seduction" not one of (Christian) love. Like the reviewer Douglas, Smith calls arguments for tolerance and understanding (and Christian love) "seductive"—a sexualized rhetoric of deceit, rather than a discourse of truth. In fact, he further sexualizes gay and lesbian literature and culture as both sexually transmitted disease and anal rape. He calls "sexually free ideas" a "rampant infection" and urges "legal prophylactics against gay rights" (L. Smith 1993, 100). He compares a gay rights movement to AIDS, calling the movement itself "a loathsome communicable disease" (1993, 14). In a truly reprehensible rhetorical move, he writes of "gays hav[ing] their way with us [Christians]" until "we finally cry out in desperation that our religious rights have been sodomized" (1993, 190).

Douglas similarly describes the presence of homosexuality in society as a "pestilence," a "plague," and a "contagion" (in Brittain 1968, 54–55). However, where Douglas imagines Hall's novel as a "poison," an image he illustrates in the image of prussic acid distributed to boys and girls, Smith reimagines those images after AIDS as sexual assault. He would protect good Christians, not from poison ingested orally, but from infected semen received in anal (or perhaps oral) rape. Both Smith's and Douglas's images fall in the context of "seductive" arguments. Presumably, Christians must protect their ears from arguments of "Christian tolerance and love" for lesbians and gay men. As Gregory Woods has written of gay poetry, "[W]hether I *whisper* in his *ear* or *come* in his *bum* makes no difference," since the "scissor-wielders" of the dominant culture will find either offensive (Woods 1990, 188). I cannot help but recall the words of Jesus ending the parable of the sower, "Who hath ears to hear, let him hear" (Mt

13:9). The image of understanding is an open ear. (One of Jesus' final miracles, in fact, was replacing the ear of Malchus [Lk 22:51].) The hermeneutic circle, it seems, becomes a vicious circle, when argument is figured as seduction, and both ears and eyes are closed, "lest at any time they should see with their eyes, and hear with their ears, and understand with their heart" (Mt 13:15). Douglas advocated the suppression of the novel, urged British officials (and specifically the Director of Public Prosecutions) to "take action," and suggested the establishment of a Censorship Board (in Brittain 1968, 57).

In Douglas's polemical construction—and in the continued opposition of religion to homosexuality—the use of language, especially Christian discourse and scripture, is (and will be) inevitably at stake in any discussion of homosexuality. In the trials of *The Well of Loneliness*, there was a battle over the use of the word of God—and literally the use of the word "God"—in a discussion of lesbianism. Although it wasn't a key part of the decision, newspaper reports of the appeal trial repeatedly referred to Attorney-General Thomas Inskip's reference to Romans 1, a chapter often used to condemn gay and lesbian sexuality and in fact the only reference in the Bible to female same-sex desire (see Brittain 1968, 129, 137). It was a critical attempt to reinstitute the prescriptive authority of Saint Paul in the context of a novel more creatively engaged with the promises of the Old Testament and the liberation offered in the story of Christ. Further, newspapers repeatedly quoted his statement of concern about the appearance of the name of God in the novel. "My lord," he said, "some may think this book corrupt because of the way it brings the name of God into the discussion of these passions" (in Brittain 1968, 130, 137). It is "corrupt," according to Inskip, to include "the name of God" in a discussion of lesbianism; it is corrupt to use religious discourse in a discussion of same-sex desire—a discussion at the time usually trapped either in the moral language of sin or at best in the sexological language of illness or congenital inversion. To collapse religious language into sexological language, as Hall emphatically did, was, to mainstream sensibilities of the period, not only offensive, but worth suppressing.

In the trial transcripts it is clear that if the character of Stephen had espoused guilt rather than virtue, or if the novel had been a medical text rather than a public fiction, or if it had not collapsed the languages of sin and sexology, it would not have had the power the judges saw to "corrupt" an innocent reader. (Douglas wrote that many things "discussed in scientific text-books cannot decently be discussed in a work of fiction offered to the general reader" [in Brittain 1968, 54].) Inskip's concern for the rhetorical insertion of the name of God into a discussion of same-sex sexuality suggests that it is not simply the rhetorical and sexological defense of lesbian sexuality that he and the other men found obscene, though they did find that corrupting; it is additionally the attempt to *morally value* same-sex desire—just as today some religious people find it unacceptable that someone might claim to be both gay or lesbian *and* Christian. Smith, for example, describes religious proponents for gay civil rights as "the spiritually-emasculated products of some of our nation's religious seminaries fraudulently cross-dressing as ministers of the gospel" and as "pandering flesh-merchants" (L. Smith 1993, 11). To advocate Christian tolerance, love, and understanding is to find oneself gay-baited, portrayed as a castrated eunuch, a transvestite, and a pimp.

One might suggest that I misrepresent the rhetorical opposition of Christianity and homosexuality by comparing such a ridiculous contemporary polemicist as Smith with Hall and her detractors. But the programmatic and categorical binarism that Douglas represents and Smith echoes hyperbolically is, in fact, mainstream and pervasive. The Bible is used in antihomosexual discourse, and the Judeo-Christian tradition is uncritically assumed to be anti-gay, even in the most influential of texts. For example, in the 1986 Bowers v. Hardwick Supreme Court decision, a decision that upheld state sodomy laws, Chief Justice Burger rather vaguely cited a "millennia of moral teaching" in his concurring opinion. Burger noted, "Condemnation of those practices [of same-sex sexuality] is firmly rooted in Judeo-Christian moral and ethical standards."[13] More recently (November 1995), a Superior Court judge in New Jersey simply cited the biblical story of Sodom and Gomorrah and "the moral law as espoused by the major religions" in upholding the dismissal of assistant scoutmaster from the Boy Scouts of America simply for being gay.[14] Even in the student newspaper at the university where I teach, a regular student columnist made the rather sweeping generalization, "Most major religions openly oppose [homo]sexual relations," adding specifically, "Christianity takes a clear, simple stand. . . . [T]he faithful Christian must oppose the act of homosexuality in a moral context."[15] In a final bid for doctrinal (i.e., scriptural) authority, the writer even inaccurately attributes such teachings to Jesus rather than Paul: "Jesus says that 'homosexuality' and 'sexual sin' separates [*sic*] us from God" (Touchberry 1995, 4).

Through literature, Hall subverted such binarism. Through *The Well of Loneliness*, Hall reclaimed Jesus and moral discourse for gay and lesbian readers in a way neither the sexologists nor the religious alone could have done. Although, in Smith's manichean scenario the Bible is the only barrier left against the queer barbarians at the gates of the citadel of Christian culture, Hall used Scripture to construct a lesbian messiah. In the margins

of the canons of literature and sexology, we may find more explicit uses of
Christian imagery and the language of Scripture. An obscure 1918 text on
homosexuality by A. T. Fitzroy, for example, is entitled *Despised and Rejected*, a title that invokes both Isaiah 53:3 and the image of a Christ ac-
quainted with human suffering—a figure of empathy and identification for
the "inverts" he discusses. Xavier Mayne's enormous 1908 sexological
study, *The Intersexes*, includes a very brief section on "Christ and Uranism"
which notes not only that Christ never rebuked homosexuality, but that "as
we study Gospel narratives . . . we [have] cause to believe that Christ was
an Uranian" (Mayne 1908, 258–59). This reclaiming of Christ as a "inter-
mediate sexual type" not only reclaims Christ for homosexual believers as
a figure of empathy, it identifies him as an exemplary model of a higher
human type, in part because of his intermediary sexual identity, his ability
to relate to all aspects of the sexual spectrum.[16]

More recently, gay priest Malcolm Boyd has written, "In Christ I find
many gay qualities. . . . He also broke many social taboos and found
sterling qualities in a number of people who were despised by the society
they lived in. He is very much a gay archetype in my understanding of
what being gay means" (in Thompson 1994, 233).[17]   Former Jesuit priest
Robert Goss has written of "Jesus, the queer Christ," not a homosexual
Christ, but an image of social justice and compassion: he says, "To say
Jesus the Christ is queer is to say that god identifies with us and our experience of injustice" (Goss 1993, 84)—a Christ who is functionally "queer"
because he is always outside social norms, resistant to religious and social
authority, always on the side of the social outcast, and a model of justice
and compassion.[18]   Although the writings of liberation theologians have
focused primarily on economics and race, gender and sexual orientation
also need to be rethought in terms of a theology of liberation.[19] Hall's novel
was an important and prescient step in that direction.

How may we then read texts such as Ellis's and Hall's, these disturbing
parables, these gospels of inversion? At a basic level, they are simply
rhetorical appropriations. Ellis uses the parable figure of the seed and the
soil for its allegorical and explanatory potential. Hall uses the images of
Christ's life, and the parabolic fragment of the good father, to craft a demand for acceptance. These figures, drawn from a familiar and dominant
cultural discourse, work well in arguments of analogy. But clearly these
appropriations are not simply methodological. They are epistemological,
ontological, theological. And they are resistant, minority narratives—hy-
brids, thefts, inversions.

In literary-rhetorical terms, such a project might be figured as a feminist strategy, a "reverse" discourse, or a minority construct. Alicia Ostriker has examined the importance in women's poetry of "stealing the language" of male authority, especially in order to revise traditional sexist mythologies (Ostriker 1986, 211). Hall "steals the language" of the Bible to write a new gospel of the messiah as lesbian apologist/martyr. If we are to read this as a feminist project, there are obvious problems, primarily the mapping of gender into theories of sexual inversion (Stephen is portrayed as quite masculine). Gender and sexuality are not identical, and yet, at the time, Hall could only read her sexual orientation as part and parcel of a gender identity.

In fact, if we read this project in historical and cultural contexts, I don't think we can help but suggest that despite its deficiencies in theorizing sexuality, and despite its portrayal of lesbianism as a stigma and a sacrifice, Hall still rewrites a primary cultural narrative in theologically and theoretically challenging ways. True, her lesbian is a butch stereotype, since she is so indebted to the texts of the sexologists who described her so, but her messiah is a lesbian. True, she may be too heavily indebted to a scriptural text for nonbelievers and those who would reject patriarchal narratives, but she inverts that narrative in striking ways, since it is the heteronormative Christian society that is evil. True, the mother figures rejection and Stephen may be too bound to good father figures (Philip or God), but Hall thus grounds social liberation—as yet unfulfilled in the novel—in religious and scriptural justifications, as well as sexological understanding. She inserts "God" in the discussion in a very new way.

Hall appropriates the language of a set of world views (Scripture, Gospel, parable, "God": Christianity) in an attempt to name and include an experience otherwise unnamed and excluded—often by the very world views and language she uses. These texts by Ellis and Hall may suggest what Foucault calls, in *The History of Sexuality*, a "reverse discourse." Although the languages of law, psychology, and sexology made possible a more extensive social control over homosexuality, he explains, "it also made possible the formation of a 'reverse' discourse: homosexuality began to speak in its own behalf, to demand that its legitimacy or 'naturality' be acknowledged, often in the same vocabulary, using the same categories by which it was medically disqualified" (Foucault 1978, 101). Although not exactly analogous—though one might argue more subversive—the use of Biblical language to justify homosexuality, to preach through the parables of Christ a gospel of inversion, is surely a similar project in what Foucault calls "the insurrection of subjugated knowledges." Ellis and Hall take the terms of a language and a world view that would deny gay and lesbian identities, sexualities, and rights, and use it to argue for understanding and acceptance. Theirs is a "will to be uttered."

In a sense, then, Ellis and Hall have queered the gospel of Christ. Hall's text, a founding moment in gay and lesbian literature, characterizes what Gilles Deleuze and Félix Guattari have called a "minor literature": "A minor literature doesn't come from a minor language; it is rather that which a minority constructs within a major language" (Deleuze and Guattari 1986, 16). Scripture and religion were dominant cultural discourses, and Hall rewrites them to justify minority identities, minority cultures, and minority spirituality. In particular, Hall's conclusion exemplifies the three characteristics of minor literature. The text demonstrates "deterritorialization" both in figures of expatriation and estrangement and in the rhetorical reterritorialization of Christian figures and language. By the end it is political rather than individual, since the martyred figure, despite its potential for individualism, stands for a larger community of disenfranchised. Similarly, if in minor literature, "everything takes on a collective value," so this novel became a lightning rod for sexual values. "If the writer is in the margins," say Deleuze and Guattari, "this situation allows the writer all the more the possibility to express another possible community and to forge the means for another consciousness and another sensibility" (1986, 17). Stephen literally is possessed by a community at the end, and her voice figures theirs; her singular prayer is their collective reinvestment of Christian theology, including the gay and lesbian community in the human community as another consciousness, another sensibility.

All of these projects—the feminist strategy, the reverse discourse, the minority construct, the *queer* gospel—in Hall's work, finally, must be further spiritualized, Christianized. For the revision Hall performs reimagines both a minority spirituality and a truer Christianity. Reimagining the parables, as Patricia Jung and Ralph Smith note of their own rewriting of the good Samaritan as a gay man or lesbian in *Heterosexism: An Ethical Challenge*, is a way of taking the Bible more seriously:

> This is not a new argument. Others who have experienced oppression make it clear that when they read the Bible it speaks to them in ways that many of the rest of us cannot hear except through their voices. Whether it is the poor in Latin American base communities, women throughout the world, or blacks in North America or South Africa, we are called to recognize the absolute necessity of letting the Bible's living voice speak through living people. This does not mean that we are "reading into the Bible" meanings that are not there. On the contrary, it means freeing the meanings that are there from the bondage of silence that our prejudices impose. (1993, 108)

In *Sexual Inversion* and *The Well of Loneliness*, the Gospel isn't simply stolen; the text isn't simply hybrid and marginal. Ellis and Hall are writing apologetics, Hall a gospel of inversion. We must reinvest these texts as theological texts, texts that attempt to question the categorical binarism of homosexuality and Christianity (or religion), texts that work by both/and logic rather than either/or. Ellis provides an understanding of sexual orientation—as a preconscious if not congenital identity—that would destabilize any easy moralizing about sexual activity. Hall pushes further, adding gay and lesbian identities to the community of believers ("We have not denied You," Stephen cries).

To conclude, I want to propose one further angle on these texts. They use parables, but they are parables. Although Ellis's theft of a figure may seem less shocking than Hall's (since a lesbian messiah has obvious shock value), rhetorically it provides a self-reflexive comment on the kind of work these texts do. Like the parable of the sower, these texts mark themselves as parabolic discourse. John Dominic Crossan says that a parable contains "a radically new vision of the world," and "it gives absolutely no information until after the hearer has entered into it and experienced it from inside itself" (Crossan 1973, 13). A hearer's (reader's) first response may be to refuse to enter that metaphorical world, to stop up his or her ears and eyes and to refuse to understand, to silence it (as Douglas would suppress Hall's novel), to refuse its implications (as contemporary Christians continue to refuse the implications of sexual identity, maintaining the status/conduct dilemma at the expense of human integrity), or to translate it into the comfortable normalcy of his or her own worldview. To refuse the shock, and the call to a new understanding.

Further, James Breech notes that Jesus' parables are usually stories without endings, to emphasize the ambiguity of human actions, despite spiritual principles (Breech 1989, 28–29), or in terms of Hall's novel, to emphasize the continued social and political oppression despite spiritual questions. Hall pushes us to move from either/or to both/and, and to reimagine our prayers for deliverance from "why not?" to "How long, O Lord, how long?" (Hall 1928, 364). Hall's use of the parable in the novel's conclusion is open-ended: If your child asks for bread, will you give him a stone? "We have asked for bread; will you give us a stone?" (1928, 437). The usage suggests the spiritual validity of lesbian identity and the promise of an eventual deliverance (grounded, perhaps, on religious principles), but it recognizes that human response might indeed be stones, not bread, hatred and condemnation, not material or spiritual sustenance. Only those who have the ears to hear, will hear. Let them hear.

Notes

1.   Johnson founded Spatula Ministries, an evangelical ministry for parents of gays and lesbians. The title refers to the fact that when parents discover their children are gay, they "hit the ceiling" and "only a spatula of love can peel them off" (1993, 92).

2.   More recently, when I was attacked by a local right-wing newspaper for teaching Winterson's novel in a British literature course, the discursive impasse of being gay and Christian became more clear. The paper accused me, of course, of "promoting homosexuality," but added that "Dr. Madden . . . purports to be a 'Christian' of some sort" (Davenport 1995, 8). The choice of the verb "purports" and the very careful placement of "Christian" in quotation marks indicated the writer's view: that someone who "promot[es] homosexuality" and is "openly gay" cannot really be a true Christian. In fact, the paper went on to say, inaccurately, "Although a former seminarian, Dr. Madden openly despises mainstream religion." Such an identity can only be explained through the writer's recourse to the languages of marginality and "mainstream"—a language of "otherness."

3.   This distinction has numerous ramifications. Restated as a status/conduct distinction, it has determined much of the discussion in the U.S. about gays in the military, a distinction blurred, apparently, by the speech-act of coming out (in the "don't ask, don't tell" policy). The distinction also furthers anti-gay rhetoric about orientation as a disease or a psychological disorder, one that should not be acted upon or should be put—through counseling or other means—under control. More importantly, this distinction obviates any claim that orientation (hetero or homo) is central or essential to identity—that it is something one is, not something one does. The status/conduct dilemma, and the corollary issue of identity, is a dilemma at work in much of the discussion of same-sex sexuality, be it scriptural interpretation, pastoral advice, or military policy.

4.   I suggest that this image is *epistemic*, meaning that it has force as a means toward understanding something—just as the images of viruses and computers appear so frequently in our own culture. Steam was an important source of power, and Great Britain and the United States became major dam-building countries during the first half of the nineteenth century; the earliest hydroelectric developments in Great Britain began in 1894. (See N. Smith 1971, 191, 230.) So the image of sexual drives as streams (of water or perhaps steam) forced into new directions echoes a primary cultural image of drive, power, and production.

5.   Although I do not specifically develop here Crossan's analysis of the parable (in 1980, 25–64), his discussion of the parable's polyvalence and self-reflexivity informs my reading of Ellis's appropriation.

6.   Many of these other parables are parables of seed, growth, and harvest—the parable of the wheat and tares (Mt 13:24–30), the parable of the seed growing secretly (Mk 4:26–39), the parable of the mustard seed (Mt 13:31–32,

Mk 4:31–32). The parable of the wheat and tares suggests the possibility of hybrid teaching, of false teaching among the true; the other two are about the "kingdom" community's ability to bear fruit.

7.   For an extended analysis of the novel as a reconfigured gospel featuring a lesbian messiah, see my "*The Well of Loneliness*, or the Gospel According to Radclyffe Hall," in *The Journal of Homosexuality*, fall 1996.

8.   Not only do many gays and lesbians face such familial rejections from our own parents, but repeatedly that rejection may be figured in such physical terms—"I'd rather you be dead," or "you make me sick." For example, Barbara Johnson writes of her own experience on discovering her son was gay, "I felt as if someone had shoved a shag rug down my throat and I was gagging on it," and she finds herself unable to swallow (1993, 37). According to therapists, some parents experience the fact of their child's homosexuality "as if that person had died" (Switzer and Switzer 1980, 25). There is surely further theoretical work to be done on the gay child as the abject(ed) other of the family and of the church.

9.   The eunuch is repeatedly invoked in contemporary gay and lesbian theology as a figure of the sexually marginal.

10.   Ironically enough, Hall collapses Ellis's stream and sowing metaphors in a scene from metropolitan London, in which she describes the Thames being plowed by a passing tugboat, but concludes "a field of water is not for the sowing" (1928, 209). This image appears after Stephen has accepted her unprocreative sexuality, and written her first novel.

11.   In an attempt to convey the "shock and challenge" of the parable, John Dominic Crossan suggests reimagining the telling of the story as a Catholic priest in Belfast telling the story of a good IRA terrorist who helps a wounded (Catholic) man on Falls Road (Crossan 1975, 106–8). See also the use of the parable in Patricia Jung and Ralph Smith's *Heterosexism: An Ethical Challenge* (1993, 106-8).

12 .   Psalm 13 is also invoked in Christ Glaser's *The Word Is Out: The Bible Reclaimed for Lesbians and Gay Men*, in a meditation on liberation for June 4 (liberation being the theme for the month of June in his text, the month of the Stonewall Riots).

13.   The Bowers v. Hardwick U. S. Supreme Court decision, 478 U. S. 186 (1986), is reprinted in *Lesbians, Gay Men, and the Law*, edited by William Rubenstein, pages 132–48. (See pages 135–36 for Burger's concurring opinion.)

14.   The story, "Scout's dishonor," may be found in *The Advocate* 696, 12 December 1995 (11).

15.   Notice that the student columnist emphasizes "the act of homosexuality" rather than the identity or the orientation. The writer obviates the status/conduct or identity/activity dilemma by comparing homosexual orientation to alcoholism and stressing "activity" as the issue, a not infrequent tactic of the politico-religious right. He thus explicitly ignores what many consider obvious: that being gay or lesbian is something you are, not simply something you do.

16.   As Sallie McFague demonstrates at length in her *Models of God: Theology for an Ecological, Nuclear Age*, the images we have of God, especially the personal and relational metaphors (such as parent images), profoundly affect both our theology and our ways of living ethically, politically, and socially in the world (1987, 86–87).

17.   Those "gay qualities" include "vulnerability, sensitivity, someone who emptied himself of power, who lived as a gentle but strong person" (in Thompson 1994, 233).   Boyd also wrote a 1990 essay in the *Advocate* entitled "Was Jesus Gay?"   And the *Advocate* recently featured a cover story, "Is God Gay?" (December 13, 1994).

18.   Chris Glaser writes, in his collection of biblical meditations for gays and lesbians, "Jesus was queer. Not in our sense, perhaps. But queer enough to be mocked, scorned, despised, shamed, and forsaken" (February 18).

19.   For an analysis of the place of gay and lesbian liberation within the contexts of both Scripture and liberation theology, see George Edwards's *Gay/Lesbian Liberation: A Biblical Perspective.*

Works Cited

Baker, Michael. 1985. *Our Three Selves: A Life of Radclyffe Hall.* London: GMP.

Boswell, John. 1980. *Christianity, Social Tolerance, and Homosexuality: Gay People in Western Europe from the Beginning of the Christian Era to the Fourteenth Century.* Chicago: University of Chicago Press.

Breech, James. 1989. *Jesus and Postmodernism.* Minneapolis: Fortress.

Brittain, Vera. 1968. *Radclyffe Hall: A Case of Obscenity?* London: Femina Books.

Comstock, Gary David. 1993. *Gay Theology Without Apology.* Cleveland, OH: Pilgrim.

Crossan, John Dominic. 1973. *In Parables: The Challenge of the Historical Jesus.* San Francisco: Harper and Row.

———. 1975. *The Dark Half: Towards a Theology of Story.* Niles, IL: Argus Communications.

———. 1980. *Cliffs of Fall: Paradox and Polyvalence in the Parables of Jesus.* New York: Seabury.

Davenport, Vernon C. 1995. "Homosexual Professor Indoctrinates Students." *The Carolina Spectator* 4 (September): 8.

Deleuze, Gilles and Félix Guattari. 1986. *Kafka: Toward a Minor Literature.* Trans. Dana Polan. Foreword by Réda Bensmaïa. Minneapolis: University of Minnesota Press.

Edwards, George R. 1984. *Gay/Lesbian Liberation: A Biblical Perspective.* New York: Pilgrim.

Ellis, Havelock. 1897 [1975]. *Sexual Inversion.* With appendices by John Addington Symonds. New York: Arno.

Faderman, Lillian. 1981. *Surpassing the Love of Men: Romantic Friendships and Love Between Women from the Renaissance to the Present.* New York: Morrow.

Foucault, Michel. 1976 [1978]. *The History of Sexuality, 1: An Introduction;.* Trans. Robert Hurley. New York: Vintage.

Frontain, Raymond-Jean. 1995. "The Bible." In *The Gay and Lesbian Literary Heritage: A Reader's Companion to the Writers and Their Works, from Antiquity to the Present.* Ed. Claude J. Summers. New York: Holt. 92–100.

Glaser, Chris. 1994. *The Word Is Out: The Bible Reclaimed for Lesbians and Gay Men.* New York: HarperSan Francisco.

Glasgow, Joanne. 1990. "What's a Nice Lesbian Like You Doing in the Church of Torquemada? Radclyffe Hall and Other Catholic Converts." In *Lesbian Texts and Contexts: Radical Revisions.* Ed. Karla Jay and Joanne Glasgow. New York: New York University Press. 241–54.

Goss, Robert. 1993. *Jesus Acted Up: A Gay and Lesbian Manifesto.* New York: HarperSan Francisco.

Hall, Radclyffe. 1928 [1990]. *The Well of Loneliness.* New York: Doubleday.

Johnson, Barbara. 1990. *Stick a Geranium in Your Hat and Be Happy!* Dallas: Word.

———. 1993. *Pack Up Your Gloomies in a Great Big Box, Then Sit on the Lid and Laugh!* Dallas: Word.

Jung, Patricia Beattie and Ralph R. Smith. 1993. *Heterosexism: An Ethical Challenge.* Albany: State University of New York Press.

Krafft-Ebing, Richard von. 1886 [1965]. *Psychopathia Sexualis.* Trans. Harry E.

Wedeck. New York: Putnam.

Kristeva, Julia. 1982. *Powers of Horror: An Essay on Abjection*. Trans. Leon S.
Roudiez. New York: Columbia University Press.

LaHaye, Tim. 1984. *What Everyone Should Know About Homosexuality*. Wheaton, IL:
Living Books.

Mayne, Xavier. (pseud. Edward Irenaeus Prime Stevenson) 1908 [1975]. *The Intersexes: A History of Similisexualism as a Problem in Social Life*. New York:
Arno.

McFague, Sallie. 1987. *Models of God: Theology for an Ecological, Nuclear Age*.
Philadelphia: Fortress.

Mooney, Carolyn J. 1994. "Religion vs. Gay Rights: Attack on Homosexuality
Angers Divinity Students." *Chronicle of Higher Education* 11 (May):A38.

Ostriker, Alicia Suskin. 1986. *Stealing the Language: The Emergence of Women's
Poetry in America*. Boston: Beacon.

Robinson, Paul. 1976 [1989]. *The Modernization of Sex: Havelock Ellis, Alfred Kinsey,
William Masters and Virginia Johnson*. Ithaca: Cornell University Press.

Rubenstein, William B., ed. 1993. *Lesbians, Gay Men, and the Law*. New York: New
Press.

Scanzoni, Letha Dawson and Virginia Ramey Mollenkott. 1978 [1994]. *Is the Homosexual My Neighbor? A Positive Christian Response*; San Francisco: HarperSan
Francisco.

"Scout's Dishonor." 1995. *The Advocate* 696 (12 December):11.

Showalter, Elaine. 1990. *Sexual Anarchy: Gender and Culture at the Fin de Siècle*.
New York: Penguin.

Sinfield, Alan. 1994. *The Wilde Century: Effeminacy, Oscar Wilde, and the Queer
Moment*. New York: Columbia University Press.

Smith, F. LaGard. 1993. *Sodom's Second Coming: What You Need to Know About the
Deadly Homosexual Assault*. Eugene, OR: Harvest House.

Smith, Norman. 1971. *A History of Dams*. London: Peter Davies.

Stimpson, Catherine. 1982. "Zero Degree Deviancy: The Lesbian Novel in English."
In *Writing and Sexual Difference*. Ed. Elizabeth Abel. Chicago: University of
Chicago Press. 243–59.

Switzer, David K. and Shirley Switzer. 1980. *Parents of the Homosexual*. Philadelphia:
Westminster.

Thompson, Mark. 1994. *Gay Soul: Finding the Heart of Gay Spirit and Nature*. New
York: HarperSan Francisco.

Touchberry, Tommy. 1995. "Frowning upon Homosexuality Justified, Natural." *[Uni-
versity of South Carolina] Gamecock* 19 (October):4.

Winterson, Jeanette. 1985 [1987]. *Oranges Are Not the Only Fruit*. London: Pandora;
New York: Atlantic Monthly.

Woods, Gregory. 1990. "'Absurd! Ridiculous! Disgusting!': Paradox in Poetry by
Gay Men." In *Lesbian and Gay Writing: An Anthology of Critical Essays*. Ed.
Mark Lily. Philadelphia: Temple University Press. 175–98.

Yingling, Thomas. 1990. *Hart Crane and the Homosexual Text: New Threshholds, New
Anatomies*. Chicago: University of Chicago Press.

7

Active Readers, Obverse Tricksters: Trickster Texts and Recreative Reading

Bradley John Monsma

> If [the trickster] is the image of the ironically imaginative mind of polymorphous humans, he is equally the image of the adaptability of transcendence, for which no material thing is too trivial to become hierophany, not even that little gust of tongue-shaped breath known as the human word.
>
> —Robert D. Pelton

The first oral stories of tricksters take place in mythic time cued by the observed world. The stories of Raven, Hare, Spider, and Coyote in tribal North America help groups of people to place themselves in specific landscapes, to articulate and critique social values, and to define their relationships with "others"—other species, other people, and the sacred. Tricksters continue to be a vital presence in contemporary literatures. Like the first stories of tricksters, contemporary trickster narratives and characters invoke a border-crossing spirit that evidences an awareness that "[l]anguage . . . lies on the borderline between oneself and the other. The word in language is always half someone else's" (Bakhtin 1981, 293). The dialogic language of contemporary trickster narratives has its roots in oral storytelling traditions that have always theorized intersections of differences within and between cultures and encouraged self-reflexive discourse on interpretation and its difficulties. Contemporary trickster narratives mediate between culturally coded discourses by confronting various readers with their own potential for misunderstanding even while compelling participation in the act of creating meaning from shifting texts.

Since tricksters both inhabit the oral literatures of almost all cultures and often articulate human relationships to the sacred, much scholarship on tricksters has come from the perspective of comparative religious studies. More recently, many scholars have found postmodern vocabularies helpful in describing the paradoxical, marginal, liminal, multivocal, and multivalent qualities of tricksters. Tricksters, therefore, seem to provide fertile ground for discussion of the intersection of postmodern and religious discourses. Typically disruptive. tricksters function as a double mirror, intro-ducing to postmodernism understandings of difference and heterogeneity predating and unconnected to Western philosophy, and to Christianity un-derstandings of multivalency and contingency that support truth claims and ethical actions.

Some Christian thinkers have seen postmodernism as directly in con-flict with traditional Christian assertions concerning truth and redemptive history. Most often, they confront a postmodernism directly linked to European philosophy—Lyotard's "incredulity toward metanarratives," Derrida's deconstruction of logocentric positivism and humanism, and Foucault's claims concerning the textual mediation of history and of all knowledge. Roger Lundin, for example, writes that "the postmodern self no longer harbors hopes of discovering truth or secure principles. . . . [I]t strives to reduce all individual moral actions to matters of choice for which there are no authoritative guidelines" (1993, 75). Since Lundin sees the postmodern emphasis on perspective and interpretation as rooted in no-tions of the power of language and the individual will, he overlooks con-ceptions of powerful language that grow from sources other than a cri-tique of enlightenment and modernist epistemologies. Lundin's analysis of postmodernism, like many others, confines itself to the Western philosophical tradition and to examples taken from canonical European and American literature. Therefore, his argument fails to account for texts with non-Western roots that can be described as postmodern in form yet that retain moral commitments rooted in community and history.

However, other Christian analyses of postmodern culture, more at-tuned to the imperatives of diversity, begin by acknowledging "new" reali-ties, as when Walter Brueggemann suggests that Christian interpretation is contextual, local, and pluralistic by "describing how it is with us" (Brueggemann 1993, 10). "We claim a voice that rings true in our con-text," writes Brueggemann, "that applies authoritatively to our lived life. But it is a claim that is made in a pluralism where it has no formal privilege" (1993, 9). Brueggemann sees less danger in this sort of "perspectivism" than in the kind of "objectivity" described by Richard Rorty as "an agree-ment of everyone in the room" (Brueggemann 1993, 8). Brueggemann's adoption of a postmodern epistemology promotes a Christian discourse free from triumphalism by acknowledging not only that some who might see and say things differently have been excluded from the room, but also that there are conversations in other rooms altogether. What is less clear in such a tolerant and respectfully distant pluralism is how those from differ-ent contexts might speak to and hear each other.

In many cases, Christian efforts to articulate a space for dialogue between those marked by cultural, national, religious, and economic differences has been spurred by the need to acknowledge Christianity's complicity with colonialism. "First-world" Christians listening to voices from the "third world" have become aware not only of the ways biblical texts were made to justify cultural, psychological, and technological domination of non-Western regions, but also how biblical texts influenced resistance to domination (Gallagher 1994). In a climate defined by biblical interpretations relevant to specific places, cultures, and experiences, some theologians have reevaluated the foundations for interpretation. Sandra M. Schneiders suggests that positivist objectivity has increasingly given way to "a hermeneutical paradigm of understanding by participatory dialogue" that extends to the relationship between reader and text, even the biblical text:

> Interpretation, in other words, is not a matter either of dominating the text by method or of submitting to the text in servile fideism, but of entering into genuine dialogue with it as it stands. Through this dialogue reader and text are mutually transformed. The reader is transformed not by capitulation but by conversion; the text is transformed not by dissection but through multiple interpretations to which it gives rise by its surplus of meaning, but which can only be actualized by successive generations of readers whose interpretations enrich the texts themselves. (Schneiders 1989, 62)

Christian and non-Christian critics who are concerned with hearing voices from indigenous, postcolonial, and marginalized cultures may be more inclined to consider that what is true shifts according to one's perspective, or at least that "truth" is articulated differently from alternative contexts.[1] Nevertheless, the labeling of postcolonial texts as postmodern is controversial: Susan VanZanten Gallagher points out that "most postcolonial writers are deeply committed to the notion of the subject," and "affirm . . . the possibility of truth claims" (Gallagher 1994, 14). Similarly, bell hooks asks, "Should we not be suspicious of postmodern critiques of the 'subject' when they surface at a historical moment when many subjugated people feel themselves coming to voice for the first time?" (hooks 1995, 121). However, accounts of literary postmodernism that attend to racial, social, sexual, and gendered "margins" tend to recognize the complex subjectivities as well as the new historicity and ethical discourses embodied in many postmodern manifestations. Linda Hutcheon, for example, regularly refers to postmodern texts by Maxine Hong Kingston, Toni Morrison, Ishmael

Reed, Margaret Atwood, Salman Rushdie, and others, arguing that postmodern parody, unvexed by paradox, both enshrines the past and opens it to question (Hutcheon 1988, 126). Far from ignoring or solely mocking history, parody depends upon historical imagination. Because she supports her argument with culturally heterogenous examples, Hutcheon can claim, "Postmodernism clearly attempts to combat what has come to be seen as modernism's potential for hermetic, elitist isolationism that separated art from the world, literature from history" (1988, 140). In much postmodernist practice, the "'performativity' of the text . . . leads to the acknowledgment, not of truth, but of truths in the plural, truths that are socially, ideologically, and historically conditioned" (1988, 18). Similarly, Arnold Krupat, a scholar of Native American literature, describes his *Ethnocriticism* as being characterized by the oxymoron defined as "that figure which offers apparently oppositional, paradoxical, or incompatible terms in a manner that nonetheless allows for decidable, if polysemous and complex meaning" (Krupat 1992, 28). Such a mode of criticism does "not offer itself as a master narrative, while it does not either offer itself as just one position among others" (1992, 26).

Postmodernist critiques of language and power can clear the air for previously unheard voices crying out in wildernesses. Dialogic metaphors may signal new opportunities for prophetic words and committed actions rather than a slippery slope toward the abyss of a philosophical endgame.

Writing Tricksters

Trickster turns to wind
Trickster turns to sand, . . .
We see only his grey tail
bird-disguised
like a moving target
as he steals all the words
we ever thought we knew

                                        Wendy Rose

According to the latest
survey, there are certain
persons who, in poetic
or scholarly guise,
have claimed me like

a conqueror's prize.

> Let me just say
> once for all,
> just to be done:
> Coyote,
> he belongs to none.

Peter Blue Cloud

The history of trickster studies suggests that scholars of oral literatures have become ever more tolerant of the contradictions of tricksters and less inclined to limit individual tricksters to a single significance or to generalize about the meaning of trickster phenomena. Indeed, scholars now solve the problems of definition and description by composing long lists of characteristics, each characteristic possessed at least some of the time by a particular trickster in a set of stories from a certain culture, place, and time. Such lists attempt to avoid sublimating the differences between tricksters (or even between different moments of the same trickster) and thus limiting their shifting meanings.[2]

Most recent studies attempt to understand the immediate cultural contexts of trickster tales and the perspectives of their first audiences. This task has been spurred by the work of those who might be called postmodern ethnographers. Writers such as James Clifford, Renato Rosaldo, and others have reexamined the history of anthropology and retheorized their own work, focusing on "ethnographic authority," on how their constructed meanings are conscribed by their own rhetoric, social positions, cultural politics, and audiences (see Rosaldo 1989). Clifford writes, "Ethnography is actively situated *between* powerful systems of meaning. It poses its questions at the boundaries of civilizations, cultures, classes, races, and genders" (Clifford and Marcus 1986, 2). Constructions of culture as processual and negotiated have created institutional space for the voices emerging from "border" cultures previously ignored.

Contemporary literary tricksters can be seen as part of this "writing back"—not in the sense that these fictions ought to be read as informant ethnography (such readings would be especially ironic at a time when ethnographies are often described as fictions), but in that they assume control over their own representations and question the notion of representation itself. By suggesting that cultures are inevitably heteroglot and exist in perpetual transition, the metacritical awareness of postmodern ethnography clears the way to hear contemporary trickster tellings as part of the storytelling continua from ancient times to the most recent present.

A number of ethnographic studies have interpreted tricksters as mediating figures constructed in response to a culture's continuing perceptions of opposition and difference. Barbara Babcock-Abrahams, for example, cites both Mikhail Bakhtin and Julia Kristeva in describing the trickster as "a tolerated margin of mess," a dialogic phenomenon that resists monologic interpretation. Trickster narratives therefore induce symbolic phenomena that spark new perspectives on current realities and lead to "a rediscovery of essential truths, a transvaluation of values, and the affirmation of a primal order" (Babcock-Abrahams 1985, 181). As the terms *marginal* and *liminal* have continued to shift further from their structuralist beginnings, they have retained their popularity (perhaps to the point of being fetishized) and power to describe locations of special insight and alternatives to various centers.

Another example of the influence of critical theory on trickster studies is the work of Anne Doueihi, who uses a deconstructive approach to reinterpret a well-known Winnebago tale collected by Paul Radin. For Doueihi, to use deconstructive methods is not to force a Western critical paradigm onto Native American stories, but rather to reveal the critical discourse within the stories themselves. Doueihi's perceptive close reading reveals moments of undecidability, of semiotic play which reveals the tale to be less a story than a linguistic invention, a "complex weaving of voices" that would be understood by an informed Winnebago audience (Doueihi 1984, 305). The trickster resides "between discourse and story," "the features traditionally ascribed to Trickster—contradictoriness, complexity, deceptiveness, trickery—are the features of the language of the story itself" (1984, 308). Doueihi's conclusion resembles a point made by Gerald Vizenor concerning the inherent multivocality of trickster performances. Vizenor explains through Dennis Tedlock's work that listeners (and readers) collaborate with a storyteller who plays the leading roles, the narrator and the critical commentator (1984b, 8).

From another complex cultural standpoint, Henry Louis Gates, Jr., also begins to mark the space of what might be called an "indigenous postmodernity." Even as Gates often relies upon a poststructuralist vocabulary, his central arguments concerning African and African American dual-voiced parody grow from careful attention to trickster tales themselves.[3] The trickster plays the liminal role of translator between the literal and the figurative, drawing attention to the indeterminacy of interpretation. Gates writes that "Esu [the West African trickster] endlessly displaces meaning, deferring it by the play of signification . . . He is 'a deceiving shadow,' true to the trickster, 'which falls between intent and meaning, between utterance and understanding" (Gates 1988, 42). Gates's criticism insists upon dialogic discourse and indeterminate interpretation within the imperatives of African American history and culture.

In writing as in oral storytelling, trickster narratives both define values and reveal points at which value systems become static and the authoritative institutions supporting them become repressive. In sites of cultural contact, tricksters tend to appear as mediators between conflicting value systems—revealing power relations, suggesting survival strategies, and reinforcing values that resist or subvert oppressive power. As Ralph Ellison writes, "Change the joke, slip the yoke." But as Ellison's line suggests, trickster narratives do more than subvert power, they suggest alternative orders in which meaning proliferates and multiplicity is the norm. Each of these studies deals with culturally specific oral traditions, but together they indicate how tricksters, as liminal translators and irrepressible border-crossers, provide suggestive images through which to think about cross-cultural negotiations and diverse understandings of faith.

Creation Stories

> In that "ensemble of texts, themselves ensembles," which is the culture of any people, the trickster is only one text among many; yet as master of all language, [the trickster] is the ensemble of ensembles, the meeting-place of all words.
>
> —Robert D. Pelton

The ethnologist Basil Johnston of the Anishinaubae (often called the Ojibway or Chippewa) tells the story of the trickster Nana'b'oozoo, who finds himself trapped by the rising waters covering the whole earth. (In some versions of the story, the trickster's mischief is responsible for the flood.) To save himself and other creatures from starvation and drowning, Nana'b'oozoo remembers a story: Once before during a flood the mother of the Anishinaubae had restored the earth by blowing on (speaking to) a bit of soil from the bottom of the sea. Since he has no options, Nana'b'oozoo tries to imitate the story, and with the help of the earthdiver muskrat he is successful. The story of Nana'b'oozoo, originally a communal oral performance, is itself about the recreative power of language and the responsibility of humans as co-creators. Following his own version of the flood story, the author/theorist Gerald Vizenor (mixedblood Anishinaabe—his spelling) writes:

> The past is familiar enough in the circles of the seasons, woodland
> places, lakes and rivers, to focus a listener on an environmental
> metaphor and an intersection where the earth started in mythic
> time, where a trickster or a little woodland person stopped to imag-
> ine the earth. The tribal creation takes place at the time of the telling
> in the oral tradition. (Vizenor 1984b, 7)

As the stories return with differences throughout his writing, investing printed texts with a sense of the variance of oral performance, Vizenor unites mythic and historical times and places. His printed voice invites diverse audiences to join the storyteller to play the part of the compassionate trickster who casts about to create new places that might survive future floods. Stories such as Johnston's and Vizenor's reveal the constructedness of physical and social realities while foregrounding the responsibility of humans to continue to imagine and create.

Vizenor, in order to place oral traditions in a continuum of "survivance" rather than in translation as "the aesthetic remains of reason in the literature of dominance," often uses a postmodern vocabulary to describe his own work and the situation of tribal literatures generally (Vizenor 1993, 7). He writes, "The ironies and humor of the postmodern are heard in tribal narratives; the natural reason of tribal creation has never been without a postmodern turn or counterpoise, a common mode that enlivened the performance and memories of those who heard the best of their own experiences in stories" (1993, 8).

Many contemporary authors, especially those with ties to oral literatures, use tricksters in ways similar to Vizenor. Such well-known writers as Toni Morrison, Maxine Hong Kingston, Gary Snyder, Ishmael Reed, Louise Erdrich, and many others commonly use trickster characters to invoke in their fictions spirits of parody, disruption, indeterminacy, expectancy, and reconciliation. Simultaneously, trickster fictions often introduce a didacticism that calls for ethical action based on truths proclaimed locally. In the polyphonic world of trickster discourses, truths are articulated provisionally in an ever-evolving process that refuses to become monologic. Contemporary tricksters, like those in oral cultures, proficiently call everything to question, upsetting orthodoxies by revealing social and moral codes to be humanly constructed and therefore revisable for better or worse. Since trickster narratives have always defined moral universes it is not surprising that more recent stories frequently engage Christianity in their playfully serious discourse. In such instances contemporary trickster narratives inform theological discussions concerning the fate of faith in a postmodern world that these narratives (oral and written) have always taken for granted, where knowledge is contextual, local, and pluralistc, and where interpretation is a precursor to transformation.

Reading Tricksters

> Well, I'll tell you something [said a turd named Harvey to Coyote]. There are people living around here. If I was you, I'd keep quiet. Cause those people will believe anything.
>
> —Peter Blue Cloud

Maybe Harvey's right about humans' capacity to believe anything. Yet, perhaps the fear of gullibility and the desire for certainty causes some to believe too little when faced with many options. Faced with religious difference, orthodoxies often resort to sealing off the borders of belief, thereby excluding those who mediate, who shuttle between codified understandings of the sacred. Chippewa writer Louise Erdrich devotes one section of her book of poetry *Baptism of Desire* to prose tales of the trickster Old Man Potchikoo, who dies and begins walking toward the white peoples' heaven. Though his progress is temporarily hindered by his appetite, Potchikoo arrives at the pearly gates where St. Peter looks up his name in the book. Potchikoo becomes frightened at what he expects will be a long list of awful deeds, but it turns out there is just one word: "Indian." St. Peter tells him to keep walking, and after more detours Potchikoo passes by a withered gate where he becomes curious about hell for white people. He manages to slip through the gate while Peter is checking in a busload of Mormons. Potchikoo's curiosity overcomes his fear, and he finds a giant warehouse with a sign marked "ENTRANCE HELL" (Erdrich 1989, 53). He puts his ear to the door "expecting his blood to curdle," but all he hears is the rustling of pages. He looks through the keyhole and sees that hell is worse than flames: everyone inside is chained hand, foot, and neck to old Sears Roebuck catalogues which they drag around, collapsing now and then to flip through the pages. Erdrich writes, "The words of the damned, thin and drained, rang through his ears all the way home. *Look at that wall unit. What about this here recliner? We could put up that home gym in the basement*" (1989, 54).

Erdrich allows Potchikoo to wander between racial and spiritual positions in a sort of trickster limbo. Being Indian keeps him out of white heaven, but it doesn't send him to white hell. Materialism—greed, sloth, and vanity—damns the souls of white folks, but poverty doesn't save Potchikoo. Erdrich's historical/mythological tone puts a comic spin on

Indian Country's first contact with a Christianity tied to Anglo–American capitalism and life-ways. At the same time, her contemporary references reveal the power of the wall unit altar and home-gym genuflecting. It is important to note that Potchikoo's curiosity motivates the tale's insights into the racial, historical, and economic construction of redemption and damnation. In Bakhtinian terms, the trickster reveals the heteroglossia surrounding and including the monological religious discourse.

The dialogizing voice of the trickster appears similarly in the work of Chinese American author Maxine Hong Kingston. Readers of Kingston's most well-known book, *The Woman Warrior*, will recognize that the text itself functions as a trickster, mediating between the past and present, reality and fantasy, necessity and extravagance. Kingston's unreliable narrator must find her way amidst a proliferation of voices that call to question authoritative perspectives, including her own. *The Woman Warrior*'s shiftiness tends to expose the essentialist thinking of readers wishing to separate clearly the Chinese from the not-Chinese. Readers become dupes to the extent that they read ethnographically and unquestioningly accept the unreliable narrator's momentary strategies for achieving ethnographic authority. The book functions like a traditional trickster tale by denaturalizing the narrator's multiple social worlds and by placing readers in the position of the narrator who must interpret relationships between the literal and the figurative so as to fit her own stories with those of the past.

In her second book, *China Men*, Kingston uses narrative strategies similar to *The Woman Warrior* to mediate between fact and fantasy. For example, she often tells different versions of the same story without clarifying what "really" happened. *China Men* also contains trickster tales told as such. These narratives provide important suggestions for interpreting the stories that surround the tales, and one tale in particular engages colonial Christianity in a resistant, reordering discourse.

Kingston tells the story of the "talk addict" Bak Goong who invents a number of trickster-like responses to Hawaiian plantation rules banning the Chinese workers from talking. He can't help but curse the overseers on horseback, so he covers his curses with coughs. He also tells scatological tales about the trickster Chan Moong Gut who dupes others so completely they falsely think they've gotten the best of Chan. Chan so abuses the weak and unsuspecting that "[p]eople with the name Chan have asked storytellers to change the trickster's name, or to forget those stories in America" (Kingston 1980, 114). These people understand Chan stories as they functioned in their original social context—as providing negative models of behavior. But unlike those who are embarrassed to be associated with the trickster, Bak Goong recognizes in the stories potent, vocal ways to respond to his present oppressive circumstances.

Bak Goong therefore acts out a traditional trickster tale, "The Story of Chan Moong Gut and the Gambling Wives," when he serves a group of missionary women tea—and serves them and serves them—until they must finally retreat to the outhouse where he has painted the rim of the seat red. From Bak Goong's perspective, the kind but "pesky" missionary women are, whether they know it or not, implicated in the power dynamics of the plantation system where converts "got extra days off on demon holidays" (1980, 112). Some of the workers pretend to be converts to get free food at the church services, but Bak Goong's more active performance breaks through the silence imposed upon him and gives voice to his creative expression. In a new land, the Chan story no longer reinforces the values of the larger society but becomes relevant to the present through Bak Goong's performance by subverting the dominant power structure. However, Bak Goong's performance reveals even more about social relationships than he intends. After all, the joke comes to fruition only when the missionary women's husbands see the red rings and beat their bottoms redder. Patriarchal social structures render the trick translatable across cultures. Ironically, Bak Goong makes use of the same forces that feminize and silence him and other Chinese men.[4] The critical discourse of Kingston's tale moves beyond the strategy of inverting the oppressed and the oppressor. Rather, it reveals social relations within both the center and the margin.[5] In the trick's reliance upon intersections between racial and gendered social positions, that of officially silenced Chinese men and that of the white Christian women, it resonates beyond the desires of the inferior for structural superiority.

The presence of Christianity is crucial to the narratives of Potchikoo and Bak Goong because it allows them to focus upon how interpreters within locatable social contexts expose the dominant culture's highest authority where it is least conscious of its abuses, where its social constructions have masqueraded as transcendence. Certain ironies of the tales might therefore be most resonant with Christians who are inclined to interpret the biblical narrative as favoring the lowest, the least, and the last. However, criticizing religious institutions is only one part of the larger role of trickster narratives, both in oral and textual cultures, in defining moral universes and revealing possibilities for their revision. When the ethnographer Barre Toelkin asked Navajo storyteller Yellowman why he tells Coyote stories, Yellowman replied, "'[I]f my children hear the stories they will grow up to be good people; if they don't hear them, they will turn out to be bad.' Why tell them to adults? 'Through the stories everything is made possible'" (Toelkin 1969, 221). According to Toelkin, Yellowman sees Coyote as an enabler whose antics bring certain ideas into a "field of possibility" (1969, 222). Similarly, Robert D. Pelton describes the social function of West African trickster stories:

> [Children] are not meant to imitate the trickster by rebelling, lying, or cheating, in greed, lust, irreverence, or incest, but they are meant to learn from him what a human really is: an imaginer of life. The purpose of the stories is to put an adult mind in a child's heart and a child's eye in an adult head. They mean to shape the imagination by revealing this image of the human power to mold the world by language and to compose human life by the willingness to engage every reality in intimate conversation. (980, 279)

In the stories of Erdrich and Kingston irrepressibly playful interpreters reveal to themselves and to readers that the world around them is created and therefore potentially transformable by creative beings. Again, the link between interpretation and transformation in written trickster narratives can be clarified by studies of oral narratives. For example, the contemporary stories function in ways similar to the oral stories of Brazil's Kalapalo described by Ellen Basso whose analysis emphasizes "the connections between the content of trickster stories, their tellings, and lives as actually lived; each is an inseparable dimension of a single process during which meaning, at once personal and social, is constructed" (Basso 1987, 4). Robert Pelton writes that the trickster in West Africa is "the reflection in the processes of the human mind not of a Jungian archetype, but of the world experienced as an active subject" (Pelton 1980, 257). Only by acknowledging the specificity of the narratives can Pelton understand the trickster as "a symbol of the transforming power of the human imagination" (1980, 256).

In addition to retaining many of the social functions of oral narratives, written trickster texts place the spoken word in dialogue with the written word. In textual cultures this most often means that the presence of the endlessly flexible and revisable oral word questions the authority and stability of the text. Indeed, as the stories of Potchikoo and Bak Goong demonstrate, trickster mediation between the literal and the figurative, the human and the divine, tends to emphasize the creative potential and responsibility of the interpreter.

Interpretation, orality, and the sacred text come together in the enigmatic trickster sermon on John 1:1 by the Right Reverend John Big Bluff Tosamah in N. Scott Momaday's novel *House Made of Dawn*. Momaday describes the sermon in contradictory terms that could describe a trickster narrative: "Conviction, caricature, callousness" (Momaday 1968, 92). The Right Reverend Big Bluff Tosamah believes that John should have stopped after that first sentence: " 'In the beginning was the Word. . . .' Brothers and Sisters, that was the Truth, the whole of it, the essential and eternal Truth, the bone and muscle of the Truth" (1968, 93). But by tying truth to human physicality and experience—by giving airy "other" local habitation—the trickster suggests the dialogic nature of his vision, which is whole even while specific and local. Ironically, Tosamah makes his point in a flood of words condemning John for making a sermon and a theology out of a simple truth revealed in his vision. Tosamah's interpretation of the gospel rests in his understanding of the role of language in oral cultures where sacred words form the basis of communal storytelling and retain their ability to transform earthly reality. "The white man," says Tosamah, "has diluted and multiplied the Word, and words have begun to close in on him. He is sated and insensitive; his regard for language—for the Word itself—as an instrument of creation has diminished nearly to the point of no return" (1968, 95). Those who understand the significance of oral language have a privileged perspective on John: "And from that day the Word has belonged to us, who have heard it for what it is, who have lived in fear and awe of it. In the Word was the beginning; 'In the beginning was the Word . . .'" (1968, 98).

Walter Ong's research reinforces Momaday's understanding of the Word in oral cultures as generative—an idea of language and sound as power and event (Ong 1982, 31). Ong suggests that most oral peoples consider language not simply as a sign of thought but as a mode of action. "Sound cannot be sounding without the use of power," he writes (1982, 32). "A hunter can see a buffalo, smell, taste, and touch a buffalo when a buffalo is completely inert, even dead, but if he hears a buffalo, he had better watch out: something is going on" (1982, 32). Oral utterance is dynamic. In the oral literatures of many cultures, tricksters bring about (often through their self-interested bungling) the creation of the visible world. Both oral and contemporary written trickster narratives maintain this relationship to the physical world by suggesting that it as well as human culture must be continually recreated through storytelling. For Christian readers, trickster narratives might therefore provide models for the transformation of the world that are rooted in play and that balance Christian traditions of social change rooted in hard work and earnestness.

By reflecting and refracting our understanding of both human and other-than-human worlds, trickster narratives place active storytellers and interpreters within a web of relationships that must be continually enacted. Within this web that is larger than any person or perspective, they reveal, critique, and suggest possibilities for action. William Hynes and Thomas J. Steele describe how cultures of the American Southwest meld biblical stories of the Apostle Peter together with indigenous trickster narratives. To explain the significance of such folkloric expansions of biblical material Hynes and Steele look beyond an interpretation of tricksters as "social safety valves" that reaffirm existing orders by releasing pressure caused by constrictive belief systems. They write that "beyond the surface affirmation of a given belief system there is a broader, meta-affirmation that life is more than its socially constructed representations. . . . [T]he trickster makes the cyclopian eye of monoculturality swivel in its socket; he roils the tribal waters of life lest they go stagnant" (Hynes and Steele 1993, 170). Kenneth Lincoln suggest that "a truly sacred world allows for a sense of mockery and play that turns the weight of the world around" (Lincoln 1993, 49). Gerald Vizenor writes, "[T]ricksters and warrior clowns have stopped more evil violence with their wit than lovers with their lust and fools with their power and rage" (Vizenor 1990, 15).

Divine Comedies

> The tribal trickster is a liberator and healer in a narrative, a comic
> sign, communal significance and a discourse with the imagination.
> —Gerald Vizenor

Few contemporary writers depend more than the Anishinaabe author Gerald Vizenor upon the reader's willingness to engage language as a medium of transformation. Throughout his three decades of writing, Vizenor has worked out something of a theory of trickster discourse and aesthetics and sought ways that writing can approximate the performative effects of oral storytelling. The Anishinaabe scholar Kimberly Blaeser explains this with regard to his haiku. First, Vizenor's haiku mimic oral traditions by remaining "unfixed," that is by advertising absences and requiring readers' responses (Blaeser 1993, 348). A poem does more than give voice to a salient moment or image, its power "lies in its engagement of the reader's imagination and its ability to move the reader beyond the world to an individual moment of illumination" (1993, 351). The haiku dissolves or deconstructs as "art" and transforms into experience (1993, 354). Second, Blaeser points out that Vizenor uses in his haiku methods similar to traditional tribal trickster tales "to shake up the self-satisfied reader" (1993, 361). Vizenor's poems not only present an image, they evaluate implicitly as they reveal the human flaws of his audience and question accepted social orderings. Experiencing Vizenor's haiku from *Matsushima: Pine Islands* will make Blaeser's argument clearer:

Sliding in the loft
The mice complained all Winter
About the course hay.

The old man
Admired the scarecrow's clothes
Autumn morning.

Against the zoo fence
Zebras and Sunday school children
Hearing about Africa.

Vizenor himself writes, "The reader becomes the active listener, the creator, set free in a wordless natural place" (1984a, pages unnumbered). Vizenor's concern, exemplified in his haiku, with inviting readers of his trickster texts to their own experiences also manifests itself in his prose. His novel *Dead Voices* collects a series of stories envisioned from the perspectives of animals finding ways to survive in urban landscapes. Vizenor frames the book with a troubled narrator's account of how he heard stories from an old trickster, Bagese, whose stories come alive in her words and in the mirrors of her dirty Oakland apartment. The unnamed narrator begins the book by telling us that he has written the stories down and published them against Bagese's wishes and his own promises. Readers turn the page at the end of the narrator's chapter to find Bagese's transcribes stories.

If Bagese's warning at the outset places the narrator in a problematic position, it does the same for readers, especially those with any knowledge at all of the history of appropriation and misleading translation of Native American words.[6] Readers cannot enter *Dead Voices* through its frame without being implicated in the power dynamics of reading: the book traps readers like the double-binding sign "Don't read this!" In being displaced from their comfort zones, readers are placed in a relationship of difference to the text. Yet in the advice Bagese offers when she tells the narrator to imagine his own stories, the book suggests a way for readers to continue with increased awareness: "The secret, she told me, was not to pretend, but to see and hear the real stories behind the word, the voices of the animals in me, not the definitions of the words alone" (Vizenor 1992, 7). By suggesting that the narrator create his own stories, the trickster Bagese makes it possible for him to understand not just her stories but also his own desires with regard to her texts. To the extent that he is able to create his own tellings and figure himself in his readings, the narrator may like Bagese have "the power and the stories to bring back the dead, even dead voices at a great distance . . . to transform the world" (1992, 19). And in a wonderful conditional to keep us wondering about relationships between the figurative and the literal, the narrator adds, "at least in my mind" (1992, 19). Elsewhere, Vizenor writes that "[t]he most active readers become obverse tricksters, the waver of a coin in a tribal striptease" (1988, x).

Readers, like the narrator, may come to see tricksters in their mirrored image looking back. This does not mean that the difference of the text is sublimated or effaced; rather, active readers of shifting texts may come to know how they tell stories in the act of interpreting. As with Vizenor's haiku, readers who are counterpart with or complement to the trickster move, compelled by the text toward their own experiences. Instead of trying to eliminate the difference of the text or appropriate it as their own, readers begin to understand their relationship to it.

Gustavo Perez Firmat refers to the act of reading as a liminal activity; the critical act of limning notes in the margins is by nature eccentric (Perez Firmat 1986, xxi). As an antistructural moment and place in which values can be scrutinized (Turner 1969, 67), liminal reading becomes the source of recreative power. Trickster texts invite this liminality and cause us to continually question the knowledge and motivations we bring to texts as well as what we wish to take from them. Tricksters in texts alert us to the ways texts invite and repel readers at once. In making us more aware of the stories we tell in our marginal scribblings, trickster texts remind us of both the dangers and possibilities for revelation in our readings.

Notes

1. I include within the label "postcolonial literature" texts from North American indigenous cultures as well as those from the African diaspora.
2. Henry Louis Gates, Jr., writes, "A partial list of these qualities might include individuality, satire, parody, irony, magic, indeterminacy, open-endedness, ambiguity, sexuality, chance, uncertainty, disruption and reconciliation, betrayal and loyalty, closure and disclosure, encasement and rupture" (1988, 6). William Bright's table of contents forms a list: "Coyote the wanderer—Bricoleur—Glutton—lecher—thief—cheat—outlaw—spoiler—loser—clown—pragmatist—(horny) old man—survivor." Dell Hymes writes, "be-

fuddled, besmirched, beleaguered, belittled, begetter—/ profane, prophylac-
tic, prolix, procrustean precursor—/ WANDERER / MISCREANT / FORNI-
CATOR / BUNGLER / PRONOUNCER—" (Lincoln 1993, 133).

3. Since Gates limits his study of indigenous tricksters to those of Africa, he passes over Doueihi's precedent in reading traditional oral stories through contemporary critical theory.

4. For debate concerning masculine images in Asian American literature, see Cheung, Chin, and Wong.

5. Although Gates's tale of the signifying monkey is not structurally analo-gous to Bak Goong's trick, Gates's comments may pertain here: "While other scholars have interpreted the Monkey tales against the binary opposition between black and white in American society, to do so is to ignore the *trinary* forces of the Monkey, the Lion, and the Elephant. To read Monkey tales as a simple allegory of the black's political oppression is to ignore the hulking presence of the Elephant, the crucial third item of the depicted action" (Gates 1988, 55).

6. Vizenor has written frequently concerning the consequences of the textual fixity imposed upon tribal stories in translation. In the preface to *Narrative Chance*, he writes, "The immanent pleasures of an aural performance are unbodied in translation, the tribal experiences that were heard in stories, and natural variations on stories, are transformed in publications that are seen as cultural information, some with imposed significance. . . . [P]ostmodern is a pose in a language game that would convert the institutional power of trans-lation—what is seen and published is not a representation of what is heard or remembered in oral cultures" (1989a, x).

Works Cited

Babcock-Abrahams, Barbara. 1985. "'A Tolerated Margin of Mess': The Trickster and His Tales Reconsidered." *Critical Essays on Native American Literature.* Ed. Andrew Wiget. Boston: Hall. 153–85.

Bakhtin, M. M. 1981. *The Dialogic Imagination: Tour Essays by M. M. Bakhtin.* Ed. Michael Holquist. Trans. Caryl Emerson and Michael Holquist. Austin: University of Texas Press.

Basso, Ellen. 1987. *In Favor of Deceit: A Study of Tricksters in an Amazonian Society.* Tucson: University of Arizona Press.

Blaeser, Kimberly M. 1993. "The Multiple Traditions of Gerald Vizenor's Haiku Poetry." *New Voices in Native American Literary Criticism.* Ed. Arnold Krupat. Washington, DC: Smithsonian Institution. 344-369.

Blue Cloud, Peter. 1982. *Elderberry Flute Songs: Contemporary Coyote Tales.* Trumansburg, NY: Crossing.

Bright, William. 1993. *A Coyote Reader.* Berkeley and Los Angeles: University of California Press.

Brueggemann, Walter. 1993. *Texts Under Negotiation: The Bible and Postmodern Imagination.* Minneapolis: Fortress.

Cheung, King-Kok. 1990. "The Woman Warrior Versus The Chinaman Pacific: Must a Chinese American Critic Choose Between Feminism and Heroism?" In *Conflicts in Feminism.* Ed. Marianne Hirsch and Evelyn Fox Keller. New York: Routledge. 234–51.

Chin, Frank. 1991. "Come All Ye Asian American Writers of the Real and the Fake." *The Big Aiiieeeee!: An Anthology of Chinese American and Japanese American Literature.* Ed. Jeffery Paul Chan, Frank Chin, Lawson Fusao Inada, and Shawn Wong. New York: Meridian. 1–61.

Clifford, James and George E. Marcus, eds. 1986. *Writing Culture: The Poetics and Politics of Ethnography.* Berkeley and Los Angeles: University of California Press.

Doueihi, Anne. 1984. "Trickster: On Inhabiting the Space Between Discourse and Story." *Soundings: An Interdisciplinary Journal* 67 (3): 283–311.

Ellison, Ralph. 1981. "Change the Joke and Slip the Yoke." *Mother Wit from the Laughing Barrel: Readings in the Interpretation of Afro-American Folklore.* Ed. Alan Dundes. New York: Garland. 56–64.

Erdrich, Louise. 1989. *Baptism of Desire.* New York: Harper and Row.

Gallagher, Susan VanZanten, ed. 1994. *Postcolonial Literature and the Biblical Call for Justice.* Jackson: University Press of Mississippi.

Gates, Henry Louis, Jr. 1988. *The Signifying Monkey: A Theory of Afro-American Literary Criticism.* New York: Oxford University Press.

hooks, bell. 1995. "Postmodern Blackness." In *The Truth About the Truth: Deconfusing and Re-constructing the Postmodern World.* Ed. Walter Truett Anderson. New York: Putnam. 117–24.

Hutcheon, Linda. 1988. *A Poetics of Postmodernism: History, Theory, Fiction.* New York: Routledge.

Hynes, William J. and Thomas J. Steele, S.J. 1993. "Saint Peter: Apostle Transfigured into Trickster." *Mythical Trickster Figures: Contours, Contexts, and Criti-*

cisms. Eds. William J. Hynes and William G. Doty. Tuscaloosa: University of Alabama Press. 159–73.

Johnston, Basil. 1995. *The Manitous*. New York: HarperCollins.

Kingston, Maxine Hong. 1976 [1989]. *The Woman Warrior: Memoirs of a Girlhood Among Ghosts*. New York: Vintage.

————. 1980 [1989]. *China Men*. New York: Vintage.

Krupat, Arnold. 1992. *Ethnocriticism: Ethnology, History, Literature*. Berkeley and Los Angeles: University of California Press.

Lincoln, Kenneth. 1993. *Indi'n Humor: Bicultural Play in Native America*. New York: Oxford University Press.

Lundin, Roger. 1993. *The Culture of Interpretation: Christian Faith and the Postmodern World*. Grand Rapids, MI: Eerdmans.

Momaday, N. Scott. 1968. *House Made of Dawn*. New York: Harper & Row.

Ong, Walter J. 1982. *Orality and Literacy: The Technologizing of the Word*. New York: Methuen.

Pelton, Robert D. 1980. *The Trickster in West Africa: A Study of Mythic Irony and Sacred Delight*. Berkeley and Los Angeles: University of California Press.

Perez Firmat, Gustavo. 1986. *Liminality and Literature: Festive Readings in the Hispanic Tradition*. Durham, NC: Duke University Press.

Rosaldo, Renato. 1989. *Culture & Truth: The Remaking of Social Analysis*. Boston: Beacon.

Rose, Wendy. 1993. "Trickster." In Bright, 88.

Schneiders, Sandra M. 1989. "Does the Bible Have a Postmodern Message?" In *Postmodern Theology: Christian Faith in a Pluralist World*. Ed. Frederic B. Burnham. San Francisco: Harper. 56–73.

Toelkin, Barre J. 1969. "The 'Pretty Language' of Yellowman: Genre, Mode, and Texture in Navajo Coyote Narratives." *Genre* 2 (3): 211–35.

Turner, Victor. 1969. *The Ritual Process: Structure and Anti-Structure*. Ithaca: Cornell University Press.

Vizenor, Gerald. 1984a. *Matsushima: Pine Islands*. Minneapolis: Nodin.

————. 1984b. *The People Named the Chippewa: Historical Narratives*. Minneapolis: University of Minnesota Press.

————. 1988. *The Trickster of Liberty: Tribal Heirs to a Wild Baronage*. Minneapolis: University of Minnesota Press.

————, ed. 1989a. *Narrative Chance: Postmodern Discourse on Native American Indian Literatures*. Albuquerque: University of New Mexico Press.

————. 1989b. "Trickster Discourse: Comic Holotropes and Language Games." In Vizenor 1989a, 187–211.

————. 1978 [1990]. *Bearheart: The Heirship Chronicles*. Minneapolis: University of Minnesota Press.

————. 1992. *Dead Voices: Natural Agonies in the New World*. Norman: University of Oklahoma Press.

————. 1993. "Ruins of Representation Shadow Survivance and the Literature of Dominance." *American Indian Quarterly* 17 (1): 7–30.

Wong, Sau-ling Cynthia. 1993. *Reading Asian American Literature: From Necessity to Extravagance*. Princeton: Princeton University Press.

8

Whole "Altarity":
Toward a Feminist A/Theology

Ned Dykstra Hayes

she is an ocean emptying
she is no longer a part of his body
no longer a word in his language
— Jessica Simpson, "All Women Write Left-Handed"

What are we to feel towards Mark C. Taylor's a/theologizing? The style of his texts implies that we ought to feel something; emotion permeates his parapraxis. His a/theology begins—if he begins—with *Deconstructing Theology*, where the deconstructive process lays bare critical problems in "the death of God, the disappearance of the self, the erasure of the (A)uthor, and the interplay of absence and presence."[1] Taylor then moves into further deconstructive examinations of theology, literature, art, science, popular music, architecture, and media philosophy. The play of his language traces the presence of continual absence in the ontotheological. The tracing of this absent image reveals No-thing in the sacred; he writes that "God is an aftereffect or symptom of the sacred" (1994, 608). Through an "erring," "mazing," "Bacchic" (Bakhtinic?) carnival of language Taylor explores a divine figure which is revealed within the identity loss of all subjects (1987, 125, 130–81).

Taylor tells us to enjoy this experience: he speaks of *jouissance* and semen, of clowning and ecstatic laughter (1984, 117, 129; 1987, 49–50;1990, 144; 1993, 114). He states that he wishes to radicalize "the process of incarnation by redeeming the body [of text] itself" (1984, 196). Therefore his texts "plunge into the horizontality of pure surface" in which language is shifting, friable, perverse, comedic, hilarious, carnal, orgiastic, intoxicated, delirious, bewildering, stupefied, and deluded (1984, 158–69). Only through such interminable play can a postmodern rebirth of the sacred occur (Meltzer and Tracy 1994, 14). Thus, he urges his readers to joy in the corporeality of language, to embrace the Other which is ab(sense). Yet beneath these cries of pleasure, a profound discomfort permeates Taylor's experience of the Other.

This discomfort can be understood through a particular trope that Taylor employs to describe his a/theological activity. In *Nots* he focuses upon the body's "linguisticality," arguing that the lacunae of "the body . . . must be read as a text" (1993, 221). Through the symmetry of logical identity, he thereby treats *text* as body. After God, the subject, and the author have ceased to exist, there is indeed *Il n'y a pas dehors texte* (Derrida 1976, 158).[2] Taylor is left only with the inarguable materiality of writing itself in his corpus of texts. Deconstructed text seems to function as erotogenic body, horrifying to him in its riotous secretion of contradictory signifiers. For Taylor, the "sickness of language" becomes a "diseased" corpse, which continually bleeds, breaks, and dies before his eyes (1984, 171; 1990, 64, 230–32; 1993, 215–55). In *Disfiguring*, for example, he physically enters an archi(text) of breakage and absence. He describes that experience as "haunting," "inhuman," even "terrifying" (1992, 272). This feeling of terror seems at odds with his playful attempts to show that all ontotheological bodies are fields of such (absense) signifiers.

In *Powers of Horror*, Julia Kristeva identifies such a reaction to uncontrollable semiotic corporeality as "abjection." In simplified form, the process of abjection is the behavior of expelling "impure" disorderly material from the structured "proper" body. It is the symbolic's necessary attempt to reject or expel its own attachments to corporeality. The abject is not classifiable, for it is both inside and outside the body, violating boundaries, structures, and identity. Within this psychoanalytic register, Taylor's voice functions as a speaking "subject recoiling from its own materiality," fearful of the sundering of textual flesh. When confronted with the abyss of "altarity" (Taylor [1987] uses this spelling), it seems that he is brought in contact with the abject itself; he is tied again to a pre-objectal "maternal entity."[3] His "terrified" reaction is an attempt to repress those maternal, liminal associations. In fact, given the context of the a/theological motive, Taylor's fearful abjective reaction may demonstrate a continuing penumbra of phallogocentric tendencies within the shifting limen of a/theology.

In order to trace this tendency, this reading will focus first upon Kristeva's most extreme example of the abject—a corpse emptied of signifying life—a body. Next, we will explore the signifying flow of blood's semantics to demonstrate that Taylor's repressive action toward the abject is not the only possible a/theological reaction. Entering through the body and blood, an "a/theological christology" of sorts, we will then follow Kristeva's conception of (O)ther poetic writings that strategically employ feminine abjection. In readings of Hélenè Cixous, Ntozake Shange, and Lucille Clifton we see finally demonstrated feminine a/theologies that become whole altarity by embracing the threshold of the abject.

Taylor does not come close to embracing the abject. In a chapter on

Paralectics, for example, he avoids it. This ninth chapter of *Tears* begins by quoting two passages about rats that "emerged from the city's underground conscience as the demonized Other." The quotations go on to describe rats as "transgressors of boundaries," semiotics of "fascination as well as horror" (1990, 123; see also Serres 1982, 12). Rats here bear all the signs of Kristevan abjection. The rats act as Other, as semiotic chora, emerging from archaic corporeality, giving rise to the fascination of desire and to revulsion. Yet what disruptive abject do the rats represent? In the course of the chapter Taylor discusses many semantic elements, but he seems to almost forcibly ignore the semiotic of the rat as consumer of dead flesh, as a parasite on corpses. It seems it is not the rotting physical corpses of life that Taylor evinces abjection to, although such bodies appear throughout his books.[4] Yet his repeated references to the dead subvertly attest to the nature of the abjection that disturbs him. After stating that "there is no system without parasites," Taylor makes the connection explicit by placing a stream of small identical rat figures through the chapter, breaking apart the text (1990, 124–44). The rats are on the page; the rats are parasites on this textual body. The text is the disruptive semiotic that Taylor elides. In fact, as in our earlier glossing of Taylor's emotional reaction to his work, the text itself produces abjection in this "author."

Taylor's reaction to the text becomes credible when we remember that according to a/theological readings, the text is a "radical christology" embodying the "incarnate word" (1984, 158). It is the corpse-like site of God's death. Physical death does not seem to have abjective power over the author; instead, it is the putrefying carcass of God that causes him discomfort. As the divine corpus breaks apart, Taylor states that he is "anguished," and "distressed," even "revolted."[5] The monumentally rotting body of phallogocentric text is to him what Kristeva calls "the most sickening of [abject] wastes." In his horror, Taylor repeatedly identifies with Nietzsche as he invokes the abject fear of God's murder.[5] Such a reaction is a defense, according to Kristeva, against the corpse's psychic threat against the subject's boundaries:

> For the border encroaches upon everything. . . . The border has become object. The corpse seen without God [—or the corpse as God—] and outside of science, is the utmost of abjection. It is death infecting life. Abject. It is something rejected from which one does not part, from which one does not protect oneself *as from an object.* (Kristeva 1982, 3–4; italics mine)

The corpse is an intolerable abject because the body before death represented the boundary line between life and death—between meaning and nonmeaning. Now the body's death has infected the flow of all text. Once the corpse becomes object, the speaking subject has lost the possibility of feeling any anchor in the object; "The release of desire . . . decenters the subject" (Taylor 1993, 196). The textual corpse encroaches on the speaking subject's identity and capacity for desire. Without desire, we pass into an abyss of nonmeaning. In Lacanian terms, the *objet petit a*, the object of the drives, is supposed to stop up this lack the subject feels at the appearance of the *"M-Other."*[7] When the border—that is, death—becomes the object, then the subject's anchor in "objective reality" is repugnant and "infectious." As Kristeva points out, "It is no longer "I" who expel, "I" is expelled" (1982, 3).[8] If Taylor continues to feel "disgust" and "horror" toward the divine corpus he feeds on, he thus demonstrates an attachment and identification with that body. The living "self" is caught up in disgust at the Other, at the materiality of death. Abjection occurs now, at the moment that the *objet a* activity can no longer stop the lack. Unanchored, the subject attempts to expel, or reject, his own identity. When abjection appears, the speaking subject is thrown to this threshold of unspeakable loss.

A/theological acts force the subject to disappear in an act that is similar to Kristevan abjection. In fact, Taylor mentions that among feminine thinker, "it is probably Kristeva who comes closest to what I have been trying to do."[9] In this light, we can observe that the a/theological process questions identity in much the same way as Kristeva postulates that an abject "identity catastrophe causes" God, the text, the self, and "the Name to topple over into the unnameable that one imagines as femininity, non-language, body" (Kristeva 1989, 187). But the destruction of naming does not imply that the abject Other must necessarily be repressed or expelled. Instead of a(void)ing the abject, we can balance on this limen between femininity and catastrophe. Kristeva suggests, "We, as feminine, live on that border, crossroads beings, crucified beings." The latter, feminine, borderland of alterity is "natural" observes Kristeva, "for such an Other has come out of myself, and is myself" (1989, 189).[10] Those who exist on this abject threshold construe them "selves" as Other and continue to produce an endless stream of possible Others, of Otherness that flows in and out of the words of the text. The liminal abject is a body that is always flowing, continuously secreting fecund signifiers. Taylor's text also locates this site in the feminine when he comments that "the death of God the Father is the sacralization of woman" (Taylor 1993, 202). The further we move from a revalidation of the subject, the further we travel into the flow of feminine mat(t)er.

However, we have seen that as Taylor's a/theology approaches altarity, his activity shows signs of abject dis-ease. Yet this fearful tendency toward avoidance and repression is not a function of the a/theological motive. The borderland is not a site of what Kristeva characterizes as "symbolic" phallic control; in fact, Taylor understands that "[f]eminine power disarms men, thereby rendering all Boy Toys [male phalluses] impotent." Perhaps, as Taylor often implies, the erring, phallic marks on a/theology may be a Mark.[11] Therefore, if we are to continue to read a/theologically, we must be willing to erase and un-read phallogocentric presumptions that continue to limit and conceal abjection. Because of these assumptions, abjection in Taylor's a/theology pervades the text as a subverted, repressed trace. As we have read, his work sometimes signals the textual moment when abjection is about to bleed its fearful seepage into his text. In this kind of moment, Kristeva observes that the abject discharges its power in a stream "of conflict [which] attempts to release the hold of maternal entity" (Kristeva 1982, 13; italics in original). Therefore, if our un-reading is to bring this trace of a sign from the oblique margin to the textual surface, we must focus on a site of overt abjection. One of these sites is located in Taylor's (mis)reading of Kristeva's reading of the semiotics of blood.

Menstrual blood is one of Kristeva's primary examples of the abject. The flow of its wound signifies an "umbilical" debt of life that is never able to be paid. Yet even as Taylor quotes her metaphor of birth—the "wound, which gives birth"—he avoids the maternal semiotic of blood from that fertile "wound." In a display of castration anxiety, Taylor represses the sexual abject by characterizing the "dissemination of the word" as "dismemberment inflict[ing]" incurable pain and loss (Taylor 1984, 120). Phallic fear continues to haunt his readings; there is no regeneration of textual life. "Blood," he states, "is associated with violence, and by extension, with death" (1984, 91; 1987, 173). Seminal images serve Taylor as an overt way of once again repressing the feminine Other, and subliminally reinscribing phallogocentrism. Repeatedly, he describes the generation of text and the act of creation as a violently phallic dehiscence, "dripping with blood and semen" (1984, 88, 92, 103, 117, 120, 142, 173, ff; 1987, 170). There is no multiple orgasmic play, no contact with vaginal secretions or blood, and—of course—no vaginal orgasm at the joyful pain of birth. The pen(is) in one man's hand; thus, the generation of text becomes "violence," and "dismemberment." Taylor's a/theology joins the empty body of language and the specter of death when he fearfully tells us that sexual flow is deadly: *"Eros* and *thanatos* mix in blood" (1987, 170, 172). Through this trope, he follows other poststructuralist thinkers by performing a "death-fuck" with language.[12]

In contrast, Kristeva's semantics of blood does not privilege death. Instead, she observes a feminine flow which is "a continuous separation, a division of the very flesh. And consequently a division of language—and it has always been so" (Kristeva 1989, 188). This partition is not a violent dismemberment, but a birthing process in which language itself generates new signifiers. Texts bleed in a libidinous gush. And in fact, Taylor follows his stated *thanatos* abjection by acknowledging that other semantics are present in Kristeva's description of this flow: "[B]lood also refers to women, to fertility, to the promise of fecundity . . . a fascinating semantic crossroads" (Kristeva 1982, 96, 116; quoted in Taylor 1987, 173; italics in original). Yet his a/theological texts fail to follow up on this "fascinating" semantic. Instead, his text dwells on "defilement" and "deadly influence" (Taylor 1987, 168–72). Elsewhere, when he examines the carnality of the body, Taylor entirely avoids the life-giving semantic of blood as fertile *auter*. Instead, we observe only a "body that eats, drinks, shits, pisses, and fucks."[13] The Lacanian essentializing of sexual difference to a fear of phallic castration represses menstruation as abjection that cannot be named. Thus, birth's incarnation and menstruation's flow are ignored. However, Kristeva's reading finds such semantic implications absolutely necessary in order to understand the power of abjection. The body and blood are the site where the "cessation of life and vitality all come together" (Kristeva 1980, 238–40). In the semiotic of giving birth, there is a breach in the symbolic, a *jouissance* which flows beyond phallogocentric control.

Kristeva acknowledges that this breach is threatening to identity. Yet there is more than fear in her reading. Curiously, in its chapter on "Kristeva," *Altarity* elides the complete text of her commentary on blood as the semantic of sexual difference:

> [D]ecay, infection, disease, corpse, etc.[,] stand for the danger to identity that comes from without; the ego is threatened by non-ego . . . life by death. Menstrual blood, on the contrary, stands for the danger issuing from within identity (social or sexual [or textual]); it threatens the relationship between sexes . . . and through internalization, the identity of each sex. (1987, 169–72)[14]

The body's natural flow of signifiers no longer functions as a threat of abjection from without, from *thanatos* and decay. Blood becomes for Kristeva that fluctuating boundary between life and non-life. Sexual identity is founded here upon the possibility of the Other, on the generation of the other as a function of *différance*. The flow of menstrual blood becomes the material embodiment of a threshold between existence and alterity which is other yet not entirely separate. Because it creates the possibility of M-Other, the semiotic of blood threatens identity with alterity.[15] Thus, the feminine reader can see "the other as arbitrary," and "inevitable," but not deadly.   In fact, Kristeva tells us there may be M-Other reactions— ways of making strategic use of archaic maternal ties in order to explore the possibilities of alterity as abjection.

Instead of logocentric thinkers that reinscribe the phallus even on that feminine limen, Kristeva suggests turning toward "feminine" "poets and artisans of sorts who tap that pre-verbal" abjection by playing within the flowing signifiers of words. "Poetic language," says Kristeva, is "contrary to . . . the univocity of verbal message [*ton* logocentric *texte*], a reconciliation with what murder as well as names were separated from" (1982, 61– 62).[16] The separation she speaks of here is part(ur)ition from the maternal semiotic. The "reconciliation" does not incorporate the other but rather allows *(la) langue* to represent the abject to the symbolic. Such representation refuses presence, as can be seen in Kristeva's "revolutionary" linkage of "madness, holiness, and poetry" (Kristeva 1982, 10-11). Ab-sense becomes sacred through poetic language. Writers who don't speak of the abject as such, but refuse to name it thus refuse to establish a grounded structure in opposition toward the abject. They speak around it, about it, but never of it as "object." Kristeva points out that such a "poet . . . challenges the closure of meaning by bringing to light [opening] this 'space' prior to the sign" (1980, 281).[17] By tearing wombs in words, feminine writing refuses to be co-opted by the symbolic's necessary distance from the M-Other.   Texts inscribed by Hélène Cixous, Ntozake Shange, and Lucille Clifton are useful here as examples of writing that challenge phallogocentric closure. On the borderland between the symbolic and the semiotic, these artists push against a permeable membrane of abjection, and trace the absent space of feminine a/theologies.

In the theology of not, altarity is not only other but feminine other; "altar," Taylor tells us, "signifies the female pudendum" (1993, 204). Thus, a/theological activity figures an-other locale not only sacredly fertile, but also as a nakedly feminine place. Hélène Cixous's "Laugh of the Medusa" becomes such a fertile site in its very title (1993, 260–61). The laughter of the "medusa" is the female genitalia in grotesque, parodic ecstasy, in laughter, dis(playing) its carnality in a profane mockery of containment and stricture.   Such a laughing alterity is produced not from the subject, but from the abject. As Kristeva writes, paradoxical laughter which echoes out of abjection is "[n]either request nor desire, it is an invocation, an anaclisis" toward the maternal other (Kristeva 1980, 281–84). This invocation is not directed at a present divine, but towards the sacred as an open flowing space: *la mèr(e)*.[18] With writers like Cixous "we are ourselves sea, and can know the other without violence, bypassing loss, struggle" (Cixous 1976, 260). By refusing to struggle against loss, Cixous's *l'écriture feminine* flows continually, creating a place that flows over and out of limits. Her discourses function as "witnesses to the perviousness of the limit" (Kristeva 1982, 61–62).[19] Continually, she inscribes that limit between the maternal semiotic and the containment of the symbolic. Her work flows in and out of abjection, and thus takes us into the eye of a whole altarity:

> We're stormy, and that which is ours breaks loose from us without our fearing any debilitation. Our glances, our smiles, are spent; laughs exude from our mouths; our blood flows and we extend ourselves without ever reaching an end; we never hold back. (Cixous 1976, 248)

To release oneself into the storm of altarity is to break free from the tracings of ontotheological structures. It is also to break the self into a constant spill and flow of spent substance, to bleed "without ever reaching an end." Abjection is recognized in substance that exudes from the body, and in the semiotic of *la mère*. Yet it is not repressed. Instead, Cixous's text becomes an active womb of generating signifiers that give way.

Cixous says that this feminine textual process is an act that is never "afraid of lacking" the subject, because it is lack itself. In fact, such an activity, which continually gives way, allows the subject to disappear with no threat, for it expects no return. Such "feminine" activity can be characterized as a textual *agape*. "Even when appearing as agape, the sacred is not a subject" (Taylor 1994, 607). *Agape* "is" only in its own lacking, its emptying. This process becomes a place of uniquely sacred, even divine activity, as Keiji Nishitani notes. In fact, one can see such in such a self-releasing site as the self-lacking giving of God, *kenósis*. Nishitani describes the absent Christ emptying into transcendence as "[s]elf-emptying, ego-negating love . . . agape, that loves even enemies. . . . [I]n a word, it is 'making oneself empty'" (Nishitani 1983, 58-59).[20] *Kenósis* does not give emotion toward an(other). It is not a nostalgia for the lost subject. Instead, this laugh is an outflow toward what cannot be held or named. On the feminine limen, "Love, here, is only for the impossible" (Kristeva 1989, 202). For as soon as an other is conceived and appears, it no longer exists. The womb laughs on, bleeds on, gives birth again and again, without taking, utterly without care or cure. Names and words disappear into it, and emerge in rebirth. Cixous plunges into the abject abyss, laughingly dragging all down with her into the wound of joyful spent giving. In this she joins that madman of poets Zarathustra when she acts in "[j]oy that accepts everlasting flow" (Nietzsche 1957, 38).

In Cixous's work, the a/theological sacred cannot be held onto, cannot be sensed, and thus cannot be present except in the flow of absence. This negated ab(sense) allows us to experience what Derrida calls "*une différence affirmative*" and characterizes as that which *échappe dun saut et vienne signer en riant ce qu'elle laisse faire et défiler*" (Derrida 1977, 119). [21] Only and always in releasing do we laugh, and only in laughing do we begin to trace and erase the sign of that which does not exist except in absence:

> Flying is woman's gesture: flying in language and making it fly. . . . [F]or centuries we've been able to possess anything only by flying; we've lived in flight. . . . It's no accident that *voler* has a double meaning, that it plays on each of them and thus throws off the agents of sense. It's no accident: women take after birds and robbers. . . . They (*illes*) go by, fly the coop, take pleasure in jumbling the order of space, in disorienting it, in changing . . . dislocating things and values, *breaking them all up*, *emptying* structures, and turning all . . . upside down. (Cixous 1976, 258; italics mine)

The feminine flies, creating absence behind, seeing absence in front, giving without caring about the balance of power, the taking of subject away. Thus, Cixous uses *illes* to describe the feminine, for once we move into the abject we create absence, like all birds, and yet once we come into the phallogocentric place, we bring absence, as robbers, taking away. All "things and values" must be broken, and are broken, including the language and the self. "[T]he element of self is broken through again and again."[22] The revelatory nature of this re(*voler*)ution is nearly indescribable. In her "revolutionary" terminology, Kristeva writes that language only contains this *agape* when "the love of God and for God resides in a gap: the broken space made explicit" (1989, 186). This space of broken language is the feminine membrane between symbolic and the semiotic.

Ntozake Shange creates her feminine texts upon the same pervious threshold where language breaks. Often, it is "feminine" in the way Kristeva describes such w(riot)ing as "the most immediately erotic, sexual, and desiring mainspring of abjection" (1982, 20). Appropriately, Shange situates herself in a textual borderland; she is a dramatist who will not admit to writing drama. She condemns language as a constraining "straightjacket over the minds of all," and illustrates divine abjection by writing "chorapoems" (1981, xii). Shange's poetry continually shatters the forms of English language, and breaks propriety, "turning all *à l'envers*" in constant breakage. Like Cixous, Shange finds in the repeated loss of the divine not a deadly wound, but the bleeding into life of constant absenting. Shange speaks of the wounding/wombing of language in her poem "We Need a God Who Bleeds Now" (Shange 1983, 51):

> we need a god who bleeds now
> a god whose wounds are not
> some small male vengeance
> some pitiful concession to humility
> a desert swept with drying marrow in honor of the lord

Shange's poem is not a plea for "a god" who bleeds to appear to women; it is not a poem of desire or loss. If we remember "To try to lose loss," Taylor looked into the closed wall of a desert absence like that in Shange's last line. In that text, he found only "terror" (Taylor 1992, 186). Yet this poem is a cry for the place of the language to recognize what Shange already knows: that "small male vengeance" is no true "honor of the [ab-sent] lord." Instead, she (un)names a divinity who keeps on bleeding, whose "wounds" never close. Shange's god does not lose anything in giving. Shange wishes to "break this place" of language open, as she has emphasized on numerous occasions. But instead of fearing the loss of abjection, Shange tells us to look beyond the desert, into the abject blood which signifies fertile life:

> we need a god who bleeds
> spreads her lunar vulva & showers us in shades of scarlet
> thick & warm like the breath of her
> our mothers tearing to let us in
> this place breaks open
> like our mothers bleeding
> [. . . .]   / i am
> not wounded i am bleeding to life
>
> we need a god who bleeds now
> whose wounds are not the end of anything[23]

As we have seen, the abjection of birthing blood represents the embodi-ment of that abject, semiotic link between mother and child. By illustrating the sacred as an enactment of that link, Shange's poem does not refuse abjection, but embraces it. Yet the activity of her "god" is not an incorpo-ration of the abject, because her flow is not constrained within the body; it "showers" outward. It is also not wholly without the body, because the "vulva" continues to bleed its own substance, tearing "to let us in" to her fertile language. As Kristeva writes, abjection thus is located in such ambiguous merger/ruptures, which is "the non-distinctiveness of inside and outside unnameable, a border passable in both directions by pleasure and pain" (1982, 61). The hymenal field is a place of birthing, full of the emotion of change and discovery. Shange's poem exploits and re(presents) the maternal semiotic by finding in her a sacred absent space. "A gift that is never (a) present cannot be received" (Taylor 1994, 606). The "breaking open" of this place locates the present, or its presence, outside of the naming of logocentrism.

The gifting flow of the a/theological may be the reason, in fact, that deconstructed text allows us to see, from "the vantage of laughter," "on the other side of nostalgia . . . Heideggerian hope." And Derrida states this "without excluding any of its implications" (quoted in Taylor 1986, 420; emphasis in original). What are the implications of hope? *Espérance* in the English translation is "hope," derived from the Old English *hopa,* and the German *hoffa:* the expectation of something desired. "Hope" *(hopa)* also means a "bay," or "haven"; a place you go into for safety and sustenance, a safe and sacred place much like that threshold of abjection where Shange envisions going (with)in a warm-breathed god "tearing to let us in." This immanent and eternal process of dialectical tearing is the (un)birthing of the divine. In the work of female poets like Shange and Lucille Clifton, we can see that this "process" is more accurately a passage, an endless abjection of birthing, a continuous breaking of language into the absense of the divine. Birthing is the immanent dialectic.[24]

The transgressive abjection of flesh which tears and breaks into new signifiers is further elaborated in Lucille Clifton's poetry. Specifically, Clifton addresses a series of poems to a god that functions only within the abject (Clifton 1985).[25] In her work, she uses the dark, bloody, bleeding, black trope of the Goddess Kali to approach a god who transgresses limits. To open the "Kali" section of poems, Clifton gives us "the lesson of the falling leaves" (133):

> the leaves believe
> such letting go is love
> such love is faith
> such faith is grace
> such grace is god
> i agree with the leaves

In this poem, the articulation of "belief," "faith," and even "grace" seem to be reinscriptions of traditional theological language. Yet the logocentric decisions implicit in such theological activity are embodied not in the mouth of a speaking "subject," but in the fragile, friable bodies of inanimate leaves— dead things. When they drop from the tree, it is as refuse, prey to decay, the essence of abjection. Such an abject faith is "grace," which—as Clifton states—can also be written as divine *agape*.   Thus, by the end of the poem, when we enter the space of a personal narrator, she has "agreed" that abjection and "grace"full emptying are her entrance to the space of the hol(e)y. Here language is spent without taking, without fear. The letting go and abject breakage of Clifton's fragile "leaves" recalls to us Taylor's "glass man" who sees through everything. However, for Taylor, the letting go was also a *glas(s)* breakage (Taylor 1990, 35–53).[26] Clifton's feminine incorporation of the abject is able to say that "such grace is god," without finding in that loss any *thanatos*.

Continually in her poetry, Clifton restates such themes of loss and of change as emotions of pleasure. Always, "the wind is eating the world again," yet despite the image of abject consumption, there is no fear of the maternal semiotic (Clifton 1985, 116). And always, she "lets go" with a sense that such loss is inevitable, unstoppable, and pleasurable. In her *Next* book of poems, this is made explicit when she writes "the fact is the fall-ing" (Clifton 1987, 39). Her poetry identifies this ceaseless falling flow with a God who is beyond language, a god who knows intimately the abject feminine.

In "she understands me" (1987, 137), Clifton speaks of this empty a/ theological space who has presence only in the bleeding and breakage of language:

> it is all blood and breaking
> blood and breaking. the thing
> drops out of its box squalling
> into the light. they are both squalling,
> animal and cage. her bars lie wet, open
> and empty and she has made herself again
> out of flesh and out of dictionaries,
> she is always emptying and it is all
> the same wound the same blood the same breaking.

The images of explicit abject "improper" flow and rupture are here em-ployed to trace the movement of a feminine understanding. As Clifton writes from the vantage point of the feminine threshold between utter

abjection and the structural constraints of the symbolic, she is able to release the burden of the maternal abject that is repressed within language.
Her "God" thus breaks all the boundaries of language, losing all meaning(s).
However, once again, in breaking the language the divine is not "murdered,"
as Nietzsche would have it. Instead, a feminine divine births herself anew
even as she breaks open into absence. In absenting the meaning from
language, she fills it with newly friable signifiers, which are in turn broken
away. "She has made herself again / out of flesh, out of dictionaries." As
Kristeva observes of other feminine writing, this maternal flesh overwhelms
the individual in "the fantasy of loss in which [s]he is engulfed" (1982, 20).
This feminine divine makes the carnality of play her body; she incorporates
the whole abject body, pain and pleasure. As Cixous writes elsewhere, we
must continually "tear off this skin of language" (Cixous and Clement 1986,
91). The textual flesh, for feminine readers, is continually flowing, continually bleeding, continually breaking. This is a "bleeding to life," not to
death. For she is not there; she is "out" of the dictionaries that contain and
kill words. Yet as the divine absents itself, what does it give birth to?

"The thing" drops out of its box, out of the wound/womb. It is a loud,
and uncontrollable, "animal." This embodiment of textual abjection becomes "a vast field of powers; a sea of energy; unknown forces" (Taylor
1984, 122). What is it? It is an(Other) thing that constantly turns one way
and another in its cage of meaning, always finding a new way of breaking
out of "her bars." Slippery, bloody, changeable, this multifarious creature
is the bleeding body of signifiers themselves, it is the re-birth, again, of
divine absence in text. As Taylor saw, signs are animalistic and unpredict-
able, "sly, slippery, and tricky" (Taylor 1984, 146). Her signs come "squall-
ing into the light." In other poets, light might be clarity. However, throughout
Clifton's poetic texts, "light" is something breakable, changeable, and unstable.[27] Thus, to birth a "thing" into light is to birth it into flux and play,
into breath and movement. As we saw in Shange's bleeding "god," the
continually torn away skin/thing of abjection is something mutable and
live. As with all live birthings, this is a m(o)ment of joy; it is also as close
as we can come to embracing the unnameable abject. For though the
absence of Presence takes place on the border of the symbolic and the
semiotic, the divine continually transcends and transgresses these boundaries of the sacred and the profane. "She comes in again, without the fear
of ever reaching a limit" (Cixous 1976, 263). "The wind eats the world"
and she is always "vomiting" material from one space into the site of another. Thus, Clifton shows us that feminine a/theologians like herself,
Cixous and Shange birth a textual hole that is (*auter*)ity; a whole fabric
which is a sacred altar; a feminine altar which is an erotogenic hole; a

whole altarity. Yet this text will not end; there is no way of closing—no one will finish. The end is a(void)dance.

As we begin, we find fertility in

Notes

1.   Mark C. Taylor, Introduction to *Deconstructing Theology*. (New York: Crossroad, 1982), xix.
2.   This is Derrida's well-known summation: "There is no(thing) outside language."
3.   Julia Kristeva, *Powers of Horror: An Essay on Abjection* (New York: Columbia University Press, 1982, 310); see also Elizabeth Grosz, *Sexual Subversions* (Sydney: Allen and Unwin, 1989, 71–78). Several of my statements here are paraphrases or clarifications of Grosz's insightful analysis of Kristeva's concept of the "abject."
4.   Representations or references to corpses appear here (and on many more unlisted pages): Taylor 1982, 47, 114, 120; 1984, 1, 29, 92, 117, 141; 1987, 85, 114, 151, 170, 184; 1990, 62, 85, 87, 105, 126; 1992, 37, 113, 272; 1993, 59, 76, 188, 249, 255.
5.   Mark C. Taylor, *Erring: A Postmodern A/Theology* (Chicago: University of Chicago Press, 1984), 168–71, 175; and *Tears* (New York: State University of New York Press, 1990), 230. Regardless of how Taylor manipulates or construes text, it becomes obvious that he feels dis-ease at its breakage. However, note that Taylor does not subscribe to an essentialist reading of body = text. In *Nots* he writes: "The idealism/realism opposition or polarity is as problematic as every such binary or dialectical contrast. Nor does the suggestion that the body is structured like a language inevitably imply the reinscription of logocentrism. Everything turns on how language is construed" (220).
6.   Friedrich Nietzsche, *Thus Spake Zarathustra* (Chicago: Regnery, 1957), 38. Taylor often quotes Nietzsche's fear (see Taylor, *Erring*, 1, 19, 25; and *Nots* [Chicago: University of Chicago Press, 1993], 202).
7.   Taylor also mentions Lacan's concept of the "M-Other" (see Mark C. Taylor, *Altarity* [Chicago: University of Chicago Press, 1987], 87).
8.   Kristeva, *Powers of Horror* 3.   For this analysis of the subject's abject relation to the archaic maternal, I am indebted to Grosz, *Sexual Subversions,* 73.
9.   Mark C. Taylor, e-mail to the author, <ndhayes@cc.wwu.edu>.   January 19, 1995.
10.   In the open field of the borderland, there are many more feminine possibilities and positions than I am able to enumerate here.   Gloria Anzaldua, for example, explores some of these (O)ther possibilities in her extraordinary text

Borderlands: The New Mestiza.
11.   "Impotent": Taylor, *Nots,* 202. Taylor here is analyzing Madonna's video "Like a Prayer." Within the text of the video, he finds a latter-day "Antichrist who repeats the call of Nietzsche's madman." "Mark" puns off his name as mistake in *Erring* (see 12, 131–32, 137–39, 174).
12.   Kate Millett characterizes the "death-fuck" as the expectation of seeing the face of God in another's pain; see Kate Millett, *Sexual Politics* (New York: Equinox, 1971), 292.
13.   Taylor ignores Kristeva's conception of generative textual flow. Instead, for several pages he pursues Kristeva's linking of "food and the feminine" (Taylor, *Altarity,* 163–65). It is possible that this topic is relevant insofar as women who stop eating also stop menstruating. But Taylor never returns to the life-giving potential of this blood.
14.   In *Altarity*, Taylor separately quotes parts of Kristeva's commentary. Yet the portions of Kristeva's text that appear in *Altarity* (169–72), are fragmented, and Taylor does not pursue Kristeva's notion of sexual *différance* as essential to abjection. Instead, Taylor's text moves on to notions of "defilement," "poison," and "death." Thus, he elides the full import of Kristeva's discussion of menstrual blood as a sexual *pharmakos* that is not necessarily deadly.
15.   Kristeva readily acknowledges that menstruation is not straightforwardly related to the confusion of sexual difference, as Grosz points out (1989, 76). However, I am not interested in any actual maternity, but rather in the textual space of life and fertility. The metaphor that Taylor, Kristeva, and I employ to describe that site is characterized as feminine because of its *capacity* for nurturing *différance* and for its continual transgression of corporeal boundaries—its possibility of flow. Therefore, menstrual blood is only one of the possible signifiers that can emanate from this hymenal site.
16.   In order to approach the other as other, we must also avoid the trap of using the violence of comprehension to reduce the other to self, thus depriving the other of its very alterity. Levinas and Derrida warn us of this. (See Levinas 1969, 33–34; Derrida 1978, 117–228.)
17.   Although in *Powers of Horror* Kristeva uses (other) writers who happen to be male to illustrate "revolutionary" writing, she also characterizes their activity as limited and constraining. Kristeva describes the work of such writers as "an attempt to name the other facet of taboo: pleasure, pain" (1982, 62). In naming the desires evoked by abjection, Kristeva explains that the "feminine" writings of Artaud, Borges, Proust, and Joyce attempt to *name* the abject. Thus, they continue to restrain and sublimate the abject other.
18.   Taylor also speaks of *la mèr(e)* in *Altarity* 1987, 163, 176.
19.   Although any use of Cixous is necessarily limited by questions Kristeva has raised regarding the usefulness of *l'écriture féminine* as a description of the "feminine" body of articulation, it seems evident that Cixous illustrates—at the least—Kristeva's strategy of discourse which provocatively opens the "dark continent" of abjection. Whether or not she essentializes that *différance* is not the subject of this paper.

20. Note also Taylor's critique of Nishitani in *Nots* (1993, 3–5, 61–70).
21. Such paradoxical *différence* that affirms, says Derrida, "is that which escapes with a leap and laughingly signs that which it lets go, that which it makes and unmakes" (1977, 93).
22. Nishitani, commenting on Meister Eckhart's breaking *kenósis*, (1983, 62). It is interesting to note that Kristeva uses Eckhart as one of her primary examples of writers who inscribe themselves as "feminine," allowing themselves (as a subject) to be "broken through again and again" (1989, 190).
23. As Shange writes: "i found god in myself & i loved her / i loved her fiercely." These are the last lines of Ntozake Shange's "chora-poem" (cf. Kristeva) *For Colored Girls Who Have Considered Suicide / When the Rainbow Is Enuf.*
24. For Taylor's description of dialectical development, see Taylor 1982, 102. For cautions against linking the feminine too closely to *mater*, see Jones, 1985. I speak of the "maternal" without any desire to contribute to "the coercive glorification of motherhood that has plagued women for centuries" (Jones 1985, 89). A/theology is not limited to any one perception of the feminine. I use this trope *only* as a way of opening a discussion of feminine a/theolog(ies) that will reach beyond Taylor's fear of M-Other.
25. Lucille Clifton, *good woman: poems and a memoir (1969–1980).* All further references to Clifton's poetry, cited simply by page number, are drawn from this volume. There is one noted exception, that is, the reference to her *Next* (1987). Notes upon poem placement are equally valid in all earlier editions of Clifton's work. Susan Friedman brought Clifton's startling use of the childbirth metaphor to my attention in her article "Creativity and the Childbirth Metaphor: Gender Difference in Literary Discourse."
26. As Taylor hints in surrounding pages, *"glass"* is a punning reference to Derrida's *glas* of the self; "in seeing through everything, the glass man sees himself."
27. "[B]reaklight" (Clifton 1985, 154) is one pertinent work. In this poem, Clifton writes "light keeps on breaking. / i keep knowing / the language of other nations. / . . . light just keeps on breaking." Her poetry contains similar approaches to light throughout.

Works Cited

Anzaldua, Gloria. 1987. *Borderlands: The New Mestiza*. San Francisco: Spinsters.

Cixous, Hélène. 1976. "The Laugh of the Medusa." *Signs* 19 (5–6):245–64.

Cixous, Hélène and Catharine Clement. 1986. *The Newly Born Woman*. Trans. Betty Wing. Minneapolis: University of Minnesota Press.

Clifton, Lucille. 1985. *good woman: poems and a memoir (1969–1980)*. New York: Brockport.

———. 1987. *Next*. New York: Brockport.

Derrida, Jacques. 1976. *Of Grammatology*. Trans. G. C. Spivak. Baltimore: Johns Hopkins University Press.

———. 1977. *"Ja, ou le faux-bond."* *Diagraphe* 11 (March):83–121.

———. 1978. *Writing and Difference*. Trans. Alan Bass. Chicago: University of Chicago Press.

Friedman, Susan. 1989. "Creativity and the Childbirth Metaphor: Gender Difference in Literary Discourse." In *Speaking of Gender*. Ed. Elaine Showalter. New York: Routledge. 45–55.

Grosz, Elizabeth. 1989. *Sexual Subversions*. Sydney: Allen and Unwin.

Jones, Ann Rosalind. 1985. "Writing the Body: Toward an Understanding of *l'écriture féminine*." In *Feminist Criticism and Social Change*. Ed. Judith Newton and Deborah Rosenfelt. New York: Methuen. 86–101.

Kristeva, Julia. 1980. *Desire in Language*. New York: Columbia University Press.

———. 1982. *Powers of Horror: An Essay on Abjection*. Trans. Leon S. Roudiez. New York: Columbia University Press.

———. 1989. "Stabat Mater." In *Contemporary Literary Criticism*. 2nd ed. Ed. Robert Con Davis and Ronald Schleifer. New York: Longman. 186–203.

Levinas, Emmanuel. 1969. *Totality and Infinity*. Trans. Alphonso Lingis. Pittsburgh: Duquesne University Press.

Meltzer, Françoise and David Tracy. 1994. Editorial introduction to "Symposium on 'God.'" *Critical Inquiry* 20 (4):14.

Millett, Kate. 1971. *Sexual Politics*. New York: Equinox.

Nietzsche, Friedrich. 1957. *Thus Spake Zarathustra*. Trans. M. Cowan. Chicago: Regnery.

Nishitani, Keiji. 1983. *Religion and Nothingness*. Berkeley and Los Angeles: University of California Press.

Serres, Michel. 1982. *The Parasite*. Trans. L. Schehr. Baltimore: Johns Hopkins University Press.

Shange, Ntozake. 1977. *For Colored Girls Who Have Considered Suicide / When the Rainbow Is Enuf*. New York: Bantam.

———. 1981. *three pieces*. New York: St. Martin's.

———. 1983. *A Daughter's Geography*. New York: St. Martin's.

Simpson, Jessica. 1994. "All Women Write Left-Handed." Spoken poem, Women's Writing Collective, Capitol Hill. Seattle, Nov. 9. 3.

Taylor, Mark C. 1982. *Deconstructing Theology*. New York: Crossroad.

———. 1984. *Erring: A Postmodern A/Theology*. Chicago: University of Chicago Press.

———. 1986. *Deconstruction in Context*. Ed. Mark C. Taylor. Chicago: University of Chicago Press.

———. 1987. *Altarity.* Chicago: University of Chicago Press.

———. 1990. *Tears.* New York: State University of New York Press.

———. 1992. *Disfiguring: Art, Architecture, Religion.* Chicago: University of Chicago Press.

———. 1993. *Nots.* Chicago: University of Chicago Press.

———. 1994. "Denegating God." *Critical Inquiry* 20 (4):592–610.

9

Mallet-Joris's *Divine:*
A Twentieth-Century Mystic

Susan Petit

Where is my fat of yesteryear?
My enticing double chin?
I've lost it all by getting so thin
My extra pounds and lovers so dear.
—Françoise Mallet-Joris, "Mes Bourrelets d'antan"

Eternal beatitude is a state where to look is to eat.
—Simone Weil, *Gravity and Grace*

In Françoise Mallet-Joris's novel *Divine* (1991), a high school science teacher in Paris in 1988 goes on a diet and finds herself becoming a mystic. The book starts out as a representation of ordinary contemporary life, and the protagonist, Jeanne-Ludivine Grandier, is a clear-headed, intelligent, and scientifically trained woman firmly anchored in the physical, sensory world. As the book's events become less normal, they remain believable because the third-person narrator uses humor and concrete detail to trace Jeanne's journey in the steps of such mystics as Saints Teresa of Avila and John of the Cross. Jeanne's mysticism, however, unlike theirs, is largely secular and pagan, as is much mysticism in our century (Borchert 1994, 314-20), and it is acted out in the grocery store and the kitchen. Because of her life's resemblance to and difference from the lives of famous mystics of the past, Jeanne's journey may lead us to reexamine our understanding of mysticism.

Postmodern literary and philosophical theories provide particular insight into this book. If Linda Hutcheon is right that postmodernism, at least in art and literature, finds its main expression in parody and pastiche because it "both incorporates and challenges that which it parodies" (Hutcheon 1993, 251) while opening new dialogue between past and present, then Jeanne, whose story replays classical mystical experience in a modern key, can be called a postmodern mystic because of the dissonances between her outer and her inner life. This conflict can also be interpreted using philosophers like Derrida, Foucault, and—particularly relevant here—Jean-François Lyotard who are interested in how what is often called the Enlightenment project and its totalizing systems are challenged by "others" who are usually partly within that system but marginalized by it.

Lyotard, in particular, for whom postmodernism can exist in any time period, has famously defined it as characterized by "incredulity toward metanarratives" (Lyotard 1987, 74), or *grands récits*, such as political emancipation and freedom from toil, but also including Christianity seen as a quest for the salvation of souls (Lyotard 1986, 37). He opposes to such metanarratives various little narratives, or *petits récits*—ways of understanding appropriate to only a particular time and place, and/or produced by marginalized people. He thinks that the *grands récits* and *petits récits* should engage in dialogue in order to achieve "paralogy," or new ways of thinking that are not logical in the normal sense—hence "paralogic" or fallacious—but that bridge the aporia between logical and totalizing Western thinking and local "language games." In *Divine*, Jeanne's mystical experience can be read as a *petit récit* that is radically "other" in regard to the rationalism of her scientific training and of her society, and which is also in conflict with a normative Christian conception of God. As this discussion will show, this is the situation generally of mysticism, which by its nature is not a social but an individual phenomenon, however much it may be influenced by one's society and one's religious training, and despite the similarity of much mystical experience.

Before we consider the novel in detail, some information about its author and a description of mysticism will be useful. Françoise Mallet-Joris is best known in North America for realistic modern novels including *The Illusionist, The Red Room,* and *House of Lies,*[1] but she has also set works in the Middle Ages and the Renaissance.[2] In 1978 she published a biography of Jeanne Guyon, the French mystic. Besides fifteen novels, she has published poetry, short stories, biography, autobiography, children's fiction, prefaces, translations, and essays; she is also a lyricist for the French popular singer Marie-Paule Belle. Mallet-Joris is a member of the Académie Royale de Belgique, past member of the jury for the Prix Fémina, and, since 1970, member of the Académie Goncourt, of which she is now vice-president. She has been an Honorary Fellow of the Modern Language Association since 1973, and on 31 December 1997, Jacques Chirac promoted her from *chevalier* to *officier* of the Legion of Honor. Her writing has become increasingly concerned with spiritual issues, but, though she is a late convert to Catholicism—she was baptized at 24—she is not what is generally meant by a "Catholic writer." Rather, she is a Catholic who writes. *Divine,* like much of her other fiction, illustrates a spiritual journey that does not conform to any particular creed.

This approach is appropriate, for "mystical truth," according to Evelyn Underhill, cannot be limited by "the formulæ of any one religion" (1930, 96). In fact, many mystics have been suspected of heresy because their experiences did not correspond to the dogma of their churches. Mysticism, defined as the experience of "union with the divine" (Graef 1965, 9; see also Corbishley 1967, 175), need not be based on organized religion but may reflect "a sense of the immanence of the One or God or soul in Nature" (Happold 1970, 43). Though mystics differ greatly, they tend to share four experiences. First, they generally undergo a painful period of purgation which often is not chosen, such as a prolonged illness, and which involves what St. John of the Cross called "the dark night of the senses" (Happold 1970, 60). Second, they experience union with the divine, which they typically can describe only through metaphors and/or paradox. Third, they commonly suffer what St. John of the Cross called "the dark night of the spirit" (Happold 1970, 60), a period in which they may feel deserted not only by God but also by friends and relatives, and during which they may suffer undignified humiliations (Underhill 1930, 382 ff.). These trials bring about a "remaking of character and the liberation of a new, or rather latent, form of consciousness" (Underhill 1930, 81). Fourth, many of the great mystics worked actively in the ordinary world, whether it was Saint Teresa finding God "among the pots and pans" of the convent kitchen (Underhill [1938?], 71), Saint John of the Cross escaping from imprisonment in Toledo by making "a rope . . . from his bedclothes, and walk[ing] as fast as he could" to safety (Graef 1965, 243–44), or Hildegard of Bingen treating the sick, writing scientific treatises, and composing music (Lagorio 1984, 163–64).

The protagonist of *Divine* undergoes all four of these experiences— the dark night of the senses, nearly incommunicable union with the divine, the dark night of the soul, and combining mysticism with practicality—but she does so in ways that simultaneously undercut and affirm them. This duality is typical of postmodern art generally, which "uses and abuses, installs and then subverts, the very concepts it challenges" (Hutcheon 1993, 243). Though Jeanne's spiritual experience is classic in outline, its content is not, because it takes place in what Julia Kristeva has called "our mascara and soap-opera age" (Kristeva 1992, 203), which is permeated with popular culture, leaves us little physical or spiritual dignity, and provides few absolute truths. In addition, the novel's mixing of genres, which Florence Noiville has pointed out in her review, is a typical postmodern technique used here partly to open up a dialogue with the past, partly to make Jeanne's experiences more believable by placing them in our mass-culture society, and partly to show that spiritual life includes all sorts of events, even the lurid and the ludicrous.

The novel's plot is simple. Jeanne, aged thirty-five, a high school science teacher, of average height (about 5 feet, 7 inches [246]) but weighing around 187 pounds (15),[3] goes on a diet when she realizes that other people feel sorry for her because she is heavy. Nearly all of the external action is mundane: in the spring Jeanne teaches her biology classes; over the summer, alone, she reworks her class notes; and in the fall she receives a declaration of love from a colleague, Didier Schmidt. She also maintains relationships with others, including her mother, her friend and colleague Evelyne Berthelot, and the school's Turkish concierge, Selim. The real action, though, takes place within Jeanne. Reviewers have said that Jeanne is on a "rocky road to sainthood" (Lathers 1993–94, 166) or is "a saint who had [at first] chosen the wrong faith and law" [un saint qui s'était trompé de foi et de loi][4] (Nourissier1991, 127), and that is true enough if by "saint" one means a person "who, by heroic virtue, [has] learned to love without possessiveness" (Dupré 1987, 255). It is more accurate, though, to say that Jeanne makes a mystical journey in the midst of messy contemporary life.

There is nothing mystical in the novel's first half, but it establishes Jeanne's heretical tendencies, her "otherness." Her heresies are secular ones; she defies the beliefs of her relatives, friends, and colleagues about how women should look and act. Even her intelligence has about it "something a little suspicious, a little heretical" [quelque chose d'un peu suspect, d'un peu hérétique (200)], and she has chosen to commit "the sin of obesity" [le péché d'obésité (142)] as well as the sins of being careless about her appearance and of being too independent. She sees her defiance of society's beliefs in religious terms, for when she goes to the school doctor, Pierquin, for guidance in dieting, she hopes he will give her "absolution" (97); that is, pardon her for having previously refused to diet. She considers Pierquin's questions an "Inquisition" (102) and feels that he treats her like a confessed sinner who has "become indicted and emptied of his substance"[devenu inculpé et vidé de sa substance (103)]; she even thinks that his questions of her are like the "torture" of Ravaillac (103–4), horribly killed for assassinating Henri IV. However, Jeanne will not stop smoking, dressing in tents, wearing tennis shoes, and acting and thinking as she wishes, nor does she wear makeup or manage to keep her hair from falling out of its chignon. Though she diets, Jeanne remains a heretic, not because she is a woman and thus marginal or "other" by virtue of her gender, but because she refuses to fill the marginal role she has been assigned.

Historical references give Jeanne's acts a religious context from the start and open up the dialogue with the past. Both Jeanne and the narrator refer frequently to the sixteenth century Wars of Religion, when, in the novel's words, "blood flowed, abundant, on meadows strewn with flowers" [le sang coulait, abondant, sur les prés "émaillés" de fleurs (162)]. Partly because she is helping Didier research a thesis on "Realism and Poetics of the Suffering Body in the Literature of the XVI Century" [Réalisme et poétique du corps souffrant dans la littérature du XVIᵉ siècle (53)].[5] Jeanne knows how both John of Leiden (40, 58) and the assassin of William the Silent of Orange (53) were killed by torture, and she still remembers her shock at seeing, years earlier, the Iron Maiden, the boot, and other torture instruments (57). Jeanne thinks about the St. Bartholomew's Day Massacre (79) and religious poets of the period including Agrippa d'Aubigné (140), Pontus de Tyard (79, 156, 162, 237), and Honorat de Racan (160).[6] Her interest in the Wars of Religion, clearly, connects suffering with heresy. As Jeanne's own suffering due to her diet is hardly on a level with the martyrdoms mentioned, it is, in a sense, a parody of such torture. However, it is still real suffering. Jeanne and the martyrs with whom she identifies suffer because a totalizing society is trying to make them either renounce or assume their otherness; that is, they must either convert (lose weight, change religion) and so give up at least some of their marginality, or pay the penalty of their otherness (be pitied and denigrated, be martyred). They might also do both: convert (or diet) *and* suffer for having done so.

Jeanne's religious quest becomes central about halfway through the novel, as she remains alone in Paris over the summer and her diet makes her undergo purgation such as often precedes mystical experience—an experience, in her case, ironically counterpointed by her scientific work preparing notes for her fall classes. The novel is well aware of the humor inherent in finding God through weight loss, but food deprivation has often been part of religious purification. Women are particularly likely to choose to fast even when religion does not require it, and in the Middle Ages and during the Renaissance refusing to eat was the chosen path to salvation for many women. Caroline Walker Bynum persuasively argues that "food was . . . a more important motif in [medieval] women's piety than in men's" (Bynum 1988, 4) because women were the food preparers and servers (as is still largely true today). Bynum also explains that women were more likely than men to give up food because, if they were well-to-do, it was often the only thing their families and spiritual advisors permitted them to renounce (1988, 24–25, 193), and if they were poor, it may have been the only thing they *could* renounce.

These women, who were by virtue of their gender "other" in the eyes of medieval churchmen, were sometimes suspected of witchcraft, and they frequently disobeyed their spiritual advisors by not eating more, which is why, according to Rudolph M. Bell, they often "came to be seen variously as insane, demoniacal, and heretical" (Bell 1985, 170); however, many have since been designated by the Catholic Church as holy, blessed, and even saints.[7] Saints Teresa of Avila and Catherine of Siena are probably the best known of such women. The possibly pathological character of such deprivation does not necessarily undermine its religious nature, according to Bruno Borchert, who says that "mysticism and mental disturbance are not mutually exclusive" (Borchert 1994, 14), and even Hildegard of Bingen, who lived to be over eighty, was a "sickly creature" with "psychosomatic troubles" (Zum Brunn and Epiney-Burgard 1989, 5). Because of these historical parallels, the reader cannot help thinking that Jeanne's diet both parodies the deprivations of celebrated mystics and reenacts their stories realistically in a contemporary context. As Jeanne spends her days alone counting carbohydrates, she, like other mystics, becomes more and more detached from the physical, like them "turning away from what is not God in order to come to God" (Corbishley 1967, 176).

Jeanne's deprivation makes her increasingly reject her body, even while she seems to be suffering to make it more attractive. Though an atheist, she has been affected by Christianity, and at first she wants only to ignore her bulging, overweight body, to be like "the saints of the old Byzantine icons . . . whose head and hands only are visible" [les saints des vieilles icônes byzantines . . . dont seules la tête et les mains sont visibles (63)]. Her desire to think of her body merely as a prison for her soul (61) reflects a tradition, going back at least to Plato and continuing in medieval and Cartesian theology, in which, according to the philosopher Susan Bordo, "the body is experienced as *alien*, as the not-self" (1993, 144), "*the enemy*" (145), or a "jail" (147). In other words, Jeanne is discovering that she is alienated not only from her friends and colleagues but also from her body. Somewhat similarly, the psychologist William N. Davis says that medieval holy women starved themselves because they "detested their bodily desires and were terrified at the possibility of their unbidden appearance" (Bell 1985, 182).[8] Jeanne, too, wants to dominate her body, for her diet becomes a "reconquering of her freedom" [une reconquête de sa liberté (143)]. Although her friend Evelyne points out that Jeanne's rejection of her body is "a little contrary to the dogma of the Incarnation" [un peu contraire au dogme de l'Incarnation (235)]. Jeanne's attempt to tame her bodily desires is in line with Christian tradition. Yet it is in keeping with a tradition found more in the margins of Christianity than in the mainstream; ascetics are necessarily "other" in relation to ordinary believers, who may fast but not so rigorously.

Unlike most dieters, Jeanne does not focus on her appearance; she is well aware that her goal is spiritual. Kept awake by hunger, she compares herself to an imaginary monk who stays awake to watch and pray, and she wonders

> if all these privations have a meaning, or if they are good in them-
> selves . . . [if the] faith [of the imaginary monk] (him, the recluse,
> the hermit, the stylite perhaps), [if] the loss of weight (her, to the
> goal she blindly set for herself), if all that has truly any importance.[9]

Despite such doubts, Jeanne continues to diet and to stay alone in her high-rise apartment. (In French, it is called a *tour* [tower], a name suggesting both sequestration and spiritual elevation.) Finally, the dark night of the senses is alleviated, as her "hungers began to leave, like dismissed servants" [les faims s'éloignaient, comme des servantes congédiées (157)]. Her hungers for knowledge and for love also lessen, leading her to decide, "There is only one hunger" [Il n'y a qu'une faim (154)], as Teresa of Avila thought, "There is only *one* love" (Borchert 1994, 39; emphasis in original). If in the past Jeanne had been more satisfied in friendship and love, she would not have wanted to overeat.

Having gone through this purgation, Jeanne has her first mystical experience—in a grocery store. The situation may be a parody of traditional mystical experiences, but it is a serious parody, what Hutcheon would call a "critical reworking" (Hutcheon 1993, 245) of the past, in that it implies that the context of mystical experience has always been the quotidian. It is only because we shroud the past in nostalgia and romanticism that we cannot see its ordinariness for those who lived in it. As a result of Jeanne's purgation in a Paris "desert" (139),[10] she has become aware of her spiritual needs, but, because her sensibility is essentially pagan and because she has been dieting, her experience is of union with food. (In fact, Borchert shows that mystical experience can be evoked by nearly any stimulus. He says that the "usual stimuli in non-believers are: first, sex; second, nature; and third, art" [Borchert 1994, 27].) Having decided, in one of the paradoxes common in mysticism, that "if there is possession, it is in lack" [s'il est une possession, c'est dans le manque (170)]—a phrase echoing Simone Weil's "We only possess what we renounce" (Weil 1952, 80)—Jeanne tests her insight one day by going into a supermarket and merely looking at, smelling, and touching the cheeses, meats, and produce. The scene is both funny and serious as Jeanne uses sight, smell, and touch to invoke taste, "brushing, like Tantalus' torture, like a Tantric torture, the irritating down of a peach's buttocks" and so finding "a minuscule recess of the mystery of the Incarnation" There, "between the strawberry and the artichoke" [entre la fraise et l'artichaut (183)],[12] the Incarnation, "the most dangerous mystery in the world, waited for her":

> And like . . . Saint Lydwina [who] stammered in God's honor child-like words . . . [s]o Jeanne, in the childish enchantment of essential discoveries, reaching out her hand . . . murmured to herself these heavy words which from then on weighed more than everything: "So one can do without these? And without this? And without that? And one has them all the same? So can one do without everything?"[13]

Weil saw beauty as a trap God sets so he can enter one's soul (Springsted 1986, 42); for Jeanne, the trap is not esthetic but gustatory.

The novel validates this mystical experience in the supermarket by explicitly comparing Jeanne to mystics from the Middle Ages and the Renaissance, including Joan of Arc (99, 142), Hildegard of Bingen (84, 182-83), Hadewijch of Antwerp (251), Teresa of Avila (258), Marie des Vallées (251), Joseph Surin (251), and John Ruysbroeck (251). Jeanne-Ludivine's two given names also relate her to mystics.[14] "Jeanne" connects her to Jeanne Guyon, who also exercised what Mallet-Joris has called a "will not to will" [volonté de ne pas vouloir (1978, 505)], and perhaps also to Joan of Arc [Jeanne d'Arc]. But a more important name is one she has abandoned. Throughout childhood she was called "Divine," a nickname for "Ludivine," and by dropping that name she has symbolically denied the divine in herself.[15] Through dieting, however, she comes to identify with her namesake, the mystic Saint Lydwina of Schiedam,[16] who represents victory over hunger. Confined to bed for her entire adult life by illness, Lydwina is said not to have eaten for the last nineteen years of her life except for the Communion host (Delaney 1980).[17] Lydwina's story can be called a *petit récit* (in Lyotard's sense) because it is about individual experience in a particular time and place, and it is neither rational nor normative. However edifying her experience, few would wish to emulate her. She has found her place in Catholic hagiography (the *grands récits* of the Church), but the strangeness of her life marks her as ineradicably "other," and the fact that she has not actually been canonized may indicate her alterity. Jeanne, too, remains other to those around her; she has begun to *look* more average, but her attitudes since she has begun the mystic's journey are more alien than ever.

After school starts in the fall, Jeanne discovers, like many mystics, how difficult it is to explain her insights. She tells Evelyne: "One doesn't *lose* weight: one *gains* lightness, willpower. . . . [I]t's a sort of turning inside out, like a glove."[18] It is especially hard for Jeanne to explain her experiences because she rejects Christianity, which could have given her words Evelyne would have understood. Instead, Jeanne's mysticism is linked to conscious atheism and initially unconscious paganism, both common in today's mass-culture society but "other" in relation to Christianity. Ludivine, the atheistic grandmother who raised Jeanne and for whom she was named, taught Jeanne to distrust sexual desire (both Jeanne's mother and her grandmother were unmarried mothers deserted by their lovers), and just as Jeanne has formerly eaten heartily while ignoring the effects on her waistline, she has satisfied her sexual desires while refusing to think about her acts' meanings or consequences. As the novel opens, she is in a strange sexual situation which is explicitly compared to a soap opera (236). She has been having an affair with Selim, her school's concierge (a rationalist who is in love with cartesian philosophy), without even knowing who her lover is: she simply turns out her lights and leaves her door unlocked from time to time so that an unknown man can have sexual relations with her. But once she starts dieting, she leaves her door locked. No doubt partly as a result of the ensuing sexual frustration, she one day has a mystical union with Didier, if one can give that name to a sexual fantasy culminating in orgasm. (One might in fact see this episode as a parody of erotic mystical experiences such as those of Hadewijch of Antwerp [see Borchert 1994, 40].) Jeanne imagines that in the fall she and Didier will make love for the first time, not because she will be slender—in her fantasy she is huge—but because he will desire her maternal, milky body (167-69).

Jeanne's paganism also connects her with past mystics. It also comes from her grandmother, a chef who gave "herself to cooking as one gives oneself to God" [se donna à la cuisine comme on se donne à Dieu (29)]. Just as Jeanne imagines that her grandmother's lover was like a pagan god (249), she comes to think of Didier as one of those deities that are "half-gods, half-animals, the god Pan's satyr friends, flute or penis upraised, making the countryside fertile!"[19] To the child Jeanne, Ludivine was "a rough-hewn goddess, lare, penate, or road-marker—but a sacred one—which delimit[ed] the space in which [Jeanne] move[d]."[20] Jeanne concludes that Ludivine's seduction left her "burned to the heart and not trying any more, respectfully, to understand, than a little country girl who thinks she is seeing the Virgin or Saint Michael speaking to her in the local dialect."[21] Ludivine's paganism is thus linked with that of such Catholic saints as Bernadette of Lourdes and Joan of Arc, uneducated girls who were from villages steeped in pagan beliefs but who had Christian visions. The novel thus suggests that paganism has been a step to Christianity, while nearly equating Ludivine's seduction with a vision of the Virgin.

Having experienced both purgation through dieting and a nearly incommunicable mystical experience in the produce department, Jeanne finds herself in the third common stage of mystical experience, the dark night of the soul, which she undergoes in the context of catty gossip and seemingly unrequited love. Because she has lost about 26 pounds since spring, her colleagues at school assume that she is trying to attract Didier, who has taken an extended vacation, and they speculate about how he will react when he returns and sees her. Hurt and puzzled by the whispering around her, Jeanne then suffers two blows in quick succession. First, she discovers that her mother has never loved her: "Painful [is] the loss . . . But more terrible the lack" [Douloureuse la perte... Mais plus terrible le manque (213, ellipsis in original)]. To lose—weight, friends, or love—is one thing; to discover that there has been nothing *to* lose is more painful. Then, the same day, she gets a letter from Didier. Afraid that he is either breaking off their friendship or declaring his love, and unable to face either possibility, she burns his letter without reading it. All of this is the material of a sentimental novel or a soap opera, but Jeanne's spiritual suffering and isolation are real:

> Suddenly she was again traveling in the summer's desert. Solitude. God, perhaps. God [is] this void, this lack? The thing one cannot turn inside out, which has no right or wrong side, neither density nor extension? . . . Emptiness which is not the opposite of fullness?[22]

When Didier later visits Paris and proposes that they live together, it is too late: "He had hesitated [to declare his feelings earlier] because of those few pounds too many. She had lost them, and was no longer the same."[23] The seeming triviality, the soap-opera quality of the plot, helps initiate what Hutcheon would call "an ironic dialogue with the past" (1993, 244)[24] because these events are consistent with events in the lives of other mystics; for example, the dark night of the Blessed Henry Suso began when he was accused of fathering a child (see particularly Underhill 1930, 409-12), and the turning-point in Saint Lydwina's life was an ice-skating accident when she was a teenager.

In her dark night of the spirit, Jeanne no longer finds satisfaction in mental *or* physical life. She is alienated from her mother, friends, and colleagues; even Evelyne seems different. And Jeanne feels that she must

renounce Didier, partly because she believes that the only way to keep her
love for him from changing is to lose him (222), to "lose what [she] has
never had" [perdre ce qu['elle] n'a jamais eu (217)], and also so she can
"prevent the Spirit from touching him" [éviter que l'Esprit ne le touchât
(249–50)] so he can continue to live happily in an uncomplicated physical
world. She has reached a state of nearly total renunciation, even though on
the surface she seems to be living a sentimental romance. Then in the last
week of October, Jeanne comes through this dark night. Her mysticism
reaches a climax, amusingly but appropriately, as she is defrosting her
refrigerator, which is not merely empty, or *vide,* but a symbol of *le vide*—
the void. She now uses Christianity as a reference, a fact that explains the
narrator's statement that Jeanne "was thinking of God for the first time"
[pensait à Dieu pour la première fois (249)]. Jeanne decides that "God, the
terrible thing which is hidden behind all vain nourishment . . . was surely
Hunger,"[25] and she speculates that "if Christ really did visit us" [si le Christ
vraiment nous visita (250)], he discovered that people have hungers that
can never be satisfied: "And the Human, in him, for an instant, won out:
he decided to be eaten, he tried to believe that one could satisfy the hunger
of men, him, the son of Hunger!"[26] Jeanne is thinking that not merely the
Eucharist but Christianity itself is a lie created by God to keep people from
feeling their true hungers, which can never be satisfied but only acknowledged and transformed. At this point Jeanne, "like Saint Lydwina asking
for her wounds to be more numerous and more painful,"[27] stands in front
of her dripping refrigerator contemplating "the divine absence, the Hunger
which alone can satisfy one and, in the icy water which had now spread
around on the tiles, slowly bent her knees."[28] To experience God as hunger
is to see him as radically other, as that which we would normally fear and
avoid, while Jeanne's own increasing difference from those around her is
underscored by her loving acceptance of this lack, which she experiences
as fullness.

Having come through the dark night of the spirit, Jeanne faces the
fourth step on the Mystic Way, combining practicality with mysticism.
She is helped when Evelyne's husband, Xavier, arrives to complain that
Evelyne's attempts to imitate Jeanne are breaking up their marriage. Jeanne
renounces the last thing she has, the privacy of her spiritual experience, by
telling him about her "intuitions, her weaknesses, the brief flashes of light,
the descents into darkness,"[29] and Xavier unexpectedly gives her the key to
coming to terms with it by saying, "Oh, what a subject! . . . You should
write about it" [Ah! c'est un sujet, ça!... Vous devriez l'écrire (261)].
Xavier, an actor whose specialty is historical romances and *feuilletons*, or
television serializations of sentimental and sensational stories, is urging her

to put her mystical experience to use, as did his namesake Saint Francis Xavier.[30] If Jeanne could create a *petit récit*, a little narrative of her own experiences, perhaps she could reach some sort of Lyotardean paralogy, an accommodation between official rationality and individual experiences, much as Jeanne Guyon in writing of her mystical experiences reached thousands of readers. The Catholic Church finally silenced Madame Guyon, but many people both then and now are eager to hear of experiences they do not necessarily want to share. We may not want to be Saint Lydwina, Jeanne Guyon, or Teresa, but we may want to learn from them. Xavier's profession, in fact, helps him understand Jeanne, and Jeanne in her own mystical growth has developed and moved "as he did on stage, between the marks which keep us from . . . going out of the narrow space given to us, limited on each side by the darkened wings which lead to madness or nothingness."[31] If we accept this statement by the narrator, life *is* actually a sort of soap opera and the lives of mystics may be especially strange and dramatic. Jeanne now decides to reestablish an "equilibrium" (263), to be sure not to skip meals, to stabilize her weight, to lead a normal life.[32] In doing so, not only would she be imitating the most celebrated mystics, she would also be following the advice of virtually every diet and self-help book.

She never gets the chance, though, for, like sixteenth and seventeenth century heretics of all stripes, she is martyred, though in a way more suggestive of a *fait divers* than the *legenda aurea*. The concierge Selim, who has been fired by the school, believes that Jeanne is responsible for his dismissal and presumably is also angry because Jeanne no longer leaves her door unlocked for him. This once rational, cartesian thinker has jumped to unsupported conclusions and is now motivated by his own "little narrative" drawn from his marginalization as a Turk in French society. He arrives at Jeanne's apartment, which she has carelessly left unlocked after Xavier's visit, and enters it, this time not to have sexual relations but to kill her. Jeanne is as helpless as any martyr, and she dies equally lightly: "two furious hands squeezed her throat, unaware that what they were smothering forever, and so easily, was a burst of laughter."[33] These are the novel's last words. Jeanne is laughing at the thought that, after all her colleagues' speculation about her romantic life, her mate has turned out to be "the concierge" (265), and she may also be laughing because her spiritual journey is ending in what will seem to be a banal crime story.[34] Jeanne dies without dignity and, in a sense, as the victim of her own misjudgment, and she will end up being the subject of still more school gossip. At the same time, this ending reminds us that the most dangerous conflicts may take place between marginalized people.

The circumstances of Jeanne's murder do not, however, necessarily negate her spiritual journey. Psalm 48, as quoted by Jeanne in Racan's verse translation, stresses the unimportance of the physical world: "do not be envious to see that in this world the sinner receives abundantly all good things; [for] he leaves it as naked as you."[35]   In her struggle to come to terms with her body, like most mystics, Jeanne has gone through purification, union with the divine, and the dark night of the soul, and she has decided to try to balance the spiritual and the practical. Yet unlike the other mystics mentioned in the novel, she lives in a contemporary world hostile to mysticism, and she does not belong to a church to help her cope with her experiences. The main guides to life she has are history, particularly the Wars of Religion, and popular culture, both of which seem to trivialize her experience, the former by making her concerns seem petty by contrast and the latter by seeming to reduce her life to soap opera. Lyotard has said that the postmodern writer's works "cannot be judged according to a determining judgment, by applying familiar categories to the text or to the work" because "those rules and categories are what the work of art itself is looking for" (1992, 149). This is certainly true of *Divine,* which mixes high and low culture, seriousness and humor, the past and the present. In it we see how a woman who is marginalized both by her gender and by her refusal to assume the stereotypes evoked by that gender becomes still more "other" because of a mystical experience. That same mystical voyage, however, reveals to her a vision of God as even more radically other: God as lack. If Jeanne had lived to write of her experiences, perhaps creating what would be her own postmodern work with its own rules and categories, she might have helped bridge for others that aporia between an unfathomable divinity and human thought, making Enlightenment logic and rationality come to a new accommodation with a mystical experience of God.

Notes

The first epigraph to this chapter is a free translation trying to capture some of the spirit of the original lines; a more literal translation would read: "Where are my rolls of fat of yesteryear? / My attractive double chins? / I've lost everything with this diet: / My extra pounds and my lovers" [Où sont mes bourrelets d'antan? / Mes doubles mentons séduisants? / J'ai tout perdu / Avec ce régime: / Mes grammes superflus / Et mes amants]. The lines are from "Mes Bourrelets d'antan," a song written by Françoise Mallet-Joris for the popular singer Marie-Paule Belle.

The second epigraph is from Simone Weil's *Gravity and Grace* (1952,

153). Weil's early death in England in 1943 by tuberculosis was precipitated by her refusal to eat more than rationing permitted her compatriots to eat in occupied France at the time. Robert Coles devotes an entire section of his biography of Weil to the theme of hunger in her life and in her writings, and he quotes her as having written, "Religion is a form of nourishment" (Coles 1989, 28).

1.   *The Illusionist.* Trans. Herma Briffault. New York: Farrar, Straus, and Young. 1952 [*Le Rempart des béguines* (1951)]; *The Red Room.* Trans. Herma Briffault. New York: Farrar, Straus, and Cudahy. 1956 [*La Chambre rouge* (1955)]; *House of Lies.* Trans. Herma Briffault. New York: Farrar, Straus, and Cudahy. 1957 [*Les Mensonges* (1956)].

2.   *The Witches: Three Tales of Sorcery* [*Trois Ages de la nuit: Histoires de la sorcellerie,* 1968] is set in the Middle Ages; *The Favourite* [*Les Personnages,* 1961] and *The Uncompromising Heart: A Life of Marie Mancini, Louis XIV's First Love* [*Marie Mancini, le premier amour de Louis XIV,* 1964] take place in the seventeenth century.

3.   Jeanne's height is just under 1.70 meters, and her initial weight is 85 kilos.

4.   This and all other translations, unless otherwise noted, are mine.

5.   Didier's last name, Schmidt, suggests the French scholar Albert-Marie Schmidt, who wrote a thesis on sixteenth century French poetry (Kanters 1967, 14). Didier's home town, Blois, was the scene in 1563 of a famous event in the Wars of Religion, the murder of the Catholic Duc de Guise by a Protestant.

6.   John of Leiden, an Anabaptist, was tortured to death by Catholics in 1536; William the Silent was assassinated in 1584 by a French Catholic, who was then tortured to death by Protestants. The St. Bartholomew's Day Massacre, in 1572, was of Protestants who were in Paris to celebrate the Protestant (later Catholic) Henri IV's wedding to the Catholic Marguerite of Valois (Queen Margot), daughter of Henri II. Agrippa d'Aubigné (1552–1630) was a Calvinist poet; Pontus de Tyard (1521–1605) was a Catholic bishop as well as a poet; Racan (1589–1670) was a Catholic.

7.   See also Underhill 1930, 59. Mallet-Joris is familiar with Underhill's study, which she refers to it in *Jeanne Guyon* (1978, 488).

8.   Bynum disagrees with this reading, however, and emphasizes the wide variety of ways in which women experienced their relationship to food in the Middle Ages.

9.   si toutes ces austerités ont un sens, ou si elles sont bonnes en soi. . . . [Si] la foi [du moine imaginaire] (lui, le reclus, l'ermite, le stylite peut-être), la perte de poids (elle, au but qu'elle s'est fixé à l'aveuglette), si tout cela a vraiment une importance (107–8).

10.   Just as hagiographers in the Middle Ages sometimes "compared their [female] subjects favorably to the Desert Fathers of antiquity" (Bynum 120), the narrator is drawing an implicit comparison between Jeanne and those hermits, the male saints and other holy men most commonly associated with fasting.

11. le toucher effleurant, supplice de tantale, supplice tantrique, le velouté
     agaçant d'une fesse de pêche . . . un minuscule recoin du mystère de
     l'Incarnation (182).
12.   This phrase echoes (or parodies) the famous French Christmas carol
     "Between the Ox and the Gray Ass" [Entre le boeuf et l'âne gris], whose
     various stanzas all begin with *entre*. What is found between each of these
     things in the song is the Incarnation, the Christ Child in the manger.
13.   le plus dangereux mystère du monde, l'attendait, elle. . . . Et telle . . . sainte
     Lydwine, [qui] balbutiait en l'honneur de Dieu des mots d'enfant. . . . Telle
     Jeanne, dans le puérile enchantement des découvertes essentielles, tendant
     la main . . . se murmurait ces mots qui pesaient, pesaient dorénavant plus que
     tout: "On peut donc s'en passer? Et de ceci? Et de cela? Et on les a tout de
     même? On peut donc se passer de tout?" (183).
14.   Jeanne's last name, Grandier, suggests Urban Grandier, canon of Sainte-
     Croix de Loudon, who was suspected of being a cause of the Ursuline nuns'
     possession in the affair of the "Devils of Loudon" and who was burned alive
     in 1634 ("Urban Grandier," in *Dictionnaire,* 1967).
15.   The name "Divine," which provides the book's title, may also allude to *The
     Divine Comedy,* particularly as Jeanne's spiritual journey, which she makes,
     like Dante, at the age of thirty-five, takes her from suffering through purga-
     tion to a mystical vision.
16.   Technically, she is the "Blessed Lydwina," or "Blessed Lydwine," not a
     saint, but she is commonly referred to as a saint. She lived from 1380 to 1433.
     Her most famous biography is that by Karl-Joris Huysmans, but Bynum also
     treats her extensively (1988, 124–29).
17.   Lydwina is only one of many holy medieval women reported to have eaten
     nothing or almost nothing except the Host for years at a time (Bynum 1988,
     86–93).
18.   On ne *perd* pas du poids: on *gagne* de la légèreté, de la volonté. . . . [C]'est
     une sorte de retournement, comme d'un gant" (191; emphasis in original).
19.   mi-dieux, mi-animaux, satyres amis du dieu Pan, la flûte ou le pénis dressé,
     fécondant les campagnes! (250).
20.   une fruste déesse, lare, pénate ou simple borne—mais sacrée—qui délimite
     le territoire où elle se meut (98).
21.   brûlée jusqu'au coeur, et n'essayant pas plus, respectueuse, de comprendre,
     qu'une petite fille de campagne qui croit voir la Vierge ou saint Michel lui
     parler en patois du lieu (99).
22.   Tout à coup elle fut de nouveau dans le désert de l'été, cheminant. La
     solitude. Dieu, peut-être. Dieu, ce vide, ce manque? La chose qu'on ne peut
     pas retourner, qui n'a ni envers ni endroit, ni densité ni étendue? . . . Le vide
     qui n'est pas le contraire du plein? (218).
23.   Il avait hésité à cause de ces quelques kilos de trop. Elle les avait perdus,
     et n'était plus la même (241).
24. Hutcheon's specific context for this phrase is that of the 1980 Venice Biennale
     of architecture, but she also applies the principle to other situations and arts.

25. Dieu, la chose terrible qui se cache derrière toutes les vaines nourritures . . . c'était bien la Faim (250).

26. Et l'Humain, en lui, un instant, l'emporta: il voulut être mangé, il voulut croire qu'on pouvait rassasier les hommes, lui, le fils de la Faim! (251).

27. telle sainte Lydwine implorant plus nombreuses et plus douloureuses ses plaies (251).

28. ". . . la divine absence, la Faim qui seule comble et, dans l'eau maintenant répandue, glacée, sur le carreau, ployait lentement les genoux" (251).

29. intuitions, ses défaillances, les brusques éclairs de lumière, les plongées dans la nuit (260).

30. Xavier Berthelot may owe his last name to Pierre Berthelot, a French sailor who became a Carmelite in Goa at a mission established by Saint Francis. He was martyred in 1638 ("Pierre Berthelot," in *Dictionnaire*, 1967).

31. comme lui sur scène, entre les marques qui empêchent . . . de sortir de l'étroit espace qui nous est dévolu, borné des deux côtés par les coulisses sombres qui mènent à la folie ou au néant (260).

32. If Jeanne had lived to write of her experience, she would have resembled more strongly Madame Guyon: "Before she had written a line, Jeanne Guyon had already begun on herself an interior work half-perceived since childhood, and similar in its slow development to a secret and precious alchemy" [Avant qu'elle ait écrit une ligne, Jeanne Guyon a déjà commencé sur elle-même un travail intérieur dès l'enfance, et semblable dans son long cheminement à une alchimie secrète et précieuse] (Mallet-Joris 1978, 493). Jeanne Guyon, after many trials, lived a quiet life with her family in Blois. Could the fictional Jeanne have done the same with Didier?

33. deux mains furieuses la serrent à la gorge, ignorant que ce qu'elles étouffent à jamais, et si facilement, c'est un éclat de rire (265).

34. This violent ending has been prepared for by Jeanne's earlier memory of a lurid news story about a Japanese man who killed and ate his Dutch lover. Jeanne speculates that he wanted to possess her forever but realizes that she does not know his motive. The text is especially piquant in French, where a Dutchwoman is "une Hollandaise," like the sauce except for the capital letter: "Maybe he was simply a weirdo, and he didn't love his Dutchwoman/ Hollandaise at all. He just got a little ravenous, that's all" [C'était peut-être un dingue pur et simple, et sa Hollandaise, il ne l'aimait pas du tout. Une petite fringale l'avait pris, c'est tout (170)].

35. ne soyez pas jaloux / De voir qu'au pêcheur en ce monde / Le bien de toutes partes abonde, Il en sort aussi nu que vous (161; Racan 1857, 142–43).

Works Cited

Bell, Rudolph M. 1985. *Holy Anorexia.* Epilogue by William N. Davis. Chicago: University of Chicago Press.

Borchert, Bruno. 1994. *Mysticism: Its History and Challenge.* Trans. Transcript, Ltd. York Beach, ME: Samuel Weiser. Originally published as *Mystiek: geschiedenis, en uitdaging* (Bloemendaal, Netherlands: Uitgeverij J. H. Gottmer/H. J. W. Becht, 1989).

Bordo, Susan. 1993. *Unbearable Weight: Feminism, Western Culture, and the Body.* Berkeley and Los Angeles: University of California Press.

Bynum, Caroline Walker. 1988. *Holy Feast and Holy Fast: The Religious Significance of Food to Medieval Women.* Berkeley and Los Angeles: University of California Press.

Coles, Robert. 1989. *Simone Weil: A Modern Pilgrimage.* Radcliffe Biography Series. Reading, MA: Addison-Wesley.

Corbishley, T. 1967. "Mysticism." *New Catholic Encyclopedia.* Vol. 10. New York: McGraw-Hill. 175–79.

Delaney, John J. 1980. "Bl[essed]. Lydwina." *Dictionary of Saints.* Garden City, NJ: Doubleday.

Dictionnaire de spiritualité ascétique et mystique doctrine et histoire. 1967. Ed. M. Viller et al. Paris: Beauchesne.

Dupré, Louis. 1987. "Mysticism." *The Encyclopedia of Religion.* Vol. 10. Ed. Mircea Eliade. New York: Macmillan. 245–61.

Graef, Hilda. 1965. *The Story of Mysticism.* Garden City, NY: Doubleday.

Happold, F. C. 1970. *Mysticism: A Study and an Anthology.* Rev. ed. Baltimore: Penguin.

Hutcheon, Linda. 1993. "Beginning to Theorize Postmodernism." In *A Postmodern Reader.* Ed. Joseph Natoli and Linda Hutcheon. Albany: State University of New York Press. 243–63.

Huysmans, Joris-Karl. 1901. *Sainte Lydwine de Schiedam.* Paris: Stock.

Kanters, Robert. 1967. Tribute to Albert-Marie Schmidt. In Albert-Marie Schmidt, *Etudes sur le XVIe siècle.* Paris: Albin Michel. 13-14.

Kristeva, Julia. 1992. "A Feminist Postmodernism?" In *Modernism/Postmodernism.* Ed. and Intro. Peter Brooker. London: Longman. 197–203.

Lagorio, Valerie M. 1984. "The Medieval Continental Women Mystics: An Introduction." In *An Introduction to the Medieval Mystics of Europe.* Ed. Paul E. Szarmach. Albany: State University of New York Press. 161-93.

Lathers, Marie. 1993–94. Rev. of *Divine. French Review* 67:166–67.

Lyotard, Jean-François. 1986. *Le Postmodernisme expliqué aux enfants: Correspondance 1982–1985.* Paris: Galilée.

———. 1987. "The Postmodern Condition." In *After Philosophy: End or Transformation?* Ed. Kenneth Baynes. Cambridge: MIT Press. 73—4.

———. 1992. "Answering the Question: What Is Postmodernism?" In *Modernism/Postmodernism.* Ed. and Intro. Peter Brooker. Trans. Régis Durand. London: Longman. 139–50.

Mallet-Joris, Françoise. 1978. *Jeanne Guyon.* [Paris]: Flammarion.

———. 1987. "Mes Bourrelets d'antan." In *Marie-Paul Belle.* Paris: Seghers. 135–36.

———. 1991. *Divine.* [Paris]: Flammarion.

Noiville, Florence. 1991. "Maigrir, dit-elle." *Monde* (13 September): 22.

Nourissier, François. 1991. "Dieu aime les gros." *Figaro Magazine* (12 October): 127.

Racan [Honorat de]. 1857. "Le XLVIIIe Pseaume." In *Oeuvres complètes de Racan.* Vol.2. New ed. Ed. M. Tenant de Latour. Paris: P. Jannet. 141–43.

Springsted, Eric O. 1986. *Simone Weil and the Suffering of Love.* Preface by Robert Coles. Cambridge, MA: Cowley.

Underhill, Evelyn. 1930. *Mysticism: A Study in the Nature and Development of Man's Spiritual Consciousness.* 12th ed. London: Methuen. Rpt. New York: Meridian, 1974.

———. [1938?]. *The Spiritual Life.* New York: Harper.

Weil, Simone. 1952. *Gravity and Grace.* Intro. Gustave Thibon. Trans. Arthur Wills. New York: Putnam.

Zum Brunn, Emilie and Georgette Epiney-Burgard. 1989. *Women Mystics in Medieval Europe.* Trans. Sheila Hughes. New York: Paragon. Originally published as *Femmes, troubadours de Dieu.* (Belgium: Brepols, 1988).

10

Reconceiving God:
Luce Irigaray's "Divine Women"

Sam McBride

Luce Irigaray has spoken strongly against traditional Christianity, particularly the Roman Catholic Church which has figured prominently in French culture. The traditional Christian view of God as male, she believes, supports the patriarchal privileging of men and a corresponding devaluation of women. She implies that Christianity neglects women, and that in the moments when it does consider women it mystifies them; "God knows women so well," she points out with more than a little sarcasm in *Speculum of the Other Woman*, "that he never touches them directly, but always in that fleeting stealth of a fantasy that evades all representation" (Irigaray 1985, 236). Irigaray's opposition to theism has extended beyond Christianity. In the introduction to *Sexes and Genealogies* the model for Freud's Oedipal triangulation (which gives creative, originative abilities exclusively to men) is briefly traced to Greece and shown to depend on a God-Father, whether Greek, Roman, Hebrew, or Christian (Irigaray 1993, v).

From this perspective, however, Irigaray's essay "Divine Women" (from *Sexes and Genealogies*) seems surprising in its attitude toward theism. Irigaray says, "Divinity is what we [women] need to become free. . . . If women have no God, they are unable either to communicate or commune with one another" (Irigaray 1993, 62). Given the patriarchal Christian assumption that God is male, such statements appear startling to readers familiar with Irigaray's habit of deconstructing patriarchal structures. Graduate students in a 1993 seminar on feminist discourse (in which I first encountered the essay) concluded that Irigaray had "gone overboard" into mystical spirituality; she was jokingly dubbed by the seminar professor "the Shirley MacLaine of theory."

Yet Irigaray's interactions with theism do not stem from a conversion to mysticism, whether "new age" or otherwise. In another essay from *Sexes and Genealogies* ("Women, the Sacred, Money"), Irigaray notes that "it seems we are unable to eliminate or suppress the phenomenon of religion." As a result, "it is crucial that we rethink religion, and especially religious structures, categories, initiations, rules, and utopias, all of which have been masculine for centuries" (1993, 75). "Divine Women," therefore, describes, very briefly, Irigaray's concept (or perhaps conception) of a feminine god, one that, of course, contrasts with the traditional Christian God. While Irigaray's essay has not sparked a massive conversion to theism on the part of feminists (even Irigaray, as far as I know, remains an atheist), and while the essay has had even less impact on Christianity,[1] it should be recognized as unique among contemporary secular feminist theoretical writings in the extent to which it uses theistic concepts and terminology as a source for women's progress and development.

In this chapter, I want to examine the implications of Irigaray's intervention into theism, particularly in "Divine Women." Irigaray's strategy in this essay involves two simultaneous gestures: deconstructing a patriarchal structure (specifically, the philosophy of Ludwig Feuerbach, which itself reconstructs theism), and reconstructing the deconstructed structure for women. I also want to examine three difficulties inherent in Irigaray's strategy. First, the problem of essentialism: does Irigaray rely on an essential nature of "woman" that better suits and even privileges some specific women? Irigaray's work has been an important site in the feminist essentialism/anti-essentialism debate; "Divine Women" suggests Irigaray is on both sides. The second problem concerns the difficulties surrounding feminist appropriation: does ideological, or in this case gender, residue from the appropriated resurface in the appropriation? Any act of verbal borrowing raises this question (as Wright's essay on Midrash in this collection points out), but Irigaray's essay suggests that effects transpire in both directions between the appropriated and the appropriation. Third is the question whether Irigaray proposes a "kyriocentric" (master-centered, to borrow Schussler Fiorenza's term) totalizing structure: does Irigaray lay the groundwork for a new and potentially oppressive theistic system? In fact, Irigaray avoids such a system by denying the mastery of her feminine god and even her own mastery as 'theologian' of such a god. I will conclude by acknowledging some further implications from Irigaray's involvement with theism.

Deconstructing Feuerbach

Irigaray's work stems from an extensive cultural project she proposed many years ago. Irigaray has articulated feminists' "need to ask ourselves how to give an identity to scientific, religious, and political discourses, and how to situate ourselves in these discourses as subjects in our own right" (Jardine and Menke 1991, 101).[2] She also describes her work as "focusing at times on one section of culture, at times on another, in order to rethink the way in which culture is constituted" (1991, 103). In other words, Irigaray's movement into and through religion is part of her strategy for examining what happens to culture, and what would need to happen to culture, if women were recognized as subjects.

Furthermore, almost always Irigaray's writings are actually feminist deconstructive readings. That is, when Irigaray writes she reacts to, and in a sense writes over, a preexisting text, typically by a prominent male philosopher. To understand Irigaray's writing, one must also encounter the text she is working with (or perhaps working against). In the case of "Divine Women," Irigaray is reacting to Ludwig Feuerbach, as she makes clear in a footnote to the essay: "readers interested in an exact understanding of 'Divine Women'" should read the introduction of Feuerbach's *The Essence of Christianity*.

Feuerbach developed an atheistic explanation of Christianity, one that has influenced contemporary critical theory through Freud and Marx. Feuerbach claims man's nature as man's absolute (Feuerbach 1957, 5), with the nature of God simply the nature of man's emotion (1957, 9). God is always within man, in the same way that consciousness is within man: "consciousness of God," he says, "is self-consciousness" (1957, 12), though, generally speaking, man will not be aware of that fact. Religion is an indirect form of self-knowledge, and man's earliest such form; before man perceived his own nature, he projected that nature out of himself, as an external god (1957, 13). Of course, when man projected god out of himself, he made god appear better than what man appeared to himself; the divine being was "purified, freed from the limits of the individual man" (1957, 14). Feuerbach posits an evolutionary religious progression, in which man's earlier assumptions of an exterior god will someday be realized for what it is, man himself. Feuerbach, of course, claims to have reached that ultimate stage, awareness that "the antithesis of divine and human is altogether illusory" (1957, 13).

The significance of such a belief system to a post-Lacanian psychoanalyst such as Irigaray should be apparent, and by significance I mean not simply "importance," but quite literally its ability to communicate meaning through signs. Feuerbach's belief that man unconsciously constructed god by positing himself as an other, better than himself, is fundamentally similar to Lacan's explanation of the mirror stage, where the infant sees her image in a mirror and posits that image as a whole, complete entity, and therefore because it is whole and complete, better than herself. For Lacan, of course, that mirror image is not God, but then again the god Feuerbach posits isn't God (in the traditional sense) either.

Interestingly enough, several years before writing "Divine Women," Irigaray had expressed a view similar to Feuerbach's in *Speculum of the Other Woman*: "I think, therefore God is," (1985, 186). Yet at that time,

Irigaray's use of the phrase was heavily tinged with irony. She continued, "God is, but it is the 'I' that by thinking has granted him that essence and existence that the 'I' expects from God" (1985, 187). Irigaray's understanding of the projection she termed *god* at that time was informed by Lacan's mirror stage; projecting God, she suggested, results in a lack, not only a lack of god, but a lack within the subject as well.

In fact, Irigaray, reading Feuerbach, finds a specific lack within Feuerbach's discourse, namely, his exclusive use of male nouns and pronouns. If man, at some historical moment, posited an improved version of himself as god, what was woman doing? This question becomes especially important as Feuerbach continues his dissertation on god; for if god is merely man's nature glorified, then doubting the existence of god is doubting the existence of man. Having no god at all, Feuerbach implies, suggests that a person doesn't exist.

If having no god suggests that a person doesn't exist, then women, it would seem, don't exist, or at least not as persons, as subjects. Since god is simply human nature posited as outside of humanity, if women have no god, it must be because they have no nature. This, of course, prevents women from developing a god, since one needs an originary feminine nature from which to posit a god. When women are introduced into the Feuerbachian system, in other words, they are sucked into a vicious cycle of negation. "Woman scatters," Irigaray says, "and becomes an agent of destruction and annihilation because she has no other of her own that she can become" (Irigaray 1993, 64); Irigaray might rewrite Feuerbach as saying, "To doubt of [a female] God is to doubt of [woman her]self."

Reconstructing Feuerbach

Thus far my interpretation of Irigaray's essay has focused on deconstructing Feuerbach by asking about women's place within his system. But the essay does more than read and write over *The Essence of Christianity*. After deconstructing Feuerbach, Irigaray turns to reconstructing his version of Christianity for women, a gesture Serena Jones has appropriately identified as utopian (1995, 55). She suggests that Feuerbach's system can be broken into at any point. For example, one can posit a female divinity, a projection of women's best qualities. This would provide women with an example of what their natures should be; thus, "Divinity is what we need to become free" (1993, 62).[3] Or again, women could explore their own preexisting nature(s), which, in the Feuerbachian sense, is a form of constructing a divine; Irigaray hints at this when she speaks of woman lacking "a divine made in her own image" (1993, 63).

Abandoning her earlier Lacanian assumption that projecting a god results in a subjective lack, Irigaray takes both these strategies; that is, she constructs a feminine divine, but based on what she believes is (or should be) women's natures. Irigaray's feminine divine contrasts with the attributes of the Greco-Christian "God the Father," who is traditionally thought to be unchanging, originary, hierarchically situated at the top of the chain of being, and though disembodied, more male than female. Irigaray's god/woman, in contrast, is process, always "in gestation" (1993, 63). Irigaray alludes here to "mothering," the shifting between darkness (the womb during gestation of the fetus) and light (the womb exposed during and after birth). Process also characterizes women's dual (sometimes vacillating, sometimes united) roles of mother and lover. This notion of process is "the idea of becoming" (Whitford 1991, 47). Of course, as Jones argues, a concept of women's becoming implies a focus on social ethics, rather than ontology (1995, 57).

Irigaray's god/woman will also be autonomous, rather than linked within a hierarchical chain of cause and effect. This means that the feminine divine does not require a male divine, nor any power relationship between them. With the divine as model, woman will also be autonomous from man, free from enslavement within a patriarchal cultural system. The ensuing freedom removes woman from her culturally assigned role as obligated to man.

Irigaray also defines her feminine divine/nature by means of negatives. That feminine divine involves neither suffering nor sacrifice. She requires no faith in an other, "other than the faith in the possibility of our autonomy, our salvation" (1993, 68). She is not to be a communal aspect of some future feminine culture, but should remain individual. This latter point seems calculated to interfere with the two characteristics of the feminine divine which Irigaray has spelled out. If constructing a feminine divine is an individual matter, then perhaps an individual woman could construct a feminine divine *outside of* the divine nature briefly described by Irigaray. In other words, Irigaray's emphasis on the process she wants to see women undergo, the process of constructing a feminine divine, overshadows and overpowers the divine characteristics Irigaray sets forth. Irigaray's exposition of a feminine divine is descriptive rather than prescriptive; the need to construct such a divine is "essential" (and in the context of Feuerbach, essential to humans, regardless of gender) while the characteristics are not.

The (In)Essential Nature of the Feminine Divine

Perhaps no aspect of Irigaray's writing has been more hotly debated than whether or not Irigaray is an essentialist.[4] In general, both sides of this debate have tended to agree that essentialism, positing some characteristics as identifying (yet exclusive to) all women, would be a negative practice for Irigaray to espouse. The debate, therefore, has vacillated between Irigaray's detractors, who condemn her for being an essentialist, and her supporters, who praise her for *not* being an essentialist. At least in this essay, however, Irigaray carefully positions herself as both essentialist and nonessentialist (a strategy that frustrates efforts to definitively label Irigaray, and which, I suspect, sparks her centrality to the essentialism debate in the first place).

In "Divine Women," just after arguing the need for a feminine divine, but before addressing what the feminine divine should be (in other words, *before* describing her two qualities, process and autonomy), Irigaray digresses on the subject of female beauty, particularly as revealed in a mirror or in the gaze of an "other." This digression illustrates both Irigaray's "essentialist alterity" as well as her objection to assuming a god-projection must result in subjective lack. Mirrors, she suggests, have not been used by women as tools for self-exploration; rather, women have used mirrors primarily to prepare their appearance so that they will please someone else. Mirrors, therefore, and the gaze (to the extent that it acts as a mirror), serve to enforce an obedience.[5]

Mirrors, Irigaray continues, shouldn't work that way. "The mirror should support, not undermine my incarnation" (1993, 65). This argument further interferes with Irigaray's development of the feminine divine, dispersing and deflecting the train of that thought into several directions at once. First, the thought stands alone as a critique of the ways in which women have used (or been allowed to use) mirrors. That which has been classified as narcissism by psychoanalysis has been a self-destruction imposed on women by the patriarchy.

Second, in the larger context of Irigaray's work, this digression evokes the image of the speculum mirror which Irigaray also invoked in *Speculum of the Other Woman*. The speculum mirror (because it is concave) always distorts the image it reflects. However, even a plane mirror reduces a body's volume to two dimensions. This is a phenomenon Irigaray takes as especially important, having attempted to theorize from women's anatomy (the vagina and the womb as spaces, volumes, rather than objects, like the penis), and suggests a possible direction for women in constructing a god (as volume, space, rather than being).

Third, conjoining the mirror and the gaze invokes, once again, Lacan's theorizations on those two phenomena. In the Lacanian system, men and women both travel through the mirror stage and are both equally object to the all-seeing, never-acknowledging gaze; men, however, at least have the object which "stands out as most easily seized upon in the real of sexual copulation"[6] (Lacan 1982, 82). While having the penis is not quite the same as having the phallus, having the penis, in the Lacanian configuration, seems somewhat better than not having the penis. Mirrors and gazes, it can be argued, are doubly unpleasant for women since they remind women of their (phallic and penile) lack, while men are at least reassured that they have the penis. Thus when Irigaray suggests that "the mirror should support, not undermine my incarnation" (1993, 65), she is arguing, once again, for a means of theorizing human development that doesn't depict women as even worse off than men, and that doesn't use women as simply a poor reflection of men. Constructing a feminine divine is another instance of Irigaray's project of developing a feminine imaginary; Irigaray's Feuerbachian reconfiguration works against Lacan's Freudian reconfiguration (and remember, once again, the influence of Feuerbach on Freud).

Equally significant for Irigaray's construction of a feminine divine, this discussion of mirrors offers a deconstruction of her own project. Feuerbach posited a system whereby god is actually a reflection, a mirror image of man. Within the Feuerbachian system, "woman has no mirror wherewith to become woman" (1993, 67). Appropriating Feuerbach for women involves creating an image of woman, a deity (or deities) that mirrors women. Such an image, Irigaray warns, can end up trapping women. Creating a god as a model for women to realize their subjectivities must not be confused with creating an essentialist, universal woman. "The mirror must support, not undermine my incarnation." This suggests that different incarnations of women might require different gods/models of becoming.

All of these problems regarding mirrors conflate. One reason Irigaray avoids providing a precise god-as-mirror-image-of-woman is her knowledge that mirrors always distort whatever images they reflect (if in no other way, by flattening them out). Furthermore, in order to provide women with models for becoming subjects, Irigaray appropriates (mirrors) for women Feuerbach's system whereby man posits God as a perfection of man's subjectivity. At the same time, she wants to avoid the pitfalls of the (very similar) Lacanian system, whereby positing the perfection, the wholeness, of the other in the mirror, one develops a strong sense of inadequacy and lack. Women are already provided with a strong sense of inadequacy within patriarchal systems; they will not be able to exit or diminish the influence of the patriarchy by emulating an impossible-to-emulate divine superwoman. The mirror serves as a warning, to writer and reader alike, to exercise extreme caution in universalizing a feminine divine, and in essentializing women.

Irigaray's warning, however, does not prohibit her from providing "essential" qualities for a feminine divine. I take this conflict within the essay, this opposition to an "essential" nature combined with a brief statement of an "essential" nature, to suggest a means of escape from the essentialism debate. One can invoke an essentialism for some creative, constructive purpose (the "strategic essentialism" approach promoted by Gayatri Spivak [1990, 11–12]) while opposing essentialism in general (and while, as Irigaray does, remaining aware of the dangers of such a strategy); in such a case, one is and one is not an essentialist. To oversimplify, Irigaray chooses to assert "essential" feminine characteristics, but does not assume it is "essential" that all women possess those characteristics.

The Feminine Divine Is (Not) the Goddess; Gender and Theistic Language

Irigaray's understanding of the danger of essentializing the nature of a feminine divine may explain why Irigaray tends to avoid the term *goddess* in her essay. Goddess theology may imply a preexisting entity with which women can communicate or interact, an entity roughly comparable to (though vastly different from) the traditional (male) Christian God. Irigaray suggests that, rather than finding a preexisting goddess, women must make their own. At the same time, Irigaray does not oppose goddess theology, or suggest her model of the feminine divine as an alternative to the goddess; rather than promoting an entity, Irigaray urges women to engage themselves in the process of constructing a feminine divine. This degree of openness to what can qualify as the feminine divine implies that, should a woman so choose, she could take as her model some preexisting goddess theology. Thus, while Irigaray's feminine divine is not the goddess, nothing prevents it from being the goddess.

Yet Irigaray's choice to avoid using the noun "goddess," a noun that may have suggested certain essential characteristics for the feminine divine, introduces a further risk in Irigaray's essay. Irigaray chooses, instead, to use the term *god*, a noun that (at least in Western culture) is irretrievably male. Other religious terminology in Irigaray's essay has similar male connotations, if not explicitly male denotations. The Judeo-Christian tradition has positioned its God as male, a father figure, and has restricted access to its God to men. The few instances where the divine and the feminine coexist in the Bible can be categorized in two realms: maternal qualities attributed to the male God (largely overshadowed by his paternal qualities), and wholly evil female "false gods," always contrasted with God the Spirit by their embodiment as idols. Thus when Irigaray names the Trinity, the reader remembers "father, son, and (male?) holy spirit"; when she speaks of angels, the reader thinks of Gabriel and Michael. Her terminology is historically inhabited by concepts gendered male.

A post-structural understanding of language, that all signifiers are caught up in interconnected chains or webs of meanings, suggests that Irigaray's attempt to create a feminine divine will automatically import the male connotations of her religious signifiers. When she speaks of God's touch (especially when using God with a capital G), her word choice connects that image to examples of the (male) Christian God touching: God extending his finger to Adam on the Sistine Chapel ceiling, God writing with his finger the law in stone, God "touching" evildoers by enacting their destruction, and God appropriating Adam's rib to make Eve, as well as (the male) Christ touching to heal the sick. No matter what Irigaray does with her traditional, Christian religious terms, no matter what gender she gives them, they still invoke the name of Abba, the Father God.

Thus any use or appropriation of patriarchal theistic terms is at least a partial return to the gendered bias of those terms. Irigaray seems well aware of this difficulty (which further indicates the appropriateness of the noun form of the word "divine," which by definition includes females). Irigaray's construction of a feminine divine is, in part, an effort to create a new context for theistic terminology, one developed out of the preexisting patriarchal context, and one into which women might feel (more) comfortable entering. Because this new context stems from the old, it both is and is not that older context, the patriarchal context. It connects with that older context, but it leads somewhere else, outside of the sacrificial framework of traditional religion.

That "somewhere else" toward which Irigaray moves need not be some place completely unexplored. Though Irigaray makes no mention of any postmodern theologian or school of theologic thought, her work is not incompatible with contemporary theology, a field quite foreign to most cultural theorists. In the rare moments when critics and theorists deal with religious matters, according to C. Douglas Atkins, "they tend to treat theology as if it were monolithic and naive, almost pre-Darwinian and literalist"; the result is "a caricature that the enlightened theorist has little trouble demolishing" (Atkins 1985, 92). Atkins laments that, while theologians have paralleled recent trends in philosophy, theory, and literary criticism, philosophers, theorists, and critics seem remarkably ignorant of those parallels in theology (1985, 90). One such trend in theology is a feminist-inspired movement away from the traditional Christian view of god as male. Thus while Irigaray herself might be guilty of deconstructing a mode of theology no longer considered valid by theologians, Atkins's assessment suggests a theologic space already affected by deconstruction and other postmodern theoretical practices, a space that parallels Irigaray's reconstruction.[7] Atkins, for example, cites Eberhard Jungel's assertion that God is no longer viewed as fixed or static, but rather "God is a Becoming" (Atkins 1985, 93), or as Irigaray suggests, process.

From the perspective of postmodern theology, terms such as *god* will indeed always possess male connotations (at least historically); even Atkins, while lamenting that literary critics seem unaware of theological developments, refers to God as "He." But theological terms need not continue to possess male connotations exclusively. Thus while Irigaray's use of patriarchal theistic terms will inevitably bring along masculine connotations, her use will also (perhaps less inevitably) infuse those terms with feminine connotations.

A Non-Denominational Reformation

One difficulty in creating a "new space" for feminist theistic discourse is that it will coexist with the "old space" of patriarchal discourse. This could be construed to suggest that women should develop a "separate but equal" religious tradition. At times, Irigaray seems to support such a move. Traditionally, man has "belong[ed] to the line of a Father God," she says; therefore, "does not [woman] need a Mother God? The two genealogies must be divinized in each of the two sexes and for the two sexes, mother and father, woman and man" (1991, 115).[8]

Such a development, however, would most likely mirror patriarchal religious structures with the same hierarchical, oppressive qualities. These structures tend toward totalizing systems of thought, attempting to encompass the entire universe and invariably resulting in privileging and emphasizing some elements while ignoring and subjugating others. In the case of Irigaray's work, a totalizing structure that might conceivably arise would be a religion for women with several primary deities. While Irigaray does nothing to suggest forms of worship for women within such a religion, one can imagine later commentators creating a feminist Talmud specifying what women can and cannot do, and perhaps disallowing men from access to the feminine divine (except, of course, through women).

Such a development would be constraining for women (and men), rather than liberating. Suggesting a full-scale theistic system, a theology, for women would counteract the benefits Irigaray hopes to achieve by constructing a feminine divine. If indeed Irigaray were to suggest a theologic system for women, the consequence would roughly parallel the difficulties faced by the feminist who fights for equal wages for women, while not questioning exploitative capitalist structures or suggesting that men take on traditionally "feminine" qualities.

Combating a sense of "system" within Irigaray's theology is a significant level of contradiction purposefully introduced into the text. Patriarchal religion has traditionally spurned contradiction; reams of pages of biblical commentary, for example, have argued that a given scriptural passage does not actually conflict with another passage, despite how much it might appear to. Irigaray's "theology" welcomes contradiction. She suggests (reading Feuerbach) that a god is necessary (apparently a priori) for women to complete their gender; nearby she asserts that women must construct a god in their own image. At some moments she posits a feminine divine, apparently as a nonhuman entity; at others she asserts the divine can only be within persons. Such contradictions carry their own deconstruction; rather than a totalizing structure, Irigaray constructs an ever-changing polymorphosity, a cloud rather than a cathedral.

Conclusion

For Irigaray, then, conceiving an imaginary feminine divine is a useful strategy for an individual woman to pursue. The strategy will provide a positive model to emulate, based on her best preexisting or desired qualities. Since each woman would need to determine for herself what the qualities and characteristics of her feminine divine or goddess would be, the result is not (necessarily) ontologically essentialist. As Esther D. Reed asserts, "Hers is an embracing of God for the sake of women, not for the sake of God" (1994). While a feminine divine would have an affiliation with traditional theistic understandings of a male god (in the sense that "feminine divine" calls to mind the word and concept "god"), that affiliation would not only "taint" the concept of a feminine divine, but would simultaneously affect (or perhaps infect) patriarchal theistic god-talk. And rather than launching a new religion, Irigaray's argument remains primarily a gesture, a purposeful meddling within a patriarchal cultural field which, Irigaray believes, might serve to redirect that field in a manner useful for (at least some) women.

Irigaray's essay is unique among the work of atheistic theorists in its willingness both to "take seriously" and to *use* theistic discourse. While other theorists have addressed theistic or Christian discourse, their primary purpose has been to reveal its oppressive nature in hope that the revelation would serve to counteract its oppressive force. Thus while Julia Kristeva traces the discursive history of Mariology in "Stabat Mater," she concludes that a development of a "feminine ethics" would "[swallow] up the goddesses and [remove] their necessity" (989, 202). Though deconstructing a theistic construct, Irigaray acknowledges the continued value of working within, of reconstructing, that construct. Irigaray's essay joins the work of feminist theologians in rethinking theism.[9] Whether or not it has been influenced by such work, "Divine Women" suggests the possibility of two-way dialogue between atheistic feminist theorists and feminist theologians.

Notes

1. Serena Jones's essay "Divining Women: Irigaray and Feminist Theologies" is an examination of the implications for feminist theologians of Irigaray's appropriation of theistic terminology, and is therefore one of the few published reactions to Irigaray's work within theological circles.
2. That Irigaray's interventions are having an impact on culture can be seen in recent debates over the World Wide Web concerning the validity of Irigaray's critiques of science. See, for example, Oron 1998 and Sleator, 1996.
3. Lorraine Gauthier suggests that such a project would provide women with a "symbolic language through which we can return to our origin, in order to go beyond" (1986, 44). Irigaray's essay ignores the idea of origin, perhaps in keeping with the nature of Feuerbach's construction.
4. For an excellent summary of this debate, see Kirby, 1991.
5. For a useful commentary on Irigaray's discussion of mirrors, see Peel 1986, 113–14.
6. This is Jacqueline Rose's translation. Alan Sheridan's, for *Écrits*, is somewhat more prosaic: the phallus is simply "the most tangible element in the real of sexual copulation" (Lacan 1977, 287).
7. Mark C. Taylor has begun exploring a post-deconstructive theological space in his books (notably *Deconstructing Theology*); in this regard, see the essay by Hayes elsewhere in this collection. Paula M. Cooey suggests a post-patriarchal space within Christian theology affected by feminist theory in a brief article in *After Patriarchy: Feminist Transformations of World Religions*, while Marjorie Hewitt Suchocki in *God, Christ, Church* maps out the compatibility of feminism with a post-Christian philosophy known as Process Theology; this latter theology, a form of panentheism, has potentially interesting compatibilities with Irigaray's theologic imagery, since both focus on process rather than being, and both consider god embodied. Jones examines and critiques the similarities and differences between Irigaray and process theology (1995, 49–55).
8. This quote not only goes on to suggest an essentialist need for a feminine divine, but apparently does so in order to support an essentialist heterosexuality.

9.   See Jones for an appraisal of Irigaray from the perspective of feminist
theology.   Jones unwisely chastises Irigaray for an "uncritical" use of
Feuerbach (my analysis within this chapter shows Irigaray's feminist criticism of Feuerbach), but astutely challenges Irigaray to grant her feminine
divine agency with the characteristics of self–love and wondrous responsiveness.   These are the same characteristics Irigaray seeks for women, yet
Irigaray restricts the feminine divine to a self–referential "empty sign."   Instead, Jones implies feminist theologians will be most interested in a feminine
divine that is truly an "other," rather than "really only . . . herself" (1995, 65).

Works Cited

Atkins, G. Douglas. 1985. "A(fter) D(econstruction): The Relations of Literature and Religion in the Wake of Deconstruction." *Studies in the Literary Imagination* 18 (1): 89–100.

Cooey, Paula M. 1991. "The Redemption of the Body: Post-Patriarchal Reconstruction of Inherited Christian Doctrines." In *After Patriarchy: Feminist Transformations of World Religions*. Maryknoll, NY: Orbis. 106-30.

Feuerbach, Ludwig. 1957. *The Essence of Christianity*. Trans. George Eliot. New York: Harper.

Gauthier, Lorraine. 1986. "Desire for Origin/Original Desire: Luce Irigaray on Maternity, Sexuality and Language." *Canadian Fiction Magazine* 57:41–46.

Irigaray, Luce. 1985. *Speculum of the Other Woman*. Trans. Gillian C. Gill. Ithaca: Cornell University Press.

———. 1991. "Questions to Emmanuel Levinas: On the Divinity of Love." In *Re-Reading Levinas*. Trans. Margaret Whitford. Ed. Robert Bernasconi and Simon Critchley. Bloomington: Indiana University Press. 109–18.

———. 1993. *Sexes and Genealogies*. Trans. Gillian C. Gill. New York: Columbia University Press.

Jardine, Alice A. and Anne M. Menke, eds. 1991. "Luce Irigaray." In *Shifting Scenes: Interviews on Women, Writing, and Politics in Post-68 France*. Trans. Margaret Whitford. New York: Columbia University Press.

Jones, Serena. 1995. "Divining Women: Irigaray and Feminist Theologies." In *Another Look, Another Woman: Retranslations of French Feminism*. Yale French Studies, no. 87. Ed. Lynne Huffer. New Haven: Yale University Press. 42–67.

Kirby, Vicki. 1991. "'Corpus Delicti': The Body at the Scene of Writing." In *Cartographies: Poststructuralism and the Mapping of Bodies and Spaces*. Ed. Rosalyn Diprose and Robyn Ferrell. Boston: Allen and Unwin.

Kristeva, Julia. 1989. "Stabat Mater." In *Contemporary Literary Criticism: Literary and Cultural Studies*. 2nd ed. Ed. Robert Con Davis and Ronald Schleifer. New York: Longman. 186–203.

Lacan, Jacques. 1977. "The Signification of the Phallus." In *Écrits: A Selection*. Trans. Alan Sheridan. New York: Norton. 281–91.

———. 1982. "The Meaning of the Phallus." *Feminine Sexuality: Jacques Lacan and the École Freudienne*. Trans. Jacqueline Rose. New York: Norton. 74–85.

Oron, Gadi. 1998. "Irigaray." 21 March 1997. Online. Internet. 15 Feb. Available: http://pmmh.espci.fr/~oron/bricmont/node17.html

Peel, Ellen. 1986. "The Irony of Women: Reflections of Irigaray." *Cincinnati Romance Review* 5:109–20.

Reed, Esther D. 1994. "Feminism and Love of the 'Unreal' God." *Modern Believing* 35 (October):17–22. Online. Internet. 15 Feb. 1998. Available: http://emma.cam.ac.uk/fellows/cupitt/sea_of_faith/feminism.html

Sleator, Daniel. 1996. "Manifold Theory: (W)holes and Boundaries." 6 June. Online. Internet. 15 Feb. 1998. Available: http://www.physics.nyu.edu/faculty/sokal/transgress_v2/node5.html

Spivak, Gayatri Chakravorty. 1990. *The Post-Colonial Critic: Interviews, Strategies,*

Dialogues. Ed. Sarah Harasym. New York: Routledge.

Suchocki, Marjorie Hewitt. 1982. *God, Christ, Church: A Practical Guide to Process Theology*. New York: Crossroad.

Taylor, Mark C. 1982. *Deconstructing Theology*. American Academy of Religion Studies in Religion 28. New York: Crossroad.

Whitford, Margaret. 1991. *Luce Irigaray: Philosophy in the Feminine*. London: Routledge.

11

Beastly Theology:
When Epistemology Creates Ontology

Carol J. Adams

Mortals deem that gods are begotten as they are, and have clothes like theirs, and voices and form . . . yes, and if oxen and horses or lions had hands, and could paint with their hands, and produce works of art as men do, horses would paint the forms of gods like horses, and oxen like oxen, and make their bodies in the image of their several kinds. . . . The Ethiopians make their gods black and snub-nosed; the Tracians say theirs have blue eyes and red hair.

—Xenophanes

Talking about whether or not animals feel pain, is like talking about the existence of God.

—an animal researcher

Similarities exist between discussing the other animals and discussing God, and no, it is not just that *dog* is *God* spelled backwards. Granted, some of the similarities are actually expressed in opposition: the idea of God as an unembodied, disincarnate force, while animals are seen as soulless and solely body. The charge of anthropomorphizing, often laid at the feet of animal defenders, originally referred to language about God. As Mary Midgley points out, anthropomorphism "may be the only example of a notion invented solely for God, and then transferred unchanged to refer to animals" (Midgley 1983, 125).

Our concepts of God, ourselves, and how we relate to animals are all bound together. Theologically as well as culturally positioned under man's control, animals have been devalued. While all language about God is metaphorical, animals often become reduced to metaphors that reflect human concerns, human lives.[1] The term *beast* functions in this way. Beastly theology is Christian patriarchal theology about animals, in which they are seen as "beasts" in a pejorative sense—categorized as less than, as representing the opposite of human beings.

We will explore some of the problems inherent in this Christian beastly theology, because it has influenced and interacted with Western philosophy in positing animals as usable. In this chapter, I raise some of the philosophical issues that theology must attend to so that it is not used to uphold institutional violence. I place epistemological issues central to beastly theology, both to explore the problems of Christian beastly theology and to help shape theology that does not marginalize the other animals, but affirms relationships with them, treats them according to a transvaluation of their status, and that ultimately retires the word *beast* from the English language.

Anthropomorphism can go either up or down, humanizing either the deity or animals; but if the vertical distance is closed in any way, that is, between God and humans or between humans and animals, many are disconcerted. Curious, then, that one of the few feminine images of the divine presented in the New Testament moves downward past humans entirely, drawing instead on an image from the world of animals. It is actually pollo-morphic: "How often have I desired to gather your children together as a hen gathers her brood under her wings, and you were not willing!" (Lk 13:34; see also Mt 23:37). In talking about the other animals, including whether or not they feel pain, we must bring the theological attention and skills we would bring to talking about the existence of God. We must, in other words, attend to this with as much care as a hen gathering her brood under her wings.

What Is Beastly Theology? The Patriarchal Christian Answer

> The tame animal is in the deepest sense the only natural animal
> [and] [b]easts are to be understood only in their relation to man and
> through man to God. (C. S. Lewis, quoted in Yi-Fu Tuan 1984, 69)

C.S. Lewis accepts a hierarchy of value that determines where on the continuum God, men, and beasts fall.[2] The vertical boundaries that divide human and animal are related to the boundaries that have been inscribed between maleness and femaleness, God and humans. This results in a patriarchal beastly theology that contradictorily knows that something invisible exists (God), while denying the sensory information available that indicates any sorts of relevant connections between humans and animals. Barbara Noske points to the contradictions of anthropocentric theory, and by implications, beastly theology: "I have always wondered how humans

(Marxists and others) can be so sure about their own *ability* to judge animal *inabilities*. Humans pretend to know *from within* that they themselves possess certain faculties and to know *from without* that animals do not" (Noske 1989, 77). How do we explain beastly theologies that know from within that God exists, but similarly know from without that animals' consciousness does not exist, or that it is not ethically relevant? Feminist theologian Paula Cooey offers one answer: it is "way too easy to project a God in our own image because it is simple to commit idolatry and way too difficult to project pain and pleasure on actual sentient nonhuman creatures. Thus we can project a conscious being and call it God because we perceive it as a linguistic being, but it is much harder to do this with animals because it is hard to attribute consciousness, pain, and suffering to a nonlinguistic being."[3]

Certainly the theological centrality of the Word in Christian thought militates against recognizing animals as subjects of their own lives. Whether used literally (in the sense of valuing spoken and written words over other forms of communication), or metaphorically (in the identification of Jesus Christ as God's definitive "Word"), it has the effect of marginalizing and objectifying those who have no words. Although God speaks in other, nonverbal ways in Scripture—whirlwind, fire, political upheaval, military victory or defeat—God's definitive communication is in the form of words: the Decalogue, the Law, Scripture, etc. Speaking thus becomes identified with holy power. Language provides us with both a sense of affinity with God and subject status, while simultaneously confirming the object status of those who have no speech.[4]

But this focus on language may deflect our attention from the knowledge claims that are presupposed in patriarchal beastly theologies. Language may be one of the methods for acquiring knowledge, but to stake one's knowledge claims solely on language becomes self-referential, as Cooey implies when she points to how easy it is to commit idolatry. Moreover, "the most eloquent signs of pain, human or animal, are nonlinguistic" (Rollin 1981, 32). Why, when projected God-ward, is one form of inner knowledge acceptable, but projected animal-ward, is this form of knowledge rendered unacceptable, and the external knowledge we can gain from animals eloquently expressing pain distrusted? Because anthropocentricity is inherently circular, arising from and referring to human beings. As Donald Griffin, a leading ethologist, remarks:

> I believe that with due caution it is reasonable to make some use of such analogies between human and animal behaviour and mental experience, for the simple reason that central nervous systems are

so similar in all their basic attributes, as far as we know. Against the
charge that such reasoning by analogy is mistakenly anthropomorphic, I have pointed out that such anthropomorphism is mistaken
only if there are indeed fundamental and absolute differences between human and non-human mental experiences. Since this is the
question under discussion, it is prejudicial to assume, even by implication, that one of the possible answers to the question is necessarily correct.[5]

Anthropocentric theology is inherently circular, too. When theology is
modeled upon the traditional, self-referential conceptualizations of the God–
human relationship, knowledge claims on behalf of the other animals are
most likely to be excluded.

Value Hierarchies and Dualisms

Value-hierarchical thinking, or "up-down thinking," places higher value,
status, or prestige on what is up rather than what is down. In Christian
theology, God has been up, animals have been down. And though humans
are seen to be in between, both the notion of *imago dei,* that humans are in
the image of God, and the idea that animals do not have souls place humans
much closer to God than to the other animals.

Ecofeminist philosopher Karen J. Warren also identifies value dualisms
as part of an oppressive conceptual framework: disjunctive pairs such as
human/animal, male/female, adult/child, white/nonwhite, culture/nature,
mind/body, subject/object, humans/nature are seen as oppositional rather
than as complementary. Dualisms reduce diversity to two categories: A or
Not A. They convey the impression that everything can then be appropriately categorized: *either* it is A or Not A. These dualisms represent di-
chotomy rather than continuity, enacting exclusion rather than inclusion.
Feminist theologian Catherine Keller explains how the identification of the
separative self is based on emphasizing differences: "It is *this, not that"*
(Keller 1986, 9). This phenomenon is especially true in the ontological
assumptions concerning humans and the other animals. We structure this
ontology by saying we are *this, not that;* humans, not animals. We are
people, they are beasts. We go to heaven, they do not.

Higher value is accorded the first item in each dyad. Moreover, the
second part of the dualism is not only subordinate but *in service* to the
first. Women serve men, nature serves culture, animals serve humans,
people of color serve white people. Theologically, traditional conceptions
of heaven and earth work in this oppositional, dualistic way that discour-

ages earth consciousness. Restrictive dualisms uphold a logic of domination. Central to a logic of domination is language that normalizes this domination. The hierarchical nature of the traditional conception of the Godhead sacralizes a logic of domination in our relationships.

Let us recall certain characteristics of the prevailing, fossilized "Godtalk" that relies on hierarchical images: God is imaged as a human male (father, lord, king), and as a male with authority and power; human maleness is conceptualized as being higher up on the hierarchy than human femaleness. In my research on people's attitudes to animals for *The Sexual Politics of Meat,* I discovered why animals of prey are called "she" no matter what their sex (see Adams 1990, 72–73). Because, according to linguists, the word *she* connotes a "minor power." Will "she" always be a "minor power" as long as resistance exists to seeing God—about as major a power as one can be—as anything but "He."[6] Will animals be a "minor power" and exploitable as long as the traditional conception of God ratifies hierarchy in our relationships?

Yes, according to Catherine Keller:

> The association in this epoch between separatism and masculinity is so tight that as long as God is imagined in mainly masculine metaphors, there is simply no chance for conversion to a fundamentally relational spirituality. And the reverse holds equally true: as long as divinity is externalized by the traditional perfections of self-sufficiency, omnipotence, impassionability and immutability, "God"—even were she made in name and image a woman, an androgyne, or a neuter will support the oppression of women. . . . As long as separation itself is deified, women of faith will end up in the doubly dependent role of subjugation to God and the male, who is himself subjugated to God. (Keller 1986, 38–39)

Human authority over the other animals is modeled after the notion of divine authority over humans, and men's authority over women. We recapitulate a hierarchy of control, playing God, lord, ruler, regent, dominator toward the other animals. This role is one of dispensing decisions rather than egalitarianism; it enforces rather than enhances; it highlights separation and difference rather than relationship and similarity. Concepts of God as father and animals as beasts fall at either ends of this value-hierarchical continuum. Metaphors announce and reinforce this placement.

Metaphors of Domination

Metaphors are and are not true, depict and yet cannot depict reality. As Sallie McFague explains it: "Metaphor always has the character of 'is' and 'is not'" (McFague 1987, 33). This is especially true with theological metaphors. When *metaphors* for God that offer models of relationship with God become instead *definitions* of God, they become frozen, inadequate, anachronistic. While the metaphor of "God the father" provides one way of thinking about our relationship with God based on relationships we know and understand, it is not a definition of God. God may be like a father in some ways, but God is not a father. When metaphor becomes definition, limits on relationships occur.

Metaphors for God become frozen and outdated; so, too, do metaphors for animals. When metaphors like "beast," "bestial," "brutal," "beastly," "animal desires," "animal-like" are used uncritically to provide contrast with and to glorify human behavior, we have allowed our ideas about animals to be frozen and outdated. Let us remember, as Keith Thomas points out, that "it was as a comment on *human* nature that the concept of 'animality' was devised" (Thomas 1983, 41). What we consider to be their reality becomes our metaphor. We respond to animals as though these metaphors about our behavior are true for them. In the process, a distancing akin to the distancing accomplished by envisioning a separate, individualistic, regent in the sky is accomplished. Our metaphors seem to say that God is not us; we are not animals. But much feminist theology suggests that God is us, is in us, is revealed by us, is a part of our relationships. And animal defenders declare, we are animals. As philosopher Mary Midgley says emphatically: *"They are the group to which people belong. We are not just rather like animals; we are* animals" (Midgley 1983, 114).

Maureen Duffy observes: "The truth is that we have always used animals not simply for practical purposes but as metaphors for our own emotional requirements, and it is this that we are unwilling to give up by considering them as creatures with rights and lives of their own. We refuse to recognise the sentience of other species in order that we may go on treating them as objects, projections and symbols" (Duffy 1972, 113). Similarly, while it may have helped believers of previous centuries to say that God was like a lord, king, ruler, these metaphors are not helpful today as they uphold the idea of God being separate from creation. As Sallie McFague explains:

> We live in our imaginations and our feelings in a bygone world, one
> under the guidance of a benevolent but absolute deity, a world that
> is populated by independent individuals (mainly human beings)
> who relate to one another and to other forms of life in hierarchical
> patterns. But this is not our world, and to continue doing theology
> on its assumptions is hurtful, for it undermines our ability to accept
> the new sensibility of our time, one that is holistic and responsible,
> that is inclusive of all forms of life, and that acknowledges the
> interdependence of all life. (McFague 1987, 3)

Metaphors of a triumphant, monarchical "God" are not true for our time.
But they help to explain why we see animals as exploitable. A value hierarchy that is upheld by a logic of domination places animals so low on the
hierarchy that their bodies can be viewed instrumentally. Moreover, as
long as the main images in Western culture are of "God" as ruler, lord, king
of creation, and this metaphor is derived from the experience of some
(predominantly white male) human beings, then animals cannot be ruler,
lord, kings of creation. By anthropomorphizing God, we exclude animals
from the Godhead. In addition, the value dualisms of spirit over body,
maleness above femaleness, heaven above earth become sacralized.

If images of God as king and male are incomplete, partial, and inadequate, so too are *animal* metaphors.

The "God" of the Man of Reason

> The very beginning of Genesis tells us that God created man in order
> to give him dominion over fish and fowl and all creatures. Of course
> Genesis was written by a man, not a horse. There is no certainty
> that God actually did grant man dominion over other creatures.
> What seems more likely, in fact, is that man invented God to sanc-
> tify the dominion that he had usurped for himself over the cow and
> the horse. Yes, the right to kill a deer or a cow is the only thing all
> of mankind can agree upon, even during the bloodiest of wars.
> (Kundera 1988, 286)

Feminist philosophy challenges the notion of an atomistic subject, "the
man of reason" who splits subject from object, and whose mode of being
is marked by transcending the body. Just as animals are defined precisely
as what humans are not, so, traditionally, "femaleness was symbolically
associated with what Reason supposedly left behind" (Lloyd 1984, 2).
Feminists have demonstrated that a knowing subject cannot transcend the

social structures in which he or she lives, or become abstracted from one's own history. However, the idea of the man of reason was that he could overcome body, history, social situations, and thereby gain knowledge of others he examined as objects. This idea of the man of reason was accompanied by the Western idea of a disembodied, ahistorical God the father. The Man of Reason and his God created categories for animals, categories that arise from knowledge claims about what we *believe* to know that animals are.

Human male dominance may be having a parallel influence on both the assumption of who the knower is *and* the assumption of who an animal is. As feminist philosopher Alison Jaggar explains: "Several feminist theorists have argued that modern epistemology itself may be viewed as an expression of certain emotions alleged to be especially characteristic of [human] males in certain periods, such as separation anxiety and paranoia, or an obsession with control and fear of contamination."[7] According to this insight, modern epistemology and its suspicion of emotions, dualist ontologies, rationalist bias, and concern for achieving objectivity may represent not some universal response, but a very specific one: the response to the experience of being an elite human male. Similarly, feminist theorist Barbara Noske points out that "it is really the straight Western male whose strongholds are threatened by humananimal continuity. Physical closeness, grooming, nurturance and companionship are so much part of the female *and* male primate behavioural pattern that the lack of these among heterosexual Western males is genuinely surprising" (Noske 1989, 117; see also Clark 1982, 112–15).

The patriarchal knower's fear of his own body may account for both the Enlightenment epistemology that objectifies others and the delineation of a complete and utter chasm between human and animal. In a vertically organized world, in which spatial hierarchies denote value or lack thereof (the traditional God-human-animals hierarchy), beastly theological categories are maintained. Pulsating out from the humanocentric view of the world, we both wish to make and resist making the Other in our image. The "Man of Reason" traditionally transcended both femaleness and beastliness, while viewing many female traits as linking women to other animals (see Tuana 1993). Anxious about charges of expressing sentiments for animals if they were acknowledged to have forms of consciousness, sociality, or other human-allied concepts, the man of reason deemed these emotions untrustworthy and invalid sources of knowledge. The positivistic scientific view of the other animals that arises from "men of reason," that is, traditional scientists, is one that Barbara Noske calls the "de-animalized animal." Since it is equipped only to measure observable phenomena, and its explanatory apparatus of natural selection focuses on the individual organic level, this scientific view discounts animals' culture. It strips the other animals of consciousness, inventiveness, and cultural context. What we have is "a de-animalized biological construct rather than a mirror of animal reality" (Noske 1989, 88). It becomes, however, the prevailing viewpoint. This illustrates an "objectifying epistemology," as Josephine Donovan calls it, "which turns animals into 'its'" (Donovan 1990, 353). The positivist tradition simultaneously denies animals their context and the knowing subject her emotions.

Many who experience a metaphysical shift toward animals, refusing to ontologize them as usable, discover a feeling of abiding anger contrary to the reasonable standard of patriarchal culture. Anger is a frightening and much-misunderstood expression, an "outlaw emotion" in Alison Jaggar's terms. According to Jaggar, outlaw emotions

> may enable us to perceive the world differently from its portrayal in conventional descriptions. They may provide the first indications that something is wrong with the way alleged facts have been constructed, with accepted understandings of how things are.... Only when we reflect on our initially puzzling irritability, revulsion, anger, or fear may we bring to consciousness our "gut-level" awareness that we are in a situation of coercion, cruelty, injustice, or danger. (Jaggar and Bordo 1989, 161)

While the knowledge claims arising from men of reason would disown such emotions, Jaggar points to the importance of such outlaw emotions for challenging dominant conceptions of the status quo. She perceives intertwined influences in which "appropriate emotions may contribute to the development of knowledge" and "the growth of knowledge may contribute to the development of appropriate emotions" (Jaggar and Bordo 1989, 163). In light of Jaggar's insights, we can see that anger may well be an appropriate response to the knowledge of monkeys in stereotaxic chairs, minipigs being developed for animal experimentation, debeaking so that hens do not commit cannibalism in their stressful and overcrowded cages, the capture and breeding of dolphins and whales for humans' entertainment, the transporting of one- or two-day-old feeble male calves (awkwardly walking and still with wet umbilical cord) to slaughterhouses, the dragging of old, crippled dairy and beef cows by skid steer loaders or the scooping up of downers into buckets to get them to the slaughterhouse door, and any number of creatively cruel interactions that humans have with animals. *These emotions are not only appropriate, but appropriate sources of knowledge.* By occluding these acts we hide from the truth.

In February 1994 the California Board of Education banned the use of Alice Walker's "Am I Blue?" from a statewide English test because it was "anti-meat-eating." Marion McDowell, president of the California Board of Education, reportedly said that the conclusion of the short story—when the narrator spits out the steak she had been eating because she is eating misery—"could be rather disturbing to some students who would then be expected to write a good essay while they were upset."[8] Fascinating in this decision is the epistemological control exercised here: no one challenges the fact that Alice Walker's essay may be speaking the truth; it is eliminated because the truth might be upsetting. Again, we see that emotions are related to truth and, as McDowell implies, that the growth of knowledge may contribute to the development of appropriate emotions, truly outlaw emotions.

The Categorization of Animals and the "God" of the Man of Reason

What results from an anxious knowledge stance that objectifies animals and disowns outlaw emotions is an ahistorical and disembodied view of animals. The knowledge claims gravitate to categories that would apply in most, if not all cases, across history and specific individual situations. And this is exactly their problem. The debate about what is uniquely human, and what it is about animals that makes them nonhuman, takes place precisely in the zone that theologies of liberation have shown to be false— the zone of absolutes. Definitions or categorizations regarding animals function as absolute truths. Such absolute or universal knowledge claims represent the logic and interests of the oppressor. Grounding one's claims in ahistorical absolutes demonstrates bad faith. To cling to certainty in categories such as *animals* represents a political decision and avoids a risky and potentially destabilizing discourse.

In discussing the way categories of knowing influence perceptions, Michel Foucault described a passage from the writer Jorge Luis Borges that provides a different ordering of things. Borges wrote about a Chinese encyclopedia in which animals are divided into "(a) belonging to the Emperor, (b) embalmed, (c) tame, (d) sucking pigs, (e) sirens, (f) fabulous, (g) stray dogs, (h) included in the present classification, (i) frenzied, (j) innumerable, (k) drawn with a very fine camel's hair brush, (l) etcetera, (m) having just broken the water pitcher, (n) that from a long way off look like flies" (cited in Welch 1988, 9). According to Foucault this passage "shattered all the familiar landmarks of my thought." Because these cate-

gories are alien to our experience, this example provides the vehicle for
Foucault and Sharon Welch—who cites it in her feminist theology of liberation—to explore the relativity of truth claims and of ordering experiences.
Foucault points out that the dominant culture, too, may be relying on categories that function as absolute but are actually as contingent as Borges's
fabulous organization of animals. Pushing this insight, I would argue that
such absolutes as our current categorization of animals may be as contingent and false as Borges's example. Seeing Borges's categorization of
animals only as the vehicle to expose the falsity of absolutes is one option.
While this fictional classification may operate to disrupt one's notion that
existing categories can be adequate or accurate, it could also direct us to
the fixed categorizations that still operate when we think of and interact
with the other animals. I would turn such insight about absolutes and
universals back toward that which prompts such insight—the categories
we cling to in oppressing animals.

What we perceive here is that the fabulous categorizations of animals
reflects on another level—a level that has so far been unacknowledged—
the actual situation of animals who have been categorized by humans. While
there appears to be a logic to these familiar animal categories, they may
simply represent the arbitrary logic of the oppressor: (a) animals who are
edible; (b) animals who are not edible; (c) animals who produce food for
us while living (cows, goats, chickens, bees); (d) animals living as com-
panions in households; (e) animals living in households but not wanted
(vermin); (f) animals whose bodies can be experimented upon; (g) animals
who can be worn; (h) animals who have social networks but no consciousness; (i) animals who use tools but are not humans; (i) animals who
can be hunted; (k) animals who no longer exist; (l) animals who are in
danger of extinction; (m) etcetera.[9] These examples are not fabulous and
fictional, they represent everyday relations that are predicated on acceptable boundaries arising from universal truth claims of what is uniquely
human. These boundaries and the structure of relations they legitimize are
as suspect as any other form of traditional knowledge posited as universal
and absolute. They result from what Donna Haraway calls "the god trick."

The God Trick

The *god trick* refers to the positioning of those who hold to a traditional notion of objectivity: that one can transcend body, personal and cultural history, and thereby acquire "pure knowledge." In Marilyn Frye's
terms, the god trick sees with an arrogant eye. According to Donna
Haraway, "[T]hose occupying the positions of the dominators are self-

identical, unmarked, disembodied, unmediated, transcendent, born again"
(Haraway 1988, 586). In dualistic patriarchy, those occupying the positions of the subjugated, therefore, are marked, embodied, mediated, immi-
nent. Haraway argues further that knowledge arising from this positioning
of the subjugated is situated knowledge, and because situated, therefore
responsible, whereas knowledge arising from a place where one has the
illusion of a view of infinite vision produces unlocatable and thus irresponsible—that is, unable to be called into account—knowledge claims:

> The standpoints of the subjugated are . . . preferred because in
> principle they are least likely to allow denial of the critical and
> interpretive core of all knowledge. They are knowledgeable of modes
> of denial through repression, forgetting, and disappearing acts—
> ways of being nowhere while claiming to see comprehensively. The
> subjugated have a decent chance to be on to the god trick and its
> dazzling—and therefore, blinding—illuminations. "Subjugated"
> standpoints are preferred because they seem to promise more ad-
> equate, sustained, objective, transforming accounts of the world.
> (Haraway 1988, 584)

Virginia Woolf provides an excellent example of someone engaging in the
god trick in her classic feminist text, *A Room of One's Own.* She demonstrates the way absolute and universal categories work, the way one claims
to see comprehensively:

> I thought of that old gentleman, who is dead now, but was a bishop,
> I think, who declared that it was impossible for any woman, past,
> present, or to come, to have the genius of Shakespeare. He wrote to
> the papers about it. He also told a lady who applied to him for
> information that cats do not as a matter of fact go to heaven, though
> they have, he added, souls of a sort. How much thinking those old
> gentlemen used to save one! How the borders of ignorance shrank
> back at their approach! Cats do not go to heaven. Women cannot
> write the plays of Shakespeare.[10]

How comforting to hold such firm beliefs as the bishop! Yet, in Donna
Haraway's words, how irresponsible are such knowledge claims. Irresponsible precisely because they appear unable to be called into account.
(How does one, after all, prove who does go to heaven?) How much thinking patriarchal beastly theologies used to save us! Once we believe that
any authority or our theology has decided the question of the status of the
other animals, then we can, without any qualms, safely abdicate thinking,

feeling, responding to the issues that arise concerning the exploitation of animals. The surest way to short-circuit justice is to believe that the question of exploitation has already been settled and we are not the responsible parties in the debate. We let someone else perform the god trick and then choose it as our own methodology.

The God Trick and Animals

In Woolf's description of the bishop's knowledge claims the traditional spatial hierarchy of heaven and earth recalls the literal hierarchy of humans and animals, men and women, since, as Virginia Woolf reminds us through the bishop's self-proclaimed authority, humans may go to heaven, but animals are earthbound. Of course his opinion represents a defensive position: there is self-interest in believing that animals (at least those who are consumed) do not go to heaven. To imagine that we would meet animals in heaven may be a disquieting thought for those who eat them.[11] Yet whether cats or farm animals go to heaven is not the point, to imagine heaven as separate from and above earth decanters our here-and-now relationships with all that live on earth. The parallel hierarchies of space and power (heaven over earth, humans over animals) enact a distancing that allows us to become disengaged from animals and the earth. This distancing allows us to become god-like—in Haraway's terms, "unmarked, disembodied, unmediated, transcendent."

While we may be god-like in the way we can create and dispose of animals, we actually are marked, embodied, mediated. The choice before us is to cling to the God-human-animal hierarchy and inevitably continue to see God as an old gentleman, or affirm the relevance of our own—and animals'—sensory experiences. Options other than an objectifying epistemology exist.

Agreeing Not to Play the God Trick

Among other things, theologies of liberation interpret sin as domination, and direct our attention to *structures* of domination and exploitation. Traditional, universal truth claims are exposed as false. Whereas there is a tendency to universalize animals, actually no one animal nature exists. Animals are particular, embodied, social creatures, not representatives of a measurable and thus "timeless" or disembodied quality. Moreover, developments in ethology and the other sciences are undermining the human/animal dualism by pointing to evidence of animal consciousness, language, tool use, and other attributes previously considered the sole province of human beings. Our capabilities are continuous with those of the other animals, not discontinuous.

Patriarchal beastly theologies derive from an epistemological stance that presumes universal categories and removes the knowers from any position of responsibility at all. But the god trick is an illusion. As Lorraine Code argues, we do not know "the world" as objective observers who are separate from the world. Hopefully, we wish to know the world as "moral and epistemic subjects who know and understand by positioning themselves within a situation in order to understand its *implications* and see in those implications contextualized, situated reasons for action" (Code 1991, 148). But in order to so position ourselves we must be willing to reexamine universal categories.

Not only is the dominant culture coercive—constructing universal categories and absolutes where they do not exist—it has an ability to absorb a radical viewpoint, an epistemological challenge, and eviscerate it so that it looks like the argument is about ontology. As long as we are debating ontology, the epistemological is invisible. This serves the dominant culture's perspective. What should be suspect, and a question of consciousness— for instance, universal categories that cast animals as consumable—is rendered valid and inevitable.

An Excursus on Ontology and Epistemology

Epistemological and ontological issues recur throughout this book. They are particularly pertinent to theological discussions. When feminist theologians devoted close attention to the Genesis 2 story of creation they did so in part because it provided theological justification for an ontological situation—women's subjugated status. To get at the ontological, these theologians reinterpreted Genesis 2. They argued that the story of Eve's heeding the serpent and disobeying God, thus being told that she would be subject to her husband, was not actually about the woman being untrustworthy and sinful, nor did it mandate women's subordination. Similarly, as we saw in the previous chapter, attempts are made to interpret Genesis 1 to break the ontologizing of humans as dominators of animals and the rest of nature.

But these defenses keep the debate on the ontological level, when what is needed is a focus on knowledge claims and therefore on epistemology. The epistemological is always framing a discussion, an approach, a theology. It is often invisible or actively concealed.

In *Neither Man Nor Beast* (1994, 160–78) I describe the death of an animal that I had come to know, and how it precipitated ontological questions: Why are some animals seen as consumable? What I had previously "known" rationally, that I ate animals, I now "knew" as an embodied truth—and one with serious moral implications. I felt the fact that I consumed animals resonating throughout my bodily self in a shock wave of horrified fascination and irredeemable immediacy. And a realization radiated from this felt truth, this embodied knowing: what I am doing is not right, this is not ethically acceptable. In a sense I began to ask myself: On what grounds have I accepted the ontologizing of animals as edible?

What I "knew" through my bodily self was, as Josephine Donovan states: "We should not kill, eat, torture, and exploit animals because they do not want to be so treated, and we know that" (Donovan1990, 375). This embodied knowledge involved recognizing that whereas I had ontologized animals as consumable, exploitable, violable, I could do so only through the god trick, by following the methods of any oppressor in believing the illusion that this was a universal perspective, that is, that no other ontological possibility existed such as that the other animals might want to be treated otherwise, as inviolable. As Donovan recognizes, another perspective exists, that of the animals so violated. Integrating this perspective within the reality of my life required me to change my diet and my moral framework. In this sense, mine was the sort of knowledge that feminist philosopher Lorraine Code describes when she envisions knowledge that does not seek to control "nature" but instead lets "nature" speak for itself.

I questioned the ontology that permitted oppressive actions and controlled "nature," and began to seek an alternative ontology. But I also began to recognize that what has been cast as an issue of ontology—that is, are animals "meant" to be eaten?—is much more centrally a question of epistemology. The epistemological questions feminists explore regarding the social construction of "women," knowledge, science, and culture address knowledge claims that are pertinent here. What do we know about animals? about human beings' differences from the other animals? about how the other animals experience their relationships with human beings? and how do we know it? How do we know, for instance, that animals do not suffer when being killed to become food? that animal experimentation is the only way to advance medical knowledge? Who is making these knowledge claims about the other animals and on what grounds? What do we actually know about animal consciousness? about the standpoint of animals? about what commonalities we truly share with the other animals? about the ways animals experience themselves and other animals? Questions such as these problematize the knowledge claims that accompany the acceptance of the value dualisms and value hierarchy of patriarchal beastly theology.

From questions such as these we begin to see that the current ontological condition of animals as violable has less do with their beingness, than with *our* consciousness. Animals need not be destined to become humans' food (ontology). That we see them as food or clothes is a construct of perception, cultural intervention, a forced identity (epistemology). The representation "animal" is what we are given to know.

The epistemology of the "human" who sees "animals" as usable creates the world of the human/animal dualism. The way we humans look at animals literally creates them as usable.[12] This means that in life "human" and "animal," like "woman" and "man," are "widely experienced as features of *being,* not constructs of perception, cultural interventions or forced identities." Both *species* and *gender* are "lived as ontology, not as epistemology."[13] As Catharine MacKinnnon observes, what is occurring is a "transformation of *perspective into being.*" And if it succeeds ontologically, human dominance does not look epistemological: "Control over being produces control over consciousness" (MacKinnon 1989, 238). This is why so many debates focus specifically on animals' beingness: because the shift from perspective to being (from epistemology to ontology) is, if successful, hidden from view. The role our consciousness plays in all of this remains concealed.

Catharine MacKinnon points out further that "when seemingly ontological conditions are challenged from the collective standpoint of a dissident reality, they become visible as epistemological" (1989, 240). Animal defenders offer such a dissident reality, saying, "Animals aren't meant to be eaten or experimented upon! Eating animals and experimenting upon them is not inevitable! Their meaning in life does not come from their being consumed!" Those who challenge animals' exploitation are knowing subjects who have recognized their position in, and accountability to, the animals' world. What has been hidden is brought into view.

Transforming Beastly Theology

Because women's roles were declared to be subordinate to men as a matter of God's will, a part of the feminist theological task has been the breaking of the authoritative/ontological association that predetermines questions of authentic being. Feminist theology begins with experience as a corrective to the authority/ontological situating of women as other. A similar process of beginning with experience opens new possibilities of relationships with animals. As testimonies of numerous people reveal, when people experience the realities of the slaughterhouse or the factory farm, they are less likely to want to see themselves as corpse eaters and the other animals as flesh. Outlaw emotions may prompt epistemological shifts.

Many defenders of the other animals came to their positions through radical intersubjectivity, through the second-person relationship of knowing another animal. Here, too, is the sort of knowledge that does not seek to control "nature" but instead lets "nature" speak for itself. Such resituating of nature as a speaking subject is illustrated in Vicki Hearne's *Adam's Task*: "It occurs to me that it is surprising that 'I don't know, I haven't met her' is rarely the response given to 'Can Washoe [the chimpanzee] talk?'" (Hearne 1986, 33).

Second-Person Theology

We become persons through our dependence upon other persons from whom we "acquire the essential arts of personhood" (Code 1991, 82, quoting Baier 1985). Lives begin in commonality and interdependence; thus in our acquisition of knowledge, "persons are essentially second persons" (Code 1991, 85) and our knowledge is never atomistically individualistic or "self-made." Second-person theologies are needed to upend patriarchal beastly theologies. Like second-person thinking in which "knowledge claims are forms of address, speech acts, moments in a dialogue that assume and rely on the participation of (an)other subject(s)" (Code 1991, 121), second-person theology derives from encountering the other animals as subjects. As Vicki Hearne suggests, our knowledge claims are inadequate if in discussing animals we have not included them within the dialogue.

God unfolds in relationships. Most animals are excluded from experiencing this notion of "God-in-relationship" because we use them precisely in ways that sever relationships. Many forms of animal exploitation involve caging and confining them, restricting their ability—no, their need—to enjoy social relationships, and bestow upon animals an expectation that they can exist inanimately even while alive. Does the creation of some beings solely for the purpose of being objects make sense in the face of an intrinsically and radically relational divinity? If God is process, *being,* and revealed through relationship should we not situate all beings within that divine relationship, seeing with loving eyes?

It is said that talking about whether animals suffer pain is like talking about the existence of God. But let's push this further. What if trying to have a conversation with an animal is like trying to have a conversation with God? Would we then bring a discipline of attending to our relationships with animals? Vicki Hearne refers to Martin Heidegger's suggestion of 'listening to the dog's being" (Hearne 1986, 59). Sally Carrighar in *Home to the Wilderness: A Personal Journey* offers an example of such listening to an animal's beingness: "I talked to the birds and animals and I talked sense, in a normal voice. . . . [I would say] to a very shy grouse, 'Have you thought of taking a dustbath? Look here where the earth is so fine and dry.' I knew they did not understand the words, but to such sensitive creatures a tone may convey more than we realize. . . . It seemed that they had to feel a true sense of warmth, not sentimentality but concern" (Carrighar 1974, 304). Need it be observed that such conversations are impossible with one's "steak" dinner or leather coat?

Second-person theology incorporates animals both directly through acknowledging them as subjects rather than objects, and also in its care to create knowledge claims that assume and rely on the participation of these other subjects. The result would be not only the destabilizing of flesh and leather and other forms of animal exploitation, but the retiring of the word *beast,* recognizing that its function is restricted to a vertically organized world. Liberating animals from the appellation of beast, we would also be liberated from the need to label humans as "not beasts." *Beast* would appear in dictionaries with the label *archaic* appended to it.

From Beastly Theologies to Second-Person Theologies

> I do think that one's fellow animals of other species are aware of the change in one's own attitude when one becomes vegetarian. . . . I do think that the psychological act of deciding to be a vegetarian frees one from a lot of guilt towards animals and I think they are aware of this. My impression is that one's relationship to them becomes very much less ambiguous and ambivalent and one is freer to think of them as equals. I think it's this property that they respond to. I definitely have the impression that I have a different relationship with animals since I became a vegetarian.[14]

With second-person theologies, animals would no longer be absent referents in theological discourse—metaphors for human beings—nor absent referents in theological praxis, objects whom we do not know anything about, or whom we assume to know categorically and universally. Second-person theologies are inimical to the structure of the absent referent. When animals are absent conceptually, we have eliminated the space in which our embodied knowing could encounter relationship, there is nothing for our loving eye to engage with. Whatever limits there are to knowing the viewpoints of the other animals, we can know that what matters to them is that we stop defining them and using them. We can never be in relation with all animals nor need we be, but we can work to release all animals from being ontologized as usable.

In dismantling the structure of the absent referent, second-person theologies resituate animals, resubjectifying them, acknowledging that each animal is a subjective presence in the world. As Barbara Noske argues, we need to move to a descriptive rather than definitional discourse about animals, recognizing a species boundary that is horizontal rather than vertical and hierarchical.

Second-person theologies offer alternatives to the dualistic reduction of human versus animal claims. By challenging the dualism, we refuse to accept the oppositional nature of the definitions of humans and animals. In this we are not making "animals" like "humans," only less so. We are, however, releasing both humans and animals from this reductive dualism. We may discover that our concepts of ourselves will change as our concepts of animals change. In fact, feminist challenges to the notion of the autonomous human subject will benefit from the liberating of the other animals from the category of "animal." As Barbara Noske explains:

> Nature had to be devaluated to a state where it could be useful economically and technically, though harmless ideologically. But nature could only be devaluated if and when humanity detached itself from nature and ceased to feel part of it. The Dutch philosopher/anthropologist Ton Lemaire makes clear that the two developments, namely, the objectification of nature and the autonomization of the human subject, go hand in hand, "reality could only fully become an object after humanity had collected its personality out of the unconscious intertwinement with external nature." (Noske 1989, 53)

In recognizing that we can be second persons to animals, we reinsert our personality within creation. We are not separated, autonomous "knowers" in a dominating culture but second persons with the rest of nature. The process of reengaging with creation, and particularly with the other animals, will produce a different subjectivity and a different theology.

In a culture that ontologizes animals as exploitable we must address current behavior that is predicated on this ontology. A few centuries from now people might have to do something actively to cause the harm of animals, now they must actively do something to impede the harm of animals (i.e., bag vegetarian lunches instead of buying school cafeteria lunches, inquire into the contents of soap, shampoo, etc.). As long as "meat" or "fur" or "leather" are available in stores, people have to intervene actively against the consumerism of producing, procuring, or purchasing these "products." We must resist doing something we have been taught to do.

What remains for all of us is a task of personal and mythic archaeology, the reinspection of old terrain. We ourselves are buried under layers of categories that construct species difference as a meaningful ethical determinant. We can no longer allow the bishop and other patriarchal knowers to determine our knowledge. Those issues identified by feminist theology as central to patriarchal religion—issues such as the subordination of experience to authority, the rigid conceptualization of "God" as Father and monarch, the notion of the separate, atomistic self—are also central to the idea that animals can be objects or instruments, and that our relationship with the divine trumps their inviolability. Catherine Keller proposes that "the pull toward connection, when coordinated with feminist sensibility, can and does generate a new meaning of what it is to be a self" (Keller 1986, 2). Would this pull toward connection, this new meaning of being a self, and its relationship to the ultimate in life, would this deep affinity with all beings condone using animals instrumentally, experimenting on their live bodies, and consuming their dead bodies? Given the nature of the interlocking system of oppression, can we continue to ignore this question?

Notes

1.   I develop this idea more fully in chapter 2 of *The Sexual Politics of Meat.*
2.   While Lewis inscribes a further dualism upon animals (beasts versus tame animals), I will be using beast to refer to all other-than-human animals.
3.   Conversation, February 28, 1994.
4.   This issue is developed more fully in Carol J. Adams and Marjorie Procter-Smith, "'Taking Life' or 'Taking on Life'? Table Talk and Animals," in *Ecofeminism and the Sacred* (Adams 1993).
5.   Donald Griffin, "The Problem of Distinguishing Awareness from Responsiveness," in Wood-Gush and Dawkins 1991, 6. Griffin elsewhere suggests the term *anthropomorphophobia* to convey the "apprehension that one may be accused of uncritical sentimentality if one suggests that any nonhuman animal might experience subjective emotions such as fear, or think consciously in even the simplest terms, such as believing that food is located in a certain place" (Griffin 1990, xiii).
6.   Anyone who thinks that this resistance is not keen in our day should examine the response by conservative and many mainstream members of the mainline denominations to the "Re-Imagining Conference" held in Minne-

sota in November 1993. One of the main complaints is that God was referred to as Sophia.

7.   Jaggar and Bordo 1989, 156. Jaggar is referring to the work of Susan Bordo (1987) and Jane Flax (1983).

8.   Quoted in "Second Strike Against Noted Author in California Test," *New York Times,* February 27, 1994.

9.   While many of these examples may appear to arise and apply only to specific cultures, that is, the animals deemed inedible in the West may not be deemed inedible elsewhere (dogs, for instance), what is universal is that animals are viewed as less valuable than human, and thus can be made into an object for humans' survival or pleasure, so that some kinds of animals—even if they differ within cultures—will fill these roles.

10.   Woolf 1929, 48. When Virginia Woolf grants subjectivity to a dog in her biography of Elizabeth Barrett Browning's dog Flush, she seems to get even with the Bishop's denigration of both women writers and animals.

11.   As Brigid Brophy suggests in an imagined heavenly conversation between Bernard Shaw and God: "I suppose," God said, "theology impresses them with the notion that animals have no souls—and hence no ghosts." . . . "No, what prevents people from, on the whole, seeing animals' ghosts is not theology but bad conscience. If they do see an animal ghost, it will be a dog or a cat, not an animal they are in the habit of eating. . . . [P]eople see ghosts for the same reason that they read ghost stories: as self indulgence. It is not murderers who are haunted. It is the innocent. . . . It is because people truly are guilty of murdering animals that the folk imagination has to contrive not to see the ghosts of the folk diet" Brophy 1968, 189–90. Regarding the question of whether animals have souls, see Keith Thomas 1983, 137–42.

12.   This is a paraphrase of a remark by Melinda Vadas as she analyzed Catherine MacKinnon's insights and their applicability to the issue of animal exploitation.

13.   These are Catherine MacKinnon's insights, with my addition of species construction to her analysis of gender construction. See MacKinnon 1989, 237.

14.   Brigid Brophy, interviewed in Berry 1979, 80.

Works Cited

Adams, Carol J. 1990. *The Sexual Politics of Meat: A Feminist-Vegetarian Critical Theory*. New York: Continuum.

————, ed. 1993. *Ecofeminism and the Sacred*. New York: Continuum.

————. 1994. *Neither Man Nor Beast: Feminism and the Defense of Animals*. New York: Continuum.

Baier, Annette. 1985. "Cartesian Persons." In *Postures of the Mind: Essays on Mind and Morals*. Minneapolis: University of Minnesota Press.

Bekoff, Mark and Dale Jamieson, eds. 1990. *Interpretation and Explanation in the Study of Animal Behavior, I: Interpretation, Intentionality, and Communication*. Boulder, CO: Westview.

Berry, Jr., Ryan. 1979. *The Vegetarians*. Brookline, MA: Autumn.

Bordo, Susan. 1987. *The Flight to Objectivity: Essays on Cartesianism and Culture*. Albany: State University of New York Press.

Brophy, Brigid. 1968. *The Adventures of God in His Search for the Black Girl*. Boston: Little, Brown.

Carrighar, Sally. 1974. *Home to the Wilderness: A Personal Journey*. Baltimore: Penguin.

Clark, Stephen. 1982. *The Nature of the Beast*. Oxford and New York: Oxford University Press.

Code, Lorraine. 1991. *What Can She Know? Feminist Theory and the Construction of Knowledge*. Ithaca: Cornell University Press.

Donovan, Josephine. 1990. "Animal Rights and Feminist Theory." *Signs: Journal of Women in Culture and Society* 15 (2): 350–75.

Duffy, Maureen. 1972. "Beasts for Pleasure." In Godlovitch, Godlovitch and Harris, 107–20.

Flax, Jane. 1983. "Political Philosophy and Patriarchal Unconscious: A Psychoanalytic Perspective on Epistemology and Metaphysics." In Harding and Hintikka.

Godlovitch, Stanley, Rosalind Godlovitch and John Harris, eds. 1972. *Animals, Men, and Morals: A Enquiry into the Maltreatment of Non-Humans*. New York: Taplinger.

Griffin, Donald. 1990. "Foreword." In Bekoff and Jamieson, xiii.

————. 1991. "The Problem of Distinguishing Awareness from Responsiveness." In Wood-Gush and Dawkins.

Haraway, Donna. 1988. "Situated Knowledges: The Science Question in Feminism and the Privilege of Partial Perspective." *Feminist Studies* 14 (3):575–99.

Harding, Sandra and Merrill Hintikka, eds. 1983. *Discovering Reality: Feminist Perspectives on Epistemology, Metaphysics, Methodology and Philosophy*. Dordrecht: Reidel.

Hearne, Vicki. 1986. *Adam's Task: Calling Animals by Name*. New York: Knopf.

Jaggar, Alison M. and Susan Bordo, eds. 1989. *Gender / Body / Knowledge: Feminist Reconstructions of Being and Knowing*. New Brunswick, NJ: Rutgers University Press.

Keller, Catherine. 1986. *From a Broken Web: Separation, Sexism, and Self*. Boston: Beacon.

Kundera, Milan. 1988. *The Unbearable Lightness of Being*. New York: Penguin.

Lloyd, Genevieve. 1984. *The Man of Reason: "Male" and "Female" in Western Philosophy.* Minneapolis: University of Minnesota Press.

MacKinnon, Catharine. 1989. *Towards a Feminist Theory of State.* Cambridge: Harvard University Press.

McFague, Sallie. 1987. *Models of God.* Minneapolis: Fortress.

Midgley, Mary. 1983. *Animals and Why They Matter.* Athens: University of Georgia Press.

Noske, Barbara. 1989. *Humans and Other Animals: Beyond the Boundaries of Anthropology.* London: Pluto.

Rollin, Bernard. 1981. *Animal Rights and Human Morality.* Buffalo, NY: Prometheus.

Thomas, Keith. 1983. *Man and the Natural World: A History of the Modern Sensibility.* New York: Pantheon.

Tuan, Yi-Fu. 1984. *Dominance and Affection: The Making of Pets.* New Haven: Yale University Press.

Tuana, Nancy. 1993. *The Less Noble Sex: Scientific, Religious, and Philosophical Conceptions of Woman's Nature.* Bloomington: Indiana University Press.

Welch, Sharon D. 1988. *Communities of Resistance and Solidarity.* Maryknoll, NY: Orbis.

Wood-Gush, D. G. M., M. Dawkins and R. Ewbank, eds. 1991. *Self-Awareness in Domesticated Animals: Proceedings of a Workshop Held at Keble College, Oxford.* Hertfordshire, England: The Universities Federation for Animal Welfare.

Woolf, Virginia. 1929. *A Room of One's Own.* New York: Harcourt, Brace, Jovanovich.

ETHICAL MAPS ON SHIFTING GROUNDS

On the narrow ridge, where *I* and *Thou* meet, there is the realm of "between" . . .
> —Martin Buber, *Between Man and Man*

Christianity has made the sacred *substantial*, but the nature of the sacred, in which today we recognize the burning existence of religion, is perhaps the most ungraspable thing that has been produced between men: the sacred is only a privileged moment of communal unity, a moment of the convulsive communication of what is ordinarily stifled.
> —Georges Bataille, "The Sacred"

12

Freud and St. Francis: An Ethnological Conflict over the Command to Love One's Neighbor as Oneself

Jennifer Leader

Culture has to call up every possible reinforcement in order to erect barriers against the aggressive instincts of men and hold their mani-festations in check by reaction-formations in men's minds. Hence its system of methods by which mankind is to be driven to identifi-cations and aim-inhibited love-relationships; hence the restrictions on sexual life; and hence, too, its *ideal command to love one's neigh-bor as oneself* [emphasis added], which is really justified by the fact that nothing is so completely at variance with original human nature as this.

—Freud, *Civilization and Its Discontents*

In his 1929 treatise on the nature of society, *Civilization and Its Dis-contents*, Sigmund Freud asserts that civilization preserves itself through the invention of cultural constructs which resist mankind's aggressive drives. Thus, the universal commandment to love one's neighbor as oneself, and the ancillary command to love one's enemies (Mt 5:43–44), serves the purpose of providing an equal and opposing counterbalance to man's uni-versal instinct for hostility. According to Freud's theories of the id, how-ever, "the command is impossible to fulfill" (1952, 140) because "even in so-called normal people the power of controlling the id cannot be increased beyond certain limits" (1952, 139).

Having so convincingly debunked the call for universal love within the grounds of his own psychoanalytical theory, why then does Freud raise other, more subjective objections to the commandment? After citing Saint Francis of Assisi as an example of someone who, by sublimation, man-aged to transfer his love "not to individual objects but to all men equally" and by so doing "may have carried this method of using love to produce an inner feeling of happiness as far as anyone" (1952, 69–70), Freud makes "two principle objections" against the view that St. Francis has therefore reached "the highest state of mind of which man is capable" (1952, 70). First, Freud writes, "A love that does not discriminate seems to us to lose some of its own value, since it does an injustice to its object." "And secondly," he continues, "not all men are worthy of love" (1952, 70–71). By using the two terms *value* and *worth*, Freud has moved beyond the realm of strict, psychological objectivity and into that of relative morals and ethics. This essay attempts to answer three basic questions regarding this passage in section four of *Civilization and Its Discontents*: First, and briefly, why does Freud choose to bring St. Francis into his argument, and why does he react to his example in subjective terms? Second, what is the effectiveness of this subjective polemic against the worldview that St. Francis represents, a worldview that implicitly relies upon the existence of a Divine mystery, an ultimately unquantifiable Other, outside the realm of scientific verifiability? And finally, is there, in this era of postmodern sensibilities, an imaginative space of "unknowing" in which critical thought, Christian theology, and Freudian psychology might at last converge?

To begin with, in order to fully understand the tone of *Civilization and Its Discontents*, and, concomitantly, Freud's reason for the inclusion of St. Francis, it is useful to examine one of Freud's chief sources of inspiration for the book. On the first page Freud acknowledges that he is responding to a letter from a friend (whom he identified in his second edition as Romain Rolland) regarding a common, cross-cultural source of religious feelings. Rolland, a French author, playwright, and 1915 Nobel Prize winner, carried on a collegial friendship with Freud, mostly through correspondence, during the last thirteen years of Freud's life; at the time of their correspondence, Rolland's work with Hindu mysticism had given empirical evidence to the idea that regular mystical practices were not necessarily fleeting and regressive, rather, they "could be harnessed into purposeful social and political channels" as they had been in the life of Gandhi (Fisher 1976, 32).

According to David Fisher, who has traced their relationship through a study of their correspondences and translated previously unpublished letters of Rolland's, Freud found in Rolland a friendly adversary who, as an intellectual equal, and "an accomplished critical realist . . . could not be dismissed as a mindless crackpot mystic" (Fisher 1982, 256). Moreover, Fisher notes that Freud experienced an ambivalent, emotionally invested relationship with Rolland and "perceived Rolland to be an advocate of universal love" (Fisher 1982, 265). Freud's compulsive attraction to and repulsion from the Divine mystery inherent to Rolland's subject matter is evident even in his first letter to Rolland (dated 4 March 1923), in which he writes that "for us your name has been associated with the most precious of beautiful illusions, that of love extended to all mankind" (E. Freud, 1960, 341). He continues, "[A] great part of my life's work (I am ten years older than you) has been spent [trying to] destroy illusions of my own and those of mankind." Accordingly, "Freud saw himself as a demystifier of magical and metaphysical explanations about man and his relationship to the world," and he consciously "assumed the therapeutic stance of desacralization" (Fisher 1982, 270). At the same time, Freud reacts to the younger man's popularity with what sounds like purely belittling envy; in his letter of 13 May 13 1926, he comments that "unlike you I cannot count on the love of many people. I have not pleased, comforted, edified them. Nor was this my intention; I only wanted to explore, solve riddles, uncover a little of the truth. This may have given pain to many, benefited a few, neither of which I consider my fault or my merit" (Fisher 1982, 370). Indeed, a number of scholars have suggested that Rolland was one of Freud's many alter egos, or "literary doubles," whom he idealized, competed with, and repeatedly addressed, consciously or unconsciously, in his writings (Kanzer 1979; see also Glenn 1979 and Fisher 1976).

In a broader sense, however, the conflict between Freud and Rolland represents a clash between two different world views. *World view* is an ethnographic term that is "associated with the value and belief system of a cultural group and is concerned with what that group believes to be true, valuable, and significant" (Damen 1987, 124). Moreover, the concept "refers to sets of culturally shared 'realities.'. . . Such reality is considered true and serves as a basis for action; it is often expressed in the language use of its faithful" (1987, 124). In "The Question of a Weltanschauung" ("Weltanschauung" is translated by the editors as "A View of the Universe"), Freud states that his "psychology of the unconscious . . . is quite unfit to construct a *Weltanschauung* of its own: it must accept the scientific one" (Freud 1964, 158). Working alongside a scientific naturalism as yet unexploded by the postmodern affirmation of multiple subjectivities, psychoanalysis "asserts that there are no sources of knowledge of the universe other than the intellectual working-over of carefully scrutinized observations—in other words, what we call research—and alongside of it no knowledge derived from revelation, intuition, or divination" (1964, 159). From the standpoint of this totalizing "universal view," only religion, because of its "immense power which has the strongest emotions of human beings at its service" and its "direct influence on the great mass of mankind" (1964, 161), should "be taken seriously as an enemy" (1964, 160, 161). The religious mind set, with its affirmation of the unknowable, constitutes for Freud a dangerous "rivalry" (1964, 161) with "the scientific spirit, reason" (1964, 171) for the faith of humanity. Most of its claims can already be "answered" (1964, 169), Freud assures his readers; yet "it is true," he continues, that some aspects of the religious world view "may evade refutation" (1964, 169).

While Freud based his metapsychological system on the binary strivings of the Eros and Thanatos drives, the economics of libido, and the need for pragmatic application of the reality principle, Rolland argued for a system in which it was possible to achieve a harmonious balance between reason and mysticism. Moreover, from Freud's standpoint, Rolland had already "evolved into more than a famous man of letters. He had become a contemporary idealist and prophet, in short a writer with a priestly world view" (Fisher 1982, 269). Therefore, "in debunking the imperative to love one's neighbor uncritically, Freud is directly replying to Rolland's world vision" (1982, 266). As a consequence, it is likely that Freud chose to employ St. Francis as a straw man argument in *Civilization and Its Discontents,* for two reasons: first, St. Francis is a well-known, generally respected representative of a specific organized religion that Freud was trying to demystify, and second, he serves as a stand-in both for Rolland personally and for Rolland's mystical world view. It is probable that because of Freud's engagement on this second, more personal level, he uses subjective arguments relating to "value" and "worth" instead of contenting himself with the purely "scientific," psychological explanation for the impossibility of universal love: the superego's inability to completely subjugate the id.

In section four of *Civilization and Its Discontents*, after establishing the dangers of seeking satisfaction through Eros, Freud goes on to admit that "a small minority are enabled by their constitution, nevertheless, to find happiness along the path of love; but far-reaching mental transformations of the erotic function are necessary before this is possible" (Freud 1952, 69). These few individuals are able to accomplish this feat by making themselves

> independent of their object's acquiescence by transferring the main value from the fact of being loved to their own act of loving; they protect themselves against loss of it by attaching their love not to individual objects but to all men equally, and they avoid the uncertainties and disappointments of genital love by turning away from its sexual aim and modifying the instinct into an impulse with an *inhibited aim.* The state which they induce in themselves by this process—an unchangeable, undeviating, tender attitude—has little superficial likeness to the stormy vicissitudes of genital love, from which it is nevertheless derived. (Freud 1952, 69–70)

Surprisingly, in these few sentences, Freud seems to be admitting two provisos for the partial attainability of universal love. First, loving "all men equally" and finding happiness by so doing *is* possible for at least a few people because of their "constitution," and second, this special "constitution" enables the minority to "make" or "induce in themselves" a state in which genital love is partially or wholly transformed into "an impulse with an *inhibited aim*"—in other words, these people on some level *choose* to redirect their loving impulses (1952, 70). That this transformation does include an element of overt choice is verifiable in the personal accounts of saints' lives (such as the writings of Julian of Norwich and St. John of the Cross) which mention their conscious renunciation of thoughts and actions that they considered to be sinful. More recently, in his psychobiography of Saint Ignatius of Loyola (1991), W.W. Meissner has analyzed the manner in which St. Ignatius successfully sublimated his libidinal impulses into dynamic spiritual and humanitarian endeavors. Freud uses St. Francis as an example of such a person who "may have carried this method of using love to produce an inner feeling of happiness as far as anyone" (Freud 1952, 70).

In the second half of this paragraph Freud criticizes "one ethical standpoint" which deems "this inclination towards an all-embracing love of others and of the world at large" to be "the highest state of mind of which man is capable" (1952, 70). Freud continues, "Even at this early stage in the discussion, I will not withhold the two principal objections we have to raise against this view" (1952, 70). Freud's rebuttal, then, will not be directed toward the possibility of the minority achieving happiness through loving all men equally; rather, Freud takes issue with the public's *evaluation* of those individuals as having achieved something valuable and worthy. Therefore, Freud's objections are directed at other's ethical evaluations of people like St. Francis; Freud wishes to replace their value system with his own psychoanalytically informed views. His two objections are as follows: "A love that does not discriminate seems to us to lose some of its own value, since it does an injustice to its object. And secondly, not all men are worthy of love" (1952, 70–71). What is the effectiveness of Freud's polemic, undertaken in deceptively simple, subjective terms, against the "O/other's" subjective value system?

Freud's first objection is related to value. He writes, "[M]y love seems to me a valuable thing that I have no right to throw away without reflection. It imposes obligations on me which I must be prepared to make sacrifices to fulfill" (1952, 81). Later, toward the end of *Civilization and Its Discontents*, Freud concludes that not only is the command to love one's neighbor as oneself "impossible to fulfill," but also "such an enormous inflation of love can only lower its value and not remedy the evil" (1952, 140). The word *value* here is being used in a very fluid manner. In these passages, "value" seems to refer to the actual limitations of the libido-economy and also to the connotatively related but more subjective problem that a love-object will be offended or injured by not being the sole object of love. Cathy Caruth has noted that Freud's use of the first person (e.g. "[M]y love seems to me a valuable thing that I have no right to throw away without reflection" [1952, 81]) creates "a kind of dramatization, which puts on the stage an irritable and parsimonious self, personally resentful of the ethical command it encounters. The struggle between man and civilization is thus dramatized in the struggle between the speaker in the passage and the command" (Caruth 1991, 96). Thus, the second usage, with its additional air of a moral injunction that love shared equally among all "does an injustice to its object" (Freud 1952, 70–71), compels a stronger affective reaction than the objective argument could alone.

Regarding the economics of the libido, Freud establishes that "since man has not an unlimited amount of mental energy at his disposal, he must accomplish his tasks by distributing his libido to the best advantage" (1952, 73). Culture, furthermore, "obeys the laws of psychological economic necessity in making the restrictions, for it obtains a great part of the mental energy it needs by subtracting it from sexuality" (1952, 74). Consequently, Freud posits that since man has a limited quantity of love, it has acquired value like a monetary unit and should be spent carefully. When Freud attempts to link economics of libido and value in the St. Francis passage, however, several inadequacies within his argument are revealed. To begin with, Freud has already admitted the fact that St. Francis of Assisi and others like him, through massive sublimation, have been able to distribute "their love not to individual objects but to all men equally" (1952, 69); therefore, the economics of the libido does not in itself preclude the possibility of some people being able to move "the main value from the fact of being loved to their own act of loving" (1952, 69). Moreover, Freud's stated objective here is to destroy the public's positive view of St. Francis's achievement, and arguments of the economics of libido have little relevancy toward that end.

Another problem with attributing Freud's use of the word *value* here to the value of the libido-economy is that it could also imply that Freud is attempting to dictate how individuals should ration their energy. His warning that "such an enormous inflation of love can only lower its value" borders on a moral judgment, which is inherently subjective (1952, 140). However, throughout *Civilization and Its Discontents* Freud gives hints about his own moral attitudes regarding the survival of civilization. For example, he expresses dismay over the situation of those who abuse "intoxicating substances" (1952, 31). "In certain circumstances they are to blame," he writes, "when valuable energies which could have been used to improve the lot of humanity are uselessly wasted" (1952, 31). Freud's altruism here seems at odds with his objection to the public's admiration for the rare individual like St. Francis who is able to transform his erotic function into aim-inhibited love, benefit humanity, and still obtain happiness. Although he does express concern that a high degree of sublimation is injurious to most people, Freud has still not established why the reading public should refuse to view St. Francis's actions with regard.

The use of "value" to refer to moral preference as well as to libido-economy makes possible another reading of Freud's statement "[A] love that does not discriminate seems to us to lose some of its own value, since it does an injustice to its object" (1952, 70–71). By speaking in terms of what "seems" to be an "injustice," he is appealing to the reader's conscience, to his or her personal feelings about what is naturally right in the grand scheme of things. In section five Freud's reiteration of this idea further enhances the emotional, moral objection with which he intends to fuel his argument, not against the possibility of individuals loving their neighbors as themselves, for he has already acquiesced to the example of St. Francis, but against the very *idea* of universal love. Freud's dramatic persona states that he cannot conceive of himself loving a stranger; in fact, he narrates, "I shall even be doing wrong if I do, for my love is valued as a privilege by all those belonging to me; it is an injustice to them if I put a stranger on a level with them" (1952, 82). Freud's reliance on the word *wrong* in an attempt to set the moral inner workings of universal love against itself (and so demonstrate that it is unfair and not really a virtue at all), is extremely problematic; it takes his reasoning out of the realm of psychoanalytic objectivity and into that of moral relativity, thus placing his argument on even ground with any system of morals.

Indeed, within a subjective moral universe where there is no privileging authority to refer to, Freud's attempt to appeal to humanistic morality seems actually to be an appeal to the infantile id, an appeal that a sophisticated, superego-based moral system could easily deconstruct. For instance, his claim that he would be doing an injustice to his loved ones if he were to "put a stranger on a level with them" is based on infantile all-or-nothing thinking; in a more complex moral system which allows shades of grey as well as black and white, adults are able, within their libido-economics, to have healthy, loving relationships of varying degrees with many people. The command to love one's neighbor as oneself does not, within its own moral system, imply loved ones and strangers alike are necessarily to be loved with the same *kind* of love, or *only* with the same kind of love.

In fact, with regard to types of love, Freud's offended love object sounds a great deal like the jealous recipient of genital love, not of the aim-inhibited love Freud attributes to the universal commandment. Although aim-inhibited love is derived from genital love, throughout the text Freud describes it as having a distinctly different cultural role and emotional intensity than genital love. While "genital love leads to the forming of new families; aim-inhibited love [leads] to *friendships,* which are valuable culturally because they do not entail many of the limitations of genital love— for instance, its exclusiveness" (1952, 71–72). Freud repeats the distinction between possessive genital love and aim-inhibited love, or affection, several pages later; when speaking of the attempt to love a stranger, he narrates, "I am leaving out of account now the use he may be to me, as well as his possible significance to me as a sexual object; neither of these two kinds of relationship between us come[s] into question where the injunction to love my neighbor is concerned" (1952, 81–82). Thus, from the standpoint of universal love, Freud's objection that "it does an injustice to its object" seems irrelevant since aim-inhibited love makes no claim to be genital love and has no exclusive object.

Freud's second principal objection against the view that St. Francis's aim-inhibited love should not be "regarded as the highest state of mind of which man is capable" is that "not all men are worthy of love" (1952, 70–71). His use of the term *worthy* gives rise to the question, What, then, constitutes worthiness? Freud returns to the concept of worthiness several pages later and explains that a neighbor will be worthy of love

> if he is so like me in important respects that I can love myself in
> him; worthy of it if he is so much more perfect than I that I can love
> my ideal of myself in him; I must love him if he is the son of my
> friend, since the pain my friend would feel if anything untoward
> happened to him would be my pain—I should have to share it. But
> if he is a stranger to me and cannot attract me by any value he has in
> himself or any significance he may have already acquired in my
> emotional life, it will be hard for me to love him. (Freud 1952, 82)

Since love is based on finding some aspect of the self in another, "the lover is a narcissist with an object" (Kristeva 1987b, 33).

In other words, a person's worthiness to receive love is directly related to how much he or she attracts me, that is, by how much he or she is able to represent that object which I am lacking. Connected to this definition is a de-emphasis on the amount of personal choice that is involved when one person loves another. The statement, "[I]f I love someone, he must be worthy of it in some way or other" implies that the main impetus and responsibility for love lie outside of myself and reside within the object instead (Freud 1952, 81). I am, through no conscious choice of my own, irresistibly drawn to the object because of its inherent lovableness. Yet Freud has already attributed to St. Francis the freedom of choice. By "far-reaching mental transformations" St. Francis "[made himself] independent of [his] object's acquiescence by transferring the main value from the fact of being loved to [his] own act of loving" (1952, 69). Therefore, as an objection to viewing the life of St. Francis as exemplary, Freud's use of "worth" falls short because he has already ascribed to St. Francis a power of choice that is greater than normal.

Related to the concept of worth is Freud's remonstrance to the reader that "men are not gentle, friendly creatures wishing for love, who simply defend themselves if they are attacked" (1952, 85). Rather, as Freud has frequently proven in his work by psychological investigation and historical example, they are the sort of creatures for whom their neighbor is "a temptation . . . to gratify their aggressiveness on him, to exploit his capacity for work without recompense, to use him sexually, without his consent, to seize his possessions, to humiliate him, to cause him pain, to torture and kill him" (1952, 85). As an example of how universal love might do away with necessary distinctions between good and evil by indiscriminately bestowing love on those who, by their aggressive actions, are unworthy of it, Freud relates a story about the French Chamber. When it debated the abolition of capital punishment, one of those opposed to the idea cried out, "*Que messieurs les assassins commencent!*" (1952, 85). Consequently, "[C]onformity to the highest ethical standards constitutes a betrayal of the interests of culture, for it puts a direct premium on wickedness" (1952, 84–85). The problem with this line of reasoning is that within the highly developed moral system that Freud is criticizing, loving one's neighbor as oneself is not the same thing as condoning his behavior, for one does not always condone even one's own behavior. Just as a parent punishes his or her children when they misbehave, not in spite of that parent's love but *because of* that parent's love for the children, theoretically, a society could use capital punishment as the ultimate mechanism for holding people responsible for their actions. Therefore, loving one's neighbor as oneself does not necessarily imply the creation of a lawless, permissive society as Freud intimates. The reading public need not disregard St. Francis's achievement on the grounds that he was really mandating anarchy.

Indeed, it is very possible that Freud has underestimated the complexity of both Rolland's and St. Francis's world visions. Rolland's "concept of religion did not correspond to either of Freud's two prototypes: the Catholic Church and the Jewish religion" (Fisher 1976, 44). In fact, as both a cross-cultural scholar and a mystic, Rolland believed that "European scientists and psychoanalysts were obstructing the efforts of civilizational interpenetration by waging a battle against religion on two fronts: they condemned the religious consciousness without having experimented with the *fact* of religious experience [as William James does experiment in *The Varieties of Religious Experience*], and they confused the articulation and ritualization of religious feelings with the intensity, durability, and imaginative possibilities" of mysticism (Fisher 1976, 29). Logical arguments from the subjective basis of "value" and "worth" do not explain the positive effects of mysticism that Rolland had documented in Asia.

Moreover, on its own rhetorical grounds, away from the more objective psychoanalytical foundations that Freud also posits against the possibility of loving one's neighbor as oneself, the argument for "value" and "worth" can be answered easily from within the value system that St. Francis represents. From the Christian world view it could be maintained that the command to love one's neighbor as oneself is not based on the rose-colored, "illusory anticipations with which in our youth we regarded our fellow-men" (1952, 87). Rather, all human beings are equally reprehensible sinners, and no one is deserving, in the legal sense, of receiving love. Unlike Eros, which demands a return and is dependent on finding what it lacks, the Christian concept of agape is a "disinterested gift" (Kristeva 1987b,139) which, freely given, cannot be earned. Consequently, fulfillment of the command does not "offer . . . the narcissistic satisfaction of thinking oneself better than others" (1987b, 140), because worthiness to receive love and ability to give love is based on "the gift of God; [and is] not as a result of works, that no one should boast" (Eph 2:8b–9). To the claim that "a love that does not discriminate seems to us to lose some of its own value" (Freud 1952, 70) it could be rejoined that the value of love is not based on its object, but on the Source from which it is drawn; moreover, in loving others, the believer is ultimately loving God, who created man in His image (Gn 1:26). By the same token, "love of self is an error only to the extent that one forgets one is the reflection of the Other (the Lord) (Kristeva 1987b, 122). The believer who accepts the Christian God's valuation of her selfhood is freed from the burden of "narcissism or sinful egoism" in order to agree with her Creator's love for her soul (Kristeva 1987b, 147).

To recapitulate, it is probable that Freud included St. Francis of Assisi and his resulting arguments of "value" and "worth" in an attempt to fully dismantle the world views that Romain Rolland and St. Francis represent. These two objections leave openings for criticism because they can be deconstructed from within Freud's own text as well as from within Rolland's and St. Francis's systems. This conclusion suggests a new angle for dialogue between Christianity and psychoanalysis. Defined in current ethnological terms, both Christianity and psychoanalysis could be viewed as the philosophies of specific world views, and if, as is popularly accepted, all truth is relative, the two could be compared on equal, relative terms. A profitable conversation between the two would require what cross-cultural psychologist Dr. David Augsburger labels "interpathy," which is "an intentional cognitive and affective envisioning of another's thoughts and feelings from another culture, world view, [or] epistemology" (Augsburger 1986, 31). Interpathy requires the ability to enter a foreign frame of reference and to "temporarily believe what the other believes, see as the other sees, value what the other values" (1986, 31). As Augsburger observes in *Pastoral Counseling Across Cultures*, "[M]ost counseling training is grounded in empiricism or phenomenology. Either approach focuses on observable phenomena that are replicable, measurable, and definable by either naturalistic observation or objective self-description. Neither approach offers a useful perspective on mystic, cultic, folk religions, and commonly believed perspectives that shape many cultures" (1986, 32). The counselor who attempts interpathic understanding, on the other hand,

> enters a foreign epistemology to evaluate it not by extracultural values but rather by its own internal consistency and by its contextual congruency. When the belief system of the counselee possesses an integrity within and a congruence with the cultural field, it can have integrative power for that person, and healing and growth will emerge from using that system, not from contradicting it. (Augsburger 1986, 35)

Perhaps that is the type of participatory investigation that Romain Rolland had in mind when he "called for a radical type of research, a technique which would narrow the gap between subject and object. He suggested that the observer identify with and experience the sensation of the object observed" (Fisher 1976, 31).

A successful dialogue between adherents to psychoanalysis and to Christianity would require the participants to subscribe to at least two ground rules: first, as Augsburger explains, they would need to agree that "dialogue and hierarchy are contradictory. When one person insists on defining or describing reality in exclusive terms and possesses the power to impose the definition and description on the other, a vertical violence dehumanizes both" (Augsburger 1986, 39-40). And second, "[D]ialogue can begin only when there is an openness to being fully confronted and perhaps persuaded by the other view. Thus it carries the risk of change" (1986, 40). Such an approach to dialoguing across world views is approached in the works of Julia Kristeva; in *Tales of Love* and *In the Beginning Was Love: Psychoanalysis and Faith*, Kristeva demonstrates her familiarity with the complexities and vocabulary of both world views, and so is able to begin to communicate between psychoanalysis and Christianity biculturally. Indeed, whether the self expresses herself to a therapist or to God, she is in both cases seeking unconditional love from an "Other" who enters into her frame of reference "without ideological, moral, or biased suggestions, but through a simple listening, [which is] lovingly absent-minded" (Kristeva 1987b, 382). A number of contemporary psychoanalysts, moreover, including Stanley A. Leavy and W.W. Meissner, have affirmed the healthy possibilities of sublimation through loving identification with one's neighbor within the context of religious faith. Meissner believes that gaining the ability to love one's neighbor, regardless of that neighbor's immediate "value" to oneself, is an integral part of attaining a mature ego development; for "when the ego realizes within itself an authentic love of neighbor, the spiritual identity achieves a new synthesis in which the self-realization of its humility is deepened and intensified. The ego reaches a level of development in which its control of intrapsychic dynamisms permits diversion of its energies outside itself. This extension implies an enlargement and growth to a new level of interior organization within the ego" (Meissner 1987, 77). Even Freud himself, in his friendly correspondence with the Swiss pastor and psychoanalyst Oskar Pfister, could confess "in itself, psycho-analysis is neither religious nor non-religious, but an impartial tool which both priest and layman can use in the service of the sufferer. I am very much struck by the fact that it never occurred to me how extraordinarily helpful the psycho-analytic method might be in pastoral work, but that is surely accounted for by the remoteness from me, as a wicked pagan, of the whole system of ideas" (1909; Freud and Pfister 1963, 17).

Yet it is to the degree in which any system—theological, psychoanalytical, or otherwise—is able to tolerate the cognitive dissonance involved in accepting the *possibility* of an Inscrutable Other not made in its own conceptual image that it is able to resist appropriating the notion of this Other into the confines of its own, essentializing terminology. Post-structuralist theory is by no means exempt from the temptation to exert such a totalizing reflex; as Eugene Goodheart posits in his critique of Michel Foucault's *The History of Sexuality*, even the pursuit of unfettered desire can become deified and reductive, thus limiting creative perceptions of the Other. Goodheart asserts that in the postmodern era, when concern for loving one's neighbor has receded in favor of obtaining desire itself, "desire has come to function as an essentialist trope—which means that it has become controlling, coercive, a form of self-destructive tyranny. It is no longer simply the host of desires that makes us living beings, but desire in its hegemonic version—as ruler of life" (Goodheart 1988, 398). In as much as the postmodern critic, psychoanalyst, or theologian is able to avoid "colonizing" the boundaries of her conceptions of love or desire with her own knowing, to leave room for "God in the gaps," there is space for a dynamic interplay among the disciplines. Interpathy, in short, demands not only imagination, but humility.

In his correspondences, Freud acknowledges his inability to transverse the gap between knowing and Unknowing. He writes to Rolland in 1929, "How remote from me are the worlds in which you move! To me mysticism is just as closed a book as music. I cannot imagine reading all the literature which, according to your letter, you have studied. And yet it is easier for you than for us to read the human soul!" (E. Freud 1960, 389). Certainly, *Civilization and Its Discontents* is a masterful exposition of the illusions on which humanity bases its sense of well-being. Freud fails in his attempt to dismantle the Christian ethical world view, however, because he is unable to reach a state of interpathy and, in so doing, to generate a cross-cultural argument that translates into the highly complex system of Christian morality and belief.

Works Cited

Augsburger, David. 1986. *Pastoral Counseling Across Cultures*. Philadelphia: Westminster.

Caruth, Cathy. 1991. *Empirical Truths and Critical Fictions*. Baltimore: ohns Hopkins University Press.

Damen, Louise. 1987. *Culture Learning: The Fifth Dimension in the Language Classroom*. Second Language Professional Library. Menlo Park, CA: Addison-Wesley.

Fisher, David James. 1976. "Sigmund Freud and Romain Rolland: The Terrestrial Animal and His Great Oceanic Friend." *American Imago* 33:1–59.

———. 1982. "Reading Freud's *Civilization and Its Discontents*." In *Modern European Intellectual History: Reappraisals and New Perspectives*. Ed. Dominick LcCapra and Steven L. Kaplan. Ithaca: Cornell University Press. 251–79.

Freud, Ernst L., ed. 1960. *Letters of Sigmund Freud*. New York: Basic Books.

Freud, Sigmund. 1952. *Civilization and Its Discontents*. The International Psycho-Analytical Library. Ed. Ernest Jones. Trans. Joan Riviere. London: Hogarth Press and The Institute of Psycho-Analysis.

———. 1964. "New Introductory Lectures on Psycho-Analysis. The Question of a *Weltanschauung*." In *The Standard Edition of the Complete Psychological Works of Sigmund Freud*. Ed. James Strachey. Vol. 22. London: Hogarth Press and The Institute of Psycho-Analysis. 3–182.

Freud, Sigmund and Oskar Pfister. 1963. *Psychoanalysis and Faith: The Letters of Sigmund Freud and Oskar Pfister*. Ed. H. Meng and E. Freud. Trans. E. Mosbacher. New York: Basic Books.

Glenn, Jules. 1979. "Narcissistic Aspects of Freud and His Doubles." *Freud and His Self-Analysis*. Ed. Mark Kanzer and Jules Glenn. New York: Aronson. 297–302.

Goodheart, Eugene. 1988. "Desire and Its Discontents." *Partisan Review* 55 (3): 387–403.

James, William. 1902. *The Varieties of Religious Experience*. New York: Random House.

Kanzer, Mark. 1979. "Freud and His Literary Doubles." In *Freud and His Self-Analysis*. Ed. Mark Kanzer and Jules Glenn. New York: Aronson. 285–96.

Kristeva, Julia. 1987a. *In the Beginning Was Love: Psychoanalysis and Faith*. Trans. Arthur Goldhammer. New York: Columbia University Press.

———. 1987b. *Tales of Love*. Trans. Leon S. Roudiez. New York: Columbia University Press.

Leavy, Stanley A. 1988. *In the Image of God: A Psychoanalyst's View*. New Haven: Yale University Press.

Meissner, W.W. 1987. *Life and Faith: Psychological Perspectives on Religious Experience*. Washington, DC: Georgetown University Press.

———. 1991. *The Psychology of a Saint: Ignatius of Loyola*. New Haven: Yale University Press.

13

Facing the Other:
Levinas, Perelman, Rosenzweig

Susan Handelman

Idealism completely carried out reduces all ethics to politics.
—Levinas, *Totality and Infinity,* 216

Otherness, or *alterity*, has become a fashionable term in recent literary theory. The most problematic question, however, is defining just what and who is the "other." In most post-structuralist theory, "otherness" is usually accompanied by the notion of a "radical rupture" which subverts closed identities and all-encompassing systems. Is "otherness," then, an inchoate anonymous unknown reminding us of the limits of our knowledge and thus the fount of endless skepticism? Or is it the passage through which the Otherness of divine transcendence crosses? Is it the basis for nihilism, or for a political awareness of the relation of power to knowledge and the commitment to subvert oppression? Is it Derrida's "difference," Kristeva's feminine semiosis, Lacan's Unconscious, Foucault's marginalized discourses?

Moreover, can the relation to the human other as an individual other person have anything to do with epistemological alterity in general? And what do these notions of alterity have to do with the relation of philosophy and literary theory to Judaism?

In this chapter, I want to examine the ways in which the contemporary French-Jewish philosopher Emmanuel Levinas addresses these issues, for they are at the heart of his work. Levinas is one of the few writers who are able to restore *ethical binding* in the face of the ruptures enacted in postmodern thought. His aim is to deconstruct the subject but retain it as responsible, lucid, awake, obligated. In fact, Levinas's work may be characterized as an extraordinary ethical critique of philosophy. It is a "summoning" of philosophical reason in the sense that a summons is an urgent call or order to a trial. It is also a summons of "witnesses" whose testimony will enact a judgment on philosophy, and a summons to a prior obligation of both the philosophical "knowing subject" and the subject as the "contents," or object, of philosophy.

I will analyze Levinas's work in relation to both contemporary literary theory and modern Jewish philosophy by comparing it to two other important modern theorists of language and ethics whose work, like his, needs to be brought much more into contemporary debates about these issues: the rhetorical theorist Chaim Perelman and the great German-Jewish philosopher Franz Rosenzweig. Finally, I will discuss some of the relations between Levinas's work and the Holocaust, that catastrophic event that seems to have broken all covenants between God and humanity, human and human, language and ethics.

Levinas's Background

Since Levinas's work is not as well known in America as in Europe, let me begin with some biographical facts. Though Levinas is commonly described as a "French" philosopher, he was actually born in Russia, in Kovno, in 1906, and left in 1923 for philosophical studies (especially in phenomenology) in France and Germany. He became a French citizen and was mobilized into the French army when World War II began; the French uniform saved him from deportation to the gas chambers when he was captured by the Germans. While he was held in a prisoner-of-war camp, however, all his family remaining in Russia were murdered by the Nazis. When he emerged from the camp after the war, Levinas wrote of his "profound need to leave the climate of that [Heidegger's] philosophy" (Levinas 1978a, 19). He proceeded with an extensive critique of phenomenological thought and the way it related consciousness to being.

The entire thrust of Levinas's work is to reverse the subordination of ethics to ontology (the study of Being) and the other branches of philosophy. Ethics is not something to be added on after we establish a metaphysics or logic or aesthetics or epistemology. Ethics, which he defines as the irreducible relation of obligation to the other, is prior. Prior here does not mean "coming before" in any linear chronological sense, but a realm that has not been thought and on which thought nevertheless depends for its possibility.

This search for what philosophy has not or cannot think is an enterprise common to many modern French and German thinkers, from Heidegger to Derrida. In Deconstructionist literary theory influenced by Derrida, the focus on the non-knowledge which always conditions and eludes knowledge led to a recognition of the instability of linguistic meaning, and a practice of skeptical critique as the constant unsettling of all foundations. Those more inspired by Foucault examine the hidden links of knowledge and power, force and signification. These various means of rupturing philosophical "totality" all involve a solicitation of what is "other" as what has been "marginalized, repressed, excluded" by philosophy and its modes of intelligibility. The "subject" defined as the individual perceiving self or transparent consciousness who makes meaning of the world has been put into question. Levinas, however, differs from most poststructuralist thinkers by asserting that *"l'absolument Autre, c'est Autrui"* (1961, 39). The word *"autrui"* signifies the other as personal other; in other words, absolute alterity passes or is traced through the personal human other.

But there is another sense in which what is other is the Jew, and there is this "other" side to Levinas the philosopher as well. In 1947 Levinas also became the Director of the Ecole Normale Israélite Orientale, a Jewish school which is part of the Alliance Israélite, an organization dedicated to spreading French and Jewish culture throughout Jewish communities in France and its former Mediterranean empire. He held this position simultaneously with his posts teaching philosophy in French universities and has written prolifically on Judaism and Jewish life.

He has also delivered, for the past twenty years, the annual Talmudic lecture at the Colloquium of French-Jewish Intellectuals. In these lectures he has argued that what modern Judaism needs most of all is a renewed relation to the Talmud, that vast corpus of ancient and medieval rabbinic commentary on Jewish law and lore. His work is permeated with a distrust of religious mysticism; in his view, such attempts at ecstatic fusion of "direct experience of the sacred" destroy the lucidity of an ethical metaphysics.

One of the figures Levinas uses to describe alterity in both his philosophical and his Jewish writings is "face." But the "face of the other" is not for him a visual image; it is rather a facing *relation*. The other faces my own separate and narcissistic ego, interrupts, and shames it, a calling into question that is the call of conscience as both an appeal and an order. The connotations of the Hebrew word for face (*panim*) in biblical and rabbinic tradition are all important here. The verbal root *panah* in Hebrew connotes a "turning" toward something, and also a kind of presence.[1] In Levinas, facing is being confronted with, turned toward, facing up to, being judged and called to by the other. Facing is a disruption of that free, autonomous self which through its reasoning and consciousness thinks it can construct the world out of itself, or know the world from itself.

For both Levinas and Franz Rosenzweig (1886–1929), the great German-Jewish philosopher whose work deeply influenced Levinas, that presumption is the archetypal gesture of philosophy: idealism. Indeed, Richard Cohen has persuasively argued that the very notion of the "face" in Levinas may have its source in the culminating pages of Rosenzweig's great work *The Star of Redemption,* wherein Rosenzweig describes the apotheosis of truth with the figure of a face.[2]

The facing relation in Levinas is not, however, a relation of free reciprocal exchange, and *not* a Buberian I–Thou dialogue. Instead, this facing traumatizes and empties the subject. It binds the self to the other despite the self's will in an obligation prior to freedom, a heteronomy or "difficile liberté," to use the title of one of Levinas's books on Judaism. Identity comes not from the coincidence of self with self but from the recurrence of the call of obligation to the other. On the one hand, Levinas seeks within the philosophical tradition for moments of recognition of this ethical otherness (for example, in Plato's notion of the "Good beyond Being," and Descartes's "Idea of the Infinite"). On the other hand, I think he is also calling philosophy to this recognition in what I would characterize as a kind of prophetic and rhetorical appeal that coincides with Levinas's understanding of Judaism.

Rhetoric and Politics in Literary Theory

The relations of Levinas's Jewish thought to his philosophical thought and to his personal biography are highly complex matters which I can only touch upon here. Levinas never directly mentions his own experience of World War II in his philosophical work, but it seems to me to be one reason why he "brings philosophy to trial" and part of the explanation for the kinds of witnesses he summons in that trial and for his very notion of signification as a kind of witness, of language itself as summons, judgment, apology, and teaching. That devastating experience must also have been one motivation for his attempt to construct a philosophy that itself is not based on war (even as a game) but on justice and peace—peace defined as that very moment of renunciation, apology, welcome, and vulnerable exposure to the other.

It is not fortuitous that Levinas begins and ends both his great philosophical books *Totality and Infinity* and *Otherwise Than Being* with meditations on war and peace. The very first sentence in the preface to *Totality and Infinity* is "Are we duped by morality?" Isn't war the very "truth of the real" as Heraclitus long ago argued when he said, "War is king of all"? If so, politics as the art of foreseeing and winning war would be the "very exercise of reason" and moral consciousness would have no recourse against the mocking gaze of the political man" (1961, 21). Needless to say, that mocking gaze is found in much recent literary theory which has taken an intensely political turn through schools of criticism variously dubbed the

New Historicism, cultural materialism, or cultural poetics.[3] What might be some of the relations of Levinasian ethics to this new literary politics?

Both right-wing pragmatists such as Stanley Fish and left-wing Marxists such as Terry Eagleton argue that truth is a variable social construct connected to the interests and ideologies of particular social groups. The key question, however, is, What is the sociality of this social relation? For the political critics it is at bottom a contest for power, a struggle between domination and subversion wherein different social forces endlessly vie for control of meaning. The aim of this kind of criticism is to reveal the "social constructedness" (or what some critics call the "rhetoricity") as opposed to the "ontological groundedness" of these historical and social versions of truth. This act of "demystification" is intended to empower other voices which have been muted or repressed to contest these accounts. Roland Barthes's "pleasure of the text" has been turned into the "war of discourse."

Yet for most of the cultural-political critics there is no space "outside" this realm of war and negotiation, or outside the mutual implications of discourse and power and the constraints of institutions on "cultural practices." Hence they call for what they term a "rhetorical" notion of truth, and associate rhetorical criticism with the detection and deployment of language in the assertion of power, or with "textual strategies" in the war of discourse. Or, rhetoric is used—as in de Man or Derrida—to denote a form of negative epistemology and antagonism to philosophy, a language of tropes that interferes with and undercuts the philosophical logos.[4]

In any case, this is a very distorted notion of rhetoric which severs it from one of its ancient roots—what Aristotle called "dialectic" or deliberative argument, a mode of reasoning that deals with theses that are not necessary but only probable. That is, where formal logical syllogisms cannot apply, where there are not absolute grounds for truth, but in which decisions and actions still needed to be reasoned over and taken.

That is the aspect of rhetoric that Chaim Perelman revives in his masterwork *The New Rhetoric*. Rhetoric for Perelman involves a critique of modern forms of logical and mathematical rationalism which have their precursor in Descartes, but which have been overextended and misapplied as criteria for *all* argument. Perelman argues that there are many areas of human thought and endeavor—including questions of politics, ethics, religion, philosophy—which elude the methods of mathematical and natural sciences. If we restrict our notion of reason to the model of formal logic, and Cartesian intuitive self-evident truths, we create uncompromising and ineradicable dualisms such as "reason/imagination," "knowledge/opinion," "universal objectivity/incommunicable subjectivity," "judgements of reality/judgments of value," "theory/practice" (Perelman and Albrechts-Tyteca

1958, 510). These dualisms "and the assertion that whatever is not objectively and indisputably valid belongs to the realm of the arbitrary and the subjective create an unbridgeable gulf between theoretical knowledge, which is rational, and action, for which motives would be wholly irrational" (1958, 512). The consequence is that practice ceases to be reasonable, critical argument becomes incomprehensible, and philosophical reflection becomes meaningless.

Why such a fear of an "end of philosophy" or of the irrational? I suspect that Perelman's *The New Rhetoric* was written, like much of Levinas's philosophy, in response to the catastrophes and violence of World War II. Perelman was a Belgian Jew and one of the leaders of Belgian resistance; he also had a distinguished career as a professor of philosophy and law.[5] Like Levinas, he had personally experienced the effects of a massive collapse of reasonable discourse in the violence of that war. Like Levinas, he is searching for a "third way" beyond these dualisms, and for a form of reason that is itself neither violent nor injurious to the other and to the individual human responsibility. He shares the Levinasian impulse to modify the Enlightenment version of the universal light of reason rather than abandon it completely to a war of conflicting power interests and self-interested ideologies.[6]

So like Levinas, Perelman instead redefines, extends and amplifies reason to include forms of reasoning that do not involve what is conceptually self-evident, necessary, or autonomous, but that "require an other" and depend upon the relation of address and assent of the other person through discourse. (Rosenzweig makes a similar turn from what he perceived to be the violence of the Hegelian version of history and philosophy to what he called *Sprachdenken,* or "speech-thinking.")

In sum, Levinas and Perelman are both in search of a reason-of-the-other, an other-reason that is not however arbitrary, violent, or willful, but rather a non-necessary form of imperative. And that for Perelman is found in the forms of reasoning and persuasion of the rhetorical tradition from the Greeks onward, forms of discourse that were denigrated and neglected by Cartesian logicians and philosophers-described as merely "ornamental," "literary," or "sophistic." From this tradition, Perelman constructs a "critical rationalism" that "transcends the duality 'judgments of reality/value judgments,' and makes both judgments of reality and value judgments dependent on the personality of the scientist or philosopher, who is responsible for his decisions in the field of knowledge as well as the field of action" (1958, 514).[7]

In other words, for Perelman rhetoric is a form of social but non-coercive and nonviolent reason required to deliberate in areas where there are no necessary or absolute truths. That is, a realm where there are no truths that have *coercive* power, such as the "coercions" of self-evident reason or deductive logic or nonrational faith. Formal Cartesian reason is founded on the solipsistic notion of self evident truths, clear, distinct, and necessary—there is no need for deliberation with others, nor any question of varying intensities of adherence to these truths, nor the possibility of withholding one's assent from them. Such reason, like the theoretical reason of Kant, "imposes itself on every rational being" and "agreement is inevitable" (1958, 2). Rhetoric, by contrast, is defined by Perelman as that form of reason which involves the freely given and responsible commitment of a deliberating audience. Perelman's "new rhetoric" is then a "third way" between the compulsions of formal autonomous reason and the coercions of violence. To deliberate or argue with another

> implies that one has renounced resorting to forces alone, that value is attached to gaining the adherence of one's interlocutor by means of reasoned persuasion, and that one is not regarding him as an object but appealing to his free judgement. Recourse to argumentation assumes the establishment of a community of minds, which, while it lasts, excludes the use of violence. (1958, 55)

This is a notion of rhetoric quite at odds with the way the term is used in much contemporary literary theory, to denote the ineradicable political biases and ideologies involved in language use and interpretation. Rhetoric is then the deployment of "textual strategies" in the war-game of interpretation; and/or linguistic self-consciousness and self-reflexivity; and/or critical self-consciousness of the interpreter, who recognizes that there is no ontological or transcendent foundation to language or truth, that all truth is embodied in the social constructs of linguistic practice. To attain this critical self-consciousness is posited as an act of demystification which is a necessary part of a politically progressive practice, a kind of "postmodern ethic."

In fact, much of the recent epistemological skepticism and political criticism in literary theory justifies itself through an implicit stance of ethical and moral superiority: that is, it claims to resist by its demystifications and radical critiques the absolutism of tyrants and fanatics. But Perelman has a remarkable insight to add to the debate: the radical skeptic is often not the opposite but the counterpart of the fanatic for both equate adherence to theses with recognition of absolute truth. Both skeptic and fanatic thus foreclose deliberative argument about choice when no absolute ground exists. Writes Perelman:

> Since rhetorical proof is never completely necessary proof, the think-
> ing person who gives his adherence to the conclusions of an argu-
> mentation does so by an act that commits him and for which he is
> responsible. The fanatic accepts the commitment, but as one bow-
> ing to an absolute and irrefragable truth; the skeptic refuses the
> commitment, but under the pretext that he does not find it suffi-
> ciently definitive. He refuses adherence because his idea of adher-
> ence is similar to that of the fanatic: both fail to appreciate that
> argumentation aims at a choice among possible theses; by propos-
> ing and justifying the hierarchy of these theses, argumentation seeks
> to make the decision a rational one. This role of argumentation in
> decision making is denied by the skeptic and fanatic. In the absence
> of compelling reason, they both are inclined to give violence a free
> hand, rejecting personal commitment. (1958, 62)

This passage might be used to gloss the painful political controversy that
has so troubled many contemporary literary critics—the connection between Paul de Man's radical skepticism and his pro-fascist writings in
World War II.[8] Many of de Man's defenders have argued that his
deconstructive skepticism was an implicit repudiation and overcoming of
his earlier ideological writings, a posture of critical self-reflexiveness whose
notions about "undecidability" and the "impossibility of reading" are intended to guard against all violent engagements. But Perelman's analysis
indicates that such radical skepticism, which denies the grounds for any
choice between meanings, is overly restrictive in its definition of truth and
knowledge. Foreclosing deliberation and choice in endless aporias and
"undecidabilities" is an act as absolutist and open to violence as that of the
fanatic who refuses to debate due to her or his conviction of possessing
that absolute truth.[9]

The same criticism could be made of the "ideological" critic, who
holds that all values are masks for self-interested power plays; or the rela-
tivist who is intent on constantly undermining any and every claim to a firm
foundation for a given value or truth, and refuses to allow for any deliberative argument about the hierarchy of values or criteria for making choices
among them. For as the jurist knows, regardless of the lack of any absolute, clear, or unambiguous ground, choices still must be made and decisions rendered.

In Perelman's view both the fanatic and skeptic relieve themselves of
the burden of personal responsibility, action, and commitment to choices
made. Rhetorical argumentation, though, is oriented toward decision and
the future: "it sets out to bring about some action or prepare the way for it
by acting, by discursive methods, on the minds of the hearers" (1958, 47).

Argumentation, Perelman reminds us, is not merely an intellectual exercise divorced from practical preoccupations. "Language is not only a means of communication: it is also an instrument for acting on minds, a means of persuasion" (1958, 132). That is precisely why argumentation is a substitute for the violence that attempts to obtain an action by the use of force or compulsion. I would argue that there are many lessons here for literary criticism and theory. First, restricting questions about meaning or the nature of the literary text to questions about the epistemological status of language is as artificial as the attempt to restrict all reasoning solely to formal logic. Nor is the only alternative an uncritical embrace of "politics" and the assertion that the way language acts on the world is essentially ideological and marked by relations of force, domination, and violence.

In sum, for both Perelman and Levinas, aesthetics and politics need to be subsumed to a critical rationalism which for Perelman is rhetoric and for Levinas ethics.[10] As philosopher, however, Levinas partakes of the ancient philosophical contempt for rhetoric, which he views as the approach to the neighbor through ruse, as a mode of sophistic manipulation and violence rather than as a search for truth. But Levinas's insistence on language as preeminently a call or command before it is an exchange of information, is at bottom "rhetorical."

Rosenzweig's Critique of Philosophy

In other words, ethics as the obligation and binding of the self to the other constitutes what Levinas describes as "the 'rationality' of a reason less hard on itself than the reasons of the philosophical tradition," not a decline of rationality, but a fuller rationality (1982, 176). Levinas's critique of reason does not negate reason but tries to formulate a "second" type of reason, a reason that is not autonomous and imperialistic or slavish and mindless. The essential point is that when aesthetics or politics become their own autonomous realms, obliterating the prior realm of the ethics, they inevitably convert into forms of violence and tyranny. They deny the alterity and singularity of otherness, which for Levinas passes through the human other and is the essence of the ethical relation.

To explain this idea more clearly and consider the relation of Levinasian ethics to Jewish thought, we need to examine Levinas's relation to Rosenzweig. Along with Rosenzweig, Levinas saw (long before Foucault) the complicity of power and knowledge, of philosophy and violence. Rosenzweig's work was a fierce attack on Hegelian philosophy and especially Hegel's assertion that "History is the judge of history," that is, that immanent history was the dialectical Life of the Spirit on its road to the consummation of self-knowledge. In Rosenzweig, there is a devastating critique of philosophical idealism, but also an attempt to reconstellate the shattered fragments of that idealism in a new way. And this way involved Rosenzweig in a new relation of philosophy to theology.[11]

What World War II was for Levinas, World War I and its catastrophic slaughter had been for Rosenzweig. For both thinkers, it became imperative to judge the violence of that history and to give its victims voice. That meant locating an "elsewhere" or "beyond" or "other" that could enact a judgment upon immanent history, even while recognizing that there can be no recourse to traditional theology or traditional notions of transcendence to secure this judgment.

This project ultimately involves both Levinas and Rosenzweig in a kind of prophetic eschatology. And this search for such an elsewhere, or "otherwise than being," or time of the other, is central to the project of many other modern Jewish thinkers—even those who are highly secularized such as Walter Benjamin. One line could be traced that goes from Rosenzweig to Levinas, and from Levinas to Derrida on into post-structuralism; another line goes from Rosenzweig to the Frankfurt School of Critical Theory through Benjamin and T. W. Adorno, both of whom were influenced by Rosenzweig's critique of totality.[12] Levinas mentions his profound debt to Rosenzweig in the very first pages of *Totality and Infinity*: "We were impressed by the opposition to the idea of totality in Franz Rosenzweig's *Stern der Erlösung*, a work too often present in this book to be cited" (1961, 28).

To briefly (and too simplistically) explain this reference: Rosenzweig's great undoing of "totality" in *The Star* was a critique of the pretensions of Western philosophy from, as he puts it, "the Ionean Islands to Iena" (that is, from the Greeks to Hegel) to "know the All." This project, Rosenzweig argued, has roots in the fear of death. Philosophy flees this singular human mortal self by attempting to construct impersonal death-less systems. It tries to reduce the heterogeneity of reality into single, impersonal, explanatory principles (Rosenzweig 1930, 1–15). The project culminates in Hegelian idealism where philosophy seeks to construct out of itself a completely autonomous totality, identifying the self-fulfillment of Thought with the consummation of world history, and with Hegel's claim that his own philosophy itself is the final union of Thought and Being wherein identity dialectically overcomes difference. Needless to say, Rosenzweig is only one of the countless philosophers and critics from Kierkegaard to Derrida who have devoted their energies to opposing that notion.

One of Levinas's special contributions, however, is the application of Rosenzweig's critique to contemporary forms of impersonal reason. For

example, he writes "Heideggerian ontology, which subordinates the relationship with the Other to the relation with Being in general, remains under
obedience to the anonymous, and leads inevitably to another power, to
imperialist domination, to tyranny" (Levinas 1961, 47). Levinas's critique
of Heidegger and his connection of Heideggerian philosophy to political
violence may be applied, I would add, to de Man's linguistic theory, the key
to which is the impersonality and autonomy of language. And this critique
would shed another light on both Heidegger's and de Man's own problematic relations to Nazism.

One could even say that in much literary theory of the 1970s and
1980s, "Language" or "History" has taken the role of an impersonal term
through which all is mediated or known. The alterity of the singular, personal human other is then defined only as a subordinate function or "site"
of impersonal significations or ideologies. But Levinas's critique of impersonality is not made to defend the personal ego as some individual, unified,
sovereign center of meaning—a notion most post-structuralists have also
vigorously attacked. As he puts it, "It is not I who resist the system, as
Kierkegaard thought; it is the Other" (1961, 40).

The aim of Levinas's work is to show that reason and freedom are not
autonomous but are founded on prior structures, and that freedom is justified not of itself, but *by and for the other*. In other words, what claims to
be autonomous, independent "for and of-itself" (classical reason, the dialectical march of History, reflexive self-consciousness, the impersonal world
of art, the narcissistic ego, the play of the signifiers, institutional Discourse,
etc.) in Levinas is "faced" with the other and this facing, as the very questioning and shattering or hollowing out of the subject, becomes an extra-
version into a *for-the-other*. Before the face of the other I am judged, brought
to account, accused and so made responsible.

But one cannot logically or deductively prove that the other puts me in
question; one cannot accomplish the break with totality through the very
kind of philosophical consciousness which is by definition the attempt to
grasp and master the All, or what Levinas calls an "ego-ology" [*sic*]. His
notion of the "face" is thus a rhetorical appeal, an attempt to create an
"outside" of philosophical consciousness (or the totality) by which it can
be judged and brought to account.

That is why he writes that "the call to question is not a matter of
turning around upon oneself and becoming conscious of the calling to question. The absolutely other is not reflected in consciousness. . . . We are
concerned with questioning a consciousness, and not with the consciousness of questioning" (Levinas 1966, 41). The exile of the self through the
demand of the other is not the negative "consciousness of this exile." In

Levinas, the exile of the self is a turning outward, an extraversion, a positivity, "precisely the welcome reception of the absolutely other" which summons me to reply. He redefines the subject as "for-the-other," not as a consciousness bringing objects to representation "for itself." Moral consciousness, then, is not "an experience of values" but an access to exteriority, to Being as other, and finally beyond ontology to the otherwise than being (1978a, 183).

Subjectivity as for-the-other, in sum, involves a "plural reason" commanded not by the logic of identity which itself is the return of difference to the same—a "for itself"—but instead a reason commanded and penetrated by the other, heteronomous instead of autonomous.

For Itself and For the Other

The "extra-version" of the for-itself into the for-the-other is another key move one finds in Rosenzweig. Rosenzweig models for Levinas a path by which the totality of Idealist cognition of the All is shattered, and how the subsequent fragments (subject-object-universe, or God-humanity-world) each isolated in and for themselves can then be opened up to and for-the-other. In Levinas this opening constitutes the ethical move par excellence; in Rosenzweig it is the very meaning of Revelation. And for both Rosenzweig and Levinas, it is a fundamental characteristic of Judaism.

In an essay on Rosenzweig, Levinas makes the crucial comment that the conjunction "and" used to designate the re-connections made in *The Star* among God, humanity, and world as Creation, Revelation, and Redemption means "for": God for humanity, humanity for world, etc. The unity Rosenzweig constructs is not any formal unity of philosophical logic but "is in the sense that they are one for the other, when one is placed in these elements themselves" (1963b, 128). "One for the other" is a "living" relation, not a philosophical category, or a Hegelian dialectical synthesis which empties the terms of their irreducible individuality, or perceives them from the "outside" in the all-seeing gaze of the philosopher.

For Rosenzweig, the "I" is drawn out of its mute and isolated self-enclosure, (which Rosenzweig identifies with the mythical, aesthetic, and pagan worlds) by God's emerging from God's concealment, questing for and turning to the individual human self (Rosenzweig 1930, 156). That is how Rosenzweig understands God's question to Adam, "Where are You?" in Genesis. But as Rosenzweig notes, God receives no real response from Adam to this initial question; instead, Adam hides himself, and blames Eve and the serpent; Adam remains defiant and self-enclosed. Only when God calls out to Abraham in the story of the sacrifice of Isaac in Gn 22:1—in the vocative, in direct address, not with an indefinite "you" but with his proper name "Abraham"—that is, in all his nonconceptual individuality, in love for his singularity, "now he answers, all unlocked, all spread-apart, all ready, all-soul: 'Here I am.' Here is the I, the individual human I, as yet wholly receptive, as yet only unlocked, only empty, without content, without nature, pure readiness, pure obedience, all ears" (1930, 176). For Rosenzweig, this movement of turning and opening to the other is the essence of Revelation before Revelation signifies any propositional or doctrinal content. And this "turning towards the other," as we remember, is a prime meaning of the "face" (panah, panim) and is also essential in Levinas.[13]

In Levinas's philosophical writings, a similar pattern emerges but it is derived without direct exegesis of the Bible or explicit reference to Jewish thought, although terms such as *election, creation* and *Here I am* are used. The subject is elected (the "chosen people"), called out of its narcissistic self-enclosure not by any traditional God of theology but by the "revelation of the face" of the other, the human other through whom the other-than-being "passes" or is traced. Levinas reverses, in a sense, the path of *The Star*: in *The Star*, God's immediate and pressing love as "shining countenance" (Rosenzweig 1930, 157, 164) opens up and awakens the human soul to both God and to the love of the neighbor; in Levinas, the immediate and pressing face of other opens and awakens the ego, and traces the otherness of a divinity which is otherwise than being, otherwise than any theology, escaping the revelation of any logos.

It is important to emphasize here that like Rosenzweig, Levinas claims not to base his philosophical writings a priori on any traditional "theology." He firmly maintains that he does not use the Bible or theology as his starting point, nor does he rely on or intend any orthodox theology. His "other than being" is not intended to be theological—"of the logos," or any "ology"— that is, any identification of logos and being and being or assertion of a God who is the Being behind or beyond being. Though the other "resembles God," the relation to the other and the assignation from the Good survive the death of God (Levinas 1974, 123).[14]

The face is not, he reiterates, the image of the God who has passed. "Being in the image of God does not signify being the icon of God but to find oneself in his trace":

> The God of Judaeo-Christian spirituality preserves all the infinity of his absence which is in the personal order itself [*illeity*]. He does not show himself except in his trace, as in the 33rd chapter of Exodus. To go toward Him is not to follow the trace, which itself is not a sign. To go toward him is to go towards the others who are in

the trace. (Levinas 1966, 46)

In other words, ontological absence becomes ethical presence; difference becomes non-indifference to the other. Ethics as obligation and responsibility to and for the other is the relation and Revelation of Otherness.

The Holocaust Witness

Finally, I want briefly to examine how this notion of the self emptied out and bound over to the other is radicalized in Levinas's later work, and its possible connections to Levinas as a Holocaust survivor. The famous biblical phrase "here I am" with which Abraham answers God (*hineni* in Hebrew) is also, of course, the formulaic response given by many other biblical characters and prophets when called by God. In Levinas's later philosophical works, he uses this phrase to analyze and describe subjectivity as unlocked, wholly receptive, emptied and bound over to the other: "The word I means here I am [me voici] answering for everything and everyone" as a gratuitous sacrifice (Levinas 1974, 114). He describes the "here I am" as the "I possessed by the other," a figure of inspiration and obsession, and a "reason" or "intelligibility" beyond the *cogito*. In effect, this analysis founds the "I think" of the rational Cartesian *cogito* (which itself founds modern philosophy) upon the biblical "here I am" of subjectivity and ethics.

"Here I am" is also a language of the accusative—both grammatically and as the language of "witness," of the "first person." But he emphasizes that "here I am" is a witness before any content or "truth of representation": "it is the meaning of language, before language scatters into words." This "bearing witness of itself to the other" (Levinas 1974, 119) is the "sign bearing witness of the giving of signs"—an ultimate exposure and vulnerability which is the condition for all communication.

In other words, this one-for-the-other constitutes the very ability of a sign to be a sign, to stand for something else, and the very possibility for there even to be communication, shared meaning. Signs, that is, are given, offered to the other before they can even comprise a system, a code, a contract, a game. Speech is always said *to* someone before it has any particular content. There is a prior summoning in language—before the reciprocity of exchange of information, or code, or convention. There is a primordial donation in response to a primordial command, or what he calls an "election by the Good."[15]

And there is an ongoing and continuous oscillation between this prior contentless realm, which Levinas now calls "saying," or *le dire*, and the realm of codes, systems, concrete meanings, contracts, representations, or what he calls *le dit* (the "said"). This oscillation between "the saying and the said," he affirms, is necessary to guarantee that the contracts and codes, the politics and philosophies, do not obliterate the ethical and revert into violent tyrannies.

But in these later writings the terms he uses to describe subjectivity and responsibility often become disturbing: trauma, wounding, hostage, obsession, persecution, sacrifice without reserve. In a highly charged description Levinas writes: "signification is witness or martyrdom. It is intelligibility before the light" (Levinas 1974, 77–78). Imagery of wounding now describes the way the other puts the self in question; it is a radical denuding and shattering of egoism, so that the self is not "like a stranger, hunted down even in one's home, contested in one's identity. . . . [I]t is always to empty oneself anew of oneself . . . like a hemophiliac's hemorrhage" (1974, 92). I cannot help but hear in the voice behind this voice, and in these disturbing images of bleeding wounds the "witness" of the Holocaust survivor, even though that event is never explicitly evoked. And I would argue that in Levinas, the witness of the Holocaust enters into the "reason" of philosophy. At the same time, this rhetoric of witness is indirect for he does not explicitly invoke either his personal experiences or specific historical events within his philosophical work. The most profound signification of these events for him is not their specificity for any one nation or group. On a deeper level, this is consistent with his philosophy: witness is not "confession," a witness for and of the personal experiences of the self, but a testimony *for the other.*

So Levinas does "not make a graven image" or icon of these wounds as some kind of holy stigmata upon which we should fixate in horror. The task instead is to make these traumas revert into the foundation and guarantor of language and ethics. "Hebrew" reminds, calls to, founds "Greek" not by losing its specificity or being *sublated* (to use the Hegelian term) into the "universality" of Greek reason, but by being witness to the ethical relation to the other in a prophetic call to all human beings.

But it is also almost as if this notion of signification as martyrdom is a kind of secular or philosophical equivalent of the Jewish notion of *kiddush ha-shem*—the "sanctification of the name of God" that Jewish tradition ascribes to the death of a Jew murdered for his or her faith. As if Levinas is attempting to sanctify and redeem the deaths of those murdered in the Holocaust, that event which above all expressed hatred and intolerance for the other.[16] And also as if he is making it impossible for the persecutors to escape responsibility, to forget, deny their involvement, and making it impossible for any one of us, any reader of Levinas to escape ours.[17]

For he expands his notion of substitution to an extreme responsibility that makes even "the persecuted one liable to answer for the persecutor" (Levinas 1974, 111). As if the very outrage of persecution itself inverted into a grounds of solidarity as expiation rather than violence. One can see why this becomes an almost "unsayable" position. It also has strong Christian echoes and moves beyond Jewish tradition.[18] In classical Jewish law, one is not to actively seek martyrdom; the only cases in which one must allow oneself to be killed are if one is ordered upon pain of death to commit adultery, idolatry, or murder. In these cases, one is required to choose death rather than commit any one of those three sins. In other cases, such as for self-defense, the Talmud says, "If one arises to kill you, arise and kill himself first." One does not always give one's life for the other.[19]

Yet for Levinas, finally, the "subject" so called and elected finally signifies all human beings—not just the Jews. And so, on the concluding page of *Otherwise Than Being* there are the following words: each individual of all the peoples "is virtually a chosen one, called to leave in his turn, or without awaiting his turn...the concept of the ego . . . to respond with responsibility: *me*, that is, *here I am for the others*, to lose his place radically" (Levinas 1974, 185).

Notes

1.   See, for example, Maimonides's discussion of the meaning of the trope "face" in *The Guide for the Perplexed*, part I, section 37. Among the biblical significations Maimonides enumerates for "face" (*panim*) are "the presence and existence of a person," "the hearing of a voice without seeing any similitude," that is, the inability to comprehend God's true existence as such, and "attention or regard" for the other person.

2.   See Rosenzweig's "The Face of the Figure" (1930, 418–24)and Cohen's explication of these passages in his essay "The Face of Truth in Rosenzweig, Levinas, and Jewish Mysticism." Rosenzweig notes that the face is composed of the most receptive organs in the body—nose, ears, eyes, mouth. In the inner sanctum of divine truth, the human catches sight of "none other than a countenance like his own. The Star of Redemption is become a countenance which glances at me and out of which I glance. Not because God is my mirror, but God's truth" (1930, 418). At the end of the *Star*, the shining of God's "face" signifies redemption and ultimate truth. "But for him whom he lets his visage shine upon, to him he also turns his visage. As he turns his visage to us, so may we recognize him" (418). Rosenzweig also uses "Face" or "Countenance" to signify human communion: "Nor is this brotherliness

by any means identity of everything with the human countenance, but rather the harmony precisely of men of the most diverse countenances. One thing is necessary, of course, but only one: that men have a countenance at all, that they see each other" (1930, 345). On the glance as gesture beyond word and deed related to dance and poetry, mutual recognition through processions, pageants, and carnivals, Rosenzweig writes, "The power to dissolve all that is rigid already inheres in the glance. . . . Once an eye has glanced at us, it will glance at us as long as we live" (1930, 372).

3.   A good introduction to these schools of criticism is Veeser's *The New Historicism.*

4.   See, for example, the oft-cited essay by de Man, "Semiology and Rhetoric," in *Textual Strategies* and Derrida's "White Metaphor: Metaphor in the Text of Philosophy" in *Margins of Philosophy.* In Lacan, for example, the rereading of Freud via structuralist linguistics asserts that the "unconscious is structured like a language," and that an analyst needs to understand the rhetoric of tropes to interpret these structures. Brian Vickers, in the concluding chapter of his *In Defense of Rhetoric,* lucidly explains the distortions in many of these contemporary invocations of rhetoric. In modern thought, Vickers writes, rhetoric as a discipline has atrophied to "*elocution* alone, now detached from its expressive and persuasive functions, and brought down finally to a handful of tropes" (Vickers 1988, 439). One sees this move, Vickers notes, in Vico, who in turn is the inspiration for Hayden White's tropological analysis of historical narratives; in Roman Jakobson's structural linguistics which further reduces the tropes to only two: metaphor and metonymy; and in de Man especially "whose actual knowledge of rhetoric as revealed in [his] essays is limited to a fundamentally misguided conception of the art, and to a few tropes, not always correctly understood. But this did not prevent him from making grand generalizations" (1988, 457).

5.   Foss and Trapp write that Perelman's impetus for writing his masterwork was the problems he encountered in defining the nature of justice and reasoning about values, and the difficulty of resolving questions of value on rational grounds, that is, not being able to draw an "ought" from an "is." Along with his co-writer, Lucie Olbrechts-Tyteca, he decided to investigate the ways authors in different fields actually used arguments to reason about values—from literary to political to philosophical texts and daily speech. They "rediscovered" the neglected heritage of Aristotle's "dialectical" as opposed to "analytic" mode of reasoning, that is, rhetoric as informal, nondemonstrative reasoning (1958, 102–3). This jurists' perspective has much to add, I would argue, to current questions about the nature of interpretation, the relation of the literary to the political, and recent literary interpretations of rabbinic texts. Most of these attempts to relate literary criticism to rabbinic texts have no satisfactory way of linking up their dual functions of *halakhic*, legalistic deliberation, and *aggadic*, nonlegal creative storytelling. One of the few writers to bring attention to this issue is Gerald Bruns in his essay "Midrash and Allegory" in *The Literary Guide to the Bible.* This problem is due in part

to the identification of "Law" with oppression in much French and German post-structuralist literary theory (see Kristeva, Barthes, et al.), an identification that often goes back to a Protestant antinomianism. It is also due to the separation of literary criticism and theory from the kind of rhetorical theory that Perelman is proposing, a "new" rhetoric because it returns rhetoric to its ancient rational deliberative functions and away from its demotion to a "merely literary" analysis of style and tropes. Levinas and Perelman have shown me an important dimension to the literary approach to rabbinic hermeneutics that I neglected in my earlier book, *The Slayers of Moses*—the ethical and juridical. I address it in my book *Fragments of Redemption: Jewish Thought and Literary Theory in Benjamin, Scholem, and Levinas* from which the present essay is taken. In another article on "The New Rhetoric" as a mode of practical reasoning written in 1976, Perelman even cites the talmudic tradition as an example of the kind of deliberative rhetorical model he is propounding, in contrast to a Cartesian model where rational self-evidence and necessary truth make it impossible for two persons to come to opposite decisions about the same matter without one being wrong. In the Talmud, Perelman notes, "[I]t is accepted that opposed positions can be equally reasonable; one of them does not have to be right." For instance, the schools of the sage Hillel and the schools of Shammai are in constant opposition, but in a famous passage, R. Akiva is told from above that "both are the words of the living God" (Perelman, 1976, 305). The key point here is that there are rational grounds for multiple positions about truth, not that since all language is arbitrary—or all values are relative—there therefore are multiple interpretations. Perelman's juridical is also close to Levinas' defense in his Jewish writings of the *halakha*, the Jewish legal tradition which for Levinas is the embodiment and guarantor of the ethical relation. Both Perelman and Levinas are also inspired by the Kantian notion of practical versus theoretical reason.

6.   In current literary theory, another set of dualisms is established. Those who dispute the position that all truth is socially constructed are often accused of being "essentialists"; those who disagree with the notion that the human person is constructed by and through an impersonal "Discourse" are labeled unself-conscious and uncritical ideologues of "the liberal humanist myth." These dualisms, in my view, have become a species of name-calling which often substitutes for rigorous argument. Literary theory today is itself in dire need of a "third way" beyond them. Perelman's work preceded the advent of French structuralism and post-structuralism, but Perelman most likely would have viewed the notion of language as an impersonal system in which human selfhood and action are but anonymous functions as but another abdication of rational deliberative argument to distorted notions of reality—or as Levinas puts it, of "the primacy of formal theoretical reason." Levinas seeks a "third way" between the dualisitc alternatives of classical ontology: being/autonomy/heteronomy. Nor would the post-structuralist critique of structuralism alleviate this problem; proposing the arbitrariness of the sign and the instability of the structures of signification only replaces

existentialist irrationality with linguistic irrationality. Nor does a cultural materialism that finds all structures marked by ideology, power, domination, and force provide grounds for the kind of reason Perelman seeks.

7.   I am grateful to my colleague Jeanne Fahnestock for introducing me to and helping to explicate Perelman's extraordinary work. *The New Rhetoric* is a lengthy and complex book and I only briefly touch upon it here. The central portion of the book is an extensive set of philosophical and technical analyses of the various techniques of argumentation, rhetorical strategies, and tropes. Perelman also directly addresses the problem of rhetoric used deceptively to manipulate, of propaganda and ruse, in his idea of the "universal audience" (section 7), his discussion of the "audience as a construction of the speaker" (section 4), and the adaptation of the speaker to audience" (section 5). The speaker is not obligated to persuade an audience if that audience can only be persuaded by repugnant means. As Quintillian said, rhetoric is *scientia bene dicendi*: speaking well means also speaking what is ethically good (1958, 25). Perelman's difficult and controversial idea of "the universal audience" is an hypothetical construct in the mind of the speaker of an ideal audience competent to understand the argument and give assent; it plays a normative role in judging the convincing nature of argument. It does not refer to "an experimentally proven fact" (1958, 31): "Instead of believing in a universal audience analogous to the divine mind which can assent only to the 'truth,' we might with greater justification characterize each speaker by the image of the universal audience that he is trying to win over to his view. . . . . Each individual, each culture has its own conception of the universal audience" (1958, 33). In dialogue, for example, the interlocutor is regarded as the incarnation of the universal audience. Argument is protected from being purely manipulative and unethical by the interaction of universal and particular audience. To explain the notion of the "universal audience," Perelman quotes Allen Scult, who defines it as a "metaphor which functions as an inventional tool"; this supports Perelman's notion of a "responsible rhetoric which must be systematized in such a way as to make nonscientific discourse, which is at the core of our societal life, somehow rational . . . without recourse to 'absolute truth'" (Perelman's "Universal Audience" [1958, 176]). "The universal audience is your rhetorical conscience" (958, 179).

8.   The debate over de Man surfaced a few years after his death when, in 1987, a set of his writings from 1940 to 1942 for the collaborationist Belgian newspaper *Le Soir* was discovered. See the volume of these writings translated into English by Ortwin de Graef, *Wartime Journalism, 1939–1943*, edited by Werner Hamacher and others (Lincoln: University of Nebraska Press, 1988) and the companion volume by the same editors, *Responses: On Paul De Man's Wartime Journalism* (1989). For the extensive debate on this subject, see also the two special issues of *Critical Inquiry*, volumes 14 (1988) and 15 (1989).

9.   Perelman makes an important distinction between a "disinterested" or "objective spectator" and an "impartial" one when it comes to judging discussions that must lead to a decision. (One of the most frequently heard

statements in current literary theory is that "everything is political," meaning that there is no possibility of disinterestedness, objectivity or impartiality). Perelman writes that "interference in a controversy whose outcome will affect a specific group may be made only by one who is a member of, or closely bound up with, the group in question"; "being *impartial* is not being *objective*, it consists of belonging to the same group one is judging, without having previously decided in favor of any one of them" (1958, 60). Like Levinas, Perelman wants to preserve the possibility of "dissociating our beliefs from our interests and passions" (1958, 61). Similarly, his interesting analysis of epideictic oratory reveals a fundamental relation of value to action. Epideictic oratory was classically defined by Aristotle as the rhetoric concerned with praise and blame (a eulogy, for example), the beautiful or ugly. Aristotle distinguished between epideictic and the two other forms of oratory: deliberative and legal oratory (counseling what is expedient; establishing what is best). Perelman points out that epideictic oratory—often considered merely ornamental or "purely literary"—cannot be separated from the functions of deliberative and legal oratory because epideictic oratory "strengthens the disposition toward action by increasing adherence to the values it lauds" (1958, 50); it thus establishes a sense of communion that is the very foundation for deliberative and legal discourse.

10. This "critical rationalism" is also a feature of many other major modern Jewish philosophers who stressed the rational and ethical character of Judaism (Hermann Cohen is the most outstanding example). Nathan Rotenstreich attributes this trend in part to the influence of Kant. Ethics could remain a realm unchallenged by Kant's critique of metaphysics and religion. But also, "The ethical interpretation of Judaism makes possible a further, more radical interpretation, that the ethical teaching of Judaism may be meaningful and binding apart from religious attachment. Thus the ethical interpretation can be placed historically on the borderline of the religious attitude and the secular transformation of Judaism" (Rotenstreich 1968, 3–4).

11.   While there is not space here to examine Rosenzweig's position in depth, Rosenzweig asserts that what he calls his "new thinking" is not theological in any classical sense, nor is it any form of apologetics: "If this is theology, it is, at any rate, no less new as theology than as philosophy. . . . Theology must not debase philosophy to play the part of a handmaid, yet the role of charwoman which philosophy has recently assigned to theology is just as humiliating. The true relationship of these two regenerated sciences is a sisterly one. . . . Theological problems must be translated into human terms, and human problems brought into the pale of theology" (quoted in Glatzer 1953, 201). Or, as he writes in *The Star of Redemption*: "The theologian whom philosophy requires for the sake of its scientific status is himself a theologian who requires philosophy—for the sake of his integrity. What was for philosophy a demand in the interests of objectivity, will turn out to be a demand in the interests of subjectivity for theology. They are dependent on each other and so generate jointly a new type, be it a philosopher or theologian,

situated between theology and philosophy" (Rosenzweig 1930, 106).

12.   When asked by Richard Kearney whether his search for a non-site or *u-topos* other than that of Western metaphysics can be construed as a prophetic utopianism, Derrida answers by affirming a positive moment in deconstruction as a response to the call of alterity, and says that although he interrogates the classical ideas of *eschaton* or *telos*, "that does not mean I dismiss all forms of Messianic or prophetic eschatology. I think that all genuine questioning is summoned by a certain type of eschatology." Though he does not feel the kind of "hope" that would allow deconstruction to have a prophetic function—as exodus and dissemination in the desert—"it does have," he admits, certain "prophetic resonances," but as a search without hope for hope (Kearney 1984, 118–19).

13.   For Rosenzweig, God's turn towards humanity is an opening up and act of love which simultaneously is the command to the human person to turn and open up to the other—to love the neighbor. The neighbor to whom this love is also commanded is the turning of the human toward something else, to the world, and that is redemption. Rosenzweig also connects this receptive "Here I am" and the moment of revelation with Jewish law whose foundation is love as command. That is, this summons to hear is itself the preface to every commandment, and especially of the commandment that for Rosenzweig is the essence and highest of all the commandments, to "love God with all your heart, soul, and might." In an essay on Rosenzweig, Levinas writes:

> [I]t is very curious to note what is produced in response to God's love and how revelation is prolonged. God's love for selfhood is, *ipso facto*, a commandment to love. Rosenzweig thinks that one can command love . . . contrary to what Kant thought. One can command love, but it is love which commands love. And it commands in the now of its love, so that the commandment to love is repeated and renewed indefinitely in the repetition and renewal of the very love which commands love. Consequently, the Judaism in which revelation is inseparable from commandment in no wise signifies the yoke of the Law, but precisely love. The fact that Judaism was woven from commandments attests to the renewal, at all instants of God's love for man. . . . [T]he eminent role of the mitzvah in Judaism does not signify a moral formalism but the loving presence of divine eternally renewed. . . . Two typically Jewish ideas have appeared: the idea of commandment, as essential to the relation of love . . . and the idea of the redemptive man and not a redemptive God. Even though the redemption comes from God, it has an absolute need of this intermediary man. (Levinas 1963b, 29)

14.   See Levinas's important essay "God and Philosophy" (1973) in his *Collected Philosophical Papers* (1987). Here he attempts to clarify the relationship between philosophy and religion, and define his notion of a religion that not only exceeds theology but also is not even founded on "religious experience" or faith and the loss of faith. The key question of this essay is "Can God be expressed in a rational discourse which would neither be ontology or

faith?—in a way beyond the inadequate alternative of 'the God of Abraham, Isaac and Jacob' versus 'the God of the philosophers'" (1987, 155). He traces the connections between Western philosophy and Western spirituality which share a notion of truth defined as manifestation of being, and he posits another knowing, a "knowing otherwise" where consciousness is conscience and insomnia not enlightenment and affectivity. This knowing otherwise is reflected in a religious discourse in which God does not signify to begin with as a theme, or object of a dogma. (In his Jewish writings, his talmudic lecture "The Temptation of Temptation" in *Quatre lectures talmudiques* defines the meaning of the revelation at Sinai just in these terms—as a "doing before hearing," an acceptance of an obligation prior to any "knowledge of its content," a non-naive mode of knowing otherwise.) Nevertheless, Levinas's philosophical language strongly shadows, evokes, and echoes traditional Jewish categories. To what extent we should accept his assertions that he has used no theological traditions as a starting point is another issue for which I have no space here.

15.   For Levinas, the election or calling or displacement of the subject (as Abraham was elected, called, displaced) to undeclinable responsibility and sacrifice for the other means that the subject is "unique," not because of any particular attributes of the ego, nor because it is loved by God, but by very virtue of this undeclinable assignation (Levinas 1974, 115). These terms, nevertheless, again seem not only to echo but to be founded on classical Jewish descriptions of the covenantal call. In a sense, Levinas's philosophy and language theory is a kind of phenomenological translation of the covenantal idea. Harold Fisch has similarly devoted much of his career to tracing the covenantal idea in Western literature. In chapter four of *Poetry with a Purpose: Biblical Poetics and Interpretation*, Fisch eloquently describes the nature of the biblical prophetic call and contract, which underlies the Scripture's notion of language as summons, bond, obligation, witness, judgment—and its model for the relational contract between reader and writer, text and interpreter, God and Israel. See especially his gloss on the meaning of the *Shema*, "Hear, O Israel: the Lord our God, the Lord is One" (Dt 6:4): "To accept the role of 'hearer' in the sense understood by 'Hear O Israel' is to accept an almost overpowering responsibility. It is not a simple act of response that is required of us as though we were readers of a novel called upon to assist in the creating of a fictional illusion; rather we are called upon to commit ourselves, to accept an obligation. For the word *shema* implies not only reading but also obeying; the text seizes us even against our will" (Fisch 1988, 49).

16.   In an epigraph, Levinas dedicates *Otherwise Than Being* to the memory of those killed by Nazis, both those "closest" among the six million Jews, and the "millions of all confessions and all nations, victims of the same hatred of the other man, the same anti-semitism."

17.   In the recent Marcel Ophuls film about the trial of Klaus Barbie, *Hotel Terminus*, one of the most chilling moments comes when Barbie himself after his arrest says: "I have forgotten everything. If they haven't that's their

problem."

18.　Andrius Valevicius is quite right to point out in these Dostoevskian and Tolstoyan accents, Levinas's Russian background and the connection of even his most mature philosophy to Slavic as well as Jewish thought. See his twelfth chapter, "From East to West: Levinas and Russian Thought" (1988, 146-55).

19.　There is another similar famous passage from a talmudic discussion about the meaning of Leviticus 25:36, the directive not to take interest when one lends money to sustain "your brother who has become poor" but "fear your God; that thy brother may live with you." What is the meaning of "that thy brother may live with you"? "That is what Ben-Patura expounded: Two men are journeying through the desert, and one of them has a single pitcher of water. If one of them drinks it, he (alone) will get back to civilization. But if both of them drink it, both of them will die. Ben-Patura taught that they should both drink and die, as it said "That your brother may live with you." Said Rabbi Akiba to him: "That they brother may *live with you*." Your own life comes before the life of your fellowman" (*Sifra, Behar* 5:3; 109c [ed. Weiss]; cf. *B. Metzia* 62a). This is the same R. Akiba who also propounded that the fundamental principle of the Torah was "You shall love your neighbor as yourself." See discussion of these issues in relation to Levinas by Abner Weiss, in Fox, *Modern Jewish Ethics* 139–52. See also David Roskies's compendium of Jewish responses to catastrophe, *The Literature of Destruction,* and his *Against the Apocalypse* for the typology of the historical Jewish responses to suffering. But as Robert Gibbs writes, Levinas' work would also require a Christian thinker to recast Christology for "Is not the other in the me, the other person, and not the absolute You of God? . . . Is not the truth of incarnation that we are incarnate, vulnerable in our naked skin? That we are persecuted and so expiation for others, and not that some divinity is expiation for us? I make expiation and suffer for him: not "You or even He make expiation for me". . . but then perhaps we would no longer need to worry whether it was Jewish or Christian" (1989, 185).

Works Cited

Bruns, Gerald. 1987. "Midrash and Allegory." In *The Literary Guide to the Bible.* Ed. Robert Alter and Frank Kermode. Cambridge: Harvard University Press. 625-46.

Cohen, Richard A. 1990. "The Face of Truth in Rosenzweig, Levinas, and Jewish Mysticism." In *Phenomenology of the Truth Proper to Religion.* Ed. Daniel Guerriere. Albany: State University of New York Press.

De Man, Paul. 1979. "Semiology and Rhetoric." In *Textual Strategies: Perspectives in Post-Structuralist Criticism.* Ed. Josue Harari. Ithaca: Cornell University Press. 121–40.

Derrida, Jacques. 1982. *Margins of Philosophy.* Trans. Alan Bass. Chicago: University of Chicago Press.

Fisch, Harold. 1988. *Poetry with a Purpose: Biblical Poetics and Interpretation.* Bloomington: Indiana University Press.

Foss, Sonja K., Robert Foss and Robert Trapp. 1985. *Contemporary Perspectives on Rhetoric.* Prospect Heights, IL: Waveland.

Fox, Marvin, ed. 1975. *Modern Jewish Ethics: Theory and Practice.* Columbus: Ohio State University Press.

Gibbs, Robert. 1989. "Substitution: Marcel and Levinas." Philosophy and Theology (4): 171–85.

Glatzer, Nahum. 1953 [1961]. *Franz Rosenzweig: His Life and Thought.* New York: Schocken.

Handelman, Susan A. 1982. *The Slayers of Moses: The Emergence of Rabbinic Interpretation in Modern Literary Theory.* Albany: State University of New York Press.

Kearney, Richard. 1984. "Jacques Derrida." In *Dialogues with Contemporary Continental Thinkers: The Phenomenological Heritage.* Manchester: Manchester University Press. 105–26.

Levinas, Emmanuel. 1961 [1969]. *Totality and Infinity: An Essay on Exteriority.* Trans. Alphonso Lingis. Pittsburgh: Duquesne University Press.

——. 1963a. *Difficile liberté: Essais sur le judaisme.* Paris: Editions Albin Michel.

——. 1963b. "Entre deux mondes" (biographie spirituelle de Franz Rosenzweig)." In *La Conscience Juive: Données et débats (textes des trois premieres Colloques d'Intellectuels Juifs de Langue Française).* Ed. Amado Lévy-Valensi and Jean Halperin. Paris: Presses Universitaires de France. 121–49.

——. 1965. "Franz Rosenzweig: Une pensée juive moderne." *Revue de Theologie et de Philosophie* 98:208–21.

——. 1966. "On the Trail of the Other." Trans. Daniel Hoy. *Philosophy Today* 10:34–46.

——. 1967. "Martin Buber and the Theory of Knowledge." In *The Philosophy of Martin Buber.* Ed. Paul Schilpp and Maurice Freidman. La Salle, IL: Open Court. 133.50.

——. 1968. *Quatre lectures talmudiques.* Paris: Editions de Minuit.

——. 1974 [1981]. *Otherwise Than Being or Beyond Essence.* Trans. Alphoso Lingis. The Hague: Nijhoff.

———. 1978a. *Existence and Existents.* Trans. Alphonso Lingis. The Hague: Nijhoff.

———. 1978b. "Signature." Ed. and trans. Adrian Peperzak. *Research in Phenomenology* 8:175–89.

———. 1982. *L'Au-delá du verset: Lectures et discours talmudiques.* Paris: Editions de Minuit.

———. 1983. "Franz Rosenzweig." Trans. Richard A. Cohen. *Midstream* 29 (9):33–40.

———. 1985. *Ethics and Infinity: Conversations with Philippe Nemo.* Trans. Richard A. Cohen. Pittsburgh: Duquesne University Press.

———. 1987. *Collected Philosophical Papers.* Trans. Alphonso Lingis. The Hague: Nijhoff.

Maimonides, Moses. 1956. *The Guide for the Perplexed.* Trans. M. Friedlander. New York: Dover.

Perelman, Chaim. 1976. "The New Rhetoric: A Theory of Practical Reasoning." In *The Rhetoric of Western Thought.* Ed. J. Golden. Dubuque, IA: Kendall Hunt. 298–317.

Perelman, Chaim and L. Olbrechts-Tyteca. 1958 [1969]. *The New Rhetoric: A Treatise on Argumentation.* Trans. J. Wilkinson and P. Weaver. Notre Dame, IN: University of Notre Dame Press.

Rosenzweig, Franz. 1930 [1985]. *The Star of Redemption.* 2nd ed. Trans. William Hallo. Notre Dame, IN: University of Notre Dame Press.

———. 1955 [1965]. *On Jewish Learning.* Ed. Nahum Glatzer. New York: Schocken.

Roskies, David. 1984. *Against the Apocalypse: Responses to Catastrophe in Modern Jewish Culture.* Cambridge: Harvard University Press.

———, ed. 1989. *The Literature of Destruction: Jewish Responses to Catastrophe.* Philadelphia: Jewish Publication Society.

Rotenstreich, Nathan. 1968. *Jewish Philosophy in Modern Times: From Mendelssohn to Rosenzweig.* New York: Holt Rinehart.

Valevicius, Andrius. 1988. *From the Other to the Totally Other: The Religious Philosophy of Emmanuel Levinas.* New York: Lang.

Veeser, H. Aram, ed. 1989. *The New Historicism.* New York: Routledge.

Vickers, Brian. 1988. *In Defense of Rhetoric.* Oxford: Clarendon.

14

Accusation, Responsibility, and the Scene of Justice: Reflections on the Accusatory Tone in Recent Philosophy

Robert J. S. Manning

I accuse.

I accuse you.

I accuse you, the other, for the sake of another.

My responsibility to another, to my other, leads me to say to you, the other, I accuse you.

Perhaps scholarly work and writing always involves a good amount of correcting, a certain putting things straight. Most often, this takes the form of indicating that the author in question has not gotten everything entirely correct, has unknowingly strayed into this misassumption or that misinterpretation. The tone of such correcting, though sometimes condescending, is most often gentle, courteous, respectful.

There has been quite another tone, however, to much recent philosophical writing. The tone has grown harsh, severe, condemning. Such writing has gone far beyond being merely corrective and has become accusatory. In fact, in recent philosophy there has been a lot of accusing going on, and especially related to topics where very serious issues of responsibility are at stake. The issue of Heidegger's relation to National Socialism, referred to as the "Heidegger controversy" or sometimes even as the "Heidegger case," is a prime example. There has been an absolute avalanche of literature on this topic, much of it trying to sort out and come to a conclusion about Heidegger's responsibilities, about the extent to which he failed to fulfill them, and about our responsibilities to Heidegger in determining Heidegger's responsibilities. Much of this literature grows accusatory in tone. Some of it makes accusations against those who accuse Heidegger. The literature surrounding Paul de Man's collaborationist articles during World War II, though much smaller in scale, provides another example of how the discussion of responsibilities—de Man's responsibilities and our responsibilities to him—in recent philosophy has led to accusations, has given recent philosophy an accusatory tone. And certainly there has been much discussion recently about the extent to which Jacques Derrida and the philosophy referred to as deconstruction either takes upon itself or evades political and ethical responsibilities. Again, much of this literature is accusatory in tone, accuses deconstruction of being anti-humanist, nihilistic, of being complicitous with Nazism, of providing support for Holocaust denial.[1]

Even with all the discussion in recent philosophy about responsibility, and all the accusations flying back and forth, there has been precious little philosophical reflection on accusing as a phenomenon and accusation as a certain type of discourse that it is often engendered out of the experience of responsibility. This is why I wish to analyze accusation, and more particularly events of accusation that take the form: "My responsibility to another, my other, leads me to say to you, the other: I accuse you." I wish to analyze two recent texts in philosophy that go far beyond making corrections and actually level accusations in order to explore this particular intertwining of responsibility and accusation. Of each text I am going to ask that quintessentially Derridean hermeneutical question: What is going on here in this text when the author, out of his overriding responsibility to "his" other, to the other who is his concern, says to another other "I accuse you"?[2] I hope to show that in each instance it is the author's overriding sense of ethical responsibility to his other that leads him to mount to a position of moral height where he can level accusations down upon another other. What is more, I also hope to show that even though in both cases the end result of accusing out of a sense of responsibility may appear to be the production of justice, since it is in fact an accusation out of responsibility, this is only apparently so. The end result in both cases is not the production of justice, but is in fact the production of the opposite of justice. Finally, I shall try to show how both demonstrate why Levinas— the philosopher of the Other, of responsibility, of ethics, of justice—may have felt compelled to change the scene of justice from the way he staged it in *Totality and Infinity* to the way he staged it in his later works, most importantly *Otherwise Than Being or Beyond Essence.*

I shall explore this event of accusation out of responsibility by discussing two texts in which accusation and responsibility play a large and largely unthought role. The first concerns the Heidegger-Nazism question and is, of the countless texts on this subject, one of the most severely condemning of Heidegger, George Leaman's "Strategies of Deception: The Composition of Heidegger's Silence" in *Heidegger and the Holocaust.* The second is Jacques Derrida's famous/infamous defense of Paul de Man, written upon the discovery of de Man's wartime collaborationist writings, "Like the Sound of the Sea Deep Within a Shell: Paul de Man's War."

George Leaman's "Strategies of Deception" is one of the most remarkable pieces among the great volume of writing on the question of Heidegger's relation to Nazism and the Holocaust. Leaman chooses as the epigram for his article the repulsive statement Heidegger made to Jaspers in 1933: "[T]here is a dangerous international network of Jews." This might lead one to believe that the article concerns Heidegger's attitude toward Jews, or his possible anti-Semitism that makes his political involvement with the Nazis more plausible. However, the subject of the piece is actually Heidegger's postwar silence on the Holocaust and how best to interpret this silence in coming to understand Heidegger's true views of Nazism before, during, and long after the war.

Of course the issue of Heidegger's postwar silence has been treated many times and interpreted in many ways. The question always becomes, Why didn't Heidegger after the war and in the most definitive way condemn a regime that murdered six million innocent people, and what does the fact that he never did this indicate about his feelings after the war about the Holocaust and National Socialism? This is obviously a very complex and difficult issue and is made even more so by the fact that Heidegger's postwar silence about Nazism and the Holocaust was, as Leaman puts it, only "almost complete" (1995, 1). Heidegger did break his silence on very few occasions, and it is these occasions that become the focus of Leaman's attempt to understand the import of Heidegger's silence on the Nazis, the Jews and the extermination camps. It is Leaman's interpretation of these postwar remarks by Heidegger that becomes the ground for the severe accusations Leaman levels at Heidegger.

The first of these occasions which Leaman treats wherein Heidegger refers to the Holocaust, is Heidegger's 1948 letter to Herbert Marcuse. Marcuse had written to Heidegger demanding that he clearly distance himself from a regime that had killed millions of innocent Jews and had made terror part of daily life. Heidegger responded in his letter to Marcuse:

> I can only add that instead of the word "Jews" [in your letter] there should be the word "East Germans," and then exactly the same [terror] holds true of one of the Allies, with the difference that everything that has happened since 1945 is public knowledge worldwide, whereas the bloody terror of the Nazis was in fact kept a secret from the German people. (1995, 2)

This is an amazing passage and an amazing comparison. Instead of condemning the Nazis, Heidegger basically says that the Russians are doing the same thing to the East Germans that the Nazis did to the Jews, except that what the Nazis did they did secretly whereas the whole world watches the Russians terrorize the Germans.

There is no doubt that this remark is far from what Marcuse or anyone eager to exonerate Heidegger would hope for and leaves him open to even more condemnation. The terror of Stalinism was real and many East Germans paid for it dearly, but the Russians' treatment of the East Germans came no where close to matching the Germans' attempt at genocide of the Jews. And of course Heidegger's claim that what the Nazis did to the Jews was a secret kept from the German people is both cowardly and evasive. Hitler's hatred for the Jews was obvious from the pages of *Mein Kampf* and throughout his rise to power. Hitler's rise to power meant the dehumanization and persecution of the Jews. This fact, obvious even in 1933, was not a concern of Heidegger's sufficient to prevent him from endorsing Hitler in 1933 in the strongest terms: "The Fuhrer himself, and only he, is the current and future reality of Germany, and his word is your [German students] law."[3] And while Heidegger's concern in this passage from the letter to Marcuse for his fellow Germans is understandable, one also has to point out that Heidegger had been asked to articulate his concern for the Jewish victims of the Holocaust, not for his fellow Germans. Even after this opportunity that Marcuse gave him, one is still left wondering where Heidegger's concern for the Jews is, wondering whether Heidegger has any concern at all for the Jewish victims of Nazi terror.

To be fair to Heidegger, he doesn't come close in this remark to approving of the Nazis' actions against the Jews. Given the opportunity to condemn the Nazis for what they did to the Jews during the war, he rather calls attention to what the Russians are doing now to his fellow Germans. Though somewhat understandable, this may raise even more doubts about whether Heidegger has any sympathies at all for the victims of National Socialism. Leaman, for example, doesn't find Heidegger's comparison between what the Germans did to the Jews and what the Russians are now doing to the East Germans understandable at all. "According to Heidegger's view," writes Leaman, "east Germans and Jews were equally victims of unjustified persecution. What sense does this make? Why would Heidegger choose this particular comparison?" (1995, 2).

As I have already said, it is fairly obvious why the German Heidegger concerned about the fate of his fellow Germans at the hands of the Russians would make this comparison, although this doesn't mean the comparison is appropriate, just, or beyond condemnation. To Leaman, however, this remark "makes very little sense." It only begins to make sense, Leaman argues, when one remembers that "in Nazi propaganda [the] Jews were the driving force behind Soviet communism" (1995, 2). The Soviet

Union, in Nazi propaganda, "was a communist and therefore a Jewish power." By seeing Heidegger's remark from the perspective of Nazi propaganda, and by assuming that Heidegger's perspective and Nazi propaganda are one, Leaman can now make sense of the comparison in Heidegger's remark. Heidegger's comparison now has, according to Leaman, "a certain logic." The original remark by Heidegger can now be accurately "restated as follows: during the war Nazi Germans attacked defenseless Jews and now communist-Jews were attacking defenseless Germans" (1995, 2).

So for Leaman, what Heidegger is *really* saying is that first Germans attacked innocent Jews and now Jews are attacking innocent Germans. But given that Heidegger never talks about Jews attacking Germans but only about "one of the allies," that is, the Russians, killing Germans, how does Leaman know that what Heidegger is really talking about is Jews killing Germans?

The key to understanding this is Leaman's earlier claim that he is going to do a reading of Heidegger's postwar silence that is "historically-informed." Here the information from history that Leaman uses is that in Nazi propaganda the Jews were the driving force behind Soviet communism. The assumption he makes but does not discuss is that Heidegger's thinking must have been so thoroughly shaped by Nazi propaganda that he when talked about the Russians he really meant the same thing that Nazi propaganda meant when it referred to Russians: communist Jews. With this little bit of historical information about Nazi propaganda and this huge, unstated, and unsupported assumption about Heidegger's thinking and world view, Leaman now thinks he knows what Heidegger was really trying to say, that "during the war Nazi Germans attacked defenseless Jews and now communist-Jews were attacking defenseless Germans." This extremely far-fetched interpretation of Heidegger's remark for some reason makes much more sense to Leaman than simply that Heidegger as a German was complaining about the Russians' very brutal treatment of his fellow Germans.

Even more astounding is Leaman's treatment of another remark by Heidegger that again momentarily broke his postwar silence on the Holocaust. This remark came in a 1949 lecture by Heidegger titled "The Danger." Here Heidegger is talking about the phenomenon of mass death:

> Hundreds of thousands die en masse. Do they die? They succumb. They are done in. Do they die? They become mere quanta, items in an inventory in the business of manufacturing corpses. Do they die? They are liquidated inconspicuously in extermination camps.

And even apart from that—right now millions of impoverished people are perishing from hunger in China. But to die is to endure death in its essence. To be able to die means to be capable of this endurance. We are capable of this only if the essence of death makes our own essence possible. (1995, 4)

This is certainly an odd remark, to say the least. Why the repeated question, "Do they die?" There's no doubt that those liquidated in extermination camps and the millions perishing from hunger do in fact die, so why does Heidegger keep asking this question, "Do they die?"

There is certainly no one final and authoritative way to interpret this enigmatic statement by Heidegger. However, Heidegger himself does help us out in our hermeneutical struggles by explaining that "to die is to endure death in its essence." To be truly able to die, we have to be capable of enduring death. And we are capable of this "only if the essence of death makes our own essence possible."

How does the essence of death make our own essence possible? The obvious way to understand what Heidegger might mean by this is to interpret it through the section on death as the end of *Dasein* in his *Being and Time*. Here Heidegger is quite clear as to what he means by the essence of death and how it relates to the essence of *Dasein*. He begins by describing how we misunderstand and avoid the essence of death by interpreting it as something that happens to someone else. (1962, 283). Only by interpreting death as my death can I come to know the essence of death: "By its very essence, death is in every case mine, in so far as it 'is' at all" (284). Heidegger insists that in order for death to be truly understood, death must be understood as one's "ownmost possibility." He fully explains his view of the essence of death when he declares in *Being and Time* that "the full existential-ontological conception of death may now be defined as follows: "'death, as the end of Dasein, is Dasein's ownmost possibility—non-relational, certain and as such indefinite, not to be outstripped. Death is, as Dasein's end, in the Being of this entity towards its end'" (303).

So if this is the essence of death, how does the essence of death make our essence as humans possible? Again, this language is very much in keeping with the language of *Being and Time,* and, again, in this work Heidegger is very clear on exactly this question. To truly understand death as my ownmost possibility enables me to have an authentic understanding of myself as a unique, individuated being projected toward possibilities and potentialities I can choose to actualize or not. Understanding death means understanding myself as a being toward this possibility, and "Being towards this possibility discloses to *Dasein* its ownmost potentiality for Being, in which its very Being is the issue." Anticipating death as one's ownmost possibility brings *Dasein* "face to face with the possibility of being itself . . . in an impassioned freedom towards death." Thus, for Heidegger, in *Being and Time,* very clearly "the essence of death makes our own essence possible."

Perhaps now we can better interpret Heidegger's strange remark. The hundreds of thousands and the millions who die en masse, what about them? They succumb, are done in, are liquidated, perish, but do they experience the essence of death? Do they not experience a situation in which their own death is robbed of its ultimate significance since they have long since been made into not a person but a number? Can one really speak meaningfully of one's death as absolutely individuating when one is one of millions, only an item in an inventory in the business of manufacturing corpses? And can one's awareness of the possibility of one's death in such a situation really convey to one one's own essence as a being projected toward possibilities and potentialities? Does the death that one is faced with in such a situation really bring one face to face with the possibility of one's being? Does it really open one up to "impassioned freedom towards death"?

So what could Heidegger be saying by continually asking if people who die en masse in concentration camps and of hunger really die? It could just be that Heidegger is arguing that people who perish in such situations not only die, but they are robbed of the opportunity of truly achieving their own lives. They have been robbed not only of their lives, but of their essence as humans freely projected toward death and toward potentialities and possibilities death reveals. People who die en masse, people who become mere quanta, people who have been reduced to items in an inventory in the business of manufacturing corpses, have been exterminated not only in their bodies, but in their essence. As such, they can't even die.

I advance this reading as a possible way to read this remark by Heidegger, one that relies heavily on his understanding of death as he lays it out in *Being and Time* to make sense of this remark. I certainly wouldn't want to say that this is the only way to interpret this enigmatic passage. That this odd remark by Heidegger is certainly open to multiple interpretations does not, however, make Leaman's interpretation of it, or the accusations he levels at Heidegger on the basis of this interpretation, any less outrageous.

Leaman, too, is troubled by what Heidegger might have meant by questioning whether people who die en masse really die. He, too, turns to *Being and Time* for help in interpreting this remark. Leaman, however, discusses *Being and Time* only very briefly, only, in fact, in two sentences. "The beginning of the answer" as to how to interpret this remark (note that Leaman writes "the answer," not "an answer") "is to be found in Heidegger's earlier work." Here is Leaman's entire treatment of this very enigmatic remark by Heidegger:

> In section 74 of *Being and Time* (1927) he argued that the "anticipatory resoluteness" of Being-towards-death is the necessary precondition for authentic existence. That existence cannot be realized by isolated individuals; it can only be realized in and through an historical community in which individual fates are bound together in a common destiny. In *The Self-Affirmation of the German University* (1933) Heidegger subsequently resolved this tension between individual fates and collective destiny with the help of "transcendental forces" found in the "spiritual world" of a people. This spiritual world is that which is common to all of its members, "the forces stemming from earth and blood as the power which most deeply moves and profoundly shakes our being." Although each people has its own spiritual world, according to Heidegger the spiritual world of the German *Vole* has given it a unique historical-spiritual mission to renew the possibility of authentic existence. This means that the possibility of authentic existence depends upon, and is thus reserved for, those who share the German spiritual world. In the passage from the Bremen lecture quoted above, Heidegger explicitly distinguishes between "we" (i.e., himself and his German audience) who are capable of enduring death and "they" (the liquidated non-Germans) who are not. Read against the background of these earlier texts, the meaning of this passage can be more easily discerned: those who were murdered could not really die because as non-Germans they never had the potential for "authentic" existence in the first place. (1995, 5)

The only thing that is more astounding than Leaman's conclusion—that what Heidegger is really saying is that non-Germans can't really die because they don't have the potential for authentic existence—is the way he arrives at this conclusion. He begins with the section of *Being and Time* on death, but rather than carefully analyze what that sections says about the essence of death and our human essence, he simply gleans from it that "anticipatory resoluteness" of Being-towards-death is the necessary precondition for authentic existence. This has told us nothing about "anticipatory resoluteness," about Heidegger's view of the essence of death, about how *Dasein* comes to a proper understanding of this essence and how it relates to an appropriate understanding of our essence as humans.

He then goes on to another section of *Being and Time* in order to make the point that authentic existence also involves individual fates "bound together in a common destiny," conveniently not noticing that the section of *Being and Time* dealing with death is exceedingly individualistic, not collectivist in its language. He then goes on to discuss Heidegger's certainly very chauvinistic and nationalistic idea that the Germans have a "unique historical mission to renew the possibility of authentic existence." Leaman remarkably concludes from this nationalistic belief of Heidegger's that for Heidegger the possibility of authentic existence "is thus reserved for those who share the German spiritual world," even though Heidegger never says any such thing and despite the fact that to maintain this would violate and contradict every word of *Being and Time*, where the possibility of authentic or inauthentic existence is a basic constitutive aspect of *Dasein* itself. Since Leaman now somehow knows that for Heidegger only Germans are capable of authentic existence, he also knows that when Heidegger spoke the remark and used "they" and "we," he really meant they who are incapable of death, that is, non-Germans, and we Germans who are capable of authentic existence and thus are capable of dying. Now that Leaman knows how to interpret the meaning of "they" and "we" in the remark, he knows how to interpret the meaning of the remark: "the meaning of this passage can be more easily discerned." What Heidegger is really saying is that those who die en masse in concentration camps or of hunger in China cannot really die because they aren't Germans and so aren't capable of authentic existence in the first place.

This is an astounding conclusion, an astounding way to arrive at this conclusion, and amounts to an astounding accusation of Heidegger. Even after the war, even in the face of the Holocaust with its millions of victims, all Heidegger could say according to Leaman is that the victims of the Holocaust didn't really die because they weren't capable of authentic existence because they weren't true Germans. What Leaman accuses Heidegger of is both astounding and clear. The Nazis brought millions of Jews to their deaths; for Leaman, however, Martin Heidegger, a philosopher who was also a Nazi, did his fellow Nazis one better in that in his lofty, intellectual philosophy he deprived the victims even of the dignity of death. For Leaman, Heidegger truly believes that only Germans are real, full humans; no one else has the capacity to fully be, so no one else but Germans can truly die.

Leaman renders Heidegger's postwar silence on the Holocaust anything but silent; he renders it, in fact, very loud, harsh, and jarring. Asked to condemn the Holocaust, what Heidegger really did is bitterly and harshly complain about Jews killing East Germans, although the uninitiated might think that he was talking about Russians killing East Germans. And instead of mourning the deaths of millions, the nasty, bitter old Nazi Martin Heidegger actually said that all the Jewish victims could never be full humans anyway because they weren't Germans so they didn't really die. We can hear all of this loud and clear, even in Heidegger's supposed silence, if we hear this silence the right way, if we hear it the way Leaman does. If we allow Leaman's "historically informed" interpretation to articulate in its true loud, harsh, and jarring tones Heidegger's silence.

Of course, the fact of the matter is that Heidegger's "almost complete" silence remains troubling, mysterious, and difficult to comprehend. And the times when he broke this silence are also troubling, mysterious and difficult to comprehend. They are important for trying to understand Heidegger's silence and as such are worthy of careful philosophical analysis. They qualify Heidegger's silence on the Holocaust and give us paths for thinking about it. But they do not render Heidegger's silence clear, loud, harsh, jarring. Heidegger's silence is anything but clear.

What is clear, loud, harsh, and jarring is not Heidegger's silence, but Leaman's accusations against Heidegger. The harshly accusatory tone of Leaman's essay not only prompts us not to analyze Leaman's arguments, to ask if he has been fair to Heidegger, to read these Heideggerian remarks in another way. Leaman's harshly accusatory tone also prompts us to ask, What is going on here? What is going on in Leaman, in Leaman's text, as he levels such severe accusations at Heidegger?

What is obvious in every line of Leaman's text is his very real concern for and sense of responsibility to the victims of the Holocaust. He is very clearly concerned that the Holocaust and National Socialism be understood and interpreted correctly. For example, he wants to counter the view, still widely held in Germany, he says, that all the dead from the war should be considered "victims" of the war. It is obvious that Leaman writes out of a real concern for and responsibility to those who truly merit the word "victim," to the millions of innocent Jews and others who were mercilessly put to death by the Nazis. It is quite apparent that Leaman writes this text and addresses himself to the question of Heidegger's silence out of this very real responsibility he feels to the victims of the Holocaust.

However laudatory Leaman's sense of responsibility to the victims of the Holocaust is, however, it does not prevent us from asking, Where is Leaman's responsibility to Heidegger? How can Leaman support his accusations against Heidegger? How does Leaman know that Heidegger thought just like other Nazis so that when he complained about Russians killing Germans he was really talking about Jews killing Germans? How does Leaman know that Heidegger became and remained a Nazi so thoroughly that he turned his back on his own teachings about *Dasein* and actually came to maintain that only Germans could achieve authentic existence? How is Leaman able to know *the* answer to the mystery of how to interpret Heidegger's mysterious statements? And why does Leaman not present other alternatives, other possible ways to interpret these passages, that would render very different meanings, very different Heideggers?

What happens in this text which grows to accusation? What happens in this text to Leaman's responsibilities to Heidegger? It seems very possible, at least, that what happens in this text is that Leaman's responsibilities to the victims of National Socialism override and drown out Leaman's other responsibilities, including his responsibilities to Martin Heidegger. As outrageous as Leaman's accusations are, and as irresponsible is his text in this way, Leaman does not write outside of or beyond responsibility. His text, in fact, is heavy with responsibility, responsibility to the victims of National Socialism. What happens in this text, however, at least appears to be that in fulfilling his responsibilities to the victims of the Holocaust, Leaman entirely neglects his other responsibilities, especially his responsibilities to that other named Martin Heidegger. This heavy responsibility to the victims of the Holocaust does seem to obliterate all of Leaman's responsibilities to Heidegger. Leaman's heavy responsibilities to the victims of the Holocaust do seem to carry him to his severe accusations against Heidegger, made in such a clear, harsh, and jarring tone that it does seem as if all Leaman's responsibilities to Heidegger have been overridden and made to disappear. Thus, even though the judgment Leaman passes and the accusations he makes against Heidegger appear to be out of a strong sense of responsibility, nevertheless they are anything but fair and just and are, in fact, quite the opposite.

We may observe, and explore further, this same phenomenon of leveling unjust accusations even while assuming responsibilities by analyzing another text heavy with both responsibility and accusation, Jacques Derrida's "Like the Sound of the Sea Deep Within a Shell: Paul de Man's War." This text itself is Derrida's response to accusations, accusations made against his very close friend Paul de Man for the wartime collaborationist articles he wrote for pro-Nazi newspapers, and Derrida in turn makes accusations against de Man's accusers. Thus, this text will not settle or draw to a peaceful conclusion the controversy, which Derrida labels a "war," over these articles. This war, as it is being fought out, must and should involve, says Derrida, much reflection on responsibility, on different responsibilities, on "one's own [responsibility] as well as the responsibility to which one ought to summon others" (1988, 590). In fact, Derrida claims that in this article he will not only discuss de Man's responsibilities, and his own, and the responsibilities of the press and of "certain academics" from whom the press gets its information, but he will also explore "what responding and taking a responsibility can mean" (592).[4]

Although Derrida is clear in his text that responsibilities are everywhere, that everyone—himself, journalists, other academics—has many responsibilities, and that responsibility itself needs to be thought about, it is also very clear that the responsibility that concerns him most, and that he feels is most urgent and heavy, is his own responsibility to de Man. This responsibility is all the greater because de Man is no longer alive to speak in his own name. That his responsibility to de Man is not canceled by de Man's death, that it is a "responsibility which would never be canceled" (1988, 593), Derrida states so often that it becomes a refrain in this essay:

> However obscure this may remain, we have to register it: we still
> have responsibilities toward him, and that are more alive than ever,
> even as he is dead. That is, we have responsibilities regarding Paul
> de Man himself but *in us and for us.* (1988, 593)

Derrida in this essay is put in the position of defending de Man from his accusers. Although he often says that he is not defending de Man, that he is not playing the role of the defense attorney in what Derrida constantly calls "the trial of Paul de Man," in this very long and labored piece of writing he uses all his artful, rhetorical mastery to do just that, to defend de Man. His defense of de Man is, in fact, unrelenting, as he goes to great and at times absolutely improbable lengths to fend off accusations against de Man. In this process, Derrida's tone goes in and out of moments of great bitterness and hostility to those who would, in Derrida's view, "put de Man on trial," and he levels not just corrective or even impolite but downright nasty accusations at them. Again, we need to ask Derrida's question, but this time of one of Derrida's own texts: What is going on here? What is going on in Derrida's text when he moves from a defense of de Man to harsh accusations against de Man's accusers?

The controversy in question arose from the discovery in 1987 of some 125 articles a very young Paul de Man wrote for collaborationist newspapers in Nazi-occupied Belgium in 1941 and 1942. Both academics and the press soon became interested in this possible scandal, the heretofore unknown collaborationist writings of a young Belgian who was eventually to become one of America's most important intellectuals and one of its most well-known proponents of deconstruction, whatever academics and journalists may mean by that. This occurs after Paul de Man died, which is why Derrida has such a heavy weight of responsibility in having to speak for Paul de Man. What does Derrida do with this responsibility? What does this responsibility do to him and to his other responsibilities? We will have to analyze closely Derrida's defense of de Man in order to understand and wrestle with these questions.

The first thing to notice about Derrida's defense of de Man in this controversy, which the dead de Man is now embroiled in, is the vocabulary Derrida uses to describe it. This is not a debate or a controversy or even a scandal or even an investigation. It is a "war," even "a deadly war." Obviously, since de Man is dead, he is not the one waging war. Those who attack him, those who are raising this issue, those who are asking about the significance of these articles and his silence about them, about the possible relevance of de Man's collaborationist writings and his erasing of this past for his later, mature philosophical positions, all people who are doing any of these are for Derrida waging a war on Paul de Man. Derrida's other metaphor to describe not what is happening, but what is being done to de Man, is equally revealing: Paul de Man is being put on trial. Derrida suggests at the beginning of the essay that "there are those who want to organize a trial in order to judge him, de Man" (593). He then asks: "Who has the right to judge it [the question of how de Man dealt with his past in himself], to condemn or to absolve?" The metaphors of a trial, of a defense attorney, a prosecutor, a judge, police, even "totalitarian police," will be Derrida's constant metaphors throughout the essay. And at the conclusion of the essay, wherein Derrida has been constantly picturing all who raise the issue as judges, police, prosecutors, Derrida warns us that anyone who "already thinks of staging a trial by distributing the roles: judge, prosecutor, defense lawyer, witness and waiting in the wings, the instruments of execution" (650) has already "concluded in advance," has already condemned. Thus, the way Derrida structures his discussion of this controversy, it seems as if for Derrida anyone who takes up the issue of these collaborationist articles for any other motive than Derrida's own, to defend de Man, is waging a war on de Man and subjecting him to a very unjust trial where the verdict is certain because it is determined before the trial begins.

Derrida's overwhelming sense of responsibility to his friend Paul de Man takes him to great lengths in this article to defend de Man from his accusers. We can see most clearly the obvious and at times incredible hermeneutical gymnastics Derrida's responsibility to de Man takes him to if we look at a few specific examples of Derrida's interpretations of passages from some of the collaborationist articles in question. The most notorious of these articles is one de Man wrote in March of 1941 and is titled "Jews in Present-Day Literature." In this essay, de Man discusses the extent of Jewish influence upon European literature, concluding that it is not great and that if the solution to the Jewish problem led to a Jewish colony isolated from Europe that "would not entail, for the literary life of the West, deplorable consequences. The latter would lose, in all, a few personalities of mediocre value and would continue, as in the past, to develop according to its great evolutive laws" (631).

Derrida does not discuss the significance of this reprehensible conclusion, the significance of the fact that at a time when the Nazis were brutalizing Jews, taking their possessions, their rights, sometimes their lives, sending them off in trains packed like cattle to work camps in the East, that de Man was placidly discussing this not as a human but as a literary problem and concluding that separating the Jews from other Europeans would not be too bad for European literature since the Jews have only contributed a few mediocre figures. Derrida, in fact, does not interpret this article at all in terms of its end, its conclusion, its terrible point, but rather analyzes it piece by piece, as if each piece is not part of the whole. And not only this, he goes to great hermeneutical lengths to present the most benign interpretations of the pieces of de Man's article.

Derrida's interpretation of the piece of this article wherein de Man discusses "vulgar anti-Semitism" provides a good example of the hermeneutical gymnastics Derrida's responsibility to his friend obliges him to perform. Here de Man in this article from 1941 treats "vulgar anti-Semitism":

> Vulgar anti-Semitism readily takes pleasure in considering postwar cultural phenomena (after the war of '14–18) as degenerate and decadent because they are *enjuives*. Literature has not escaped this lapidary judgment: It has sufficed to discover a few Jewish writers behind Latinized pseudonyms for all of contemporary production to be considered polluted and harmful. This conception entails rather dangerous consequences. First of all it condemns a priori a whole literature that in no way deserves this fate. What is more, from the moment one agrees that the literature of our day has some merit, it would be a rather unflattering appreciation of Western writers to reduce them to being mere imitators of a Jewish culture that is foreign to them.
>
> The Jews themselves have contributed to spreading this myth. Often, they have glorified themselves as the leaders of literary movements that characterize our age. But the error has, in fact, a deeper cause. At the origin of the thesis of a Jewish takeover is the very widespread belief according to which the modern novel and modern poetry are nothing but a kind of monstrous outgrowth of the world war. Since the Jews have, in fact, played an important role in the phony and disordered existence of Europe since 1920, a novel born

in this atmosphere would deserve, up to a certain point, the qualifi-
cation of *enjuive*. (1941; quoted in Derrida 1988, 624)

What has de Man said? Vulgar anti-Semitism posits that Jewish influence has everywhere rendered postwar culture degenerate. He opposes
this view because it is not true of literature, which both has merit and is not
all that heavily influenced by Jewish culture. And what has he said about
Jews and Jewish culture? Jewish culture is foreign to Western writers,
which can only be true if Jewish culture is considered outside of and not a
part of western culture, that Jews glorify themselves by spreading false
myths about themselves, and that the Jews "have played an important role
in the phony and disordered existence of Europe since 1920." All three of
these can certainly be viewed as anti-Semitic beliefs. They may, in fact, be
thought of as a sophisticated, intellectual anti-Semitism, in contrast to the
"vulgar anti-Semitism" de Man corrects. Derrida, however, is quick to
point out that de Man never actually mentions any type of anti-Semitism
other than "vulgar anti-Semitism." This leaves the "door open," Derrida
says, to another interpretation of the passage. "To condemn vulgar anti-
Semitism, especially if one makes no mention of the other kind," concludes
Derrida, "is to condemn anti-Semitism itself inasmuch as it is vulgar, always and essentially vulgar" (1988, 624). As comforting as this possibility
is to Derrida, it does seem quite a stretch to believe that what de Man was
really saying is that all anti-Semitism is vulgar. De Man doesn't *mention*
another kind of anti-Semitism in this passage, but he does *exhibit* what
could be considered another kind in what he himself says about Jews and
Jewish culture in this passage. And Derrida's hopeful interpretation becomes even less plausible—loses its plausibility altogether, in fact—when
this passage is considered in the context of the entire article, including its
conclusion. This is precisely, however, what Derrida never does.

Or consider the way Derrida interprets another passage, another piece,
from the same article. De Man states that Jewish influence on present-day
literature is of "extraordinarily little importance" especially given the "specific characteristics" of the Jews. He then goes on to say these "specific
characteristics" are "their cerebralness, their capacity to assimilate doctrines while maintaining a certain coldness in the face of them" and that
these "would seem to be very precious qualities for the work of lucid
analysis that the novel demands" (630).

Now to mark certain qualities, even ones that most would consider
positive, as Jewish is hardly incompatible with anti-Semitism, especially
the qualities de Man mentions. At the book burnings in Germany in 1934,
where many products of Jewish cerebralness and lucid analysis were con-

signed to the flames, Goebels proclaimed the end of the era of "excessive Jewish intellectualism." And what exactly does de Man mean by the Jews' "capacity to assimilate doctrines while maintaining a certain coldness in the face of them"? This sounds like the common anti-Semitic platitude, repeated so many times in Christian Europe throughout the centuries, that converted Jews simply assimilated the dogma of Christianity but remained cold and untouched by its spiritual essence and so never really became true spiritual Christian souls. Anyone familiar at all with the history of anti-Semitism would hardly be put off guard by de Man mentioning these specific qualities as Jewish qualities.[5]

Derrida, however, not only is put off guard by this passage, but actually is as excited as a schoolboy to hear de Man talk about Jews in this way. "One can hardly believe one's eyes," Derrida writes:

> [W]ould this mean that what he prefers in the novel, "the work of lucid analysis," and in theory, a "certain coldness" of intelligence, correspond precisely to the qualities of the "Jewish spirit"? And that the "precious qualities" of the latter are indispensable to literature and theory? What is coiled up and resonating deep within the sentence? Did one hear that correctly? (1988, 630)[6]

Or consider Derrida's treatment of de Man's conclusion to this article. After declaring that Jewish writers have always been in the second rank, de Man goes on to say that this observation

> is, moreover, comforting for Western intellectuals. That they have been able to safeguard themselves from Jewish influence in a domain as representative of culture as literature proves their vitality. If our civilization had let itself be invaded by a foreign force, then we would have to give up much hope for its future. By keeping, in spite of semitic interference in all aspects of European life, an intact originality and character, that civilization has shown that its basic nature is healthy. What is more, one sees that a solution of the Jewish problem that would aim at the creation of a Jewish colony isolated from Europe would not entail, for the literary life of the West deplorable consequences. The latter would lose, in all, a few personalities of mediocre value and would continue, as in the past, to develop according to its great evolutive laws. (quoted in Derrida 1988, 630–31)

Derrida does not discuss the many ways what de Man says here fits neatly into National Socialist ideology: Jewish influence is a "foreign force" from which the West needs to safeguard itself; Jewish influence is "semitic interference" in European life, despite which Europe has remained healthy; the harmful influence of Jewishness is the Jewish problem that needs to be solved; that one way to solve it, a Jewish colony isolated from Europe so Jewishness can no longer harm European culture, would not have deplorable consequences for European literature. Derrida never mentions or explains how thoroughly de Man echoes National Socialist ideology in this passage. He does, however, warn us of the danger of a lack of rigor, and he says that to evaluate de Man's conclusion correctly "we must understand what this allusion to 'a Jewish colony isolated from Europe' meant at that moment" (632). Derrida states that he doesn't know what solution de Man could be referring to, perhaps the Madagascar solution. One thing we do know, he says, is that he couldn't have been referring to what we now know as the "final solution" since de Man wrote the article in March of 1941 and the final solution "was conceived and put into effect later" (632). This is an astounding statement to come from one of Europe's greatest contemporary intellectuals. Is Derrida so naive as to think that the idea of exterminating the Jews as a race was only hatched after March of 1941? Is he swallowing the Nazi party line that the final solution only came out of the Wansee Conference? Has he no idea of how many thousands of German, Polish, Russian and western European Jews had already been killed by the Nazis by the time de Man pondered the effect of the separation of the Jews from European culture on European literature? And does it really matter? Do we really have to know exactly what de Man meant by "the Jewish colony isolated from Europe" to evaluate reasonably accurately de Man's conclusion? Even if he didn't mean by "Jewish colony isolated from Europe" a Warsaw Ghetto, a Dachau, a Treblinka (and certainly all three of these are different types of "Jewish colony isolated from Europe"), does that mean we can't evaluate correctly the passage? Can't we still say that de Man is here utilizing the anti-Semitic language that portrays Jewish influence as so different from and harmful to European culture that European culture needs to safeguard itself by placing this foreign, harmful people somewhere out of the way? And doesn't de Man at least come very close in this article to endorsing the idea of a "Jewish colony isolated from Europe"? And isn't he primarily concerned about this as a literary problem, and isn't he obviously more concerned about what the isolation of Jews from Europe would do to European literature than he is concerned about the isolated Jews? And doesn't he say all this at the very time when Jews were being mercilessly tracked down and exported from the occupied countries? Don't we have to say at least this much about this article by de Man? Don't we have the responsibility to say at least this much about this article?

If we analyze Derrida's interpretation of these collaborationist articles by de Man we can clearly see Derrida at great pains to fulfill his obligations to de Man, those obligations to his friend he feels so strongly even after his friend's death. But what is also clear is that in this process of fulfilling his obligations to de Man he has neglected all sorts of other responsibilities. Where is his responsibility to understand the Holocaust, to understand how it happened? Where is his responsibility to understand the role that ideas, like the idea that Jewish influence upon European culture was harmful and needed to be minimized, and intellectuals, like de Man, who espoused such ideas, played in this complex unfolding of events that led eventually to the murder of six million innocents? And where is his responsibility to all the victims of the Holocaust? Don't we owe philosophical rigor to them, too? And where is Derrida's responsibility to that intellectual task of considering alternatives and deciding which is the most reliable, the least unreliable? Does Derrida really think that de Man was attacking anti-Semitism itself? Does he think that this interpretation is just as likely, more likely than the other interpretation despite all the evidence to the contrary? Doesn't he have the responsibility to decide for himself and explain his decision to us, even if he still insists that the question is, in an ultimate and absolute sense, undecidable? Does he really think that simply to toss out possible interpretations that alleviate de Man's responsibility no matter how far-fetched they are or how less likely than other alternatives fulfills his intellectual responsibilities? If this is how he is going to use the hermeneutical maneuvers of deconstruction with its technique of multiplying possible interpretations and its emphasis on undecidability—essentially to get his friends out of trouble—doesn't he have the responsibility to think about the consequences of this, about the Pandora's box he is not only opening but providing intellectual support for? And where is Derrida's intellectual responsibility to understand himself, to understand his own motivations in his text? Does he understand what drives him to come up with even the most unlikely of interpretations that just happens to mitigate the culpability of his friend? Clearly, what Derrida does he does to fulfill his responsibilities to de Man, which he feels so acutely and strongly. His other responsibilities, however, go amazingly unfulfilled. It appears as if they have all been superseded and drowned out by his responsibilities to de Man.

One can see Derrida again forsaking multiple responsibilities in fulfilling his responsibilities to de Man in his treatment of the question of de Man's postwar silence on these collaborationist articles. Why did de Man never mention this far from admirable aspect of his past? Why did he never talk about what he did during the war, not even to his close friend

Derrida? One rather obvious possible explanation is that he purposely re-
frained from talking about it and didn't want anyone to know about it
simply for the purely selfish interests of protecting the advancement of his
own academic career. Derrida never seems to consider this as a possibility. Rather, he offers other possibilities. If de Man mentioned this publicly,
says Derrida, it would have been "pointlessly painful theatricalization." And
Derrida speculates that de Man might have found all this attention focused
on him "indiscreet" and "indecent" because of his "modesty." And if he'd
made his past a matter of public record, reasons Derrida, dealing with the
discussions about it "would have consumed his time and energy" and "would
have deprived us of a part of his work" (639).

And besides, says Derrida, de Man did publicly reveal his past in a
letter to Harvard in 1955. Derrida makes nothing of the fact that de Man
only did this when forced, when someone who was familiar with his past
in Belgium denounced him. And Derrida doesn't really explain why he
considers a private letter to the Head of the Society of Fellows at Harvard
"a public act." The fact that de Man wrote this letter shows, says Derrida,
that his silence on his collaborationist past was not complete "and thus
cannot be understood in the sense of a dissimulation" (637). Finally, a
possible interpretation Derrida rules out: de Man's silence was not a dissimulation. It can be understood in the ways Derrida proposes, just his
natural modesty for example, his desire to avoid attracting a great deal of
attention to himself, perhaps his desire simply to have as much as possible
of his time available for writing. But de Man's silence, insists Derrida,
"cannot be understood in the sense of a dissimulation" because for Derrida
the very existence of this letter which de Man was reluctantly compelled to
write means that his silence was not complete. This is a very odd and
significant conclusion for Derrida to draw from the mere existence of this
letter, a significant conclusion made even more odd by the fact that Derrida
even admits that "naturally, we are not obliged to give credence to this
presentation of the thing, his [de Man's] version of the facts, in this letter"
(637). Instead of trying to determine if de Man was entirely forthcoming
and honest in stating his version of the facts in the letter—which would
seem to be an all important question for Derrida given the great significance he attributes to the letter—Derrida instead reflects on the terrible
ordeal his friend de Man must have gone through in his life in choosing to
be almost completely silent about his past.

Again, Derrida is amazingly resourceful and diligent in fulfilling his
responsibilities to de Man. He fails, however, in fulfilling his intellectual
responsibilities to think about all the possible interpretations of de Man's
silence. He also fails, rather spectacularly, in fulfilling his intellectual re-

sponsibility to understand himself, to understand what works in him when he concludes that de Man's silence about his past "cannot be understood in the sense of a dissimulation." He fails to understand what makes him— who possesses such a remarkably sophisticated mind—at that moment in his text so naive.

What is going on here in this long and labored text, "Like the Sound of the Sea Deep Within a Shell: Paul de Man's War"? This text is an obvious, even at times painfully obvious illustration of the same phenomenon we spied in the text by Leaman previously discussed. Derrida obviously writes out of a heavy sense of responsibility to de Man. In the process of fulfilling his responsibilities to de Man, however, he abnegates all sorts of additional responsibilities to all sorts of other parties. What happens in this text is that Derrida's responsibility to de Man overrides and drowns out all of his other responsibilities.

And what happens to Derrida when this happens? What happens in Derrida when in fulfilling his obligation to one party he neglects his other responsibilities to other parties? Writing out of his sense of responsibility to de Man while forgetful of all his other responsibilities, he grows sure, certain of himself; his tone becomes loud, harsh, stentorian, accusatory. He stands on the certain, solid ethical ground of his responsibility to de Man and from this position of moral height he levels accusations. The newspapers that reported on this controversy are not merely unfair but "full of hatred" (591).[7] All who raise this issue, except those who defend de Man, are waging a war on de Man, subjecting a corpse to a trial some-how necessarily unfair. They are playing the role of "judge," "jury," "pros-ecutor," even "inquisitor." Those who disagree with Derrida and are unfair to de Man utilize the same techniques as "the worst totalitarian police" (641).[8]

What happens in Derrida and within his text is the same phenomenon that we've already suspected in Leaman and in his text. Both write out of a heavy sense of responsibility to an other—victims of the Holocaust in Leaman's case, Paul de Man in Derrida's case—and both in the process of fulfilling their responsibilities to this one other neglect their many responsi-bilities to the many others. Not only this, but the fact that they both are fulfilling their responsibility to their one other apparently gives them the self assurance of occupying the moral high ground, from which they pronounce accusations. The end result of this process for both Leaman and Derrida is the same. They both produce texts that—even though they are written out of a sense of responsibility—are quite obviously far from just.

What happens in both of these examples may well shed some light on one of the most important transitions in Levinas's ethical philosophy: the change in the way he stages the scene of justice in his later work, most importantly *Otherwise Than Being or Beyond Essence,* from the way he staged the scene of justice in his earlier work, most importantly *Totality and Infinity.*

In *Totality and Infinity*, Levinas conceives of justice always entirely within the face-to-face relation between the self and one other person, the Other. The other other, the third person, is not for the Levinas of *Totality and Infinity* at the scene of justice. Justice here involves the ethical relation between the self and the other person exclusively. The ethical relation with the Other is, says Levinas, justice. To be in truth, says Levinas, is to "encounter the Other without allergy, that is, in justice" (1969, 303). "We call justice this face to face approach, in conversation" (71). "Truth," says Levinas, "is founded on my relationship to the Other, or justice" (99). Thus, since Levinas in *Totality and Infinity* views justice as the ethical relationship with the Other as such, justice is for him in this work coincident with ethics itself, is the same as ethics, or as he sometimes says, as "goodness": "We have described the relation with the face that presents itself in speech as desire—goodness and justice" (296).

Levinas in *Otherwise Than Being or Beyond Essence*, however, entirely changes the scene of justice in that now for him justice not only has to do with the relation between the self and the other, but also has to do with the third party, the other other. In the later work, the ethical relation with the other, what Levinas in this work calls "proximity," is no longer the same as justice, is not the same scene as justice. Justice occurs only when the third party arrives at the scene. When this happens, proximity, or "my responsibility for the other, "is troubled and becomes a problem" (1981, 157). My responsibility for my other becomes a problem when it has to be measured and balanced against my responsibility for the third and by the other's responsibilities to the third.[9] The third brings to me the question: "What do I have to do with justice?" (157). Because of the third, "justice is necessary, that is comparison, coexistence, contemporaneousness, assembling, order" (157). Not only does the relation with the third party initiate a process of correcting the asymmetry of the original relation between the self and the other, but, Levinas maintains, "[T]he relationship with the third party is an incessant correction of the asymmetry of proximity in which the face is looked at" (156). This process is precisely the work of justice; when the responsibility for the other "is also a responsibility for the third party, the justice that compares, assembles and conceives, the synchrony of being and peace, take form" (156). Thus, in absolute contradiction to the way Levinas stages the scene of justice in *Totality and Infinity*, in *Otherwise Than Being or Beyond Essence* the scene of justice cannot be staged without the third party.

This very interesting and significant change in the way Levinas stages the scene of justice can help us greatly, I think, in understanding what is going on in our two accusatory texts, the one by Leaman, the other by Derrida. Both texts, we have argued, are written out of responsibility to an other. Leaman's other is Holocaust victims, while Derrida's is his friend de Man. If we conceive of justice the way Levinas conceives of it in *Totality and Infinity*, the case could be made that both these texts, written as they are out of responsibility for an other, are the scene of justice. However, it is the presence of the third party, the others to whom Leaman and Derrida are responsible, that troubles this too easy judgment. However much responsibility for their others Leaman and Derrida assume, their texts are not the scene of justice, but of justice's opposite. This is a just judgment concerning justice that we are compelled to only because of the third party, only because, as Levinas knew in *Otherwise Than Being or Beyond Essence*, the scene of justice must involve me, and my other, and the third.

Notes

1. See David Hirsch's *The Deconstruction of Literature: Criticism After Auschwitz*. Hirsch certainly has Derrida, among others, in mind when he says that the discourses of postwar philosophy in France and Germany are "self-deceiving and antihuman" and that they "resolutely mock the idea of truth itself" because they seek to turn away from the truth of their own guilty past, meaning their association with National Socialism. For Hirsch, for some reason the fact that Derrida was influenced by Heidegger and Heidegger was a Nazi means that Derrida and his philosophy of deconstruction also have a guilty past. Luc Ferry and Alain Renaut in their *French Philosophy of the Sixties: An Essay on Antihumanism*, discuss Derrida's philosophy under the rubric of "French Heideggerianism" and argue that it is an extension of Heidegger's antihumanism. Deborah Lipstadt, in her book *Denying the Holocaust: The Growing Assault on Truth and Memory*, discusses deconstructionism as part of that assault on the concept of truth that has been very beneficial to the spread of Holocaust denial. "Because deconstructionism argued that experience was relative and nothing was fixed, it created an atmosphere of permissiveness toward questioning the meaning of historical events and made it hard for its proponents to assert that there was anything 'off limits' for this skeptical approach" (1993, 18–19).
2. One text in which Derrida plays with this phrase "what is going on here in this text" is his text on/for/against Levinas entitled "At This Very Moment in This Text Here I Am." See Ruben Berezdivin's translation of this important essay in *Re-reading Levinas*, 11–48.

3.   See some of Heidegger's most important political speeches and writings of the period of his Rektorate, translated and collected together by Dagobert Runes under the title *German Existentialism.*

4.   W. Wolfgang Holdheim, in his article "Jacques Derrida's Apologia," observes that "the central theme of the prologue [of Derrida's article 'Paul de Man's War'] is the notion of responsibility, as well it might be, given the subject. Accordingly, those first seven pages swamp the reader with the word 'responsibility' to the point where they could be described as 'variations on a theme'" (785).

5.   It is interesting to compare what de Man says here, and what Derrida says about what de Man says, with what Jean-Paul Sartre, in his *Anti-Semite and Jew*, says about the anti-Semite: "But the anti-Semite adds a new touch to the portrait [of the Jew]: the Jew, he tells us, is an abstract intellectual, a pure reasoner. And we perceive at once that the terms *abstract, rationalist, intellectual* here take on a pejorative sense; it could not be otherwise, since the anti-Semite lays claim to a concrete and irrational possession of the values of the nation" (1965, 109).

6.   Holdheim, too, notes how strangely happy these words of de Man's made Derrida: "Derrida is in a state of ecstatic amazement." Then Holdheim asks: "Is Derrida really unaware of the fact that appreciation of certain Jewish qualities goes readily with anti-Semitic convictions, as does friendship for individual Jews?" (1990, 791).

7.   Jon Wiener, in his article on Derrida's "Paul de Man's War," appropriately titled "The Responsibilities of Friendship," states that the article in *The New York Times* reporting on the discovery of these articles by de Man "was hardly 'full of hatred.'" Wiener observes that 'full of hatred' is a description that applies more to Derrida, responding to those who reported the news about his friend," (1989, 797–803).

8.   Wiener states that "the article on de Man in *The New York Times* and *The Nation*—the only publications Derrida criticizes—contain nothing that qualifies as 'totalitarian.'" Wiener concludes his essay by saying: "The conclusion one is left with is that what de Man did—collaborate with the Nazi occupiers of Belgium—should be understood and forgiven, but what de Man's critics have done—commit 'reading mistakes' (647, n. 50)—should be condemned as unforgivable. Outside the circle of de Man's most committed defenders, few readers will find this argument persuasive" (1989, 802–3).

9.   Alphonso Lingis, in his Introduction to *Otherwise Than Being or Beyond Essence*, observes that for Levinas "to find that the one before whom and for whom I am responsible is as responsible in his turn before and for another is not to find his order put on one relativized or cancelled. It is to discover the exigency for justice for an order among responsibilities" (1981, xxxv).

Works Cited

De Man, Paul. 1941. "Les Juifs dans la littérature actuelle." *Le Soir* (4 March).

Derrida, Jacques. 1988. "Like the Sound of the Sea Deep Within a Shell: Paul de Man's War." *Critical Inquiry* 14:590–651.

Ferry, Luc and Alain Renaut. 1990. *French Philosophy of the Sixties: An Essay on Antihumanism*. Amherst: University of Massachusetts Press.

Heidegger, Martin. 1962. *Being and Time*. Trans. John Macquarrie and Edward Robinson. New York: Harper and Row.

———. 1965. *German Existentialism*. Ed. and trans. Dagobert Runes. New York: Philosophical Library.

Hirsch, David. 1991. *The Deconstruction of Literature: Criticism after Auschwitz*. [Providence, RI]: Brown UP; Hanover, NH: University Press of New England.

Holdheim, W. Wolfgang. 1990. "Jacques Derrida's Apologia." *Critical Inquiry* 15 (4): 784–96.

Leaman, George. 1995. *Heidegger and the Holocaust*. Ed. Alan Milchman and Alan Rosenberg. Atlantic Highlands, NH: Humanities Press International.

Levinas, Emmanuel. 1969. *Totality and Infinity*. Trans. Alphonso Lingis. Pittsburgh: Duquesne University Press.

———. 1981. *Otherwise Than Being, or Beyond Essence*. Trans. Alphonso Lingis. The Hague: Nijhoff.

———. 1991. *Re-reading Levinas*. Ed. Bernasconi and Simon Critchley. Trans. Ruben Berezdivin. Bloomington: Indiana University Press.

Lipstadt, Deborah. 1993. *Denying the Holocaust: The Growing Assault on Truth and Memory*. New York: Free Press.

Sartre, Jean–Paul. 1965. *Anti–Semite and Jew*. New York: Schocken.

Wiener, Jon. 1989. "The Responsibilities of Friendship: Jacques Derrida on Paul de Man's Collaboration." *Critical Inquiry* 15 (4): 797–803

15

Kant with Sade, Lacan with Levinas

Kenneth Reinhard

In his 1966 essay "Kant with Sade," Jacques Lacan pairs two unlikely figures of Enlightenment ethics, conjoining without comparing them through the preposition "with." In Lacan's 1959–60 *Seminar VII: The Ethics of Psychoanalysis*, where he first addresses the strange affinities of Kant and Sade, Lacan anticipates his later essay when he translates the Greek particle *meta* as "with" or "after," and goes on to suggest that "[*m*]*eta* is, properly speaking, that which implies a break [*la coupure*]" (Lacan 1986, 265).[1] Whereas the "with" of "Kant with Sade" brings together two apparently disparate thinkers, revealing the uncanny proximity of their ethical systems, Lacan shows that the very act of making this conjunction is founded on the break, limit, or blind spot that each brings out in the other's system. Moreover, the conjunction of Kant with Sade not only indicates the break that joins the two figures, but also itself marks a break in the history of ethics, a rupture that will have opened the way for the emergence of psychoanalysis—not as the elaboration of the Sadian catalogue of perversions, but as one of modernity's epochal responses to the escalating intensity of both moral law and pathological objects in the aftermath of traditional ethics based on either revelation or the common good.

Lacan's "Kant with Sade" institutes a comparative literature otherwise than comparison, insofar as the essay pursues a mode of reading logically and ethically prior to similitude, a reading in which texts are not so much grouped into "families" defined by similarity and difference, as into "neighborhoods" determined by accidental contiguity, genealogical isolation, and ethical encounter rather than ontic similarity. "Kant with Sade" articulates a principle and practice of comparative literature in which the juncture of texts or discourses is predicated not only on historical congruencies, structural isomorphisms, or dialectical contradictions, but also on the critical act through which one text takes the place of, or "neighbors" on, the other. Through this mode of reading by way of asymmetrical substitution, Lacan presents an account of Kant and Sade in which each thinker reveals hidden truths and limitations in the other, precisely in the nonreciprocity of their relationship.

At this moment in the early sixties when Lacan initiates his rectification of the history of ethics, Emmanuel Levinas is also beginning to insist on the priority of ethics to ontology and epistemology. Lacan and Levinas took no more cognizance of each other than did Kant and Sade. Despite his evident interest in phenomenology and ethics, Lacan remained strangely silent on the work of Levinas; so too, Levinas has repeatedly dismissed the insights of psychoanalysis into the structure of subjectivity and the Other as merely "psychologistic." But it is precisely as modern "neighbors," both strange and proximate, rather than as either brothers, enemies, or friends that we can read Lacan "with" Levinas. Lacan's reading of Sade as the repressed truth of Kant reveals the perverse underside of the history of Enlightenment, in which the "pathological" object of too-much enjoyment is systematically sacrificed for the sake of the desire of a universalized Other, whether instituted as Reason, Freedom, Knowledge, or the State. By in turn reading Lacan "with" Levinas, as neighbors who, although coming from distinct traditions and aiming at different ends, together articulate the primacy of responsibility and *jouissance* to being and knowing, we can begin to imagine an ethics otherwise than sacrifice, to hear the call of a good after the dialectic of Good and Evil.

I

During the late sixties and middle seventies, at the height of the so-called sexual revolution in the Western world, Lacan frequently insisted in his seminar that "there is no such thing as a sexual relationship." If the conventional critique of periods of sexual experimentation is that they represent the futile attempt to compensate for the collective failure of authentic love relationships, Lacan argues that, on the contrary, it is *love* that makes up for the lack of *sexual* relationships. Lacan's point is not, of course, that "free love" was a meager copy of some higher form of sex, but rather that sex as such is precisely such an imitation: not the falling away from an unattainable ideal, but the protective circulation of fantasy around an originary trauma or structural impasse in the very possibility of relationship. According to Lacan, human beings do not meet as fully individual, autonomous subjects, but only in their functions for each other as partial objects and lacking signifiers, incommensurate terms of a sexual logic that oscillates between a repudiating heterogeneity and an all-absorbing homogeneity. Hence for Lacan the sixties did not signal the libido's momentary liberation from the constraints of repressive cultural ideals, but the construction of yet one more line of defense against the disturbing impossibility of intersubjective sexuality, the inconsistency in the symbolic order that materializes as a *factum*, or "Thing," whose concealment, according to Lacan, both defines human relations and marks their limit.

Another way of formulating this impasse is as the incommensurability between the theory of sexuality—what our parents tell us or what we imagine they do—and the practice of sex—what we find ourselves doing in hopeless imitation of them. Sex, that is, is always "Philosophy in the Bedroom," a failed attempt to put theory into practice, to describe and then reinscribe a paradigm for desire. And insofar as the fundamental gap between the ideals of theory and the vagaries of practice can be sutured but not annealed in the various fantasmatic scenarios that pass for a sexual relationship, human relations collect around a traumatic disjunction that always threatens to reemerge as raw aggressivity.[2]

Nevertheless, Lacan argues that love not only provides an imaginary screen against but also *makes up for* the lack of coherent and predictable social, sexual, and—we may add—intertextual transactions. "Love" has at least two distinct and perhaps contradictory valences for Lacan. On the one hand, love can dissimulate the unavailability of a sexual relationship by *imagining* a relationship between the self and the other. This version of love projects a "specular mirage" that simulates symbolic interaction by addressing me from a hypothetical point where I am seen in the way I would like to be seen, thereby fostering an illusion of reciprocity that is "essentially deception" (Lacan 1978, 268). On the other hand, Lacan suggests that there is another love, a love not bound by the circulation of images, but that arises, as Juliet Flower MacCannell has written, "outside the limits of the law" (Lacan 1978, 25)—neither within nor beyond specularity, but on what we might call, after Levinas, the "hither side" of the mirror, more proximate to me than either myself or my alter-ego.[3] Insofar as it aims precisely at the traumatic lack of a sexual relationship, this love is closely allied with the sublimation of the excessive enjoyment or *jouissance* that in Lacan's *Seminar VII* forms the imperative of the ethics of psychoanalysis.[4] At the conclusion of *Seminar XI*, Lacan warns that specular love barely conceals an internecine aggressivity that culminated most horrifically in the sacrificial fury of the Holocaust (Lacan 1978, 274-76).[5] The "other" love, on the other hand, in aiming, as Renata Salecl writes, at "what remains of the object when all the imaginary and symbolic features are annihilated," sacrifices precisely those illusory characteristics of the other person that fuel the love of sacrifice.[6]

In his *Seminar VIII* on transference, Lacan presses the encomium of love in Plato's *Symposium* into the service of his argument that love is an act of metaphoric "substitution." In Phaedrus's discourse on the hierarchy of types of love, this substitution occurs in its more conventional form when it is the lover who takes the place of (or sacrifices him or herself for) the beloved:[7]

> Love as signifier—for to us it is a signifier and nothing else—love is
> a metaphor—assuming that we have come to understand metaphor
> as substitution. . . . It is insofar as the function of the *erastes* or the
> person who loves, as lacking subject, takes the place of, is substi-
> tuted for the function of *eromenos*, the loved object, that the signi-
> fication of love is produced. (Lacan 1991, 53)

Lacan writes that this version of love—in Phaedrus's example here, the
sacrifice of Alcestis (the lover) who dies in the place of her husband Admetus
(the beloved)—is "beautiful." The "signification of love" is produced insofar as the subject sacrifices him or herself for a higher meaning or purpose
(e.g. the redemption of Admetus from his fate) in an act, however, that
conceals death as the empty center of the lack of a sexual relationship, an
aestheticizing gesture of the possible that cloaks a more fundamental impossibility. Thus Phaedrus tells us that the gods rewarded Alcestis for the
magnanimity of her sacrifice by obviating the debt and restoring her, too,
to life. The legendary love of Achilles for Patroclus, on the other hand, in
which it is the beardless beloved who sacrifices himself for the older lover,
involves a less common, and truly "sublime," substitution. In avenging the
murder of Patroclus, Achilles comes to be in the place of Patroclus, choosing death as his fate, without restoring to life either himself or his lover:

> [Achilles] is *the one who will follow me*. He follows Patroclus in
> death. . . . The question is whether or not to kill Hector merely to
> take revenge for Patroclus' death. If you don't kill Hector, his
> mother Thetis tells him, you will return home in peace, and you will
> live happily to a ripe old age. If you kill him, your fate is sealed—
> it is death that awaits you . . . the choice of *Moira*, of fate, has the
> same value as the substitution of being for being. . . . Don't imagine
> for a minute that Patroclus was the beloved, as was generally be-
> lieved. It turns out, says Phaedrus . . . that it could only have been
> Achilles, who was younger and still beardless. . . . [T]hus he must
> have been the beloved. Patroclus was ten years older than Achilles.
> . . . [H]e must be the lover. . . . Indeed, what they find sublime,
> more marvelous than anything, is when the beloved behaves as one
> would expect a lover to behave. . . . It is insofar as Achilles is in the
> position of the beloved that his sacrifice is so much more admirable.
> (Lacan 1991, 61-62)

Whereas Alcestis's sacrifice of herself for Admetus constitutes a symbolic
transaction within an imaginary economy, insofar as the debt is not merely
repaid but cancelled, Achilles' sacrifice does not win Patroclus back from
death, remaining an expenditure without either reserve or return. Rather

than imagining the substitution of one-for-the-other as an equation in which the redemption of life from death reinstates the clear distinction between the two, Achilles' substitution involves the calculus of a one-*with*-the-other, an asymmetrical transaction that insists on the infinite proximity of life to death. As Phaedrus says in the *Symposium*, Achilles died "not only *for* his friend [*hyperapothanein*], but to be with his friend in death [*epapothanein*]" (Plato 1961, 179e)—to be *with* Patroclus is to be *with* death. Achilles' substitution thrusts him into the realm Lacan calls the "between-two-deaths"—less a redemptive beyond of death than once again its *hither side*: the interval between symbolic death and real death in which the trauma of the lack of a sexual relationship is encountered.[8] Whereas what Lacan calls the "specular mirage" of reciprocal love not only conceals the other-ness of the other, but also entails the violent sacrifice of what is uncannily familiar in him or her, absorbing the other into the subject's economy of identifications, the sublime modality of what we might call "substitutive love" attempts to offer a gift to the other without hope of compensation, to make a noneconomic sacrifice in which the loving-beloved gains nothing, in which the reciprocity of sacrifice itself is sacrificed.[9] The asymmetry of substitutive love, rather than constituting a kind of relationship, entails the encounter with the impossibility of relationship: love as "substitution" sub-stitutes for relationship, but does not disguise the impossibility of a sexual relationship. In refusing to reduce the distance between sexuality and sex, substitutive love bears within it the trauma of this impasse, the scandalous enjoyment or *jouissance* of the other that makes true love always a substi-tution.

II

Yet the calculus of substitutive love in the post-classical West is ori-ented not only by the light from Troy and Athens, where the bonds of the modern state are forged out of erotic and familial relations, but also toward Jerusalem, where the conflicting imperatives of the social relationship con-verge in the commandment to "love thy neighbor as thyself" (Lv 19:18), the fiercely contested prooftext in both Judaism and Christianity for the dialectics of the private and the public, the moral and the legal, and the sacred and the secular. Just as there are reciprocal and nonreciprocal responses to the impossibility of a sexual relationship, so there are at least two modes of interpreting the Levitical injunction that historically has sought to compensate for the lack of a social or "neighborly" relationship. The traditional *reciprocal* or specular reading of the injunction, as determined and exemplified by St. Augustine, claims that everybody is my neighbor:

the community of Christians is united by mutual identification grounded in the reflexivity of self-love, and guaranteed under the symbolic aegis of God.[10] It is precisely, however, the "universalist" imperative of this interpretation, its inclusion of all people as my neighbors, that requires the absorption, expulsion, or eradication of those most proximate neighbors, Jewish and Muslim, who refuse to harken to its message because they are privy to its Semitic wellsprings. But there is an ongoing history of *non-reciprocal* or asymmetrical counter-readings of neighbor-love, before and after its Christian universalization. This tradition, which links the early saints and rabbis to Kierkegaard, Freud, Lacan, and Levinas, stops short before the Levitical commandment and refuses to endorse its imaginary consolations, without, however, giving up on the difficult conjunction of responsibility and *jouissance* crystallized in its imperative. These readings insist on either the ambiguity and ambivalence of self-love, the difficulty of determining who counts as the neighbor, or the impossibility of social love as such— that is, they come up against the incommensurability of the injunction's three basic terms, the neighbor, the self, and love.

Perhaps the strongest post-foundational encounter with the ethics of the demand to love the neighbor appears in the recent writings of Emmanuel Levinas.[11] In *Otherwise Than Being or Beyond Essence* (1974), Levinas reformulates the biblical call to neighbor-love as the insistence on the priority of ethics over ontology, a relation to the other that antedates the very being of the subject.[12] The "neighbor," in its double connotation of proximity and strangeness, names the occasion of an originary responsibility that precedes both the subject who assumes or denies that obligation and the community in which responsibility will be represented or rescinded under the sign of Justice. In a 1982 interview Levinas comments that "responsibility for the neighbor" is doubtless the "strict term for that which is called the love of the neighbor" (Levinas 1991, 113, my translation), insofar as both are defined by an ability to *respond* to the other that is not predicated on the experience of self-love (as in St. Augustine) but is rather the precondition of the self.[13] Levinas argues that the subject as such is "called into being" *only insofar as it is called into question*, finding itself already guilty, already indebted to and obsessed with its neighbor:

> The neighbor concerns me before all assumption, all commitment consented or refused. I am bound to him, him who is, however, the first one on the scene, not signalled, unparalleled; I am bound to him before any liaison contracted. He orders me before being recognized. Here there is a relationship of kinship outside of all biology, "against all logic." It is not because the neighbor would be recog-

nized as belonging to the same genus as me that he concerns me. He
is precisely *other*. The community with him begins in my obligation
to him. (Levinas 1974, 87)

My responsibility for the neighbor does not arise from my acknowledgment of him or her as like me, as a member of a common "genus," where
similarity would be defined in terms of what Levinas calls "thematism"
(e.g., genealogical or familial continuity; political, ideological, or religious
identification; geographical or historical contiguity; formal, ontic, or ontological similarity; or any dialectical negation of such generalities). Rather,
it is my responsibility for the neighbor, derived from his or her simultaneous proximity and alterity—a radical otherness which precedes the relationship of the Here and the There, the Same and the Other—that forms the
basis of any possibility of community between us. Ethics takes priority
over ontology insofar as it provides the only language that can begin to
describe this proto-social relationship.[14]

Paradoxically, the subject becomes individual, unique and irreplaceable
precisely to the extent that the strange intimacy of the neighbor brings the
subject to *substitute* itself for the other, a substitution that requires that it be
fungible, interchangeable, hence without the selfsameness of identity. The
subject, that is, can only be itself insofar as it comes to sacrifice its selfhood
in substituting itself for its neighbor:

> *My* substitution—it is as *my own* that substitution for the neighbor
> is produced. The Mind is a multiplicity of individuals. It is in me—
> in me and not in another, in me and not in an individuation of the
> concept Ego—that communication opens. It is I who am integrally
> or absolutely ego, and the absolute is my business. No one can
> substitute himself for me, who substitutes myself for all. (Levinas
> 1974, 126)

The singularity of the subject's responsibility entails its subjective "multiplicity"; the call from the other is heard neither as the imperative of the
social order nor as the voice of critical self-consciousness, but as a cry of
radical exteriority that divides the subject from within.[15] My uniqueness as
a self lies not in my identity, but in the singularity and infinity of my responsibility; no one can replace me in my obligation to substitute myself for my
neighbor, but this debt cannot be either fulfilled or cancelled, since I am
always called on to enter into the place of "whatever" person is my neighbor.[16]

Moreover, because this responsibility is singular and not transferable, it can never be reciprocal; I always have one more obligation than anyone else insofar as I am not only responsible for the other, but also responsible for *the other's responsibility*:

> The knot of subjectivity consists in going to the other without concerning oneself with his movement toward me. Or, more exactly, it consists in approaching in such a way that, over and beyond all reciprocal relations that do not fail to get set up between me and the neighbor, I have always taken one step more towards him—which is possible only if this step is responsibility. In the responsibility which we have for one another, I have always one response more to give, I have to answer for his very responsibility. (Levinas 1974, 84)

Despite the structures of social representation that attempt to calculate and equalize the individual's debt by establishing "reciprocal relations" within a group, the individual *qua* subject of substitution assumes a responsibility for the neighbor that is not mutual, that cannot be amortized, that is infinite without being asymptotic, *infinitely asymmetrical*: "The more I answer the more I am responsible; the more I approach the neighbor [*j'approche du prochain*] with which I am encharged the further away I am" (Levinas 1974, 93). My responsibility for the other cannot reciprocally entail the other's responsibility for me, because to require another person to indebt him or herself would be, as Levinas writes, "to preach human sacrifice!" (Levinas 1974, 126).

For both Lacan and Levinas, substitution does not imply an act of self-sacrifice within an economy of expiation and redemption, but rather the *sacrifice of sacrifice*. The moral economy of sacrifice entails giving up enjoyment for a place in the symbolic order (always advertised as a "higher" pleasure). The sacrifice of sacrifice, on the other hand, insists not on the enjoyment that attends responsibility, but rather on the responsibility for enjoyment, the obligation to maintain the *jouissance* that makes responsibility possible. In Lacan's dictum, "the only thing one can be guilty of is giving ground relative to one's desire" (Lacan 1986, 321); renunciation in the name of the symbolic order of morality is merely a ruse, a resistance to desire and the trauma that is its cause. For Levinas, enjoyment is not simply renounced by the subject of responsibility, but remains its intimate and ongoing condition: "only a subject that eats can be for-the-other, or can signify" (Levinas 1974, 74). Levinas articulates the responsibility of "for-the-other" as a substitution that determines not one meaning among others, but rather opens the field of signification as such. Like Lacan's substitutive love, Levinasian responsibility institutes the process of metaphorization without abandoning *jouissance*, which indeed depends on the primal signification of substitution: "I can enjoy and suffer by the other only because I am for-the-other, am signification" (Levinas 1974, 90). For Levinas the subject's passive responsibility for its neighbor is experienced as a "deafening trauma" that creates the subject as the response to a call so loud or so close that it cannot be heard, cannot be fully translated into a message. In the deferred temporality that places ethics before ontology, responsiveness before being, the subject is produced as "the echo of a sound that would precede the resonance of this sound" (Levinas 1974, 111).

In his Talmudic reading from 1982, "The Pact," Levinas renders the injunction to "Love thy neighbor as thyself" as "Be responsible for the other as you are responsible for yourself," a formulation that, in asserting the constitutive primacy of responsiveness to the other, reverses and upsets the reflexive arc implied by the verse's Augustinian translation (Levinas 1994, 84). Whereas *love* of neighbor circles from subject to other and back, *responsibility* for the neighbor originates as a traumatic response to the other that brings the subject as such into being as its aftereffect; there is no love of self that could model love of the other, since the self only exists by virtue of that love. This relationship also describes the division of Levinas's writings between philosophical works coming out of the French and German phenomenological tradition and his briefer, more occasional pieces on rabbinic texts and Jewish politics. Just as in the ethical relationship there is a radical asymmetry in the priority and direction of responsibility, so in the discursive scene of Levinas's writing, religion is always the neighbor of philosophy, but not vice versa; the injunction to love the neighbor is a piece of revelation that infiltrates into Levinas's philosophical writing, but retains its scriptural heterogeneity. Similarly, Levinas reorients modern philosophy by making it respond to signal events in religious experience: creation, revelation, and redemption—aspects of transcendence that are all refracted through the this-worldly figure of the neighbor. Although Levinas's religious essays are thoroughly permeated by the insights of his philosophical writings, those insights themselves came about through the philosophical response to religion; the interpenetration is reciprocal but not symmetrical. Indeed, the interdiscursive texture of Levinas's writing is produced by this very asymmetry, in which philosophy enters into its adulthood and becomes *responsible* not in escaping religion, but by taking religion as its neighbor.[17]

III

Demonstrating that a concept of asymmetrical substitution is central to both Lacan's and Levinas's theories of responsibility establishes a relationship between them, which, despite the conceptual, personal, and institutional insulation of the two thinkers from each other, reveals hidden affinities between them. The radical notion of substitution that forms the basis of such a comparison, however, would itself seem to precede if not preempt the very possibility of comparison. Since both Lacan and Levinas insist that intersubjectivity, reciprocity, and relationship as such are theoretical lures that conceal or forget the absolute priority of the other, how can we bring Lacan and Levinas together without in turn "thematizing" them, reducing them to a set of parallel significations? What would a relationship of asymmetrical substitution between texts or discourses, prior to one of structural or conceptual similitude, be, and in what sense would it be "ethical"? What can such substitution teach us about both textuality and ethics that remains concealed by the presupposition of comparability?

My intention in the remainder of this essay is to show how Lacan's 1966 "Kant with Sade," developed from his *Seminar VII* on the ethics of psychoanalysis, presents at once a theoretical account of the ethics of substitution (derived in part from a psychoanalytic interpretation of the injunction to love the neighbor) and a kind of textual practice that eschews the love of relationship, a "comparative literature" that would operate, to echo Levinas, "otherwise than comparison." Moreover, this modality of "reading Lacan reading" itself already depends on the act of juxtaposing Lacan "with" Levinas, of having imagined a way of thinking about modernity produced by responding to Levinas and Lacan as neighbors, historically, geographically, and genealogically proximate, yet without a common discursive ground for interchange.

If what passes for relationship in the sexual and social fields is marked by a fundamental trauma or lack of relationship—the incomensurability of theory and practice, of signifier and object, of the Same and the Other— how would such an impossibility manifest in the project of a comparative literature otherwise than comparison? To perform my own act of substitution here by putting "textual comparison" in the place of "sexual relationship" in Lacan's dictum, I would like to claim that "there is no such thing as an intertextual relationship"—that is, there is no ground that can guarantee the transactions of a comparative literature, no third term that can fully adjudicate between the incommensurabilities that haunt every textual pairing.[18] The founding gesture of "Comparative Literature" envisions the literary field as a totalizable network of genealogical and formal relationships.[19] Indeed, the various classical theories of comparative literature—historical, thematic, generic, and structuralist—proceed precisely by tracing or establishing "family relationships" based on derivation and resemblance between texts and groups of texts.

But if comparison in terms of the similarity and difference of autonomous objects is only one possible set of ways in which we make up for our inability to describe fully transparent relationships between literary and theoretical texts, are there kinds of substitutive encounters between texts that precede, exceed, and condition such comparison? Can we imagine a practice of reading, not instead of, but preliminary to comparison, a mode of interpretation that would begin by asking what the *responsibility* of one text to another is, and, in turn, of a reader to a text? If the relationships produced by critical juxtaposition first imply and conceal the traumatic fact of proximity without resemblance, hence both a *singularity* of encounter and an *infinity* of responsibility for that encounter, would this nearness take priority to and restrict the selfsameness of each text, the fixity of its place in literary genealogy, the autonomy of its reader, and the rationality of possible intertextual or comparative relationships? To approach texts as "neighbors"—for example, to juxtapose Kant with Sade, or Lacan with Levinas—entails creating anamorphic disturbances in the network of perspectival genealogies and intertextual relations. That is, before texts can be compared, one text must be articulated as the uncanny neighbor of the other; this is an assumption of critical obligation, indebtedness, secondariness that has nothing to do with influence, *Zeitgeist*, or cultural context.

Rather than suggesting a relationship of simple conjunction, such as would be implied by the phrase "Kant *and* Sade," the "with" of Lacan's title indicates a disjunctive relationship, on two levels. First, Lacan's juxtaposition of Kant/Sade marks a rupture in the historical genesis and critical genealogy of morality itself. Lacan locates Sade not at the antipodes of an Enlightenment mapped by the centrality of Kant, but as its *envers*, its seamy yet continuous other side. This rift in the history of the Good is constituted as such only after the fact—not in the linear temporality of historical causality, but in the strange light left by historical catastrophe. For Lacan, Kant and Sade will have become neighbors only from the eschatological moment produced by the breakdown of Enlightenment ideals and Romantic historiography after World War II. Second, Lacan's supplementation of Kant "with" Sade marks the inadequacy or conceptual *limit* each brings out in the other. To imagine Sade as Kant's evil twin is to locate the horizon of Kant's critique of practical reason in the unreasonable enjoyment that Sade exemplifies, while to picture Kant as the angel in Sade's house is to reveal the moral legalism that determines and finally contains Sadian transgression.

Lacan's initial comparativist gesture in "Kant with Sade" is not to oppose the two figures as representatives of antithetical principles of "moral law" and "libertinage," but to oppose them as thinkers who, read together, constitute a crucial swerve in the history of ethics since Aristotle, insofar as each divorces ethics from any notion of the good derived from well-being. Invoking the uncanny temporality and causality that characterizes the encounter of ethical neighbors rather than the relationship of moral antagonists, Lacan writes that, whereas "Sade is the inaugural step [*le pas inaugural*] of a subversion, of which . . . Kant is the turning point [*le point tournant*] . . . *Philosophy in the Bedroom* . . . gives the truth of the *Critique* [*of Practical Reason*]" (Lacan 1966, 765 [1989, 55]). Kant and Sade are not only in accord with each other theoretically, but Sade paradoxically both initiates and "completes," reveals the hidden consequences of, the ethical revolution of which Kant is the "turning point." Kant, of course, rejects all ethical objects or interests as "pathological," leaving only the pure subject of a moral law the subject wills for him or herself—the project of autonomy as *auto-nomos*, a universal but self-given law (Lacan [1989, 56]). The Kantian subject, however, is not only universalized but also in a sense radically de-subjectified by this project, insofar as, in trying to instantiate a relentlessly consistent because absolutely contentless law, it becomes indistinguishable from an Other imagined as seamless, without lack.[20]

Sade, on the other hand, produces an anti-ethics centered completely on the object, an object now defined not in terms of the aim of the subject's goodwill, but as the possibility of serving the other's "happiness in evil" ([1989, 55]), of completing and fulfilling the Other. The Sadian fantasy remains locked in the Pauline dialectic of law and sin, with no place for a subject separated out of it; Lacan writes, "Sade thus stopped, at the point where desire is knotted together with the law. If something in him held to the law, in order there to find the opportunity Saint Paul speaks of, to be sinful beyond measure, who would throw the first stone? But he went no further. . . . [T]he apology for crime only pushes him to the indirect avowal of the Law" ([1989, 74]). Lacan's conjunction of Kant and Sade crosses the two figures, suggesting both the perverse insistence on the law that haunts the imperative of Kant's universal ethical subject and the categorical structure of the perversions through which Sade's thought remains indentured to the moral law. Despite their apparent opposition on the nature of the ethical object and objective, Kant and Sade both act in support of the wholeness and consistency of the symbolic order that rewrites the traditional function of the Good and challenges the very possibility of a subjective will independent of that order.

In putting Sade in the place of Kant, Lacan shows how Sade is not only the theorist of an ethical system that shares the universality of the categorical imperative, but was also himself a practitioner of asymmetrical substitution. In *Seminar VII* Lacan derives the "fundamental law" that underwrites Sade's "social system" and underscores its Kantianism from a line in *Juliette*: "'Lend me the part of your body that will give me a moment of satisfaction and, if you care to, use for your own pleasure that part of my body which appeals to you'" (1986, 202).[21] In this version, Sade's formula is "ethical" in Kant's sense insofar as it seems to articulate a purely formal and universal law free from any pathological concern for the good, whether mine or the other's. But in "Kant with Sade," written a few years later, Lacan crucially reformulates the maxim as follows: "'I have the right of enjoyment over your body, *anyone can say to me*, and I will exercise this right, without any limit stopping me in the capriciousness of the exactions that I might have the taste to satiate'" (1966, 768–69 [1989, 58], emphasis added). While Lacan's second version of the maxim is as universal as the first (which is closer to Sade's original text), the difference here lies not in the signification of the statement, but in the locus of its enunciation: Sade's original phrase and Lacan's first account of it seem to imply the reciprocity of torturer and victim, that each has an obligation to the other, as in Kant's famous definition of marriage as each partner's ownership of the genitals of the other. Lacan's rewriting of Sade's text in "Kant with Sade" insists on the right as exclusively that of *the other*. Although the maxim is in the first person, it is not mine to pronounce, but only sounds as an indirect utterance which "anyone can say to me"; hence while it remains universal, it becomes radically asymmetrical. Lacan's modification of Sade's imperative forces the one who speaks it to put himself in the place of the other, to assert its freedom as exclusively the right of the other.

Lacan writes, "it is already a point in favor of our maxim that it can serve as the paradigm of a statement which excludes as such reciprocity (reciprocity and not changing places [*la charge de revanche*])" (1966, 770; [1989, 59]). Note how Lacan discriminates here between reciprocity and "changing places." Jacques-Alain Miller glosses this distinction by commenting that, when my friend pays for me at a restaurant and I say "next time it's on me" [*A charge de revanche*], this does not establish a relationship of parity between us—since for the moment I am in his or her debt, and even in reciprocating the accounts may remain unbalanced if I take my friend to a cheaper or more expensive restaurant; hence the debt may be shifted or modified but never repaid or cancelled. Rather, on each occasion, the one who pays has absolute mastery: no matter who takes the place of the slave the next time, at any given moment the relationship is intrinsically asymmetrical, out of sync (Miller, 1989a).

Although Kant's ethical revolution seems to be based on the assertion of the subject's full autonomy, its attempt to evacuate the pathological object that would deflect the subject of practical reason from its self-given rule universalizes the subject, who is no longer distinguishable from the abstract heteronomy of the Other in religious and political ethical systems. Sade's version of the categorical imperative, insofar as it is doubly heteronomous, brings out the truth about Kant. The juxtaposition of Sade with Kant reveals, on the one hand, the Kantian universality in Sade, and on the other, the Sadian heteronomy in Kant, insofar as it speaks a law that both comes *from the other* and is addressed *to the other* (Lacan [1989], 59). Lacan writes,

> the difficulty for whoever makes it a judgment [is] not so much to make him consent to it, as to pronounce it *in his place*. It is thus indeed the Other as free, it is the freedom of the Other, which the discourse of the right to *jouissance* poses as the subject of its enunciation. ([1989], 59–60)

The sadist is not offering to swap *jouissance* with the other (it is not a case of "I'll do you if you'll do me"), nor is he trying to achieve his own *jouissance* at the expense of the other. Rather, the moral "difficulty" of the Sadian injunction, the responsibility it imposes on its agent, is to pronounce it from the place of the other, to guarantee *jouissance* as always the other's right. And this is what the true sadist does, insofar as he locates himself as the object of the Other's *jouissance*, the tool or theory designed to serve the Other's pleasure rather than his own. For the sadist, everyone but me is entitled to this freedom; this is what it means to "pronounce it in his place." Insofar as the Sadian moral maxim enjoins that we serve the *jouissance* of the Other, its ethical imperative is to become the nonspecular object for the Other's pleasure, to sacrifice the very autonomy of the Kantian subject to it.

In *Seminar VII* Lacan reads Freud's resistance in *Civilization and its Discontents* to the injunction to neighbor-love as an indication that the traumatic "Thing," the embodiment of the obscene sexual relationship or evil stolen pleasures that we attribute to the neighbor, is present in Freud—and ourselves—as well. According to Lacan, the *jouissance* of the neighborly *Ding* emerges in the empty place of reason cleared by the Kantian notion of the *Ding-an-sich*, insofar as the only positive sign of compliance with the moral law for Kant is *pain* (1986, 80). Hence, the structural resemblance of the Kantian and Sadian systems reveals not only the similarity but the *proximity* of Kant and Sade. The comparison of Kant *and* Sade reveals that Kant is *with* Sade, that Sade manifests the nearness to Kant of the pathological object *par excellence*, the Thing that renders practical reason always impure. The juxtaposition of the two figures as nonsymmetrical neighbors brings out the Sadian Thing "in Kant more than Kant." Thus for Lacan to put Kant in the place of Sade is not only to produce a chiastic series of dialectical interchanges, but to insist on the nonreciprocity of their conjunction, the weirdness of their proximity. In this sense, to say with Lacan that Kant is "with" Sade would not be to argue that he is "like" Sade, as Sade's brother or father (as in the genealogical or homological modes of comparison), nor that he is Sade's antithesis, his enemy or Hegelian double (the dialectical critique presented by Horkheimer and Adorno).[22] Rather, I would suggest that for Lacan, Kant is "with" Sade precisely insofar as Sade is Kant's *neighbor*, at once near and strange.

Towards the end of "Kant with Sade" Lacan invokes the title of Pierre Klossowski's 1947 book *Sade My Neighbor*, one of the first post–World War II studies to approach the question of Nazi rationality by retrieving the Sadian other side of the Enlightenment history of Reason.[23] Lacan's text frames this question not only as a thematic problem of the bureaucratic banality of evil, but as a question of the function of *substitution as such* (rhetorical, historical, phenomenological) as it manifests in the wake of the retrospective proximity of Kant and Sade. In his discussion of Klossowski's book, Lacan comments that if indeed the injunction to love the neighbor translates into Sade's claim to the other's right to enjoyment, the Levitical commandment nonetheless marks the limit of Sade's fantasy:

> Thus we are in a position to interrogate the *Sade, mon prochain* whose invocation we owe to the perspicacity of Pierre Klossowski.
> . . .
>
> That the Sadian fantasy situates itself better in the bearers of Christian ethics than elsewhere is what our structural landmarks allow us to grasp easily.
> But that Sade, himself, refuses to be my neighbor, is what needs to be recalled, not in order to refuse it to him in return, but in order to recognize the meaning of this refusal.
> We believe that Sade is not nigh enough [*assez voisin*] to his own wickedness to recognize his neighbor [*son prochain*] in it. A trait he shares with many, and notably with Freud. For such is indeed the sole motive of the recoil of beings, sometimes forewarned, before the Christian commandment. (Lacan 1966, 789)

Sade's refusal to be a "good neighbor" exposes the fundamentally asymmetrical structure of neighboring: I never "am" a neighbor, I only *have* neighbors to and for whom I am responsible. That is, the neighbor is not an ontological category, defining my being, but an ethical situation vis à vis the other, who always logically precedes me. Nor is it an epistemological category, insofar as it is always marked by a certain misrecognition of the "neighbor" within ourselves, the strange sadistic enjoyment that causes Freud to renounce the Levitical injunction in nearly Nietzschean terms in *Civilization and its Discontents* as the cruel joke of a world defined by unlimited aggressivity. In Lacan's rewriting of the Sadian maxim, there is no limit to the neighbor's right to enjoyment [*droit de jouir*] save the "capriciousness of the exactions that I might have the *taste* to satiate"; the only ground for Sade's ethical rule is *aesthetic*, a law that not only applies exclusively to the other, and not to me, but that also leaves that rule open to the sublime groundlessness of aesthetic judgment. The responsibility called for by the neighbor's *jouissance* is a judgment, a radical act of asymmetrical substitution where the unlimited freedom of the torturing agent's erotic "taste" is secured at the expense of that agent's subjective autonomy. To reinflect Klossowski's phrase, Sade is *my* neighbor, despite the fact that he refuses for me to be his. Sade recognizes that to have a neighbor means to put myself in the neighbor's place, to substitute myself for him or her—not to imagine myself as like my neighbor, to constitute myself as his or her mirror or antithesis, but to serve my neighbor's *jouissance*, no matter how strange or traumatic or not to my "taste" it may be.[24]

In their situation side by side, connected as ethical "neighbors" rather than either brothers or enemies, Kant and Sade open a gap in the history of ethics that unveils the place where psychoanalysis will have come to be. This is not to suggest that for Lacan either Sade's catalogue of perversions or Kant's limitation of the possibility of knowledge "anticipates" or enables Freud's discoveries. If Sade is the "inaugural step of a subversion, of which . . . Kant is the turning point," this ethical rhythm repeats itself and is only visible in the gap between Freud's death at the beginning of World War II and the resumption of Lacan's seminar eight years after the Occupation: namely, through the breach torn in the history of pure reason by the Holocaust. It is indeed the Holocaust that provides the occasion of the return to Sade, not only by Lacan, but also by such writers as Adorno and Horkheimer, Blanchot, Bataille, de Beauvoir, and Klossowski. All of these thinkers turned to Sade after the war to try to discover the failure of the project of Enlightenment, the perversion at its core; for it is only after Auschwitz that the most disturbing consequences of the failure to recognize Sade as our neighbor emerge. If Christianity defines itself as the universalization of the Levitical injunction to "love thy neighbor as thyself," the Holocaust reveals in the most horrific way both the violence and the blindspots of that totalization. In its wake, neighbor-love, once more confronted in its noncommutativity, becomes the locus of an ethics in excess of the Pauline dialectic of enlightenment which had appropriated it.

For Lacan and Levinas, the Holocaust has the force not only of a traumatic historical occurrence, but also of a rupture in historiography itself, a calamity for the very narratives on which historical continuity and ethical certainty are based.

In the psychoanalytic theory of retroactive causality, or "deferred action," historical origins are not merely understood later, but are produced only as causes after the fact, in the aftermath of their own effects. Moreover, such retroactive causality never simply disappears into the historical dialectics it sets into motion, but always leaves a residue, a trace that exceeds the very history it is meant to explain. There is no doubt that such ahistorical causality can always be recontextualized by providing a revised historical teleology that accommodates the birth of this newlyperceived aberration; but to do so, in Levinas's understanding of ethics, is *to fail to take responsibility for it*. For Levinas, responsibility requires an act not of recontextualization but of *de*-contextualization, in which another person or another idea is stripped bare of the historical processes that seem to have determined its origination, and is confronted as a material singularity, urgently appealing to a subject here and now. In this sense, the repetition of the relationship of "Kant with Sade" in "Lacan with Levinas" is not meant to provide a new chain of genealogical similarity or historical causality, but to articulate the responsibility—the encounter with the priority of the Other— that such a comparison has already assumed.

Lacan's conjunction of Kant with Sade produces a realignment of the history of ethics that is itself repeated and rewritten in the juxtaposition of Lacan with Levinas that I have set up here. Lacan's reading reveals the limits of the ethical project of the Enlightenment, insofar as both Kant and Sade ultimately demand a sacrifice in the name of the Other—Kant repudiating the object in favor of a universal law whose fulfillment is signaled by pain, and Sade disintegrating the subject in the service of the Other's right to *jouissance*. This ethics of sacrifice in the name of the Good climaxed in the strange fury to sacrifice the neighbor that appalled Lacan and Levinas, and much of the world, after the Holocaust. To think the relationship of Lacan "with" Levinas is to locate them as ethical neighbors who are conjoined, first of all, by the critique of that will to sacrifice—not by negating sacrifice in favor of its antithesis (charity, reason, utility), but by situating it face to face with its hither side, the ethics of asymmetrical substitution.

If sacrifice is always finally sacrifice of *jouissance* to the Other, *substitution substitutes for sacrifice*; asymmetrical substitution criticizes the assumption on which the symbolic order is based, that there is a radical antinomy of *jouissance* and law, and that *jouissance* must be sacrificed for the sake of the wholeness and continuity of the moral and social orders. Substitution insists that we must *take responsibility for enjoyment*, not give up on the *jouissance* that is not merely prior to the symbolic economy of sacrifice, but that makes responsibility possible. This account of ethics as the imperative to take responsibility for *jouissance* does not announce the apocalypse of the symbolic order installed and maintained by sacrifice, but calls for responsiveness to an account of the symbolic order that would no longer be opposed to the traumatic encounter with the real. This is the realm of what Lacan calls *joui-sense*: the enjoyment of signification that is crystallized in the commandment to neighbor-love, the simultaneous presence of enjoyment and signification—as manifested in the "other love" for Lacan, in "responsibility for the neighbor's responsibility" for Levinas—that determines the ethics of asymmetrical substitution.

What, then, would such an ethics of asymmetrical substitution look like between texts? What would it mean to produce an act of intertextual "neighboring" in which both *jouissance* and signification converge? How can we reapproach the traumatic proximity of a text, before or beyond comparison and contextualization? Asymmetrical substitution implies that there is no original common ground for textual comparison, but only the trauma of originary nonrelationship, of a gap between the theory and practice of reading that is only retroactively visible. This nonrelationship is the encounter with *joui-sense*, the traumatic enjoyment that attends signification but that does not need to be sacrificed to it. Hence a responsible reading would be one that attends to the ways in which texts *might have* neighbored each other in traumatic proximity before the act of comparison which symbolizes their relations, and how they *might again* neighbor each other, by momentarily de-contextualizing them, separating them from the networks of historical and tropological association. My conjunction of Lacan with Levinas has recontextualized these thinkers by reading them as respondents to the Holocaust, but only in order to de-contextualize them, to place them in the empty space left by event as trauma, as that which cannot be symbolized. Just as Lacan's reading of Kant with Sade effectively "neighbors" rather than contextualizes the two thinkers by placing them in a relation of proximity made visible by historical catastrophe yet not reducible to historicizing explanation, so too my coupling of Lacan with Levinas does not project a common framework that would explain their resonances, but rather demonstrates points of contact that occur precisely in and as the absence of such a framework. The critical act of bringing together Lacan with Levinas, a "with" marked by the figure and logic of the neighbor, points to an ethics of reading before comparison and after sacrifice.

Notes

My thanks to Bruce Fink, David Kadlec, Richard Kroll, Richard Macksey, Patrick Sinclair, John H. Smith, and especially, Julia Reinhard Lupton, for their reading and advice at various stages of this project.

1.   Jacques-Alain Miller has provided a series of glosses for Lacan's "with" in an unpublished talk delivered at the 1989 Paris/New York Workshop, including the "utilitarian" or "instrumental" sense, as in the case of the critic who reads literature "with Lacan."

2.   On the lack of a sexual relationship, see Jacques-Alain Miller, "To Interpret the Cause: From Freud to Lacan." On the antagonism constitutive of the social relationship, see Laclau and Mouffe, 1985. On the disjunction between sexuality and sex, see Zizek, *Enjoy Your Symptom!* (1992, 123–24).

3.   In *Otherwise Than Being*, Levinas describes the subject faced with its overwhelming obligation to the other, as "on the hither side [*en deçà*] of [its] own nuclear unity . . . emptied even of the quasi-formal identity of being someone" (1991, 92).

4.   In *Seminar VIII: Transference* (1991, presented in 1960–61) and *Seminar XI: The Four Fundamental Concepts of Psychoanalysis* (1978, presented in 1963–64), Lacan distinguishes between the two modalities of love in terms of two aspects of transference. The goal of analysis that emerges in the later sixties and seventies involves "traversing the fantasy," the process in which the analyst, idealized in the first moment of transference as a supposed subject of knowledge, is de-idealized, or "de-completed," in transference's second moment of "separation," in which love's effect of imaginary coherence is stripped away to reveal love as pure drive.

5.   Jean-Luc Nancy interprets Lacan's description of Nazism as a sacrifice made to the desire of the Other, the "obscure God," in terms of his own account of the subject's "sacrificial trans-appropriation" of itself: "Let another's desire, obscure, consecrate as *his* my own desire, and I am constituted in absolute Self-possession, in unlimited self-presence" (Nancy 1991, 35).

6.   Quote taken from the title page of the special issue of *New Formations* on "Lacan and Love," edited by Renata Salecl.

7.   In the middle years of his seminar (1965–70), Lacan describes the goal of analysis as the "traversal of the fantasy": an act of substitution in which the subject *takes the place of* the *objet a* of his or her own fantasy.

8.   See Lacan's discussion of the "between-two-deaths" in Sade and *Antigone*

in *Seminar VII: The Ethics of Psychoanalysis.*

9.   See Derrida's discussions of the economics of sacrifice and the gift in *Given Time: I. Counterfeit Money,* "At this very moment in this work here I am," and "*Donner la mort.*" Derrida argues in *Given Time* that Lacan's account of love as a gift of "what it does not have" remains within a transcendental economy controlled by the phallus (1992b, 2–3, 15). In the moment of transference love Lacan calls "separation," however, the imaginary circle of reciprocal love shatters, revealing the unsymbolized reality of the *objet a*: "*I give myself to you,* the patient says again, *but this gift of my person . . . Oh, mystery! is changed inexplicably into a gift of shit*" (1978, 268). For this moment of love as the "sacrifice of sacrifice," the renunciation of the economics of the gift, see Zizek, *Enjoy Your Symptom!* (1992, 167–68).

10.   See *On Christian Doctrine,* Book One, sections 22–23.

11.   Levinas's account of the neighbor and responsibility derives, on the one hand, from Heidegger's analysis of *Schuldigsein* in *Being and Time,* and on the other, from a Jewish tradition of ethical philosophy that includes most recently Hermann Cohen and Franz Rosenzweig.

12.   Levinas writes, "Responsibility for another is not an accident that happens to a subject, but precedes essence in it, has not awaited freedom, in which a commitment to another would have been made" (Levinas 1974, 114).

13.   In one of his Talmudic essays, "The Pact," Levinas distinguishes this "responsibility" from the reciprocally determined notions of "self" and "love" implicit in the Levitical injunction: "The phrase 'Love your neighbor as yourself' still assumes the prototype of love to be love of oneself. Here, the ethic is one which says: 'Be responsible for the other as you are responsible for yourself.' In this way we avoid the assumption about self-love which is often accepted as the very definition of a person" (Levinas 1989, 225).

14.   Levinas writes that "no language other than ethics could be equal to the paradox which phenomenological description enters when, starting with the disclosure, the appearing of a neighbor, it reads it in its trace, which orders the face according to a diachrony which cannot be synchronized in representation" (Levinas 1974, 193, fn. 35).

15.   The self is not, however, divided by the guilt of an "original sin," whether theological or psychological: "the self, the persecuted one, is accused beyond his fault before freedom, and thus in an unavowable innocence" (Levinas 1974, 121).

16.   For an account of substitutability in relation to the neighbor as "what is most proper to every creature," and the mark of its being as "whatever," see Giorgio Agamben 1993, 23–25.

17.   In his essay "A Religion for Adults," Emmanuel Levinas presents monotheism not as a child-like belief overturned by philosophical doubt, but rather as a position of maturity achieved only by passing through the risk of atheism: "One wonders, in fact, whether the Western spirit, philosophy, is not in the last analysis the position of a humanity that accepts the risk of atheism, which it must run, but surmount, the ransom of its majority" (Levinas 1989, 16,

trans. mod.; cf. 1969, 23). We could say that such a philosophy has taken religion as its neighbor, not as a superseded moment in the history of spirit, but as a discourse which is both independent from philosophy and bound up in it.

18.   See Samuel Weber's critique of Wellek's foundation of comparative litera-ture on a supposedly Kantian account of the unity of the aesthetic. Weber writes that "such a perspective ignores what is most obvious in Kant—his refusal to acknowledge aesthetics as a discipline capable of being 'founded'" (1988, 61).

19.   See Clayton Koelb and Susan Noakes's account of the "urge toward total-ization" characteristic of the generation of comparativist critics that included Harry Levin, René Wellek, and Erich Auerbach (1988, 9).

20.   It is precisely the residue of "pathological" desire that both constitutes the Kantian subject and is eschewed by it, makes it doubt itself. See Slavoj Zizek's discussion of "Kant with Sade" in *Tarrying with the Negative* (1993, 70–71).

21.   Cf. Sade, "Prêtez-moi la partie de votre corps qui peut me satisfaire un instant et jouissez, si cela vous plaît, de celle du mien qui peut vous être agréable?" [Pray avail me of that part of your body which is capable of giving me a moment's satisfaction, and, if you are so inclined, amuse yourself with whatever part of mine may be agreeable to you (1968, 109)].

22.   Cf. Horkheimer and Adorno, *The Dialectic of Enlightenment*, "Excursus II: Juliette or Enlightenment and Morality." I have benefited from conversations on the Lacan–Adorno relationship with John H. Smith, whose manuscript on this topic is forthcoming.

23.   The original French edition of Klossowski's work began with an epigraph in which, when asked what he though of his contemporary the Marquis de Sade, Saint Benoît Labre responded that Sade too is "my neighbor." Also see Alphonso Lingis's introduction to his translation of *Sade My Neighbor*.

24.   Sade's refusal to be my neighbor illustrates the radical strangeness of this *jouissance*, for, Lacan suggests, even he is not "neighbor" enough to himself to recognize the *jouissance* of his neighbor in himself—even Sade is caught gazing in the mirror of reciprocal love.

Works Cited

Agamben, Giorgio. 1993. *The Coming Community.* Trans. Michael Hardt. Minneapolis: University of Minnesota Press.

Augustine, Saint. 1958. *On Christian Doctrine.* Trans. D. W. Robertson, Jr. Indianapolis: Bobbs-Merrill.

Derrida, Jacques. 1991. "At this very moment in this work here I am." In *Re-Reading Levinas.* Ed. Robert Bernasconi and Simon Critchley. Bloomington: Indiana University Press. 11–48.

———. 1992a. "Donner la mort." In *L'éthique du don: Jacques Derrida et la pensée du don.* Ed. Jean-Michel Rabaté and Michael Wetzel. Paris: Métailié-Transition. 11–108.

———. 1992b. *Given Time, I: Counterfeit Money.* Trans. Peggy Kamuf. Chicago: University of Chicago Press.

Horkheimer, Max and Theodor W. Adorno. 1986. *The Dialectic of Enlightenment.* Trans. John Cumming. New York: Continuum.

Klossowski, Pierre. 1991. *Sade My Neighbor.* Trans. and Intro. Alphonso Lingis. Evanston, IL: Northwestern University Press. Originally published as *Sade mon prochain* (Paris: Seuil, 1947).

Koelb, Clayton and Susan Noakes, eds. 1988. *The Comparative Perspective on Literature: Approaches to Theory and Practice.* Ithaca: Cornell University Press.

Lacan, Jacques. 1966 [1989]. "Kant *avec* Sade." In *Écrits.* Paris: Seuil. 765–90. Trans. as "Kant with Sade" by James B. Swenson, Jr., in *October* 51:55–75.

———. 1978. *The Four Fundamental Concepts of Psycho-Analysis (Seminar XI).* Ed. Jacques-Alain Miller. Trans. Alan Sheridan. New York: Norton.

———. 1986 [1992]. *Le Séminaire, livre VII: L'éthique de la psychoanalyse.* Text established by Jacques-Alain Miller. Paris: Seuil. Trans. as *The Seminar of Jacques Lacan, Book VII: The Ethics of Psychoanalysis.* Trans. Dennis Porter. New York: Norton.

———. 1991. *Le Séminaire, livre VIII: Le transfert.* Text established by Jacques-Alain Miller. Paris: Seuil.

Laclau, Ernesto and Chantal Mouffe. 1985. *Hegemony and Socialist Strategy: Towards a Radical Democratic Politics.* New York: Verso.

Levinas, Emmanuel. 1969. *Totality and Infinity.* Trans. Alphonso Lingis. Pittsburgh: Duquesne University Press.

———. 1974 [1991]. *Autrement qu'être ou au-delà de l'essence.* Paris: Kluwer Academic (Livre de Poche). Trans. as *Otherwise Than Being or Beyond Essence* by Alphonso Lingis. Boston: Kluwer Academic.

———. 1989. *The Levinas Reader.* Ed. Seán Hand. Cambridge, MA: Blackwell.

———. 1991. *Entre nous: Essais sur le penser-à-l'autre.* Paris: Grasset (Livre de Poche).

———. 1994. *Beyond the Verse: Talmudic Readings and Lectures.* Trans. Gary D. Mole. Bloomington: Indiana University Press.

MacCannell, Juliet Flower. 1994. "Love Outside the Limits of the Law." *New Formations* 23:25–42.

Miller, Jacques-Alain. 1989a. "A Discussion of Lacan's 'Kant with Sade.'" Paper presented at the Paris/New York Workshop. Ed. Bruce Fink.

————. 1989b. "To Interpret the Cause: From Freud to Lacan." *Newsletter of the Freudian Field* 3 (1 and 2):30–50.

Nancy, Jean-Luc. 1991. "The Unsacrificeable." *Yale French Studies* 79:20–38.

Plato. 1961. *The Collected Dialogues*. Ed. Edith Hamilton and Huntington Cairns. New York: Bollingen.

Sade, Marquis de. 1968 [1987]. *Juliette* in *Oeuvres complète du Marquis de Sade*, Vol. 8. Trans. Austryn Wainhouse. Paris: Pauvert; New York: Grove/Weidenfeld.

Salecl, Renata, ed. 1994. *Lacan and Love*. Special issue. *New Formations* 23 (Summer).

Weber, Samuel. 1988. "The Foundering of Aesthetics: Thoughts on the Current State of Comparative Literature." In Koelb and Noakes, 57–72.

Zizek, Slavoj. 1992. *Enjoy Your Symptom! Jacques Lacan in Hollywood and Out*. New York: Routledge.

————. 1993. *Tarrying with the Negative: Kant, Hegel, and the Critique of Ideology*. Durham, NC: Duke University Press.

CONTRIBUTORS

CAROL J. ADAMS is an activist, writer, and frequent speaker on college campuses. She is the author of *The Sexual Politics of Meat: A Feminist-Vegetarian Critical Theory* (1996 [1990]), *Neither Man nor Beast: Feminism and the Defense of Animals* (1994), and *Woman-Battering* (1994). She has edited *Ecofeminism and the Sacred* (1993), and co-edited *Violence Against Women and Children: A Christian Theological Sourcebook* (1995), *Beyond Animals' Rights: A Feminist Caring Ethic for the Treatment of Animals* (1996), and *Animals and Women: Feminist Theoretical Explorations* (1995).

ED BLOCK, JR., is Professor of English at Marquette University. He is the author of *Rituals of Dis-Integration: Romance and Madness in the Victorian Psychomythic Tale* (1993), and editor of *Critical Essays on John Henry Newman* (1992). He is the editor of the journal *Renascence: Essays on Values in Literature*, and has published in such journals as *Victorian Studies*, *Studies in English Literature*, and *Communio: International Catholic Review*.

SUSAN HANDELMAN is Professor of English at the University of Maryland, College Park, with a research interest especially in the relation of literary theory and Jewish thought. Among her books are *The Slayers of Moses: The Emergence of Rabbinic Interpretation in Modern Literary Theory* (1982), and *Fragments of Redemption: Jewish Thought and Literary Theory in Scholem, Benjamin, and Levinas* (1991); she co-edited *Psychoanalysis and Religion* (1990).

JOHN C. HAWLEY is Associate Professor of English at Santa Clara University. He has served on the Modern Language Association's executive committee on Religion and Literature and has edited six volumes, including *Christian Encounters with the Other* (1998), *The Postcolonial Crescent: Islam's Impact on Contemporary Literature* (1998), and *Cross–Addressing: Resistance Literature and Cultural Borders* (1996).

NED DYKSTRA HAYES currently teaches in the writing program at Seattle Pacific University, and also serves as the editor of the online literary magazine *Hot Link* (hotlink.com). Recent criticism includes articles about rhetoric on the internet, several of which also reference the work of Mark C. Taylor. He is a poet and novelist.

PAUL LAKELAND is Professor of Religious Studies at Fairfield University. Among his publications are *Postmodernity: Christian Identity in a Fragmented Age* (1997), *Theology and Critical Theory: The Discourse of the Church* (1990), *Freedom in Christ: An Introduction to Political Theology* (1986), and *The Politics of Salvation: The Hegelian Idea of the State* (1984).

JENNIFER LEADER is a doctoral candidate in American Literature at the Claremont Graduate University, serves on the editorial staff of the journal *Women's Studies*, and is an adjunct faculty member at California State University in Los Angeles. Her article on Edith Sitwell, Kathleen Raine, and Marianne Moore is forthcoming in the journal *Religion and the Arts*.

ED MADDEN is an Assistant Professor of English at the University of South Carolina, where he teaches courses on modernism, British poetry, and AIDS literature. He has published essays on Radclyffe Hall, Victorian poetry, and queer theory, and is currently completing a manuscript on images of Tiresias in modernist literature. This essay is part of a larger project on Christian language, homosexuality, and literary subcultures.

ROBERT J. S. MANNING is Associate Professor of Philosophy at Quincy University in Illinois. An ordained Unitarian Universalist minister, he is the author of *Interpreting Otherwise Than Heidegger: Emmanuel Levinas's Ethics as First Philosophy* (1993) and *Beyond Ethics to Justice: Through Levinas and Derrida* (forthcoming from The Franciscan Press).

SAM MCBRIDE is a senior Professor at DeVry Institute of Technology in Pomona, California. His doctorate is from the University of California at Riverside. His research interests focus on contemporary theory and the interdisciplinary exchange between literature, music, and the visual arts. Recent publications are on C. S. Lewis.

ANDREW MCKENNA is Professor of French at Loyola University in Chicago. He is the author of *Violence and Difference: Girard, Derrida, and Deconstruction* (1992), as well as numerous articles on Molière, Pascal, Racine, Baudelaire, Flaubert, and critical theory. Since 1996, he has been editor in chief of *Contagion: Journal of Violence, Mimesis, and Culture*.

BRADLEY JOHN MONSMA, an Associate Professor of English at Woodbury University in Burbank, California, has published several essays on multicultural literary theory, landscape in contemporary Native American Literature, and Native American autobiography.

SUSAN PETIT is Professor of English and French at the College of San Mateo. She is the author of *Michel Tournier's Metaphysical Fictions* (1991) and has contributed chapters to *The Contemporary Novel in France* (1995), *Reform and Counterreform: Dialectics of the Word in Western Christianity Since Luther* (1994), and *Diet and Discourse: Eating, Drinking and Literature* (1991), as well as articles to *Oeuvres et Critiques, Literature Interpretation Theory, French Review, Children's Literature, Orbis Litterarum, Modern Language Studies*, and *Novel*.

KENNETH REINHARD is Associate Professor of English at UCLA, where he teaches classes in literary theory, psychoanalysis, and Jewish Studies. He has written, with Julia Reinhard Lupton, *After Oedipus: Shakespeare in Psychoanalysis* (1993), and is currently writing a book for Princeton University Press on the ethics of the neighbor in religion, philosophy, and psychoanalysis. He has published essays on Lacan, Freud, Levinas, and Henry James.

T. R. WRIGHT is a Lecturer in English at Newcastle University in England. He writes on nineteenth–century figures (Gaskell, Newman, Eliot, Hardy) and among his books are *The Critical Spirit and the Will to Believe: Essays in Nineteenth-Century Literature and Religion* (1989), *Theology and Literature* (1988), and *The Religion of Humanity: The Impact of Comtean Positivism on Victorian Britain* (1986).

Index